Companion Workbook

HMH

math expressions

Dr. Karen C. Fuson and
Dr. Sybilla Beckmann

Watch the toucan come alive in its tropical forest as you discover and solve math challenges.

Download the *Math Worlds AR* app available on Android or iOS devices.

Grade 6

This material is based upon work supported by the **National Science Foundation** under Grant Numbers ESI-9816320, REC-9806020, and RED-935373.

Any opinions, findings, and conclusions, or recommendations expressed in this material are those of the author and do not necessarily reflect the views of the National Science Foundation.

Cover Illustration: ©Josh Brill

Printed in the U.S.A.

ISBN 978-1-328-74495-1

5 6 7 8 9 10 0607 26 25 24 23 22

4500844798 D E F G

Contents

UNIT 1 - Rates, Ratios, and Proportions

Family Letter....1

Vocabulary Cards....4A

1 Factor Puzzles and the Multiplication Table....5

2 Solving Factor Puzzles....7

3 Rate Situations and Rate Tables....9

4 Rate Situations and Unit Rate Language....13

5 Unit Rates, Products, and Rate Tables....15

Quick Quiz 1....17

Strategy Check 1....18

6 Unit Pricing....19

7 Constant Speed....21

Quick Quiz 2....25

Strategy Check 2....26

8 Ratio as Linked Rates....27

9 Finding Linked Values in Ratio Tables....29

10 Seeing Proportions in Ratio Tables....31

11 Identify and Solve Proportion Situations....33

Quick Quiz 3....35

Strategy Check 3....36

15 Focus on Problem Solving....44

Quick Quiz 4....45

Strategy Check 4....46

Unit 1 Review/Test....47

Unit 1 Performance Task....53

UNIT 2 - Area of Polygons

Family Letter....55

Vocabulary Cards....56A

1 Units of Area....57

2 Area of Any Right Triangle....61

3 Area of Any Parallelogram....65A

4 Area of Any Triangle....69A

5 Select the Needed Measurements....74

Quick Quiz 1....77

Strategy Check 5....78

6 Area of Any Trapezoid....79A

9 Graph Polygons in the Coordinate Plane....85

Quick Quiz 2....95

Strategy Check 6....96

Unit 2 Review/Test....97

Unit 2 Performance Task....103

Contents

UNIT 3 - Operations with Whole Numbers, Fractions, and Decimals

Family Letter....105

Vocabulary Cards....106A

1 Place Value and Whole Number Division....107A

3 Multiplying by a Decimal....115

5 Multiplication or Division....119

Quick Quiz 1....125

Fluency Check 1....126

7 Equivalent Fractions or Decimals....134

9 Mixed Problem Solving....140

Quick Quiz 2....141

Fluency Check 2....142

10 Multiplying with Fractions....146

11 Dividing with Fractions and Whole Numbers....150

Quick Quiz 3....155

Fluency Check 3....156

13 Dividing Numerators and Denominators....158

14 Dividing by Unsimplifying....159

16 Is it Multiplying or Dividing?....165

17 Mixed Practice with Decimals and Fractions....170

Quick Quiz 4....175

Fluency Check 4....176

Unit 3 Review/Test....177

Unit 3 Performance Task....183

UNIT 4 - Surface Area of Prisms and Pyramids

Family Letter....185

Vocabulary Cards....186A

1 Nets and Surface Area for Rectangular Prisms....187A

2 Nets and Surface Area for Nonrectangular Prisms....193A

3 Surface Area of Prisms....195

Quick Quiz 1....197

Fluency Check 5....198

4 Nets for Pyramids....199A

Quick Quiz 2....205

Fluency Check 6....206

Unit 4 Review/Test....207

Unit 4 Performance Task....213

Contents

UNIT 5 - Algebra and Number Theory

Family Letter....215

Vocabulary Cards....218A

2 Expressions with Exponents....222

3 Interpreting and Analyzing Expressions....225

4 Modeling and Simplifying Expressions....229

5 Expressions for Area and Surface Area....233

Quick Quiz 1....237

Fluency Check 7....238

6 Equivalent Expressions....239

7 The Commutative and Associative Properties....246

8 The Distributive Property....252

9 Practice with Expressions....256

Quick Quiz 2....259

Fluency Check 8....260

10 Relating Two Quantities....262

11 Motion at a Constant Speed....266

12 Relating Equations, Tables, and Graphs....271

13 Writing Equations....275

Quick Quiz 3....277

Fluency Check 9....278

14 Inequalities....283

15 Solutions of Equations and Inequalities....288

16 Addition and Subtraction Equations....289

17 Multiplication and Division Equations....298

18 Focus on Problem Solving....301

Quick Quiz 4....303

Fluency Check 10....304

19 Prime Factorization, GCF, and LCM....305

20 Number Theory Problems....314

Quick Quiz 5....315

Fluency Check 11....316

Unit 5 Review/Test....317

Unit 5 Performance Task....323

Contents

UNIT 6 - Geometry and Measurement

Family Letter....325

Vocabulary Cards....326A

1 What is Volume? 327A

2 Fractional Unit Cubes....333A

3 Compose Rectangular Prisms with Fractional Edge Lengths 337A

5 Write and Solve Equations About Volume....343

6 Focus on Problem Solving....347

Quick Quiz 1 349

Fluency Check 12 350

7 Angles Formed by Intersecting Lines....356

9 Interior Angles in Polygons 361

Quick Quiz 2 367

Fluency Check 13 368

11 Circumference and Area of a Circle....371

12 Solve Problems about Circles....378

Quick Quiz 3 383

Fluency Check 14 384

Unit 6 Review/Test....385

Unit 6 Performance Task....391

UNIT 7 - Ratios and Rates with Fractions, Decimals, and Percents

Family Letter....393

Vocabulary Cards....396A

1 Comparing Ratios....397

2 Unit Rates....399

3 Ratios, Fractions, and Fraction Notation....403

4 Understanding Cross-Multiplication 406

Quick Quiz 1 407

Fluency Check 15 408

5 Describing Ratios with Tape Diagrams....409

6 Ratios and Multiplicative Comparisons 414

Quick Quiz 2 419

Fluency Check 16 420

8 The Meaning of Percent....421

9 Percent of a Number....425

10 Percent Calculations....429

11 Solve Percent Problems....431

Quick Quiz 3 433

Fluency Check 17 434

12 Convert Units of Length 435

13 Convert Units of Liquid Volume, Mass, Weight, and Time....440

Quick Quiz 4 449

Fluency Check 18 450

Unit 7 Review/Test....451

Unit 7 Performance Task....457

Contents

UNIT 8 - Statistics and Probability

Family Letter 459
Vocabulary Cards 460A
2 Dot Plots and Histograms 465
Quick Quiz 1 469
3 Making Data Groups Equal 472
5 The Mean as a Balance Point 475
6 Find and Use the Median and the Mode 478
Quick Quiz 2 483
Fluency Check 19 484
7 Variability in Data 488
8 Box Plots 489
9 Mean Absolute Deviation 493
Quick Quiz 3 505
Fluency Check 20 506
13 Sample Space 508
14 Probability of an Event 511
15 Experiments to Investigate Probabilities 515
16 Experimental Probability 519
Quick Quiz 4 523
Fluency Check 21 524
Unit 8 Review/Test 525
Unit 8 Performance Task 531

UNIT 9 - Rational Numbers and the Coordinate Plane

Family Letter 533
Vocabulary Cards 534A
2 Integers on a Number Line 538
Integer Number Line Game 538A
3 Compare and Order Integers 541
4 Integers and the Coordinate Plane 545
Quick Quiz 1 549
Fluency Check 22 550
5 Rational Numbers on a Number Line 551
Rational Numbers Number Line Game 552A
7 Rational Numbers and the Coordinate Plane 556
Coordinate Plane Game 556A
Quick Quiz 2 559
Fluency Check 23 560
Unit 9 Review/Test 561
Unit 9 Performance Task 567

Dear Family:

Your child is learning math in an innovative program called *Math Expressions.* The program emphasizes understanding and fluency. Your child will

- connect math to daily life.
- solve a problem by understanding and representing the situation and then finding the solution.
- work with and explain strategies to other students.

Visualizing and talking about math is very important. This approach helps children feel that they can learn math. They do learn math, enjoy doing so, and feel good about themselves as math learners.

Recent research shows that effort is important in getting smarter and in doing well in math. This is called effort-produced ability. Students who work hard, think and participate in class, and do their homework do learn math. So encourage your child to work hard and to know that he or she can learn math.

Your child will have math homework almost every day. Homework is important for math learning. Make a special time for homework in a quiet place. Ask your child to explain to you some problem he or she did.

To make concepts clearer, the *Math Expressions* program uses some special methods and visual supports. Some of these for Unit 1 are shown on the back of this letter.

If your child has problems with math, please contact me to see how we can work together to help your child.

Thank you. You are vital to your child's learning.

Sincerely,
Your child's teacher

Rate, Ratio, and Proportion in Unit 1

In our math class, we are exploring the ideas of rate, ratio, and proportion.

A rate tells how much is used repeatedly in a given situation. For example, \$8 *per package* means \$8 *for each package* or \$8 *for every package*.

The ratio of one number to another is a simple way to express the relative size of two quantities or measurements.

A proportion is an equation that shows two equivalent ratios.
It can be written 6:14 = 15:35 or 6:14 :: 15:35.

In a proportion problem, one of the four numbers is unknown.
For example:

> Grandma made applesauce using the same number of bags of red apples and bags of yellow apples. Her red apples cost \$6 and her yellow apples cost \$14. I used her recipe but made more applesauce. I paid \$35 for my yellow apples. How much did my red apples cost?

Factor Puzzle

	Red	Yellow	
	3	7	
2	6	14	2
5	15	35	5
	3	7	

The problem makes this proportion:

6:14 = c:35

To solve this proportion, we can put the ratios in a Factor Puzzle.

c is 3 × 5 = 15

The Factor Puzzle is from the rows of the ratio table that are × 2 (• 2) and × 5 (• 5) of the basic ratio 3:7. Factor Puzzles enable your child to understand and solve challenging proportion problems.

Discuss with your child how you use proportions in your life, such as when you double a recipe.

Ratio Table

	Bags	R : Y (3 : 7)
	1	3 : 7
• 2	2	6 : 14
	3	9 : 21
	4	12 : 28
• 5	5	15 : 35
	6	18 : 42
	7	21 : 49
	8	24 : 56
	9	27 : 63

Estimada familia:

Su hijo está aprendiendo matemáticas mediante un innovador programa llamado *Expresiones en matemáticas.* Este programa enfatiza la comprensión y el dominio de los conocimientos. Con este programa, su hijo aprenderá a:

- relacionar las matemáticas con la vida diaria.
- resolver problemas mediante la comprensión y la representación de diferentes situaciones.
- trabajar con diferentes estrategias y a explicarlas a otros estudiantes.

La visualización y las charlas matemáticas son muy importantes. Cuando se usan, facilitan el aprendizaje. Mediante ellas el alumno aprende, disfruta mientras lo hace, y adquiere una buena autoestima como estudiante de matemáticas.

Estudios recientes han demostrado que esforzarse es muy importante para el desarrollo de la inteligencia y el estudio de las matemáticas. A este proceso se le llama adquisición de destrezas mediante esfuerzo. Para aprender, los estudiantes deben trabajar, concentrarse y participar durante la clase, y realizar tareas en la casa. Por esto, le pedimos que anime a su hijo a completar sus trabajos.

Casi diariamente su hijo tendrá tarea para la casa. La tarea es una parte muy importante del aprendizaje de las matemáticas. Para realizarla, designe un tiempo especial en un lugar tranquilo. Al terminar, pida a su hijo que le explique cómo resolvió algunos de los problemas.

Para lograr que los conceptos sean más claros, el programa *Expresiones en matemáticas* utiliza algunos métodos especiales y refuerzos visuales. Algunos de los que corresponden a la Unidad 1 se muestran en la parte de atrás.

Si su hijo tiene problemas en la asignatura de matemáticas, por favor comuníquese conmigo para que unidos hallemos la mejor manera de ayudarlo.

Gracias. Usted es imprescindible para el aprendizaje de su hijo.

Si tiene cualquier pregunta, por favor comuníquese conmigo.

Atentamente,
El maestro de su hijo.

Tasa, razón y proporción en la Unidad 1

En nuestra clase de matemáticas, estamos estudiando los conceptos de tasa, razón y proporción.

Una tasa indica cuánto se usa algo repetidamente en una situación dada. Por ejemplo, $8 *por paquete* significa $8 *por cada paquete*.

La razón de un número a otro es una manera simple de expresar el tamaño relativo de dos cantidades o medidas.

Una proporción es una ecuación que muestra dos razones equivalentes. Puede escribirse así:

6:14 = 15:35 o 6:14 :: 15:35.

En un problema de proporción, uno de los cuatro números es un número desconocido. Por ejemplo:

> Para hacer puré de manzanas, mi abuelita usó el mismo número de bolsas de manzanas rojas que de manzanas amarillas. Las bolsas de manzanas rojas costaron $6 y las de amarillas $14. Yo usé la misma receta, pero hice más puré.
> Si pagué $35 por mis manzanas amarillas, ¿cuánto pagué por las rojas?

Rompecabezas de factores

	Rojo	Amarillo	
	3	7	
2	6	14	2
5	15	35	5
	3	7	

El problema se representa con esta proporción:

$$6:14 = c:35$$

Para resolver esta proporción, podemos hacer un rompecabezas de factores con las razones.

$$c \text{ es } 3 \times 5 = 15$$

El rompecabezas de factores se hace con las hileras de la tablas de razones que son × 2 (• 2) y × 5 (• 5) de la razón básica 3:7. Los rompecabezas de factores sirven para resolver problemas difíciles de proporciones.

Comente con su hijo acerca de situaciones de su vida diaria en las que se usen proporciones, tal como hacer el doble de alguna receta de cocina.

Tabla de razones

		R : A
	Bolsas	3 : 7
	1	3 : 7
• 2	2	6 : 14
	3	9 : 21
	4	12 : 28
• 5	5	15 : 35
	6	18 : 42
	7	21 : 49
	8	24 : 56
	9	27 : 63

basic ratio	equivalent ratios
constant rate	factor
coordinate plane (first quadrant)	greatest common factor

Ratios that represent the same comparison. Equivalent ratios have the same basic ratio.

A ratio in simplest form.

Examples:

The basic ratio for $\frac{25}{30}$ is $\frac{5}{6}$.

The basic ratio for $\frac{12}{24}$ is $\frac{1}{2}$.

One of two or more numbers multiplied to make a product.

Example:

$12 \cdot 4 = 48$

factor (12) factor (4)

In a rate table in which the units are consecutive whole numbers, the constant difference in the values shown in the second column. Also the value in the second column when the number of units equals 1.

The greatest factor that two or more numbers share.

Example:

15 is the GCF of 30 and 45.

A plane together with a pair of perpendicular number lines that intersect at 0 on each number line. The perpendicular number lines are called axes. The coordinate plane is divided into four quadrants by the *x*- and *y*-axes.

At the right is the first quadrant of the coordinate plane.

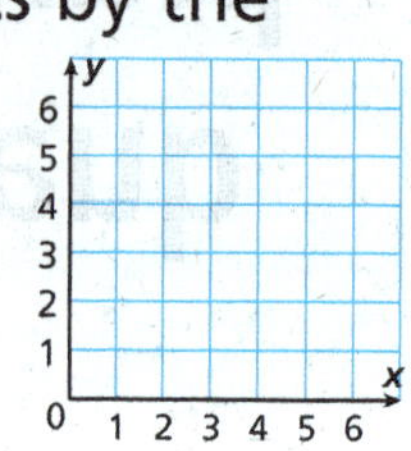

ordered pair

rate table

product

ratio table

proportion

solving a proportion

A two-column table showing the number of units in the first column and the value associated with each given number of units in the second column. When the units are listed as counting numbers in consecutive order, the values in the second column will show a constant difference; this constant difference is the unit rate.

Two numbers that are inside parentheses and have a comma in between them. Ordered pairs can represent points on the coordinate plane and are written as (x, y).

Example:

(5, 3) is an ordered pair, where $x = 5$ and $y = 3$.

A table showing equivalent ratios.

The result of a multiplication.

Example:

$12 \cdot 4 = 48$ ← product

Finding the unknown number in a proportion when one of the four numbers in the proportion is unknown.

A statement that two ratios are equivalent.

unit price

x-coordinate

unit rate

y-axis

x-axis

y-coordinate

The first number in an ordered (***x***, *y*) pair.

The unit rate associated with a price or cost.

Example:

4 dollars per pound

The vertical number line in the coordinate plane.

The value associated with 1 unit.

Examples:

5 miles per hour

3 dollars every week

2 apples each day

The second number in an ordered (*x*, ***y***) pair.

The horizontal number line in the coordinate plane.

Name ______________________________

VOCABULARY
factors
product

Discuss Patterns in the Multiplication Table

Look for patterns in the multiplication tables.

Table 1

●	1	2	3	4	5	6	7	8	9
1	1	2	3	4	5	6	7	8	9
2	2	4	6	8	10	12	14	16	18
3	3	6	9	12	15	18	21	24	27
4	4	8	12	16	20	24	28	32	36
5	5	10	15	20	25	30	35	40	45
6	6	12	18	24	30	36	42	48	54
7	7	14	21	28	35	42	49	56	63
8	8	16	24	32	40	48	56	64	72
9	9	18	27	36	45	54	63	72	81

Table 2

●	1	2	3	4	5	6	7	8	9
1	1	2	3	4	5	6	7	8	9
2	2	4	6	8	10	12	14	16	18
3	3	6	9	12	15	18	21	24	27
4	4	8	12	16	20	24	28	32	36
5	5	10	15	20	25	30	35	40	45
6	6	12	18	24	30	36	42	48	54
7	7	14	21	28	35	42	49	56	63
8	8	16	24	32	40	48	56	64	72
9	9	18	27	36	45	54	63	72	81

Strategies for Finding Factors

Write the unknown **factors** and the unknown **product**.

1 Table 3

			___		___					
	●									
___			6		10					___
___			21		n					___
			___		___					

Factor Puzzle

	___	___	
___	6	10	___
___	21		___
	___	___	

Name ______________________________

Solve Factor Puzzles

Write the unknown factors and the unknown product.

2 **Table 4**

●									
		6					21		
		16					*n*		

Factor Puzzle

6	21
16	

3 **Table 5**

●	2	4	7	1	5	3	6	8	9
3	6	12	21	3	15	9	18	24	27
1	2	4	7	1	5	3	6	8	9
4	8	16	28	4	20	12	24	32	36
2	4	8	14	2	10	6	12	16	18
7	14	28	49	7	35	21	42	56	63
9	18	36	63	9	45	27	54	72	81
5	10	20	35	5	25	15	30	40	45
8	16	32	56	8	40	24	48	64	72
6	12	24	42	6	30	18	36	48	54

Factor Puzzle

	6
35	15

Check Understanding

Explain how a Factor Puzzle is related to the multiplication table.

Name ____________________

Practice with Factor Puzzles

Solve each Factor Puzzle.

1.

20	15
8	

2.

8	14
	21

3.

	28
24	32

4.

24	
32	36

5.

20	35
	56

6.

	16
35	56

7.

21	24
28	

8.

	10
63	18

9.

35	
15	24

10.

24	28
54	

11.

56	63
	81

12.

54	63
24	

13.

36	63
8	

14.

32	36
	63

15.

	54
56	48

Name ______________________________

Make Factor Puzzles

Make your own Factor Puzzles. Exchange with a classmate.

16

17

18

19

20

21

22

23

24

25

26

27

Check Understanding

Describe the first step in solving a Factor Puzzle.

Name ______________________________

Find the Total So Far

Noreen started to save money. Every day she put three $1 coins into her bank. Write how much money she had each day.

Noreen began with an empty bank.	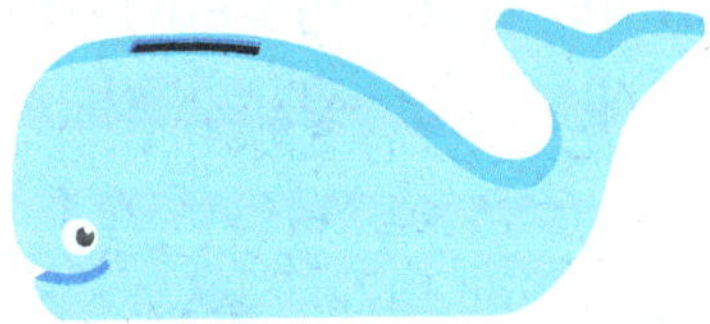	Noreen began with $0 in her bank.
1 On Day 1 Noreen put $3 into her bank.		On Day 1 Noreen had $ ______ in her bank.
2 On Day 2 Noreen put $3 into her bank.		On Day 2 Noreen had $ ______ in her bank.
3 On Day 3 Noreen put $3 into her bank.		On Day 3 Noreen had $ ______ in her bank.
4 On Day 4 Noreen put $3 into her bank.		On Day 4 Noreen had $ ______ in her bank.
5 On Day 5 Noreen put $3 into her bank.		On Day 5 Noreen had $ ______ in her bank.
6 On Day 6 Noreen put $3 into her bank.		On Day 6 Noreen had $ ______ in her bank.

Noreen continued to put $3 into her bank every day.

7 On Day 10, Noreen had ______ in her bank.

8 On Day 12, Noreen had ______ in her bank.

Name

Complete a Rate Table

VOCABULARY
rate table

This **rate table** shows Noreen's savings.

9 Fill in the rest of the table to show how much money Noreen saved each day and how much her total was each day.

Days	Dollars
1	3
2	6
3	

+ 3

10 What did you write between each row? ______

11 What does the number between each row show?

______

______

______

Identify Rate Tables

These tables show four different ways Noreen could have saved money. Complete each table. Then decide which tables are rate tables and which are not. Explain why.

12

Days	Dollars
1	2
2	
3	
4	
5	
6	

+ 2
+ 2
+ 2
+ 2
+ 2

______

______

______

______

______

Name ______________________________

Identify Rate Tables (continued)

13

Days	Dollars
1	4
2	12
3	18
4	20
5	24
6	28

14

Days	Dollars
1	7
2	14
3	21
4	28
5	35
6	42

15

Days	Dollars
1	3
2	5
3	5
4	9
5	11
6	14

Name ______________________

Practice Solving Factor Puzzles

Solve each Factor Puzzle.

16

	32
27	72

17

10	12
	54

18

	24
21	28

19

8	
12	27

20

24	30
28	

21

	12
10	8

22

56	24
35	

23

	24
28	21

24

16	56
	21

Make your own Factor Puzzles. Exchange with a classmate.

25

26

27

Check Understanding

Use the table in Exercise 14. By Day 7, Noreen will have saved _____ dollars.

Name ______________________________

VOCABULARY
unit rate
constant rate

Rates and Multiplication

1. Pedro and Pilar collect snails. Each day they add 4 snails to their tank. How many snails do they have after 5 days?

____

2. For Problem 1, we can make a rate table to find the answer for any number of days. Fill in the rest of the rate table. Write the multiplications to the left of the table.

3. Where in the rate table is the answer to Problem 1 and why is it there?

____

____

____

____

	Unit	Product	
	Days	**Snails**	
	1	4	+ 4
______	2	8	______
______	3		______
______	4		______
______	5		

Equal-Groups Multiplication and Rates

A rate problem can be thought of as an equal-groups multiplication.
The multiplier is a unit that counts the number of groups.
The **unit rate** is the amount in 1 group.

number of equal groups	•	amount in 1 group	=	total
multiplier	•	unit rate	=	product
number of days	•	4 snails each day	=	total number of snails so far

If the same rate is repeated, the rate is a **constant rate**.
Look for special words that show a constant rate.

The rate is 4 snails *every* day.

The rate is 4 snails *each* day.

The rate is 4 snails *per* day.

Name ______________________

Identify Rate Situations

For each situation, decide whether there is a constant rate. If yes, write the rate and complete the rate table.

4. In the zoo, 7 kangaroos live in each kangaroo house.

Is there a constant rate? ________

____ ________ per ________.

	Unit	Product	
	____	____	
____ •	1		
____ •	2		+ ____
____ •	3		+ ____
____ •	4		+ ____

5. In the last 3 weeks, Ben saw 3 movies, then 4 movies, and then 3 movies.

Is there a constant rate? ________

____ ________ per ________.

	Unit	Product	
	____	____	
____	1		
____	2		+ ____
____	3		+ ____
____	4		+ ____

6. Tara made 9 drawings on each page of her sketchbook.

Is there a constant rate? ________

____ ________ per ________.

	Unit	Product	
	____	____	
____ •	1		
____ •	2		+ ____
____ •	3		+ ____
____ •	4		+ ____

7. Cree makes gift bags. He puts 3 pencils in the first bag, 5 pencils in the second bag, and 4 pencils in the third bag.

Is there a constant rate? ________

____ ________ per ________.

	Unit	Product	
	____	____	
____	1		
____	2		+ ____
____	3		+ ____
____	4		+ ____

Check Understanding

Use one of the tables in Problems 4–7 to describe how a rate table shows equal-groups multiplication.

Name ______________________________

Is a Constant Rate Reasonable?

For each rate situation, fill in the rate information and the rate table. Label the columns in the table.

Discuss what you assume in order for the situation to be a rate situation in the real world.

1. Every day of this week Joanne made 3 of her free throws.

_____ __________ per __________.

Unit	Product
______	______
1	
5	

+ ____
+ ____
+ ____
+ ____

2. Efrain makes 8 sketches on each page of his drawing book.

_____ __________ per __________.

Unit	Product
______	______
1	
5	

+ ____
+ ____
+ ____
+ ____

3. Abby uses 2 cups of flour in each loaf of bread she makes.

_____ __________ per __________.

Unit	Product
______	______
1	
5	

+ ____
+ ____
+ ____
+ ____

4. Eusebio planted 7 tomato vines in each yard he takes care of.

_____ __________ per __________.

Unit	Product
______	______
1	
5	

+ ____
+ ____
+ ____
+ ____

Name ______________________

Is It a Rate Table?

Decide whether each table is a rate table. Explain why or why not.

5 ______ ______

1	9
2	18
3	27
4	36
5	45

____
____

6 ______ ______

1	4
2	5
3	9
4	10
5	14

____
____

7 ______ ______

1	11
2	22
3	33
4	44
5	55

____
____

8 ______ ______

1	3
2	5
3	8
4	10
5	13

____
____

9 Make up a story about one table and label the table.

Make Scrambled Rate Tables and Math Drawings

For each rate situation, find the unit rate and write it using *per*. Make a rate table that includes the given information as the first row in the table. Continue making a **scrambled rate table**. Then, make a math drawing for the first row of each rate table.

10 The store sold 5 sacks of oranges for $30.

______ ____________ per ____________.

Unit	Product
______	______

11 Grandpa's rectangular garden has 24 pepper plants in the first 4 rows.

______ ____________ per ____________.

Unit	Product
______	______

Check Understanding

Complete the sentence. Abby bought 3 jars of peanuts for $6.
The unit rate is ______ dollars.

Unit 1
Quick Quiz 1

Name ____________________

Solve each Factor Puzzle.

1

12	24
27	

2

	10
56	16

Is the table a rate table? *Yes* or *No*. Explain how you know.

3

Hours	Miles
1	3
2	6
3	10
4	15
5	21

4

Hours	Miles
1	6
2	12
3	18
4	24
5	30

Complete the rate table. Then write the unit rate.

5

Seconds	Feet
1	
2	4
	6
4	
	10

Unit rate: ____________________

Strategy Check 1

Name ______________________________

1 Sanaz puts 6 daisies in each bunch of flowers she makes. Fill in the rate table. Label the columns in the table.

1	
5	

2 Describe the rate using *per*.

____

____

3 Describe how the quantities in the second column change. Is the change constant?

____

____

____

____

4 Write a different story about the rate table above.

____

____

____

____

____

____

Name ______________________________

VOCABULARY
unit price
x-axis
y-axis
coordinate plane

Unit Pricing Situations

These three rate tables show the prices of three different kinds of granola. Each has a different **unit price**. Fill in the unknown values in each table.

Table 1

1

Number of Pounds	Cost in Dollars
1	3
2	
3	
	12
5	
6	
	21

Table 2

2

Number of Pounds	Cost in Dollars
1	6
2	
3	
	24
	30
10	
	600

Table 3

3

Number of Pounds	Cost in Dollars
1	
8	
	10
6	30
	100
	20
5	

What's the Error?

Dear Math Students,

I made this graph to show the first three rows from Table 1. When I tried to draw the unit rate triangle, I realized that I did something wrong.

Can you help me figure out what mistake I made?

Your friend,
Puzzled Penguin

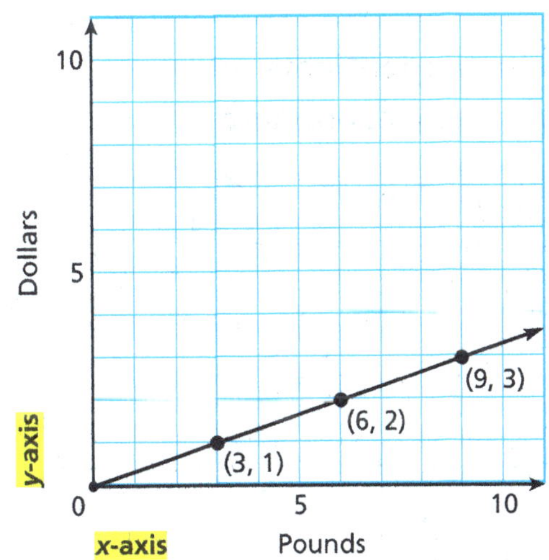

4 Write a response to Puzzled Penguin. Then draw the correct graph in the **coordinate plane** above.

____

____

Name

Relate Table, Equation, and Graph

VOCABULARY
ordered pair
x-coordinate
y-coordinate

You will now look for patterns and relationships in Table 1 from page 19.

Number of Pounds	Cost in Dollars
1	3
2	
3	
	12
5	
6	
7	21

Number of Pounds	• Unit Rate	=	Cost in Dollars
p	• r	=	C
1	• 3	=	3
2	• 3	=	☐
3	• 3	=	☐
☐	• 3	=	12
5	• 3	=	☐
6	• 3	=	☐
☐	• 3	=	21

Number of Pounds		Cost in Dollars
1	• 3	(3)
2	• 3	
3	• 3	
	• 3	12
5	• 3	
6	• 3	
	• 3	21

The unit rate is circled. Imagine the unit rate written on the vertical rule to be multiplied by the number in the left column to get the number in the right column.

Each point on the graph corresponds to an **ordered pair**. (0, 0) and (1, 3) are ordered pairs.

The first number is the ***x*-coordinate** and the second number is the ***y*-coordinate**.

In the ordered pair (1, 3), 1 is the *x*-coordinate and 3 is the *y*-coordinate.

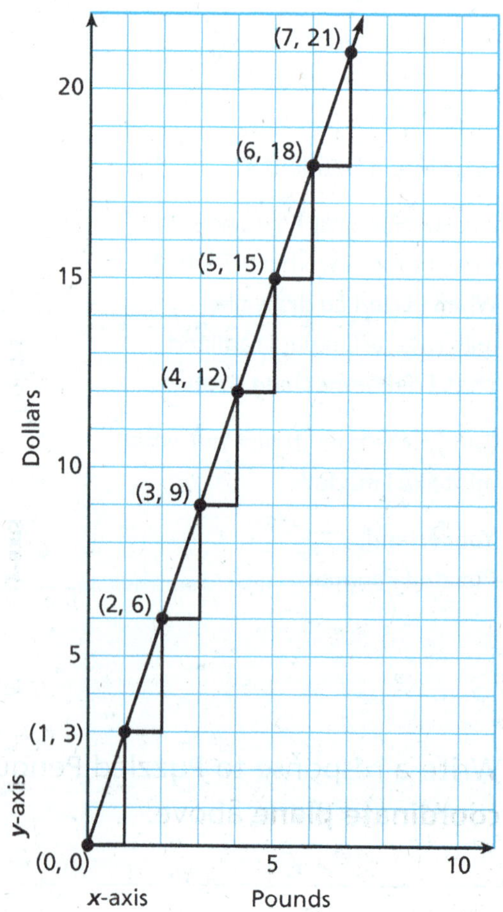

Check Understanding

On the graph, draw a line to show a unit rate of $2.

Name ______________________________

Constant Speed Situations

1. Dan ran in the Grade 6 track meet.

Time	Distance
Seconds	Yards
1	
3	15
9	
	10
50	

a. Unit rate: ___ ________ per ________

b. What are the sides of the unit rate triangle for the graph?

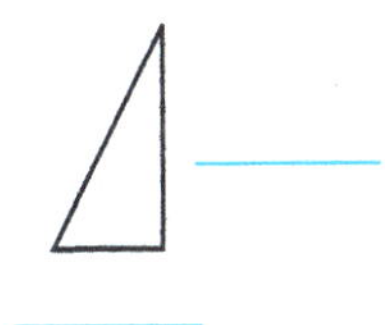

c. Draw the graph.

2. Julie rode her bike in the bike festival.

Time	Distance
Hours	Miles
1	
2	
4	44
	33

a. Unit rate: ___ ________ per ________

b. What are the sides of the unit rate triangle for the graph?

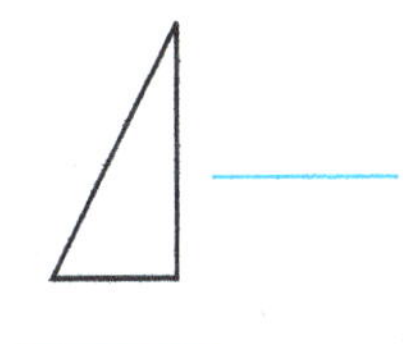

c. Draw the graph.

Name ______________________________

What's the Error?

Dear Math Students,

My friend Gavin ran in the Grade 6 track meet. His unit rate was 4 yards per second. I made this table of Gavin's times and distances. Gavin says that my table is not correct. Can you help me?

Your friend,
Puzzled Penguin

Time Seconds	Distance Yards
4	1
8	2
12	3
16	4
32	8
36	9

3. Write a response to Puzzled Penguin.

____

____

____

____

____

____

4. Show the correct table.

Name ___________________________

Review of Rate Situations

5 Use the graph to fill in the rows of the rate table. Circle the unit rate in the table. Draw the unit rate triangle in the graph.

Time	Distance
Seconds	Yards
3	
1	
	8
5	
	16

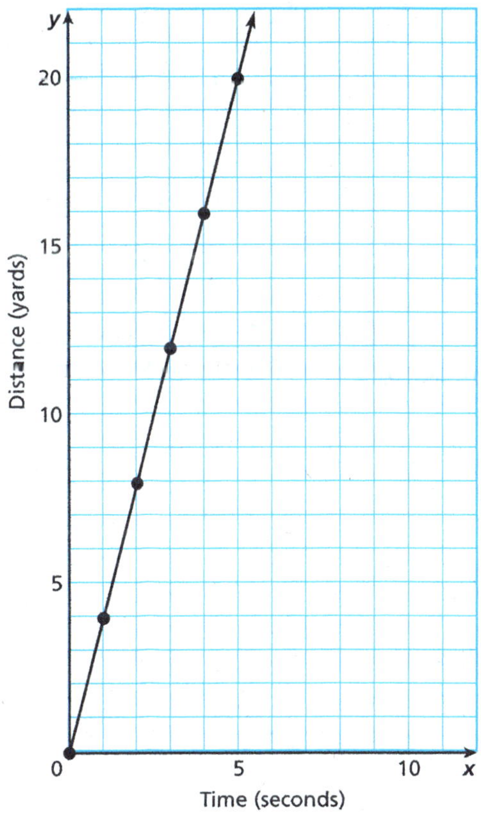

Solve each rate problem.

6 Ron earns $5 per hour for raking leaves. How much will he earn in 6 hours?

____

7 Mr. Martin makes 50 cookies per hour. How many cookies will he make in 3 hours?

____

8 Margo buys 4 pounds of peaches for $12. What is the unit rate?

____

9 Karen walks 6 miles in 2 hours. What is her unit rate?

____

10 On the Back Make a rate table for 1 to 5 pounds and draw a graph for the situation in Problem 8.

Check Understanding

Complete this sentence. If the graph for Exercise 5 is extended, it will go through the point (6, ________).

Name ______________________________

Unit 1
Quick Quiz 2

Name ______________________________

Use the rate table below for Exercises 1–4.

1. Complete the rate table.

Pounds of Tomatoes	Cost in Dollars
1	
	6
3	9
	12
5	

2. What is the unit rate for the table?

____

3. Draw the graph for the rate table.

4. Show the unit rate triangle on your graph.

Solve.

Show your work.

5. At a sporting goods store, the sale price of 6 pairs of baseball batting gloves is $54. At that rate, what is the unit cost per pair?

____

Strategy Check 2

Name ______________________________

For Exercises 1–3, use the following situation.

A catering company prepares 3 ounces of steak for every guest.

1. Label and complete the rate table.

2. Circle the unit rate in the table above.

3. Draw a graph to show the information in the table above. Show the unit rate triangle.

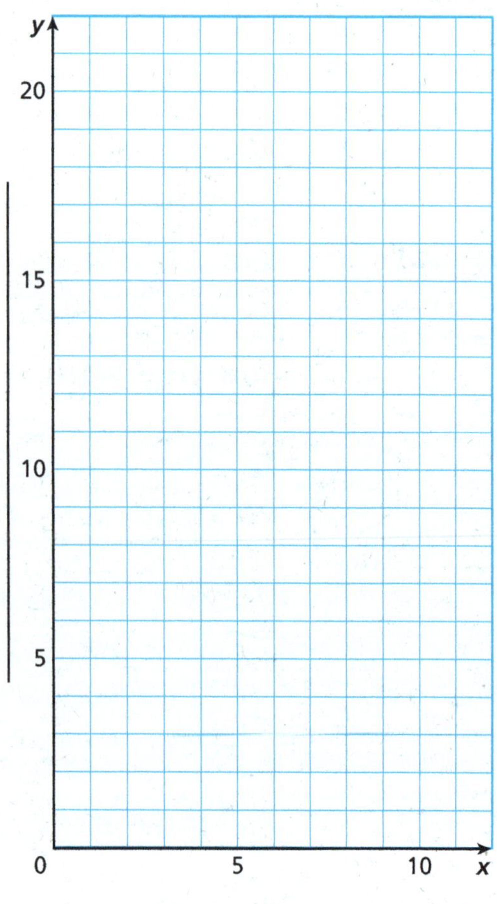

Name ______________________

VOCABULARY
ratio table

Ratio Tables as Linked Rate Tables

Noreen saves $3 a day and Tim saves $5 a day. They start saving on the same day. The linked rate table and the **ratio table** show Noreen's and Tim's savings.

Linked Rate Table

Days	Noreen (3)	Tim (5)
1	3	5
2	6	10
3	9	15
4	12	20
5	15	25
6	18	30
7	21	35

Ratio Table

	Noreen (3)	Tim (5)	
	3	5	
+ 3	6	10	+ 5
+ ___	9	15	+ ___
+ ___	12	20	+ ___
+ ___	15	25	+ ___
+ ___	18	30	+ ___
+ ___	21	35	+ ___
+ ___			+ ___

1. How are the tables alike? How are they different?

____

____

____

2. What are the numbers circled at the top of each table? ___________

3. Fill in the numbers to the left and right of the ratio table to show Noreen's and Tim's constant increases.

Use the tables to answer each question.

4. Noreen has saved $12.

   How much has Tim saved? ___________

   On which day was this? ___________

5. Tim has saved $35.

   How much has Noreen saved? ___________

   On which day was this? ___________

6. On what day will Noreen have $30 in her bank? ___________

   Why? _______________________________

   How much will Tim have then? ___________

Name ______________________

Make a Ratio Table

Make a ratio table for each situation. Be sure to label the columns.

1. Noreen makes 2 drawings on each page of her sketchbook. Tim makes 5 drawings on each page of his sketchbook.

2. Two bands march onto the football field. Band 1 marches on in rows of 5 and Band 2 marches on in rows of 7.

3. John can plant 7 tomato vines in the time it takes Joanna to plant 4 tomato vines.

Ratio Table 1

___	___

The linking unit is ______________.

Ratio Table 2

Rows	___	___

The linking unit is ______________.

Ratio Table 3

___	___

The linking unit is ______________.

Ratio Language and Symbols

4. The ratio of Noreen's drawings to Tim's drawings is ________ to ________.

5. a. The ratio of the people in Band 1 to the people in Band 2 is ________ to ________ written as 5:7.

   b. If Band 1 has 15 people on the field, Band 2 has ________ people on the field. This is ________ rows.

6. a. John and Joanna's tomato vines are in the ratio of ________ to ________.

   b. We write this as ________ : ________.

   c. If John plants 42 tomato vines, Joanna plants ________.

   d. If Joanna plants 8 tomato vines, John plants ________.

Name ______________________________

VOCABULARY
proportion
solving a proportion

Proportions and Factor Puzzles

Two equivalent ratios make a **proportion**.
Any two rows from a ratio table make a proportion.
In a proportion problem, one of the four numbers is unknown.
Solving a proportion means finding that unknown number.

Proportion problem:

Grandma made applesauce using the same number of bags of red apples and bags of yellow apples. Her red apples cost \$6 and her yellow apples cost \$14. I used her recipe but made more applesauce. I paid \$35 for my yellow apples. How much did my red apples cost?

Ratio Table

Bags	R : Y
1	:
2	:
3	:
4	:
5	:
6	:
7	:
8	:
9	:

The problem can be solved by solving this proportion:

$$6{:}14 = c{:}35$$

To solve the proportion, you need to find the value of c.

1. Fill in the ratio table for the problem.
2. Circle the rows of the ratio table that make up the problem.
3. a. What is the value of c? ______
   b. What is the solution to the problem? ______

You know how to solve Factor Puzzles. It is faster to make a Factor Puzzle than a whole ratio table.

Factor Puzzle

Red Yellow

	Red	Yellow	
___	6	14	___
___		35	___

4. Write the numbers from the proportion problem in the Factor Puzzle. Solve the Factor Puzzle.
5. Where in the ratio table are the numbers above and below the Factor Puzzle? ______________________
6. Where in the ratio table are the numbers to the left and right of the Factor Puzzle? ______________________

   Write these two numbers with a multiplication sign to the left of the yellow column in the ratio table.
7. Where in the ratio table is your answer? ______________________

Name ______________________

Solve Proportion Problems

Use Factor Puzzles to solve. Noreen and Tim both do these activities for the same amount of time but at their own constant rates.

8 a. Noreen saved $20 while Tim saved $35. When Noreen has saved $24, how much will Tim have saved? ______

b. Fill in the ratio table. Circle the rows that make the Factor Puzzle and write the multipliers for those rows.

Factor Puzzles

N T

Ratio Table

N		T
	:	
	:	
	:	
	:	
	:	
	:	
	:	
	:	

9 While Noreen plants 6 tomato plants, Tim plants 10 tomato plants. When Noreen has planted 21 tomato plants, how many will Tim have planted?

______ plants

N T

10 When Noreen had collected 6 stickers, Tim had collected 21 stickers. How many stickers will Noreen have when Tim has 56 stickers?

______ stickers

N T

11 Noreen did 72 push-ups while Tim did 32 push-ups. When Tim had done 12 push-ups, how many had Noreen done?

______ push-ups

Check Understanding

Draw your own Factor Puzzle and write a proportion it could describe.

Name ______________________________

Make Assumptions

Write the assumptions that must be stated to make the problem a proportion problem. Make and label a Factor Puzzle for the problem. Box the unknown and solve the puzzle and the problem.

1. Two bands march in rows onto the football field. When Band A has 15 people on the field, Band B has 6. When Band B has 14 people on the field, how many people will Band A have on the field?

   Problem solution: ______ people

2. An aquarium has 32 angelfish for every 12 snails. How many snails will there be when there are 72 angelfish?

   Problem solution: ______ snails

3. Ann made 35 posters while Jim made 14. How many posters had Jim made when Ann had made 15?

   Problem solution: ______ posters

Unit 1
Quick Quiz 3

Name ______________________

Complete each ratio table.

1

Boys		Girls
	:	5
8	:	10
	:	15
16	:	

2

Salt		Pepper
7	:	2
	:	4
21	:	
	:	8

Is the table a ratio table? Write *Yes* or *No*.

3 ______________

Circles	Squares
2	3
4	6
6	9
8	12
10	15

Explain why the table is or is not a ratio table.

____

____

____

____

____

Solve.

Show your work.

4 Olivia uses 3 ounces of carrots for every 4 ounces of potatoes to make soup. If she uses 16 ounces of potatoes, how many ounces of carrots should she use?

____

5 Holly and Gavin each save money at their own constant rate. Holly saved $15 while Gavin saved $20. When Holly has saved $24, how much will Gavin have saved?

____

Strategy Check 3

Name ______________________________

Solve each Factor Puzzle.

1. Hung's photograph is 8 inches wide and 12 inches long. He wants to enlarge the photograph so it is 30 inches long. How wide should the photograph be if he wants the same ratio of length to width?

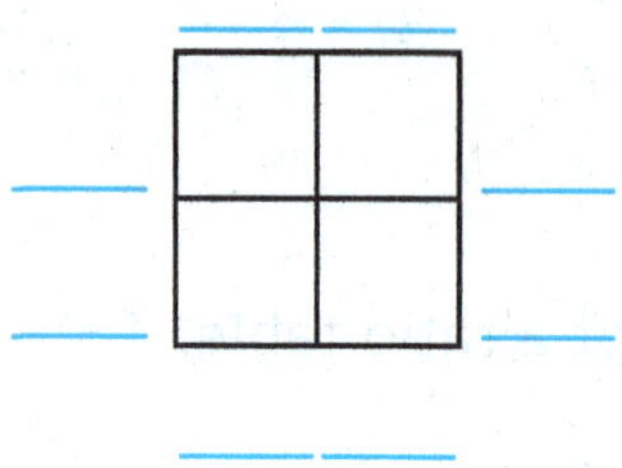

______________ inches long

2. Linda uses 15 tomatoes and 6 onions to make soup. She wants to make another batch, but she only has 2 onions left. How many tomatoes should she use to keep the ratio of tomatoes to onions the same?

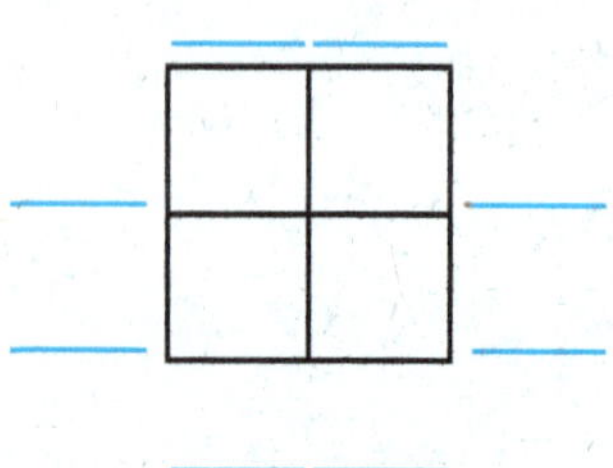

______________ tomatoes

Name ______________________

Relate Time and Distance

Each year, the Lincoln Park Conservatory in Chicago has a winter flower garden and model train exhibit. The buildings are made out of plant materials, such as twigs, leaves, bark, and seed pods.

Suppose the model train is traveling at a speed of 2 feet per second.

4. Make a table to show how far the train travels in 5 seconds.

Time	Distance
Seconds	Feet
1	
2	
3	
4	
5	

5. Graph the relationship of time and distance.

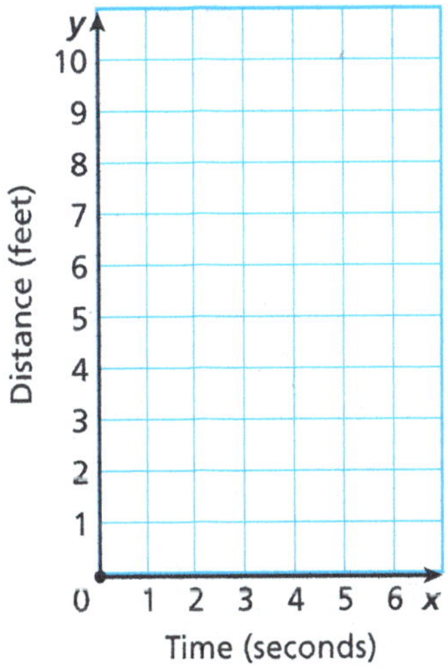

6. In the photo above, the shorter building on the right is about 3 times the height of the train. The taller building, on the left, is about 4 times the height of the train. If the train cars are 6 inches tall, about how tall is each structure?

____

____

Unit 1
Quick Quiz 4

Name ______________________________

Find the unknown value.

1. 5:c :: 30:42

   c = ________

2. 12:16 :: 3:m

   m = ________

Write the basic ratio.

3. The basic ratio for 6:21 is ________.

Solve.

Show your work.

4. A television station has 20 minutes of commercials for every 60 minutes of programming. For that station, what is the basic ratio of commercial minutes to programming minutes?

   ____

5. What is the basic ratio of red to yellow for a paint mixture of 12 cans of red paint and 27 cans of yellow paint?

   ____

Strategy Check 4

Name ______________________

Solve.

Show your work.

1. On a map, 5 inches represent 80 miles. If two towns are 400 miles apart, how many inches apart would they be on the map?

2. a. Lin uses 24 cups of vegetables for every 16 cups of stock to make a stew. What is the basic ratio of cups of vegetables to cups of stock?

   b. How many cups of vegetables should Lin use with 10 cups of stock?

3. Lachlan needs 4 drops of dye for every 30 milliliters of water. How many drops of the dye does he need if he uses 1,200 milliliters of water?

4. Write a word problem for these equivalent ratios: 4:15 = m:45.

Name ______________________________

1 Is this a problem about equivalent ratios? Write Yes or No. Explain why or why not.

Gina puts 3 cups of nuts and 2 cups of raisins in every batch of trail mix that she makes. If she uses 12 cups of nuts, how many cups of raisins will she use?

____

2 The ratios 2:3 and 8:12 are equivalent.

2a. Use words and a picture to explain why 2:3 and 8:12 are equivalent ratios.

2b. Select all the ratios below that are equivalent to the ratios in your drawing.

- ○ 4:6
- ○ 9:10
- ○ 6:9
- ○ 12:18

2c. What is another ratio equivalent to 2:3? Explain how you would change your drawing to show that ratio is equivalent.

Equivalent ratio: ______________

Unit 1
Review/Test

Name ______________________

Solve each Factor Puzzle.

3

12	20
21	

4

	63
40	35

5 Is each table a rate table? Choose Yes or No. Then explain why.

5a. Table 1

Minutes	Miles
1	5
2	10
5	25
7	35
9	45

○ Yes ○ No

5b. Table 2

Minutes	Miles
1	5
2	10
5	15
7	20
9	25

○ Yes ○ No

6 Use the table.

6a. Complete the rate table.

Pounds	Dollars
1	
	6
3	
4	12
	15

6b. What is the unit rate for the table?

____

6c. Draw the graph for the rate table.

6d. Show the unit rate triangle on the graph.

Name ____________________

Use the numbers on the tiles to complete each ratio table. You may use each number more than once.

2	3	4	5
6	10	11	12
13	14	25	28

7

Roses	Daisies
◯	◯
	9
4	
8	12
	15

8

Apples	Oranges
◯	◯
21	
6	8
	16
9	

9 When the unknown is replaced by the given value, are the ratios equivalent? Choose Yes or No.

9a. 4:9 :: 12:*a*

a = 3 ○ Yes ○ No

a = 27 ○ Yes ○ No

9b. *c*:10 :: 12:15

c = 8 ○ Yes ○ No

c = 18 ○ Yes ○ No

10 The basic ratio for 12:20 is *a*:*b*.

Choose one number from each column to identify the basic ratio.

a	*b*
○ 2	○ 1
○ 3	○ 3
○ 5	○ 5
○ 8	○ 7
○ 12	○ 9

11 Is the table a ratio table? Write Yes or No, and then explain your answer. If it is a ratio table, write the basic ratio in the top row.

Pencils	Pens
◯	◯
7	6
14	12
21	24
28	38
35	42

Name ______________________________

12 Match each situation to its unit rate.

9 boxes for $54	6 bags for $42	12 tablets for $24	4 pounds for $12
•	•	•	•
•	•	•	•
1 to 2	1 to 3	1 to 6	1 to 7

13 A baker uses 3 cups of whole wheat flour and 6 cups of white flour to bake a batch of bread.

Part A

Write a ratio that compares the amount of whole wheat flour to the amount of white flour.

____

Part B

The baker bakes a second batch of bread using 4 cups of whole wheat flour and 12 cups of white flour. Is the ratio of the two flours in this second batch equivalent to the ratio of the two flours in the first batch? Explain why or why not.

Part C

A customer wants to buy bread from the batch that contains more whole wheat flour and less white flour in it. Which batch should the customer buy from? Support your answer.

14 Tomatoes cost $2 per pound. What is the cost of 6 pounds of tomatoes?

$ __________

Name ______________________________

15 Melinda rides her bike 18 miles in 2 hours. If she rides at a constant speed, select the answers below that are equivalent ratios to the speed she rides. Select all ratios that are equivalent.

- ○ 27 miles in 4 hours
- ○ 9 miles in 1 hour
- ○ 36 miles in 2 hours
- ○ 27 miles in 3 hours
- ○ 36 miles in 4 hours

16 Grow Green Garden Center sells pots of herbs for 3 for $12. Green Thumb Garden Center sells the same herbs for 4 for $15.

16a. Which garden center has the lower unit price? Use math facts to support your answer.

16b. Suppose you want to buy 24 pots of herbs. What assumption must you make if you decide to buy them at Green Thumb?

16c. Fill in the missing numbers in each table. Then label each table with the name of the garden center it represents.

____

Pots	Cost ($)
	30
12	
16	
	75

____

Pots	Cost ($)
6	
9	
	48
15	

Name ___________________________

17 Abby saves $3 per week and Luis saves $8. Based on this ratio, complete the chart below to determine how much money Abby and Luis save over time.

Abby ($ per week saved)	Luis ($ per week saved)
3	8
	24
12	
21	
	72

18 Greg mixes 6 cans of black paint with 8 cans of white paint to get a gray paint. How many cans of black paint will he need to mix with 48 cans of white paint to get the same gray color?

Show your work in the space below.

_______ cans

19 Write and solve a word problem for this pair of equivalent ratios with an unknown:

$$6:10 = 21:d$$

Explain why your problem is about equivalent ratios.

Name ______________________________

Rates

Last week, Harry began riding his bike 4 miles every day. He wants to record the total number of miles he rides and compare how far he rides to how far his friend Peyton rides.

Help Harry by answering the questions that follow.

1. If Harry's situation is a rate situation, what is his unit rate? If it is not a rate situation, explain why not.

2. Complete the table for the number of days Harry rides and the number of miles he rides.

   - How many miles does Harry ride in 3 days? Explain and show your work.

   - How many days does it take Harry to ride 60 miles? Explain and show your work.

3. Peyton rides her bike the same number of miles every day. When Harry rides 16 miles, Peyton rides 20 miles. How many miles does Peyton ride each day? Show or explain how you got your answer.

4. How many days does it take Peyton to ride 60 miles? Explain.

Name ______________________________

5 Find the ratio of the number of days it takes Harry to ride 60 miles to the number of days it takes Peyton to ride 60 miles. How is this related to the ratio of Harry's unit rate to Peyton's unit rate? Explain why this is so.

6 Peyton and Harry want to go on a camping trip and their final destination is 20 miles away. How long would it take Harry to reach the final destination? Explain your answer.

- When should Peyton leave in relation to Harry in order to reach their destination on the same day?

7 Peyton rides a total of 50 miles and Harry rides for the same number of days. Find the number of miles Harry would have ridden. Explain your answer.

Dear Family:

Students will be learning about geometry throughout the school year. This unit is about two kinds of measurement—perimeter and area. Perimeter is a measurement of length—the distance around a figure or an object. Area is a measurement of the amount of surface enclosed or covered by a figure or an object without gaps or overlaps.

We measure area in square units, such as square inches ($in.^2$) or square centimeters (cm^2).

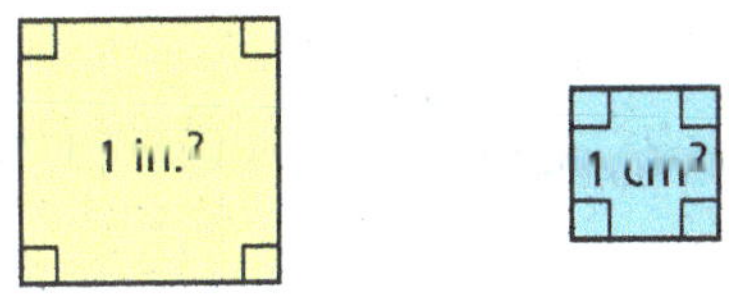

Your child will learn to calculate the area and perimeter of these figures.

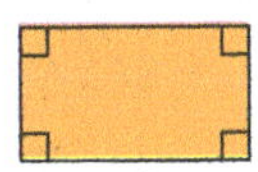

Rectangle
2 pairs of parallel sides
4 right angles

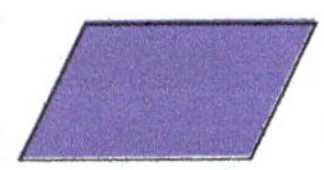

Parallelogram
2 pairs of parallel sides

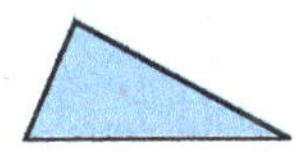

Triangle
3 sides

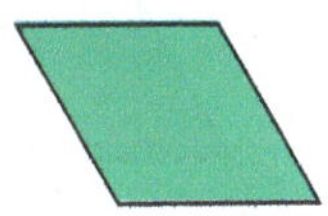

Rhombus
2 pairs of parallel sides
4 sides the same length

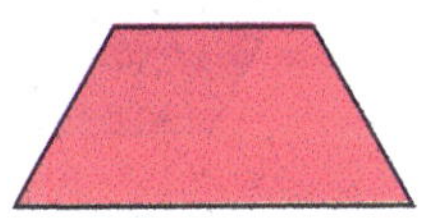

Trapezoid
exactly one pair of parallel sides

Pentagon
5 sides

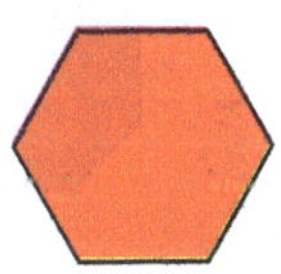

Hexagon
6 sides

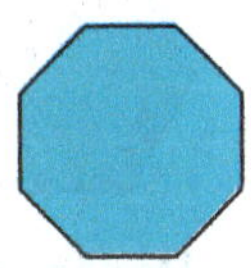

Octagon
8 sides

Complex Figure
composed of simpler figures

Students will also estimate the perimeter and area of *irregular figures* that are drawn on grid paper. Irregular figures cannot be decomposed into simpler figures that students are familiar with. So, students cannot calculate the exact perimeter or area.

Students will also graph polygons on a coordinate grid to find side lengths using x– and y–coordinates and to find perimeter and area.

If you have any questions or comments, please contact me.

Sincerely,
Your child's teacher

Calculating Perimeter and Area

Rectangle

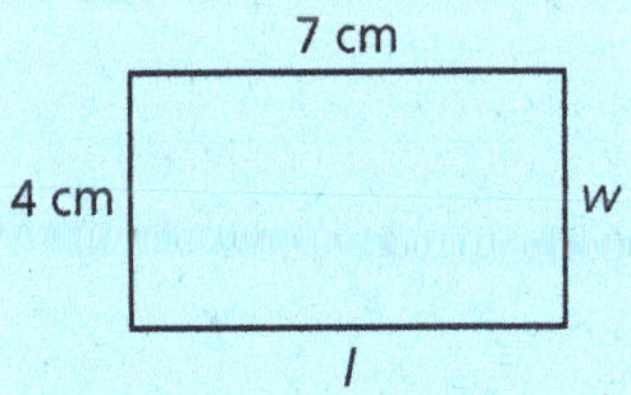

Perimeter $= 2l + 2w$
Perimeter $= 2 \times 7 + 2 \times 4$
Perimeter $= 14 + 8 = 22$ cm

Area $= l \times w$
Area $= 7 \times 4 = 28\ cm^2$

Parallelogram

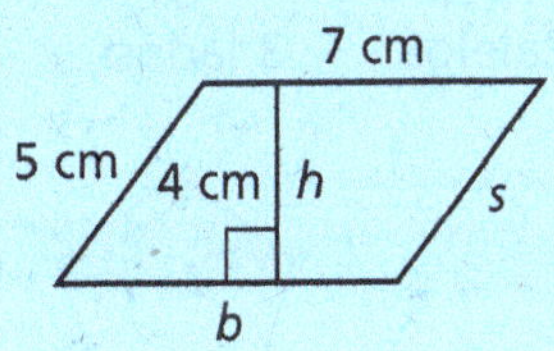

Perimeter $= 2b + 2s$
Perimeter $= 2 \times 7 + 2 \times 5$
Perimeter $= 14 + 10 = 24$
Perimeter $= 24$ cm

Area $= b \times h$
Area $= 7 \times 4 = 28$
Area $= 28\ cm^2$

Triangle

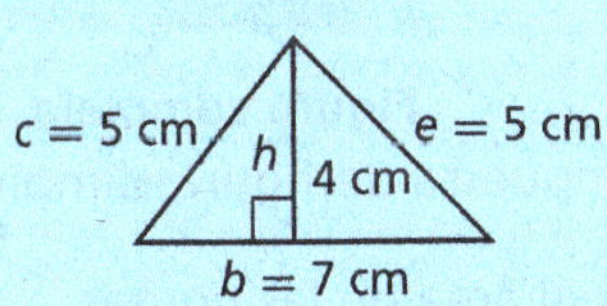

Perimeter $= c + b + e$
Perimeter $= 5 + 7 + 5 = 17$
Perimeter $= 17$ cm

Area $= \frac{1}{2} b \times h$
Area $= \frac{1}{2}(7 \times 4)$
Area $= 14\ cm^2$

Estimada familia:

Durante el año escolar, los estudiantes aprenderán geometría. En esta unidad estudiaremos dos tipos de mediciones: perímetro y área. El perímetro, que es una medición de longitud, es la distancia que rodea a una figura o un objeto. El área es la medición de la superficie que cubre un objeto sin espacios ni traslapos.

Medimos el área en unidades cuadradas, como pulgadas cuadradas (pulg²) o centímetros cuadrados (cm²).

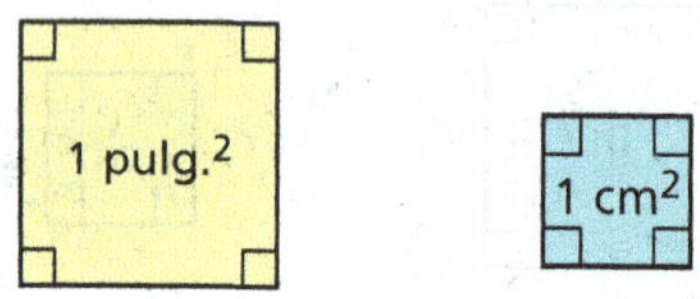

Su hijo aprenderá a calcular el área y el perímetro de estas figuras.

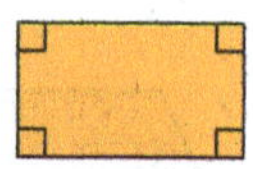

Rectángulo
2 pares de lados paralelos
4 ángulos rectos

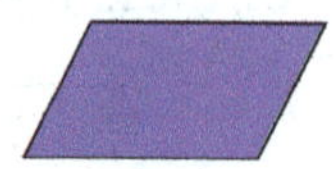

Paralelogramo
2 pares de lados paralelos

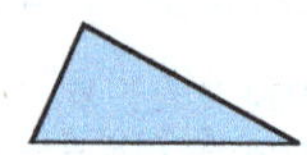

Triángulo
3 lados

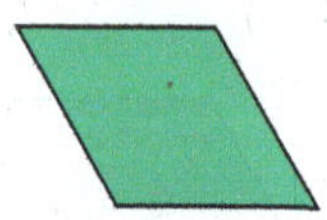

Rombo
2 pares de lados paralelos
4 lados del mismo largo

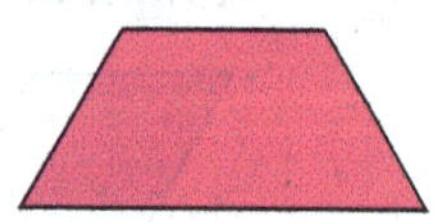

Trapecio
exactamente un par de lados paralelos

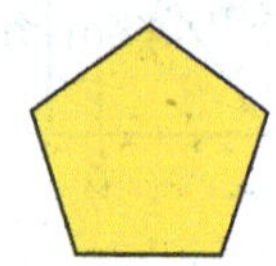

Pentágono
5 lados

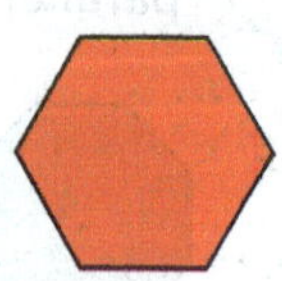

Hexágono
6 lados

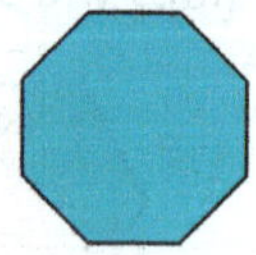

Octágono
8 lados

Figura compleja
compuesta de figuras simples

Los estudiantes también estimarán el perímetro y el área de las *figuras irregulares* que se dibujan en papel cuadriculado. Las figuras irregulares no se pueden descomponer en figuras más simples las cuales son más familiares para los estudiantes. Por lo tanto, los estudiantes no pueden calcular el perímetro o área exacta.

Los estudiantes también trazarán polígonos en una cuadrícula de coordenadas, usando las coordenadas x– y y– para hallar el largo de los lados, el perímetro y el área.

Si tiene alguna pregunta, por favor comuníquese conmigo.

Atentamente,
El maestro de su hijo

Calcular el perímetro y el área

Rectángulo

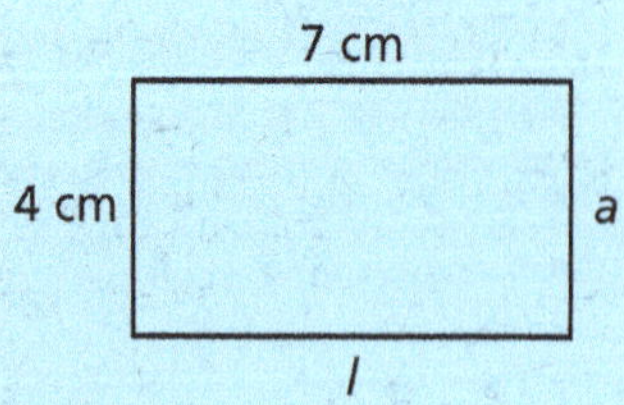

Perímetro = $2l + 2a$
Perímetro = $2 \times 7 + 2 \times 4$
Perímetro = $14 + 8 = 22$ cm

Área = $l \times a$
Área = $7 \times 4 = 28$ cm²

Paralelogramo

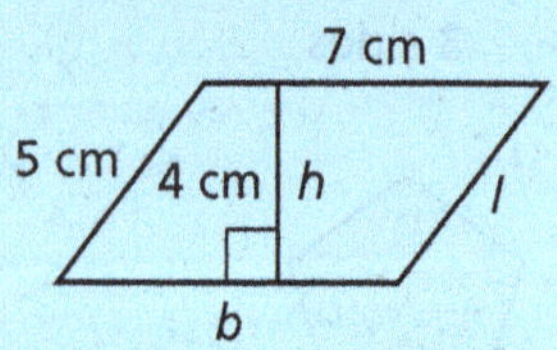

Perímetro = $2b + 2l$
Perímetro = $2 \times 7 + 2 \times 5$
Perímetro = $14 + 10 = 24$
Perímetro = 24 cm

Área = $b \times h$
Área = $7 \times 4 = 28$ cm²

Triángulo

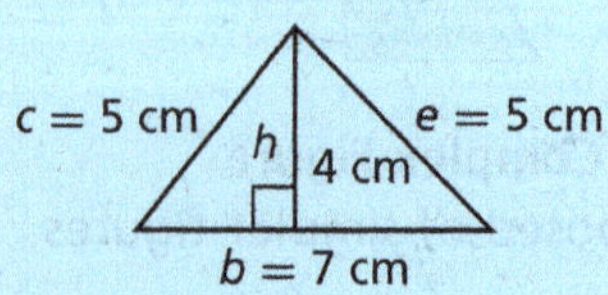

Perímetro = $c + b + e$
Perímetro = $5 + 7 + 5 = 17$
Perímetro = 17 cm

Área = $\frac{1}{2} b \times h$
Área = $\frac{1}{2}(7 \times 4)$
Área = 14 cm²

acute triangle

base of a rectangle

area

base of a triangle

base of a parallelogram

complex figure

Any side of a rectangle can be the base.

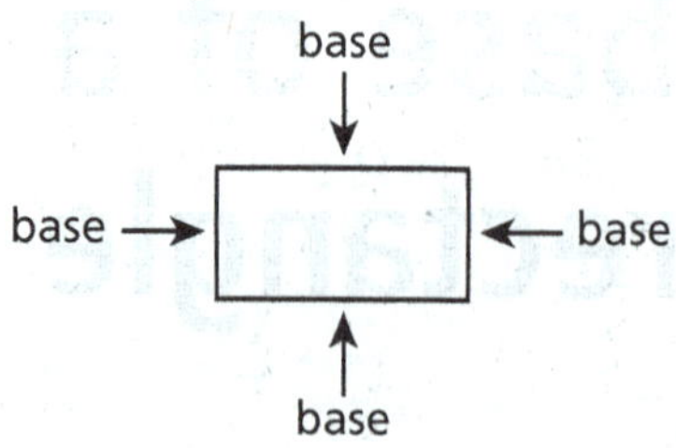

A triangle with three acute angles. An acute angle has a measure that is greater than 0° and less than 90°.

Examples:

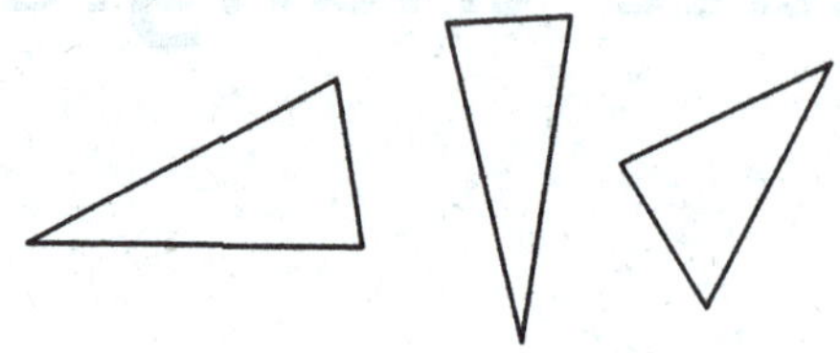

Any side of a triangle can be the base.

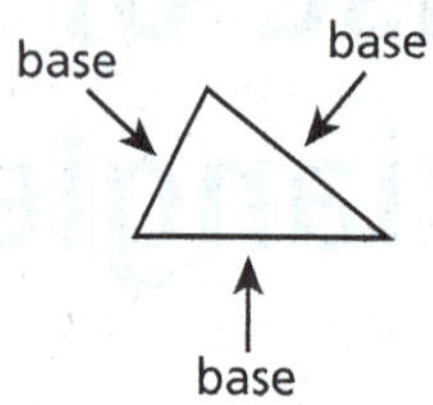

The amount of surface covered or enclosed by a figure. Area is measured by finding the number of same size units required to cover the shape without gaps or overlaps.

A figure made by combining simple geometric figures, such as rectangles and triangles.

Examples:

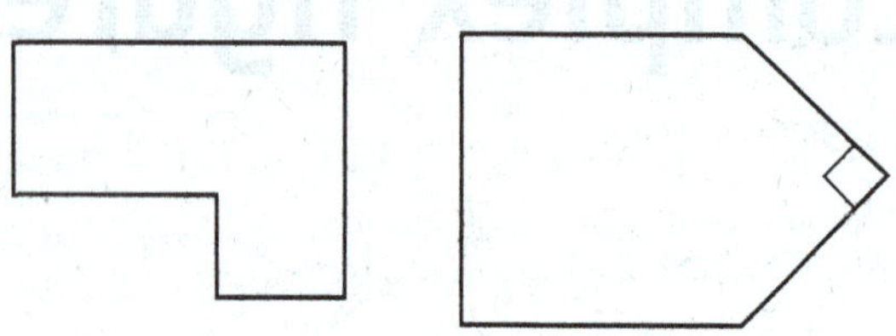

Any side of a parallelogram can be the base.

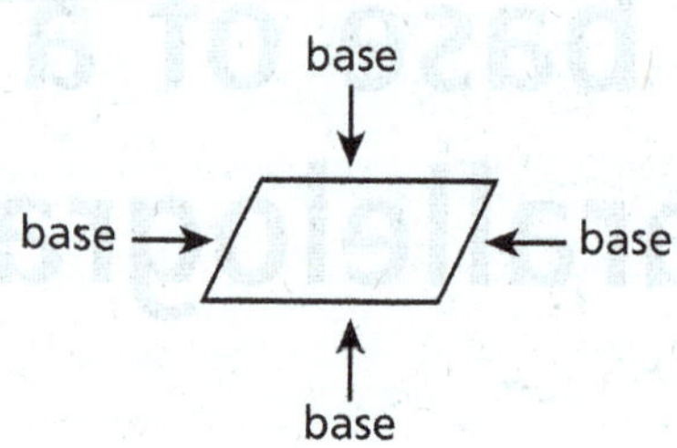

coordinates

height of a rectangle

dimensions

height of a triangle

height of a parallelogram

hexagon

Any side of a rectangle can be a height.

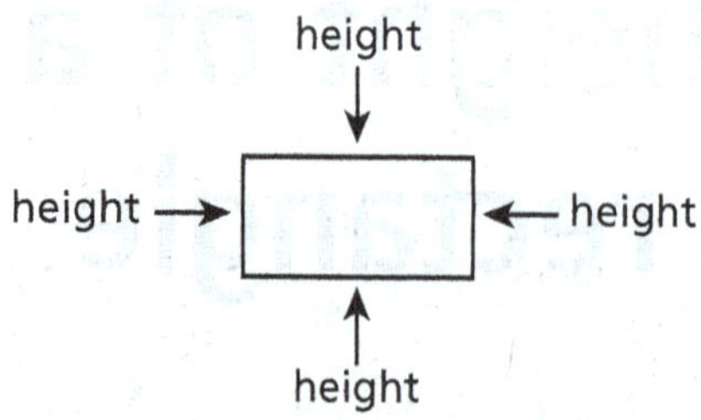

Each point in the coordinate plane corresponds to an ordered pair of numbers called its coordinates.

The perpendicular distance from a base to a vertex that is not on the base. Finding this distance may require extending the base.

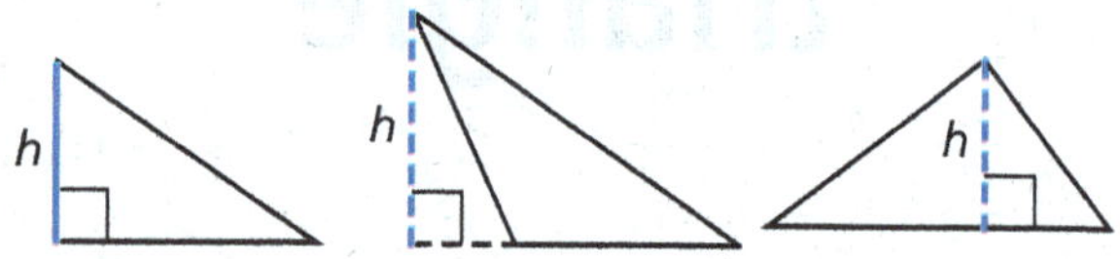

The height, length, or width of a figure.

Examples:

A line segment has only length, so it has one dimension.

A rectangle has length and width, so it has two dimensions.

A cube has length, width, and height, so it has three dimensions.

A polygon with six sides.

Examples:

The height of a parallelogram is the perpendicular distance from a base to a vertex that is not on the base. Finding this distance may require extending the base.

Examples:

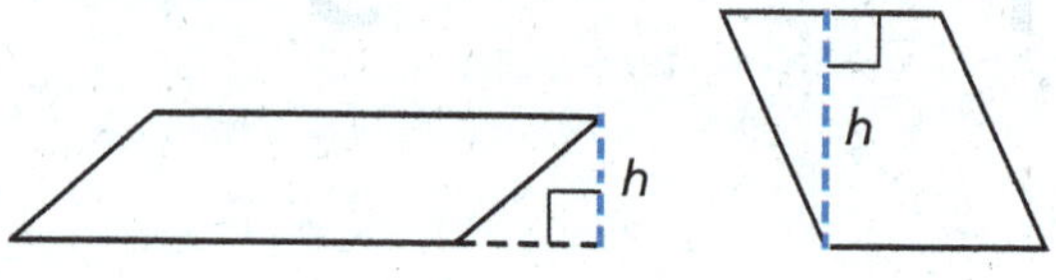

obtuse triangle	**pentagon**
octagon	**perimeter**
parallelogram	**perpendicular**

A polygon with five sides.

Examples:

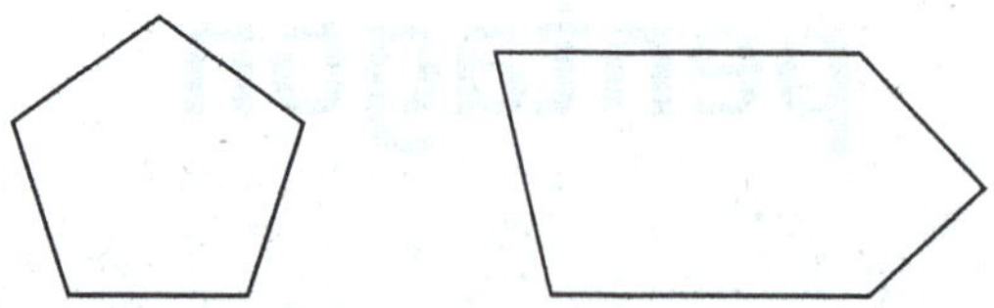

A triangle with one obtuse angle. An obtuse angle has a measure that is greater than 90° and less than 180°.

Examples:

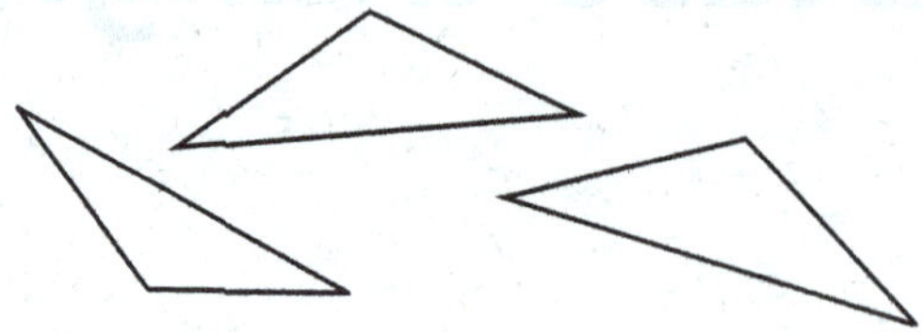

The distance around a figure. It is the total number of same size units of length required to form the sides without gaps or overlaps.

A polygon with eight sides.

Examples:

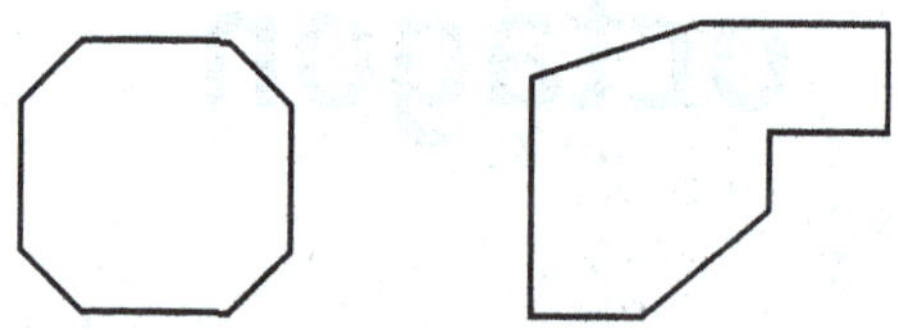

Lines, line segments, or rays are perpendicular if they form a right angle. A right angle has a measure that is equal to 90°.

Example:

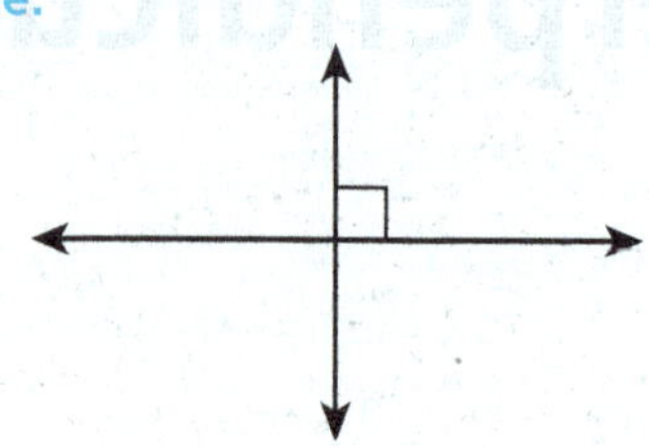

A quadrilateral in which both pairs of opposite sides are parallel and opposite angles are congruent.

Examples:

regular polygon	**square centimeter (cm^2)**
rhombus	**tessellation**
right triangle	**trapezoid**

A unit of area equal to the area of a square with one-centimeter sides.

A polygon with all sides the same length.

Examples:

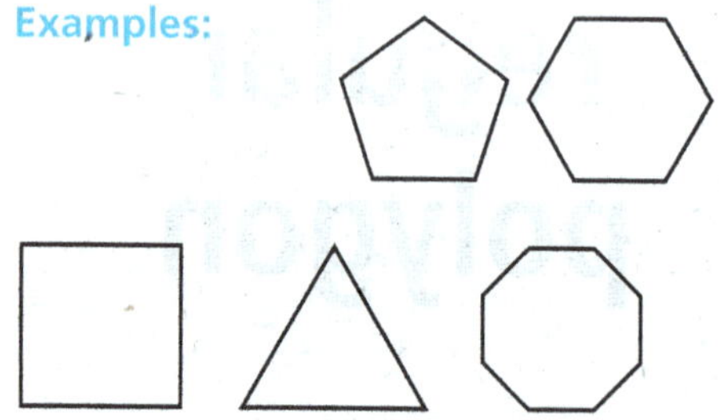

A pattern of closed figures that completely cover a surface with no gaps or overlaps.

Example:

A parallelogram with all sides the same length.

Examples:

A quadrilateral with exactly one pair of parallel sides.

Examples:

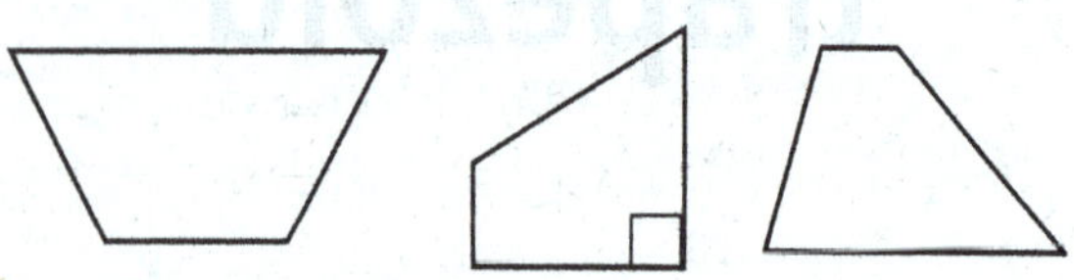

A triangle with one right angle. A right angle has a measure that is equal to 90°.

Examples:

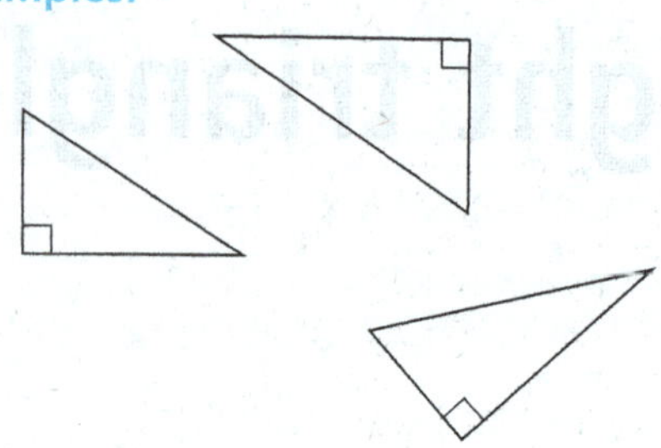

vertex

A point common to two sides of an angle or polygon, or three edges of a solid figure. The point of a pyramid.

Examples:

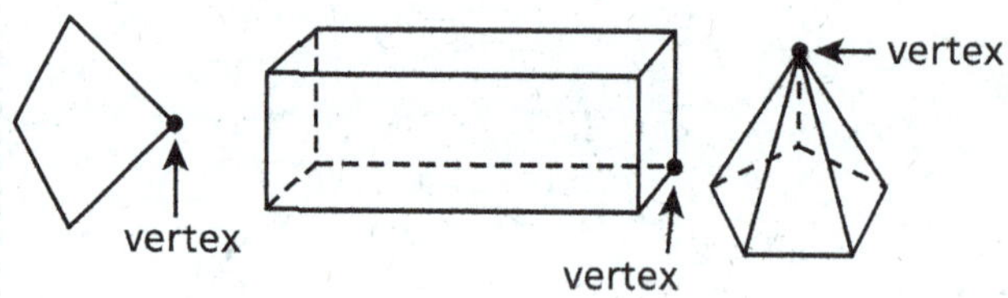

Name ______________________

VOCABULARY
perimeter
area
square centimeter (cm^2)

Formulas for Perimeter and Area

1 Look at the rectangles below.
What does **perimeter** mean?
What does **area** mean?

____

____

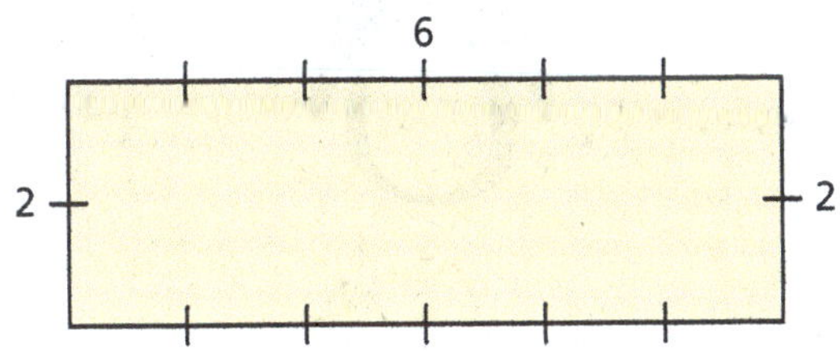

Perimeter = 16 cm

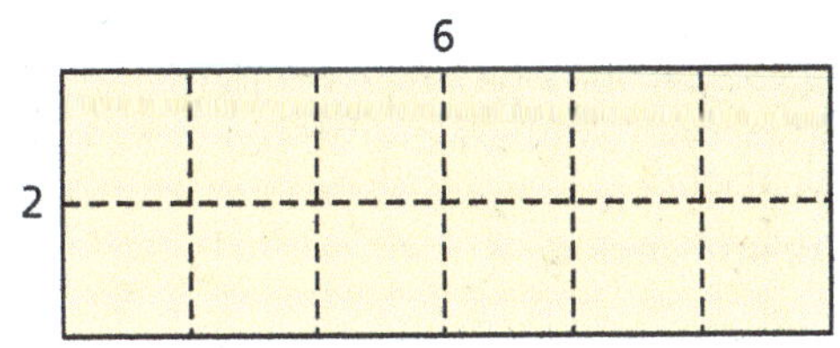

Area = 12 cm^2

On your MathBoard, draw the rectangles described in Exercises 2–5 below. Mark each centimeter with a tick mark, and write an equation that shows how to find the perimeter. Then outline and shade the **square centimeters (cm^2)** and write an equation that shows how to find the area.

	Length	Width	Perimeter	Area
	6 cm	2 cm	$2 + 6 + 2 + 6 = 16$ $P = 16$ cm	$6 \times 2 = 12$ $A = 12$ cm^2
2	4 cm	3 cm		
3	8 cm	1 cm		
4	5 cm	5 cm		
5	10 cm	4 cm		
6	l	w		

The last row of the table should show your formulas for perimeter and area.

Name ________________________________

What's the Error?

Dear Math Students,

Today I went to the paint store to buy paint for my dining room ceiling.

My ceiling is a rectangle 12 feet long and 10 feet wide. I told the clerk that I needed enough paint to cover 120 feet. He told me that I'd made a mistake.

Can you tell me what I did wrong?

Your friend,
Puzzled Penguin

14 Write a response to the Puzzled Penguin.

____

____

____

Dear Math Students,

It looks like I need your help again. I am sewing some fringe along the edge of a banner. The banner is a rectangle 96 inches long and 54 inches wide. I bought 150 inches of fringe. I started to sew on the fringe, but I ran out before I finished!

What did I do wrong in my calculation? How much fringe do I need to go around the whole banner?

Your friend,
Puzzled Penguin

15 Write a response to the Puzzled Penguin.

____

____

____

____

Name ____________________

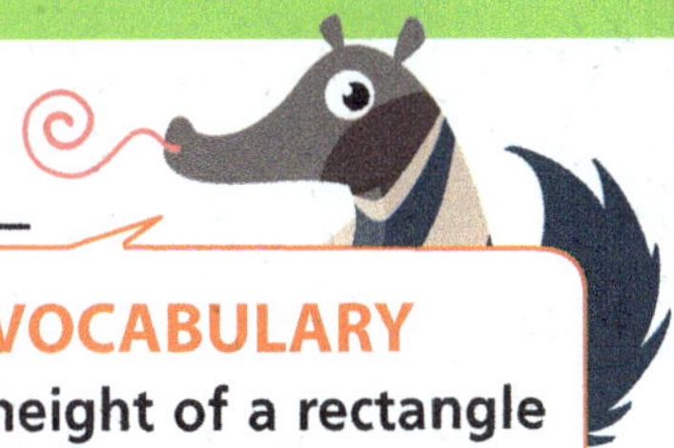

VOCABULARY
height of a rectangle
base of a rectangle
height of a triangle
base of a triangle

Relate Area of Right Triangle to Area of Rectangle

1 a. Look at Figure A. What is the area of the rectangle?

____

b. Draw a diagonal line and make two triangles. What is the area of each triangle? Why do you think so?

____

____

____

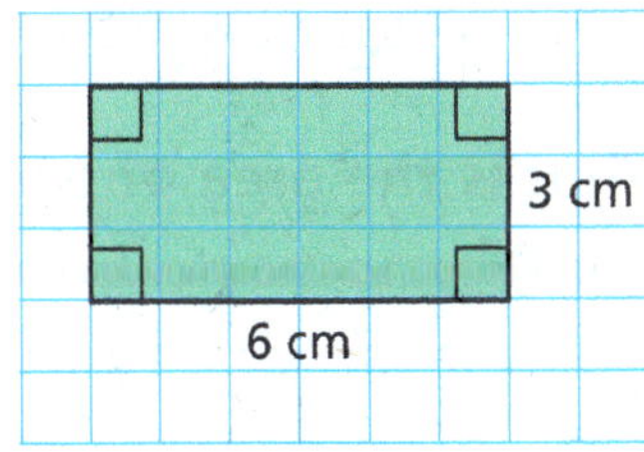

Figure A

---

2 a. Look at Figure B. How do the areas of the two yellow triangles compare? ____________________

b. How do the areas of the rectangle and the large right triangle compare? Explain your reasoning.

____

____

c. Write and use a formula to find the area of the rectangle or the large right triangle.

____

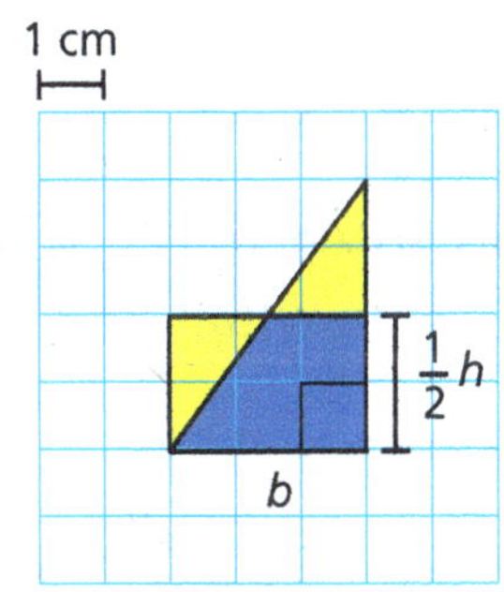

Figure B

---

3 a. Look at Figure C. Do the rectangle and large right triangle have the same areas? Explain how you know.

____

____

____

____

b. Write and use a formula to find the area of the large right triangle.

____

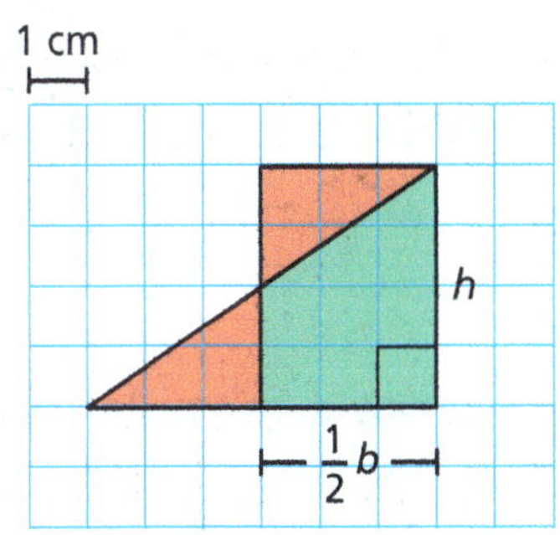

Figure C

Name ______________________

VOCABULARY
right triangle

Area and Perimeter of Right Triangles

A triangle with a right angle (square corner) is called a **right triangle**. The area of any right triangle is half the area of a rectangle with the same base and height or the same area as a rectangle with $\frac{1}{2}$ the base or height. These rectangles are called related rectangles.

What is the area of each right triangle shown below?

4
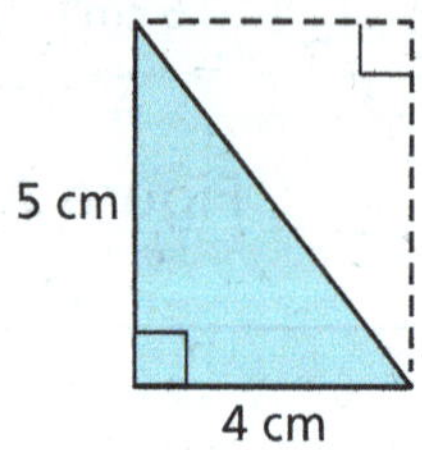

$A =$ ______________

5
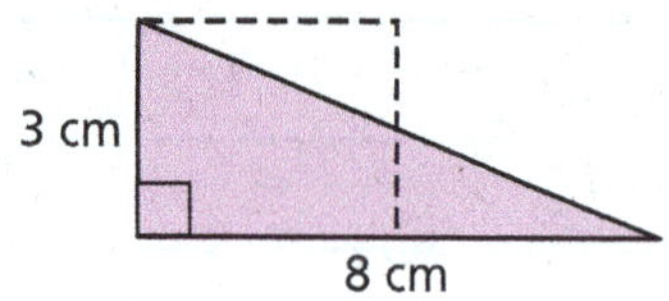

$A =$ ______________

6
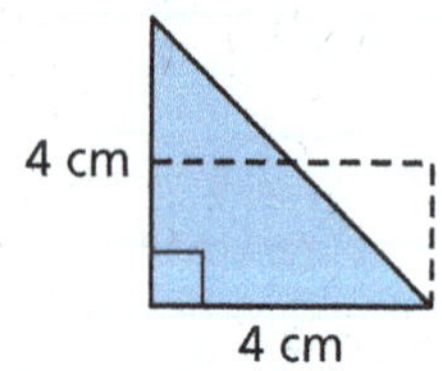

$A =$ ______________

To show that a triangle is a right triangle, mark the right angle with a small box. Find the area of each right triangle below.

7
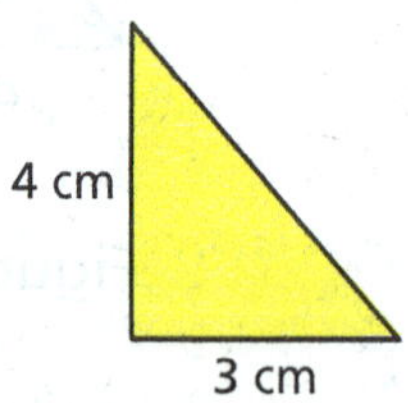

$A =$ ______________

8
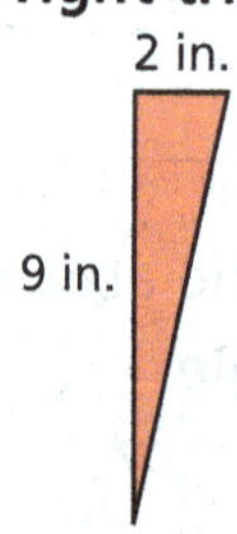

$A =$ ______________

9
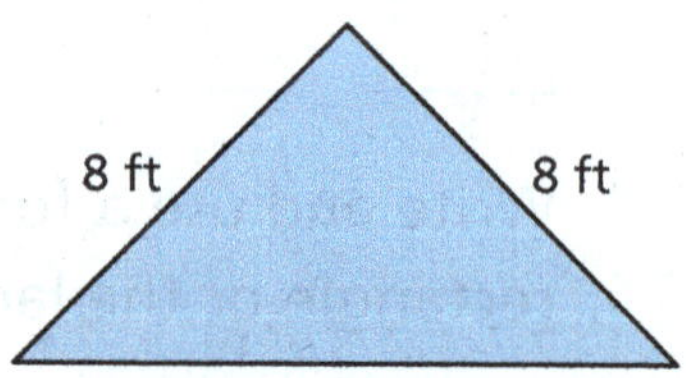

$A =$ ______________

10 This right triangle has sides of length *c*, *d*, and *e*. Write a formula for the area of any right triangle.

____

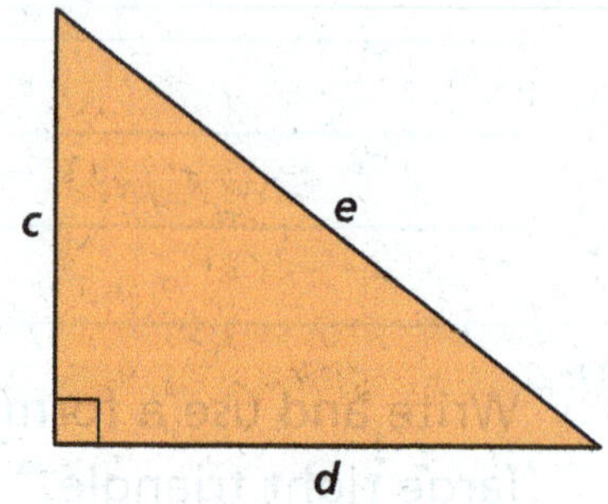

11 Write a formula for the perimeter of any right triangle.

____

Name ______________________

What's the Error?

Dear Math Students,

Today I found the area of a pennant that is in the shape of a right triangle with a base of 8 in. and a height of 6 in. Here is how I found the answer.

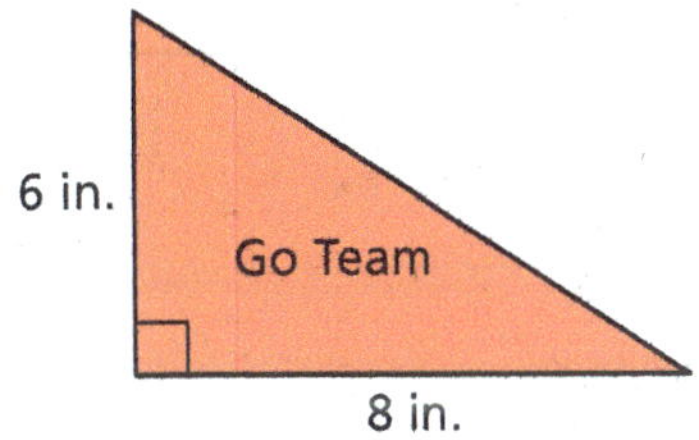

$A = \frac{1}{2}bh = 8 \times 6 = 48 \quad A = 48 \text{ in.}^2$

So, the area of the pennant is 48 in.^{2}

Am I correct? If not, please correct my work and explain below.

Your friend,
Puzzled Penguin

12 Write a response to the Puzzled Penguin.

____

____

____

____

____

____

13 Show two ways to multiply to compute the area of the right triangle.

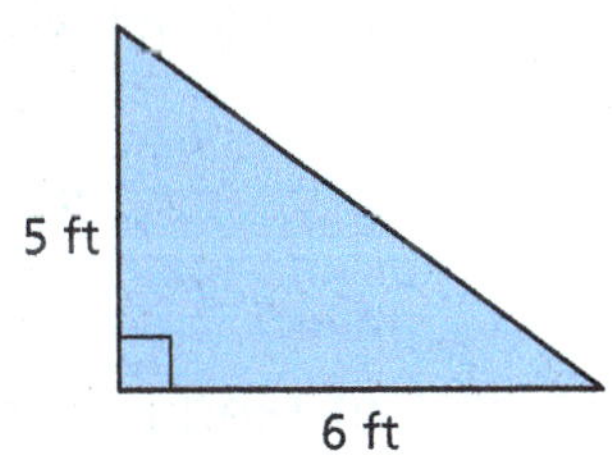

____

____

____

____

____

____

____

Name ____________________

Problems about Area of Right Triangles

Find the area of the right triangle.

14

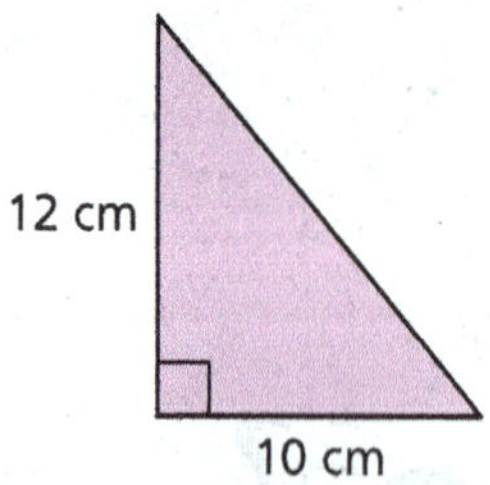

$A =$ ____________

15

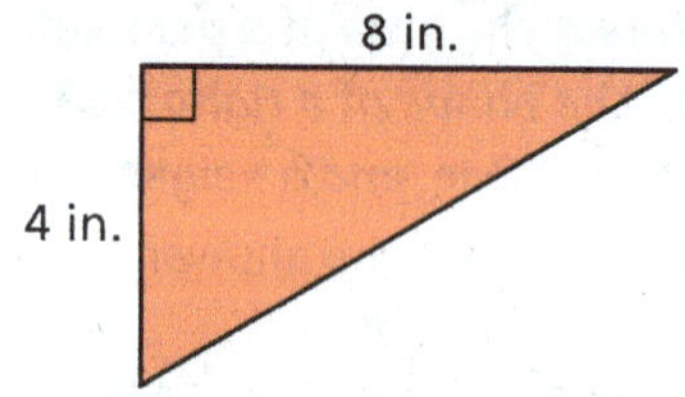

$A =$ ____________

Find the unknown side length of the right triangle.

16

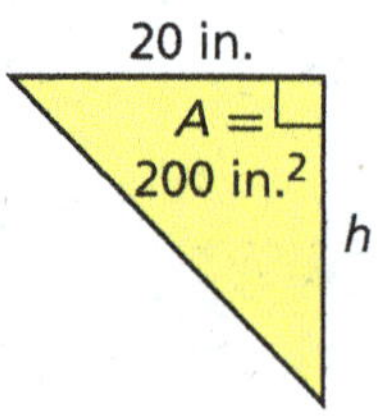

$h =$ ____________

17

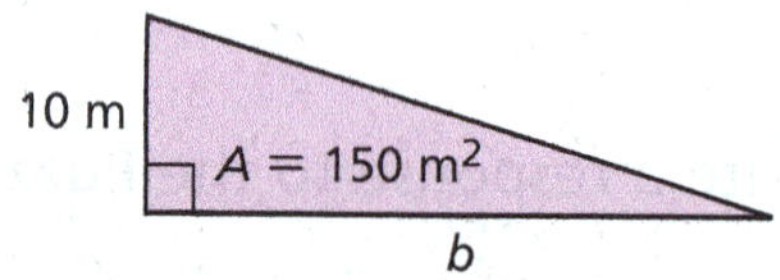

$b =$ ____________

Solve.

18 A gallon of purple paint covers 400 ft^2. How many gallons will it take to paint one side of this building purple? Allow half the area for the windows, which will not be painted.

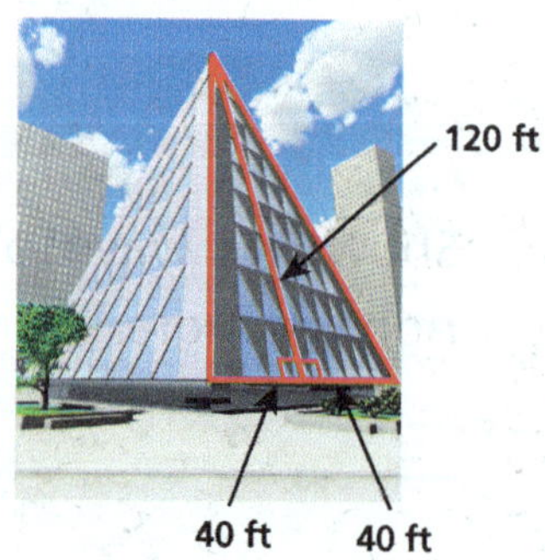

____

____

19 A plot of land is in the shape of a right triangle. The plot has an area of 2,400 square feet. The base of the triangle is 80 ft. What is the height of the triangle? ____________

Check Understanding

Draw a right triangle and one of its related rectangles. Explain how to use the rectangle to find the area of the triangle.

Name ______________________________

VOCABULARY
height of a parallelogram
parallelogram
perpendicular
base of a parallelogram

Experiment with Parallelograms

The **height** of a **parallelogram** is a line segment that is **perpendicular** to the **base**.

Cut out each pair of parallelograms below and then cut along the dashed line segment that shows each height. Switch the pieces. Put the slanted ends together.

What figure do you form?

____

Do you think this will always happen when the height connects the base and the opposite side? Why or why not?

____

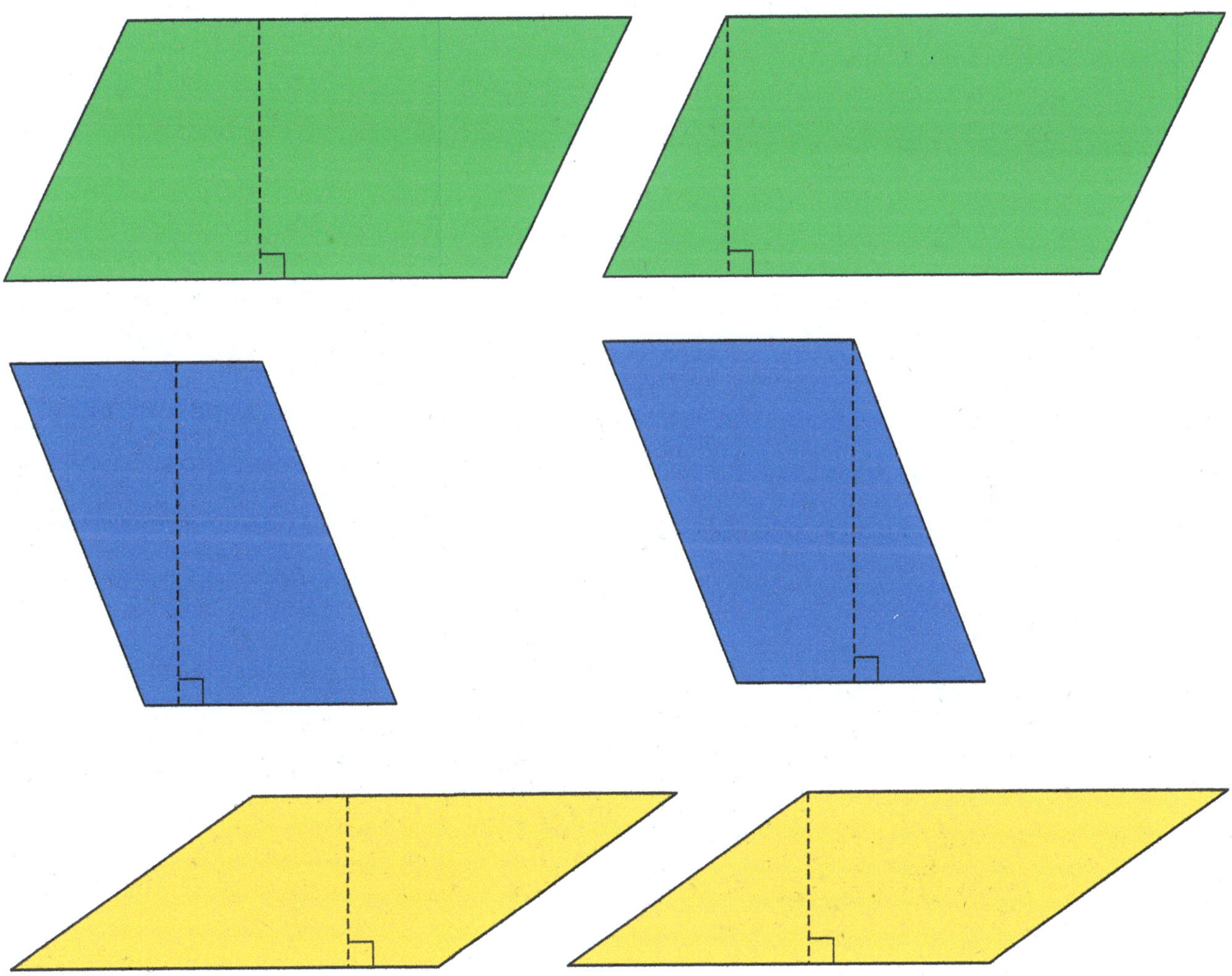

Name ______________________

What's the Error?

Dear Math Students,

Today I made a design with the parallelogram shown at the right. Then I found the area of the parallelogram. Here is how I found my answer.

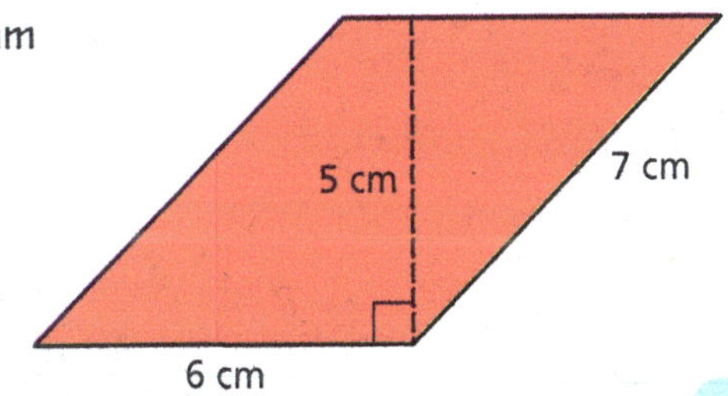

$A = \text{base} \times \text{height}$

$A = 6 \times 7 = 42$

So, the area of the parallelogram is 42 cm^2.

Am I correct? If not, please correct my work and explain below.

Your friend,
Puzzled Penguin

4. Write a response to the Puzzled Penguin.

____

____

Find the Area of a Parallelogram

This parallelogram has height *h*. The measurement of the base is *b*. The side is *s*.

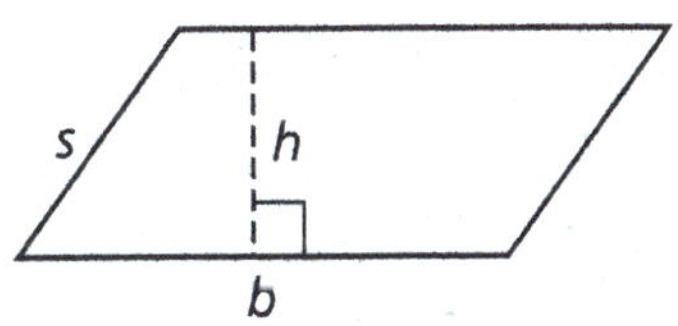

5. Write a formula for finding the area of the parallelogram.

____

6. What measurement shown is not used for finding the area?

____

7. Write a formula to find the perimeter of the parallelogram.

____

8. What measurement shown is not used for finding the perimeter?

____

Name ______________________________

VOCABULARY
acute triangle
obtuse triangle

Experiment with Triangles

The acute triangles below are exactly the same. Cut them out and rotate one so the sides labeled *a* are next to each other. What shape do you form? Do the same with sides labeled *b* and *c*. What shapes are formed?

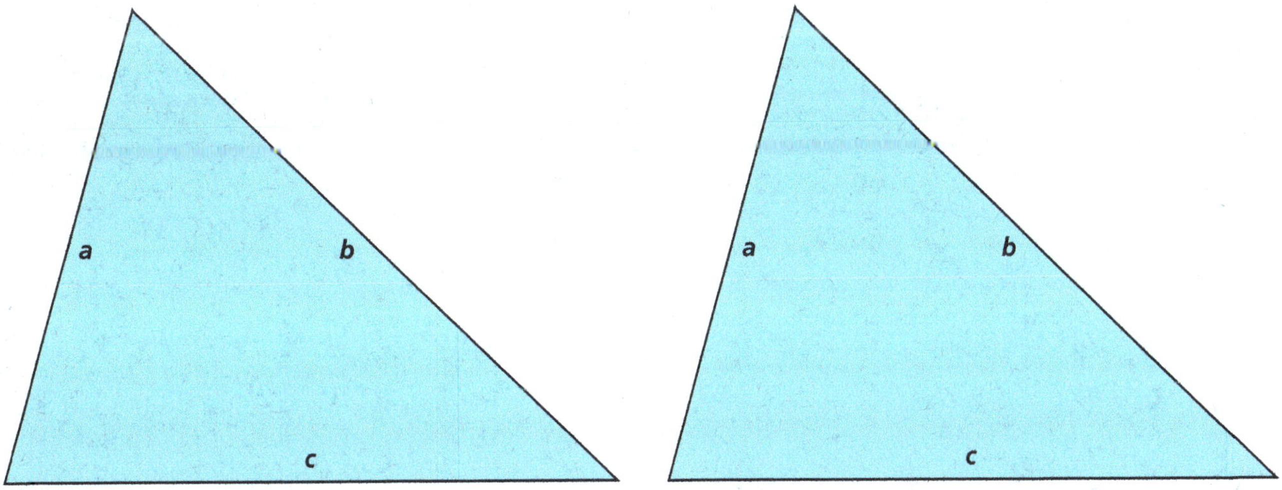

The obtuse triangles below are exactly the same. Cut them out and rotate one so the sides labeled *x* are next to each other. What shape do you form? Do the same with sides labeled *y* and *z*. What shapes are formed?

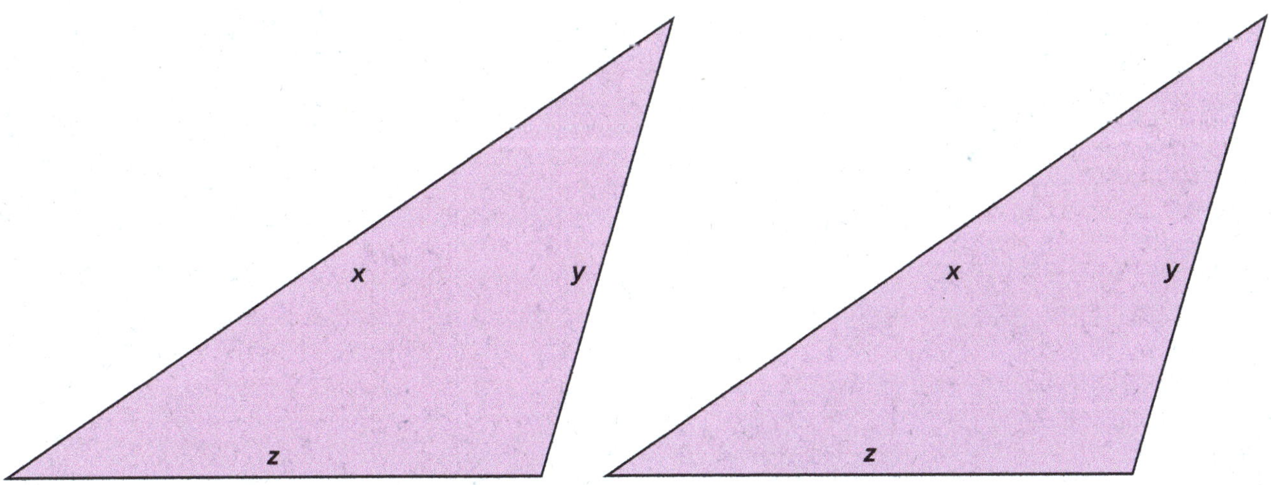

Name ______________________________

Draw Parallelograms and Triangles

Answer the following questions about triangle *ABC*.

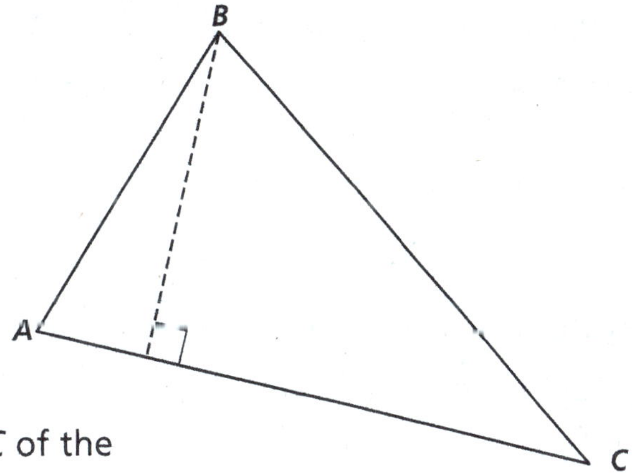

1. Measure and label side *AC* of the triangle in centimeters.
2. Measure and label the height.
3. What is the area of the triangle? ____________
4. Use your ruler to draw a line segment through *B* that is parallel to *AC*.
5. Draw a line segment through *C* that is parallel to *AB*. Label point *D* where the two new line segments meet.
6. A related parallelogram has the same base and height as its related triangle or rectangle. What is the area of related parallelogram *ABDC*?

   ____

7. Use the directions in Exercises 1–6 for this obtuse triangle. Find the area of triangle *ABC* and the area of parallelogram *ABDC*.

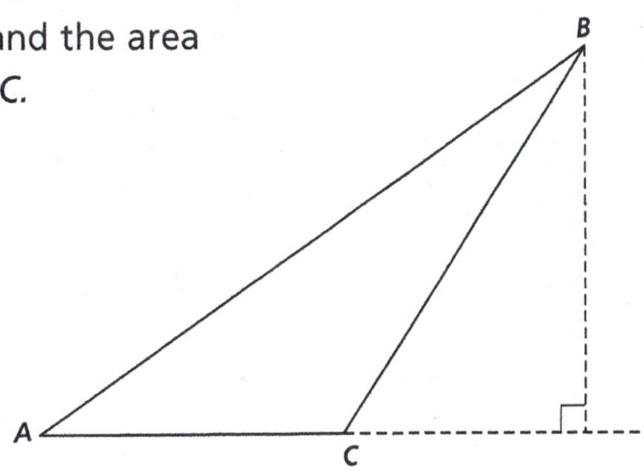

Name ______________________

Draw Parallelograms and Triangles (continued)

Complete.

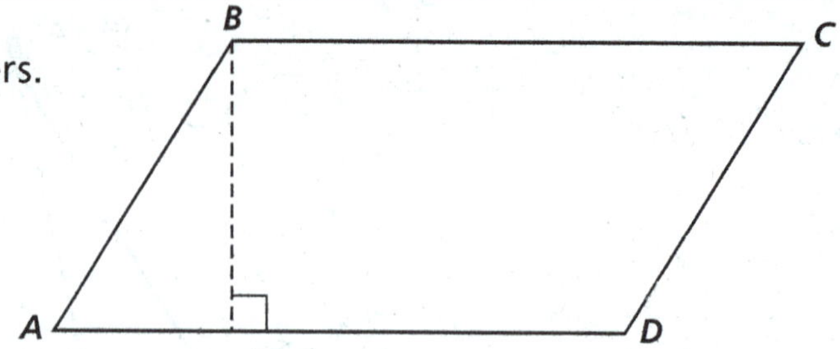

8. Measure and label side *AD* in centimeters.

9. Measure and label the height.

10. What is the area of parallelogram *ABCD*?

____

11. Join points *B* and *D*. Name the two triangles.

____

12. What is the area of each triangle?

____

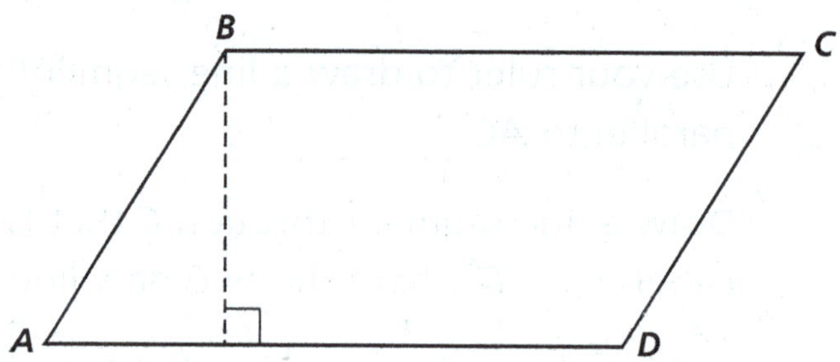

13. Divide parallelogram *ABCD* into two obtuse triangles.

14. What is the area of each obtuse triangle?

____

15. Draw two different diagonals for parallelogram *EFGH*. Name the triangles. Measure in centimeters, then find the area of each triangle.

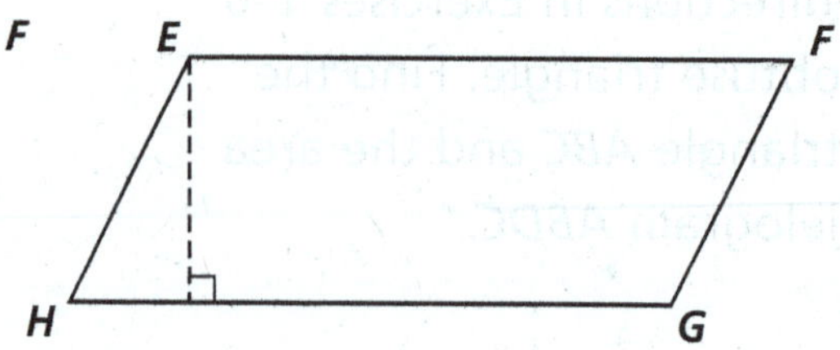

____

____

Name

What's the Error?

Dear Math Students,

Today, I found the area of the sail on the sailboat model shown at the right.

Here is how I found the answer.

$A = 6 \times 7 = 42 \quad A = 42 \text{ cm}^2$

So, the area of the sail is 42 cm^2.

Am I correct? If not, please correct my work and explain below.

Your friend,
Puzzled Penguin

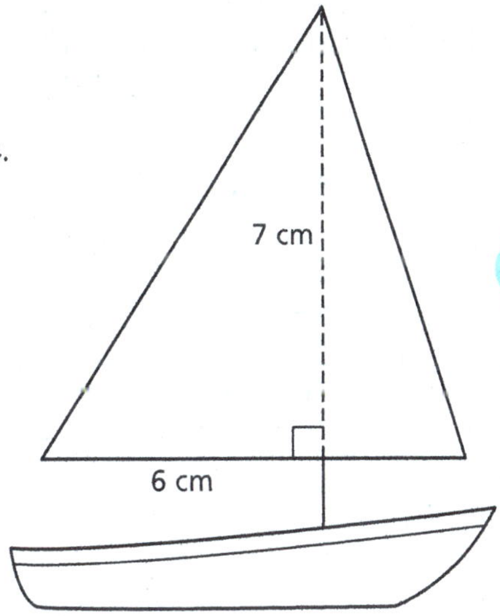

24 Write a response to the Puzzled Penguin.

Solve Real World Problems

25 Rico planted carrots in the triangular shape shown at the right. Find the area planted with carrots.

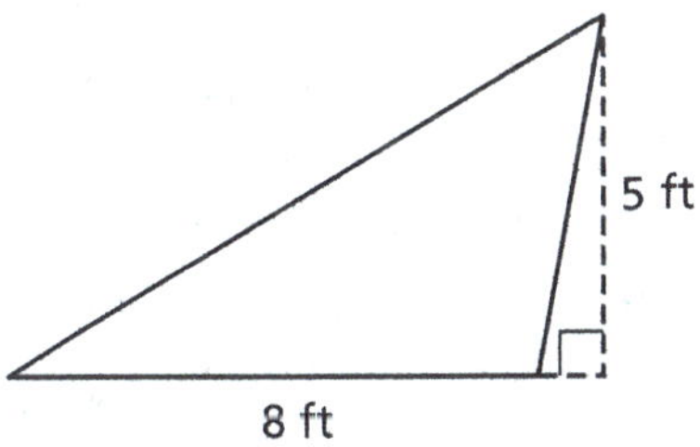

26 Katie is making a pen for her chickens as shown at the right. How much fence will she need? What is the area of the pen?

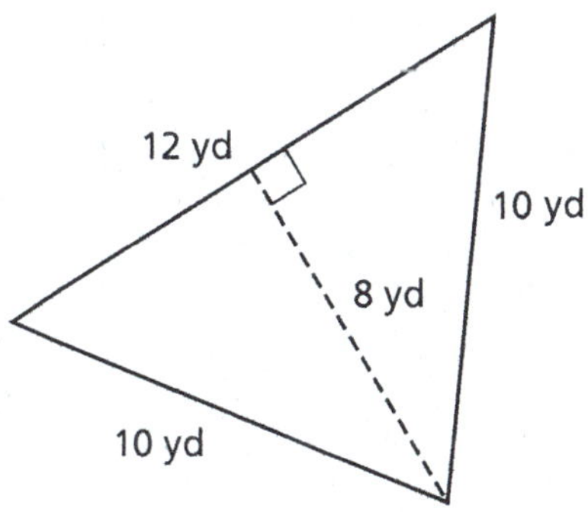

Check Understanding

Explain why the formula $A = \frac{1}{2}bh$ can be used to find the area of any triangle.

Name ______________________

Choose a Base

Choose a base and a corresponding height with lengths you can find without a ruler. Then find the area. Each square represents 1 cm^2.

13 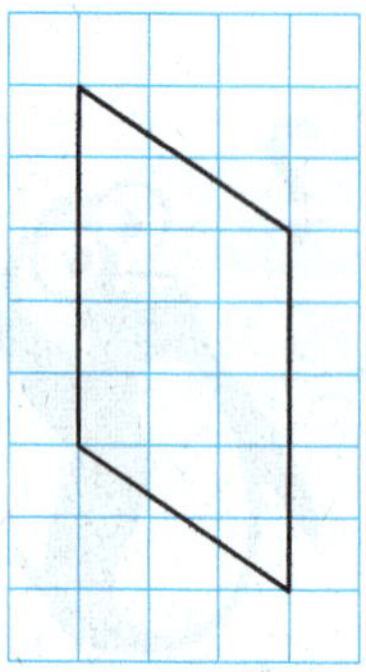

$A =$ ______________

14 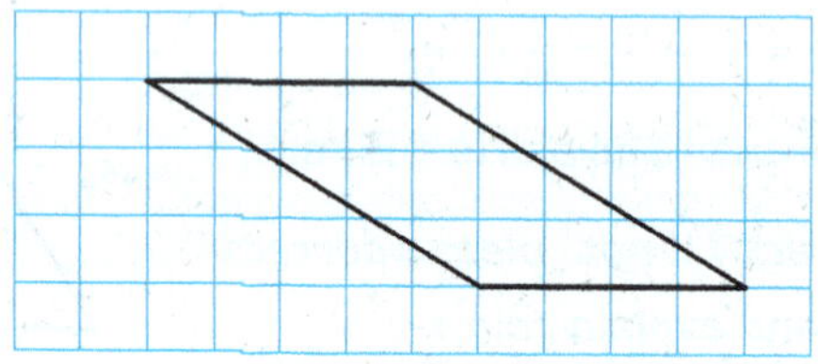

$A =$ ______________

15 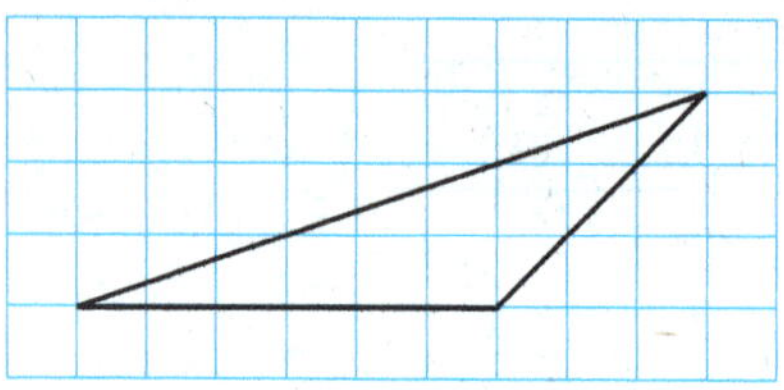

$A =$ ______________

16 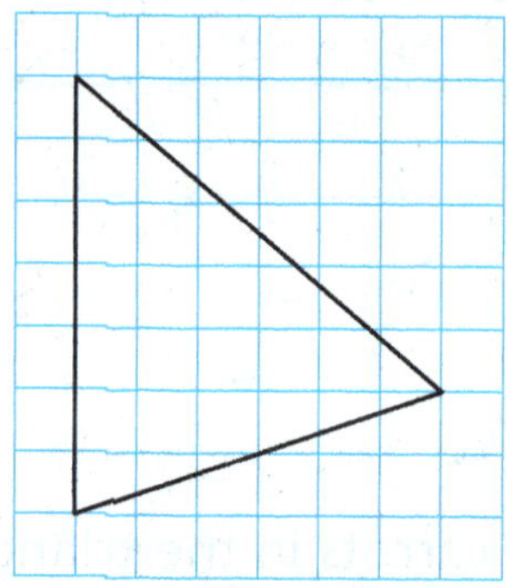

$A =$ ______________

17 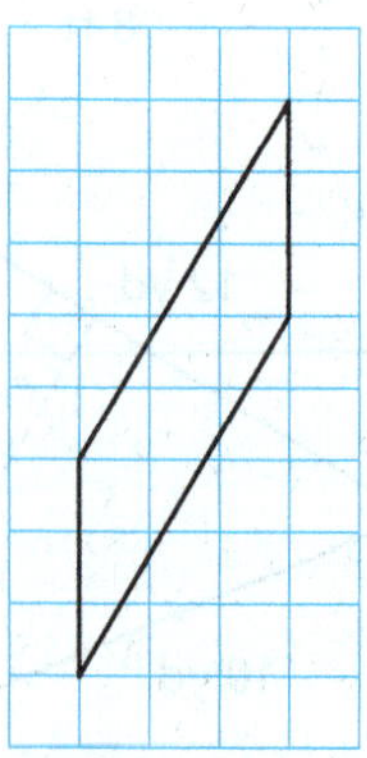

$A =$ ______________

18 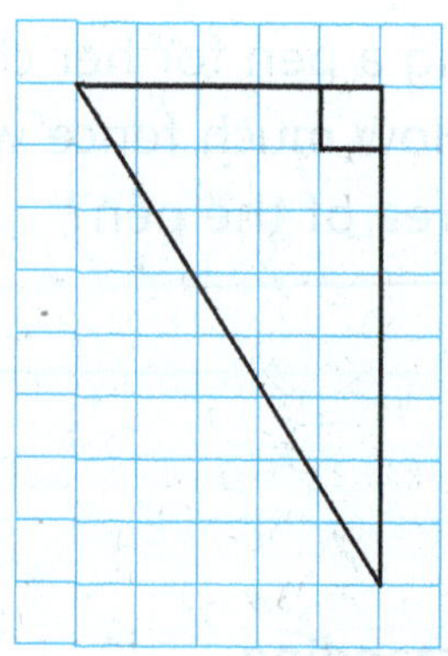

$A =$ ______________

Name ______________________

Find the unknown measurement.

1

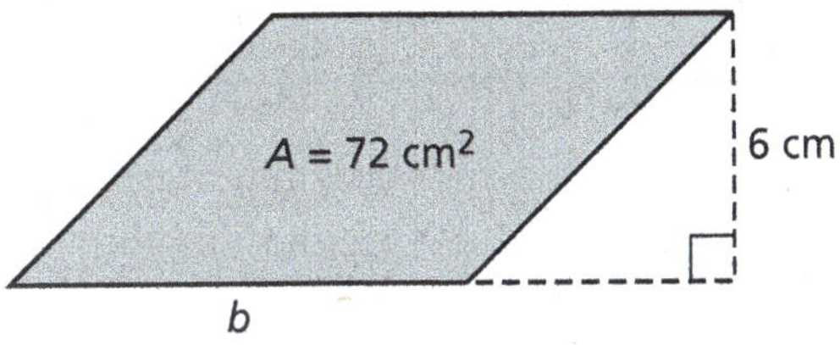

$b =$ ________

2

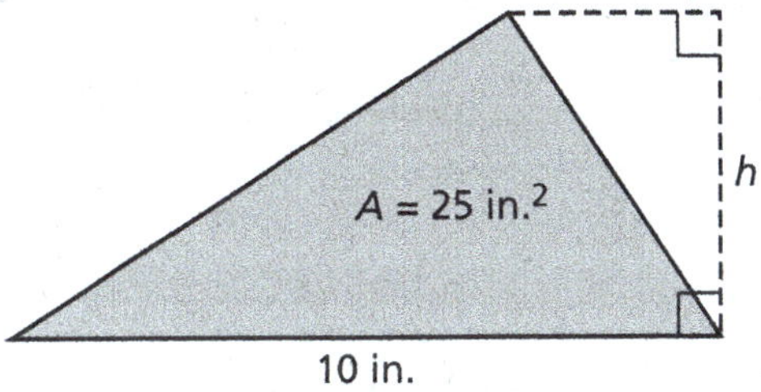

$h =$ ________

Find the perimeter and area of each figure.

3

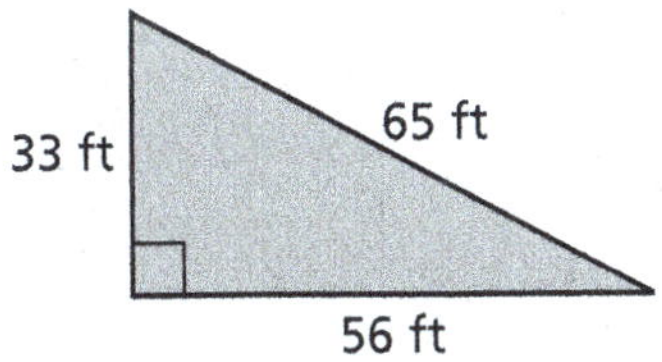

$P =$ ________

$A =$ ________

4

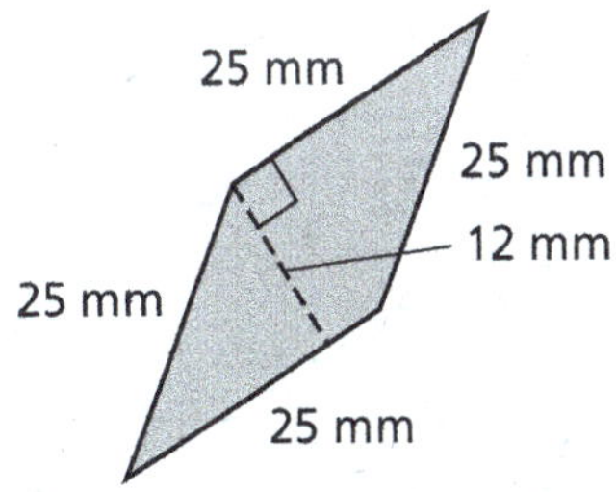

$P =$ ________

$A =$ ________

Solve.

Show your work.

5 Karen planted flowers and shrubs in a backyard garden that is in the shape of a right triangle. The garden has an area of 20 square feet. The base is 10 feet. What is the height?

____

Strategy Check 5

Name ____________________

1 Draw two parallelograms each with an area of 9 square units.

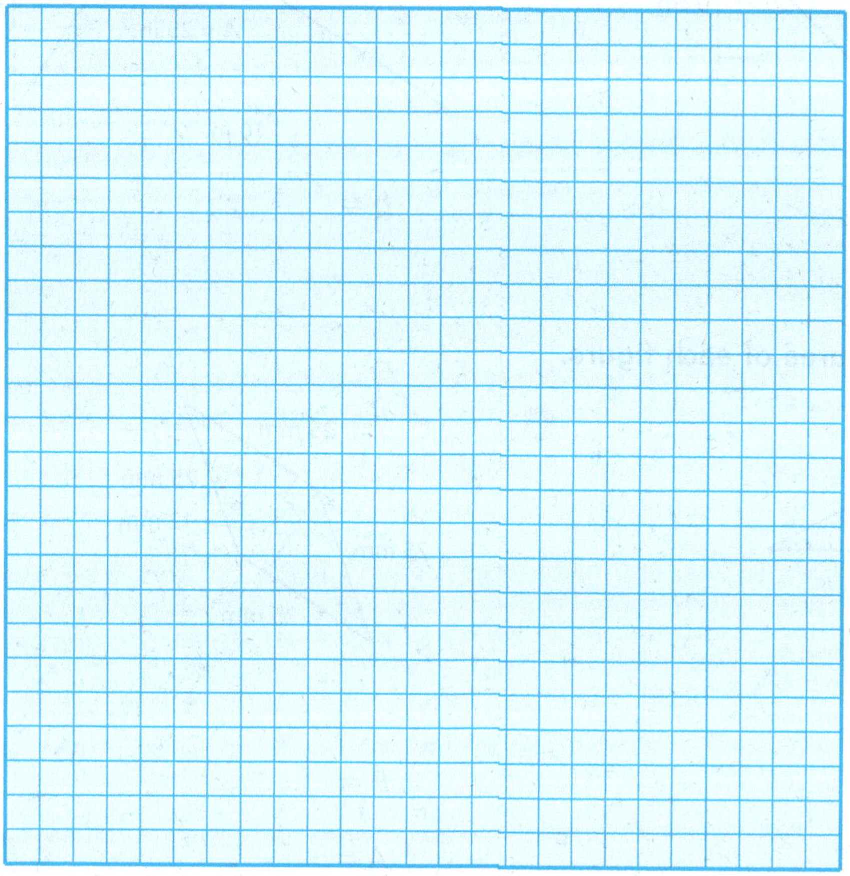

2 Explain how you selected the dimensions for the parallelograms.

____

____

____

____

____

____

Name ____________________

VOCABULARY
trapezoid

Experiment with Trapezoids

A trapezoid is a quadrilateral with exactly one pair of parallel sides. In each of the trapezoids below, the dashed line forms two triangles. How do the base and height of the two triangles compare to the bases and height of the trapezoid?

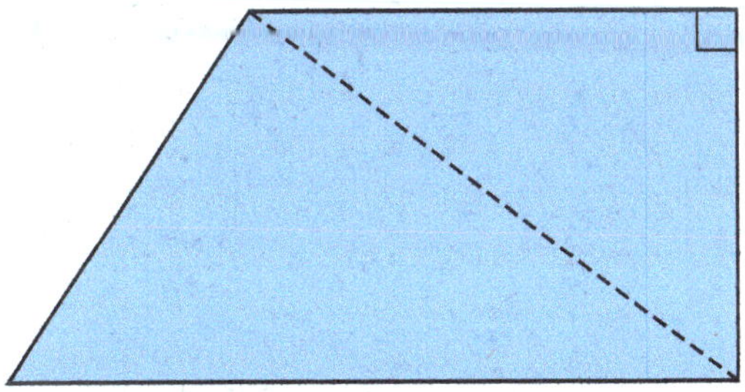

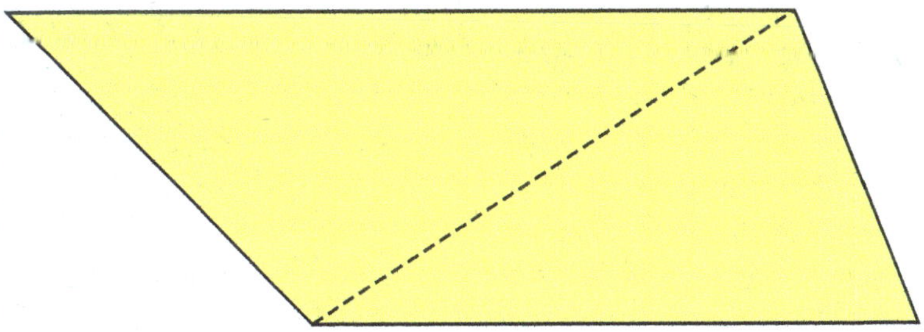

The trapezoids below are exactly the same. Cut them out and rotate one so that you can place the sides labeled *a* next to each other. What shape do you form?

The trapezoid below has a midline that connects the midpoints of the slanted sides. Measure the length of the midline and the lengths of the bases of the trapezoid. How does the length of the midline compare with the sum of the bases? Cut out the trapezoid. Then cut along the dashed lines and turn the triangles to form a rectangle.

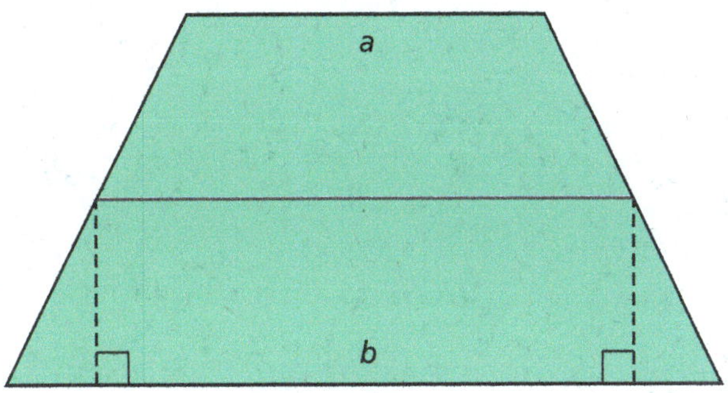

Name ________________________________

Experiment with Trapezoids (continued)

Cut each isosceles trapezoid along the dashed line. Flip one piece over. Put the pieces together to form a four-sided figure with opposite sides parallel. What figure do you form? Then put the pieces together another way to form another figure with opposite sides parallel and four right angles. What figure do you form?

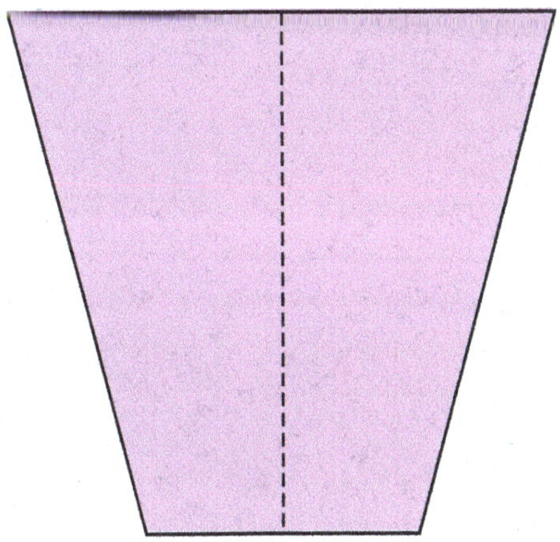

The height of a trapezoid is a perpendicular segment between its parallel bases. Draw two heights in each isosceles trapezoid. Place your heights so that you make three figures for which you know area formulas. What shapes did you form?

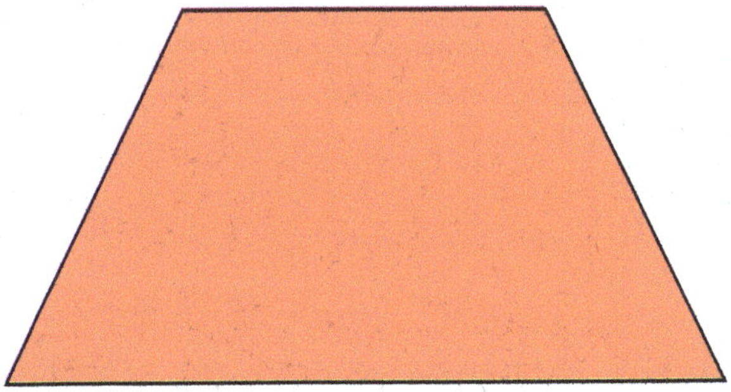

Name ______________________________

VOCABULARY
coordinates

Plot a Polygon

1. On the grid at the right, plot a polygon that you can find the area of with an even number of units for the base (or bases) and height. The vertices should be located so that they can be named by whole-number **coordinates**.

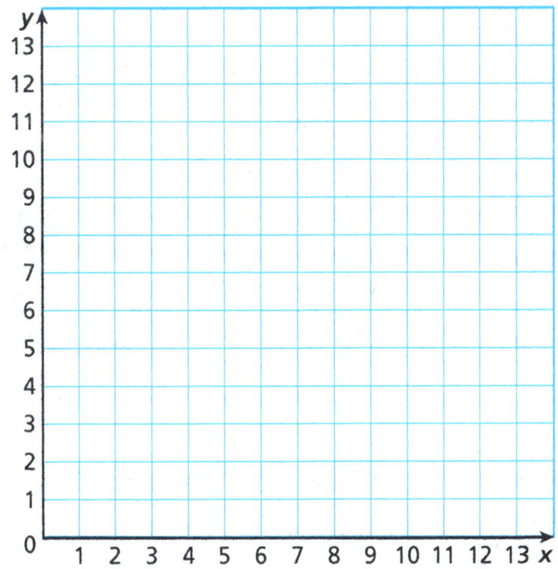

2. What polygon did you plot?

____

3. Name the coordinates of the vertices of your polygon.

____

4. Find the area of your polygon.

____

5. On the grid at the right, plot another polygon that is the same shape as the polygon above. The base (or bases) and height of the new polygon should be half as long as in the polygon above.

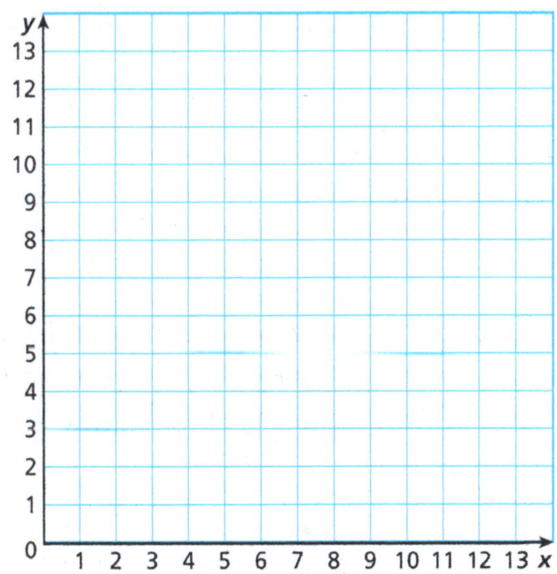

6. Name the coordinates of the vertices of your polygon.

____

7. Find the area of your new polygon.

____

8. How does the area of the polygon you drew for Problem 1 compare to the one you drew for Problem 5?

____

Name ______________________________

Find Segment Lengths

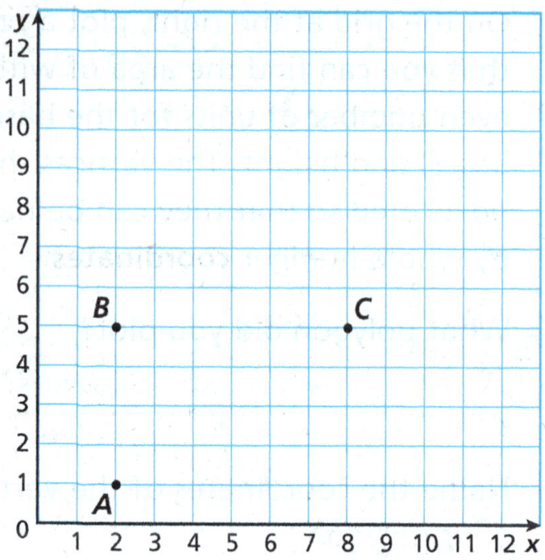

9 What point could you plot to form rectangle *ABCD*?

D is (___, ___).

10 Using your ruler, draw line segments to form rectangle *ABCD*.

11 What is the length of vertical segment *AB*?

____

12 What is the length of horizontal segment *BC*?

____

Find and label these points with the letter and coordinates given. Then connect the points and find the segment length.

13 *E* is (1, 9). *F* is (1, 12). The length of segment *EF* is _______________.

14 *H* is (6, 8). *K* is (8, 8). The length of segment *HK* is _______________.

15 Look at the coordinates of points *E* and *F* and the length of segment *EF*. How can you find the length of this vertical segment without graphing?

____

16 Look at the coordinates of *H* and *K* and the length of segment *HK*. How can you find the length of this horizontal segment without graphing?

____

17 Without graphing, find the length and direction of a line segment with endpoints at (12, 10) and (12, 2).

____

18 Without graphing, find the length and direction of a line segment with endpoints at (0, 7) and (6, 7).

____

Name ______________________

Find Perimeters and Areas of Polygons in the Coordinate Plane

19 The length of line segment *AC* is 6 units. Label the coordinates of point *C* without counting spaces.

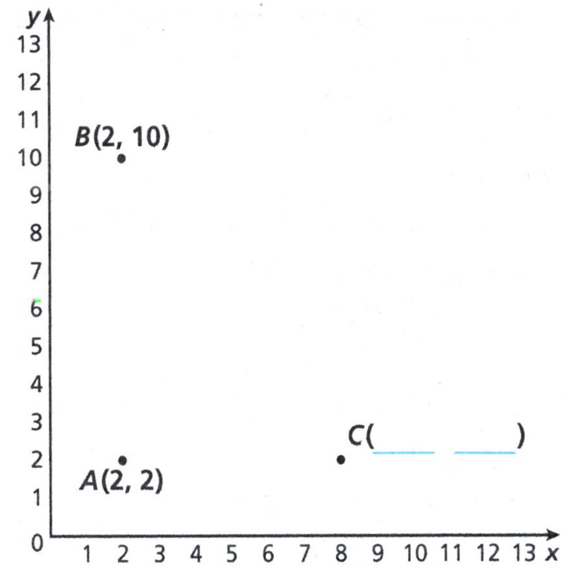

20 Using a ruler, draw line segments connecting points *A*, *B*, and *C* to form a polygon. What polygon did you form?

____

21 Segment *BC* is 10 units long. Find the perimeter and area of right triangle *ABC*.

P = ______________________

A = ______________________

22 Using a ruler, draw line segments to form polygon *DEFH*. What polygon did you form?

____

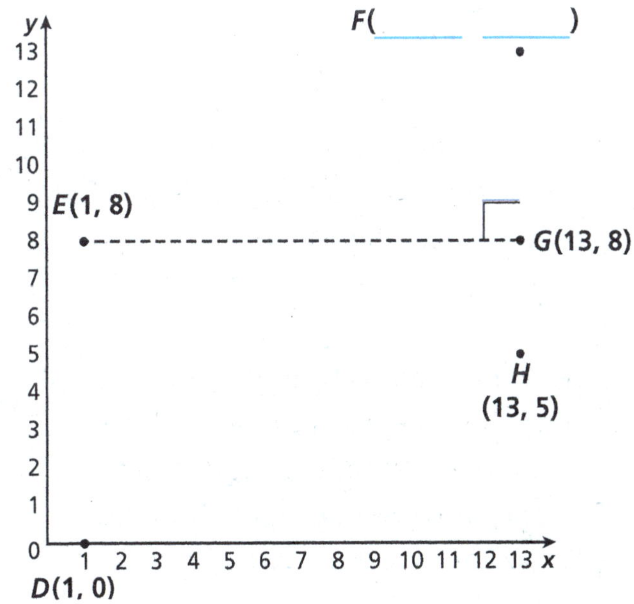

23 Segment *FH* is 8 units long. Label the coordinates of point *F* without counting spaces.

24 Segment *EF* is 13 units long. Find the perimeter and area of parallelogram *DEFH*.

P = ______________________

A = ______________________

Name ______________________

Find Perimeters and Areas of Polygons in the Coordinate Plane (continued)

25 Plot these points on the coordinate plane at the right.
K(2, 3), *L*(5, 7), *M*(13, 7)

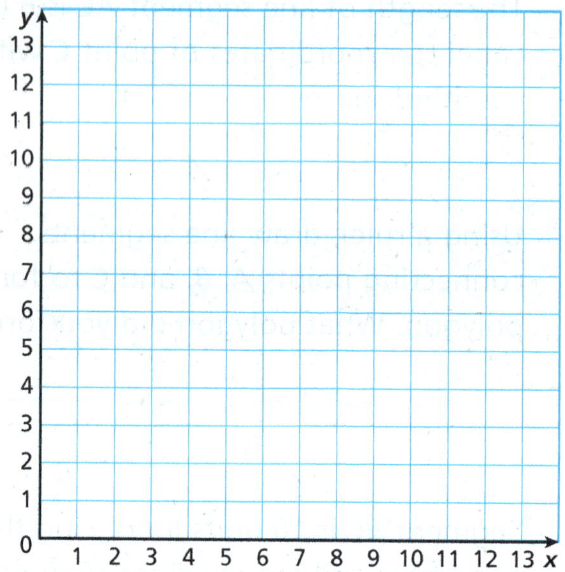

26 Using a ruler, connect your points with line segments to form a polygon. What polygon did you form?

____

27 Segment *KL* is 5 units long. Segment *KM* is 12 units long to the nearest whole unit. Find the perimeter and area of triangle *KLM* to the nearest whole unit.

P = ______________________

A = ______________________

28 Plot these points on the coordinate plane at the right.
A(2, 1), *B*(6, 7), *C*(12, 3)

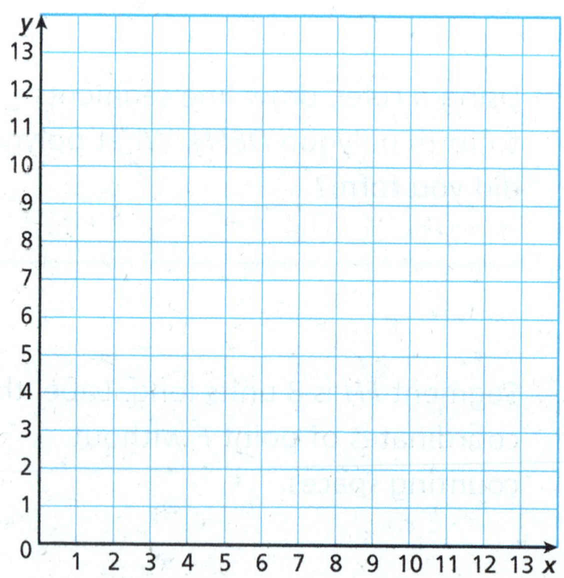

29 Using a ruler, connect your points with line segments to form a polygon. What polygon did you form?

____

30 Find the area of triangle *ABC*.
Hint: Enclose the triangle in a rectangle and take away the areas of the surrounding right triangles. Show your work.

____

____

____

Name ______________________

Solve Real World Problems

31 A surveyor marked the border of a property with metal pins at these coordinates on a survey map.

$A(1, 1)$, $B(1, 10)$, $C(7, 10)$, $D(13, 1)$

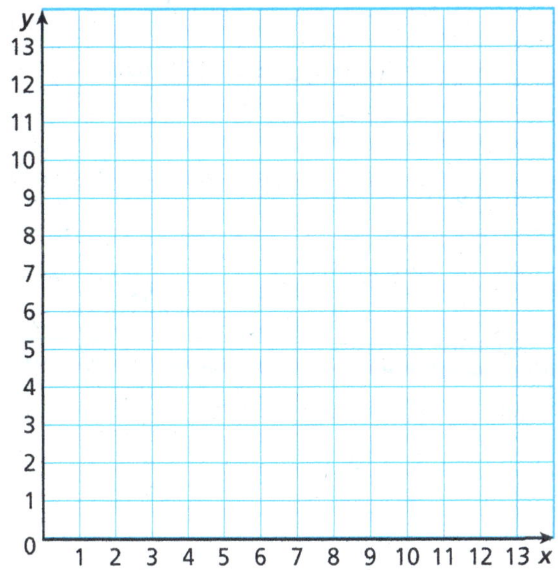

a. What is the area of the property?

$A =$ ______________________

b. A site for a house was marked off with vertices at (4, 4), (4, 6), (7, 6), and (7, 4). Find the length and width of the site without graphing the vertices. Check your answer by graphing.

____

32 An interior designer is tiling a bathroom wall with tiles that are 6 units long and 3 units wide. The bottom left corner of the first tile is placed at (0, 0). In the second row of tiles, the bottom left corner of the first whole tile is placed at (3, 3).

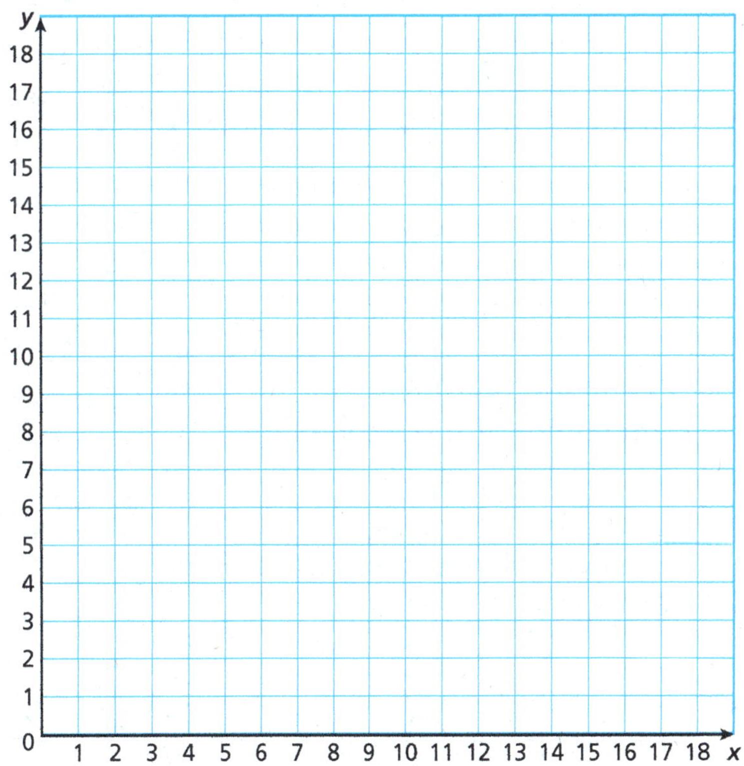

a. How many whole and how many half tiles will be needed for an 18 by 18 section of the wall?

____

b. Explain how you found the answer.

____

____

____

Name ______________________________

Solve Real World Problems (continued)

33 A city planner drew this plan for a park. Find the area of each section.

Swings: ____________________

Slide: ____________________

Picnic Area: ____________________

Jungle Gym: ____________________

Merry–Go–Round: ____________________

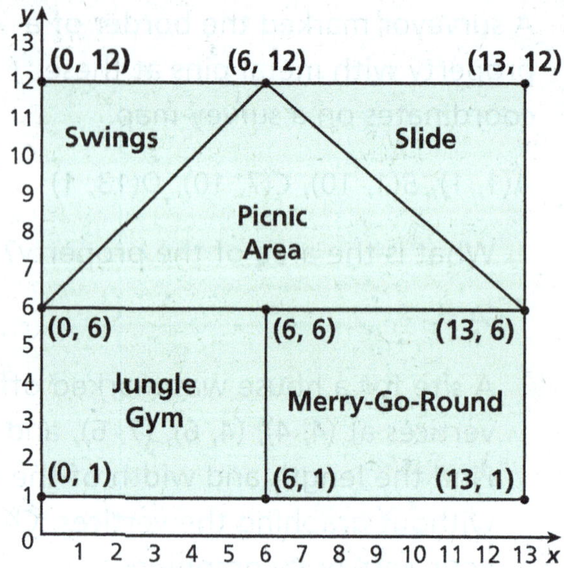

34 A land developer is dividing a section of land into building lots that are 100 ft wide and 160 ft deep. An area for gardens that is 60 ft by 160 ft will be left between each lot. Each unit on the blueprint represents 20 ft. Plot as many lots and garden areas as you can beginning the first lot at (0, 3). Each lot must touch the road.

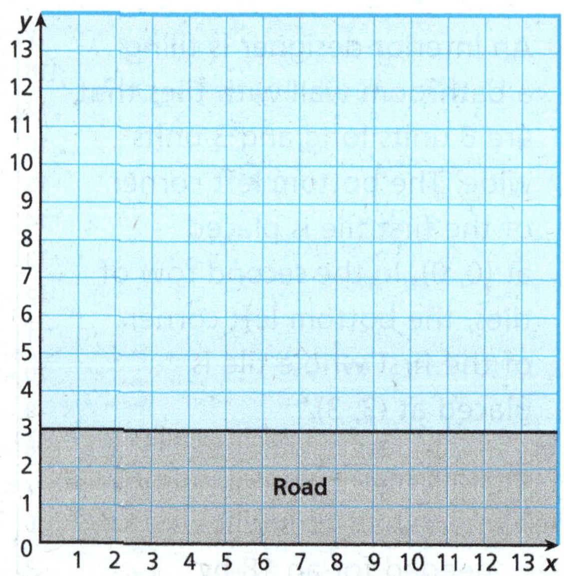

a. Name the coordinates of the bottom left corner of the second lot.

____

b. How wide is the road the developer planned?

____

c. How wide would the land need to be to make four lots and four garden areas?

____

Name ______________________________

Estimate Perimeter and Area of an Irregular Figure

Estimate the perimeter and area of each figure.
Each square on the grid measures 1 square centimeter.

35

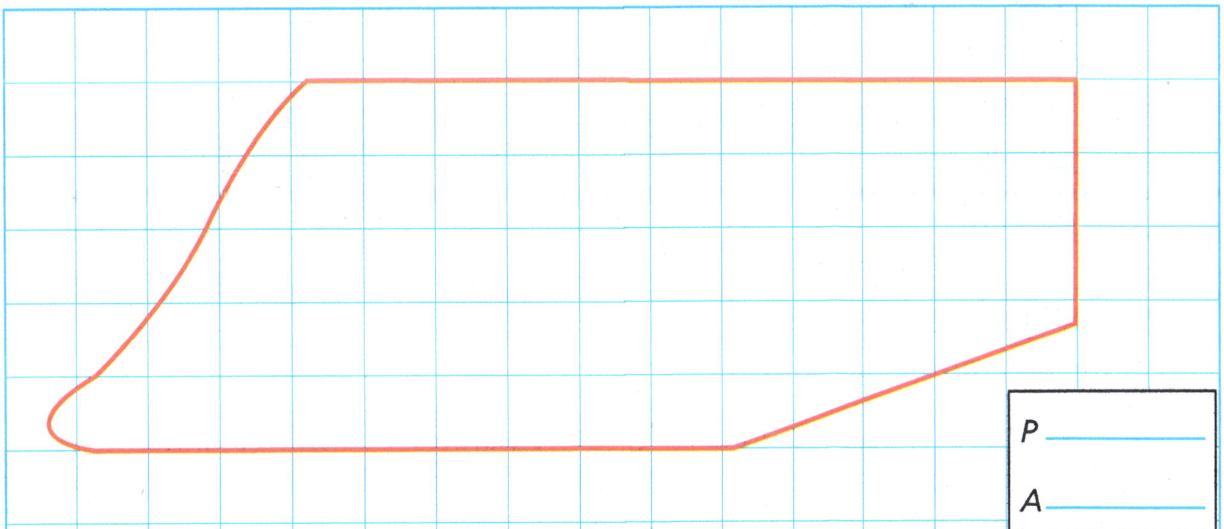

P ________

A ________

36

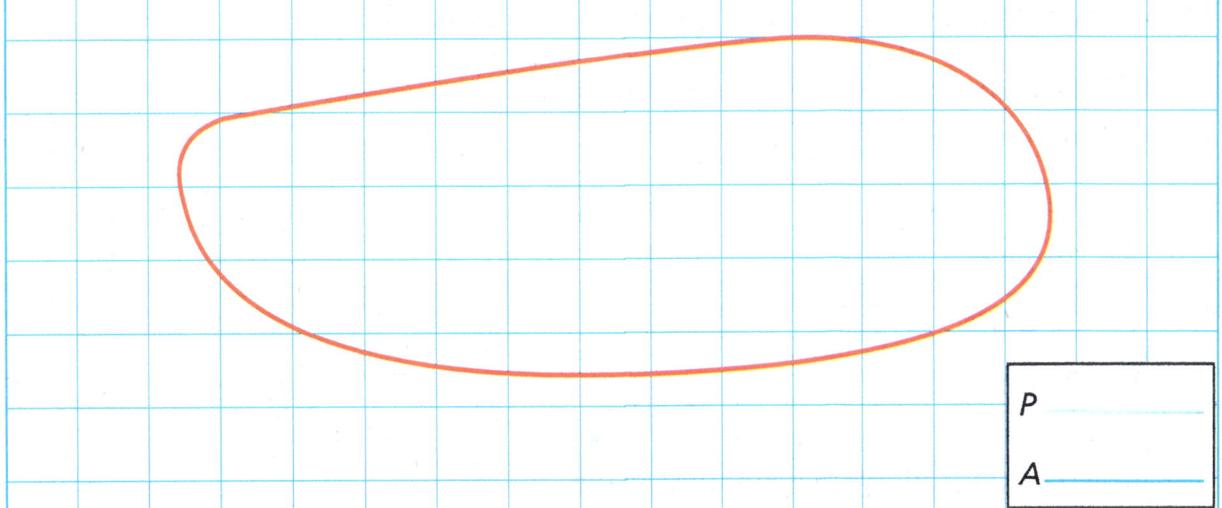

P ________

A ________

37

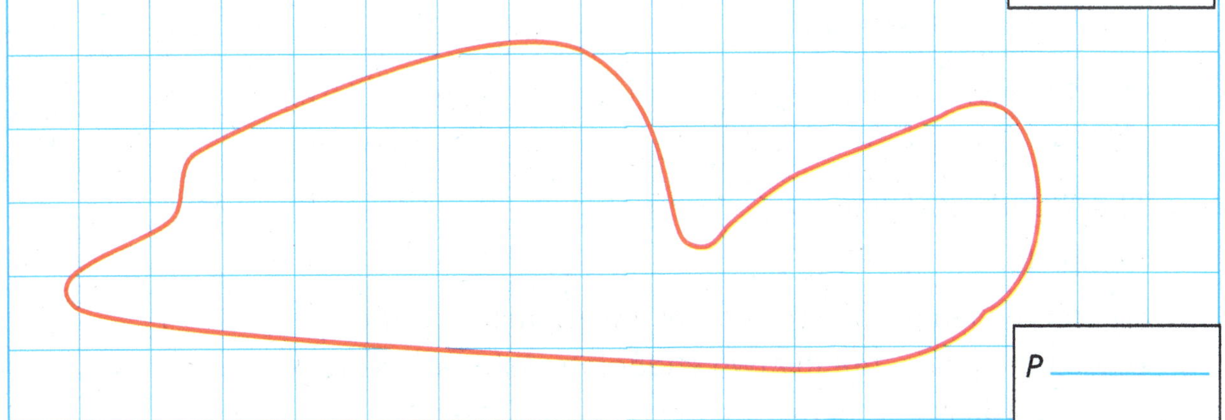

P ________

A ________

Name ______________________________

For Exercises 38–39, use the drawing to answer the questions. Fill in the circle of the letter of your answer.

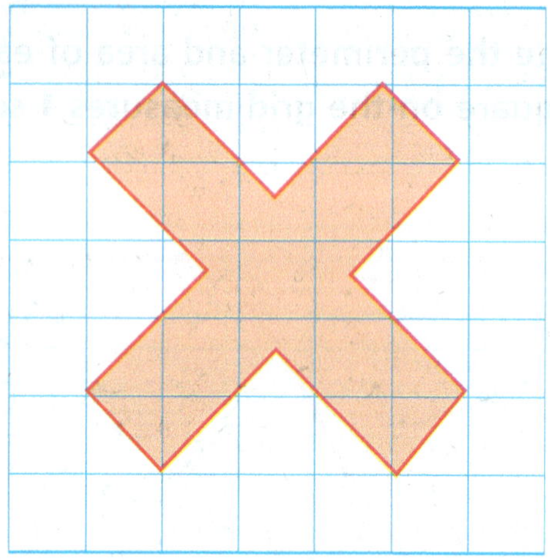

38 Which of the following is the best estimate of the perimeter of the "x" shown?

Ⓐ 10 units
Ⓑ 15 units
Ⓒ 24 units
Ⓓ 35 units

39 Which of the following is the best estimate of the area of the "x" shown?

Ⓐ 8 units^2 Ⓑ 13 units^2 Ⓒ 25 units^2 Ⓓ 30 units^2

For Exercises 40–41, use the drawing to answer the questions. Fill in the circle of the letter of your answer.

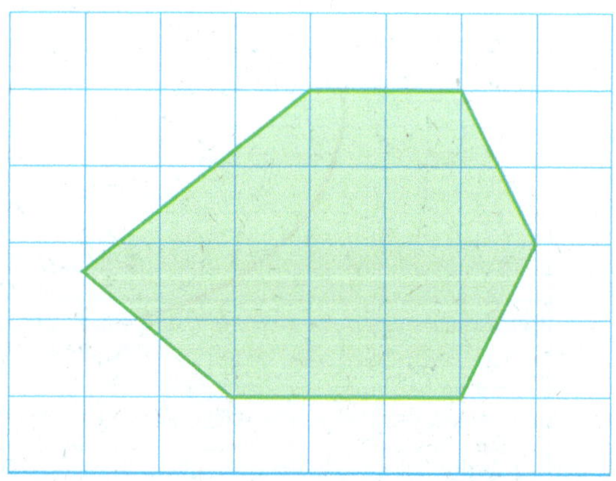

40 Which of the following is the best estimate of the perimeter of the figure?

Ⓐ 8 units
Ⓑ 10 units
Ⓒ 15 units
Ⓓ 20 units

41 Which of the following is the best estimate of the area of the figure?

Ⓐ 10 units^2 Ⓑ 12 units^2 Ⓒ 18 units^2 Ⓓ 25 units^2

Check Understanding

Complete.

To find the length of a horizontal line segment on the coordinate plane, use the two endpoints. Subtract the lesser ____ -coordinate from the greater ____ -coordinate.

Unit 2
Quick Quiz 2

Name ______________________________

Solve.

1. A right triangle has the following vertices.

   Point *A* at (2, 6), Point *B* at (5, 2), Point *C* at (2, 2)

   On the grid, draw and label the triangle. Which coordinates of Points *A* and *C* can be subtracted to find the height of the triangle?

   ____

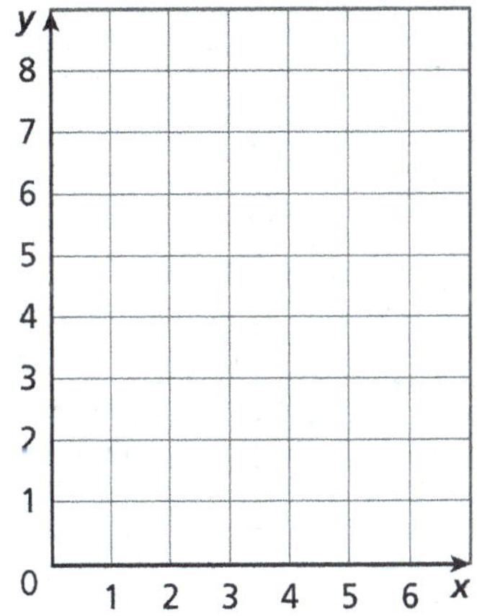

Show your work.

2. Find the area of the right triangle you graphed.

   ____

3. Find the area of the figure below.

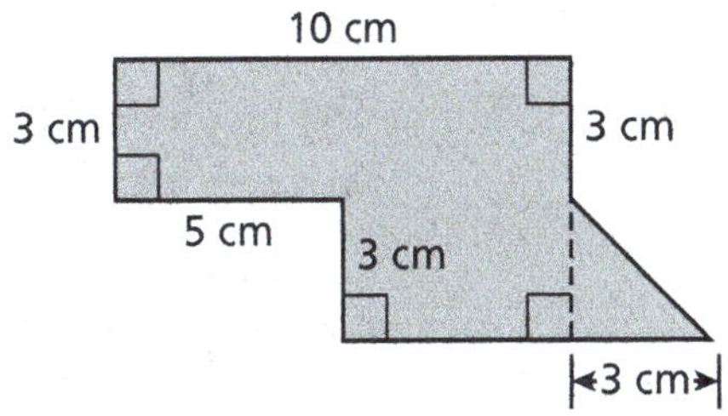

   $A =$ __________

4. The floor of a gazebo is shaped like a regular pentagon. Each side of the floor measures 12 feet, and the height of one of the isosceles triangles in the regular pentagon is about 17 feet. How many square feet of carpeting would be needed to carpet the floor?

   ____

5. A garden is shaped like a regular hexagon. Each side of the hexagon measures 10 meters, and the height of one of the isosceles triangles in the hexagon is about 5 meters. Using these measurements, what is the area of the hexagon?

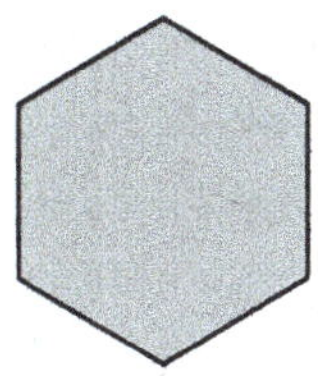

   ____

Strategy Check 6

Name ________________________________

Use the coordinate grid for Exercises 1–3.

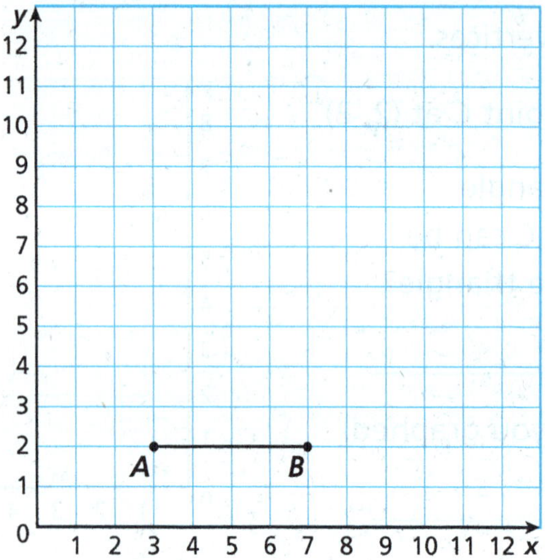

1. Find the length of line segment *AB*. How can you find the length of line segment *AB* without counting the spaces?

   ____

   ____

2. Plot a point *C* on the coordinate grid. Triangle *ABC* should have an area of 6 square units.

3. What are the coordinates for point *C*?

   ____

4. Draw a complex figure with an area of 12 square units.

Name ______________________________

1 Choose the correct unit for each measurement. Then write your answer.

linear units	square units	cubic units

1a. the area of the surface of a table ____________

1b. the perimeter of a fenced-in field ____________

1c. Explain your answer choices. Include a sketch in your explanation.

2 Mark each statement about the parallelogram as True or False.

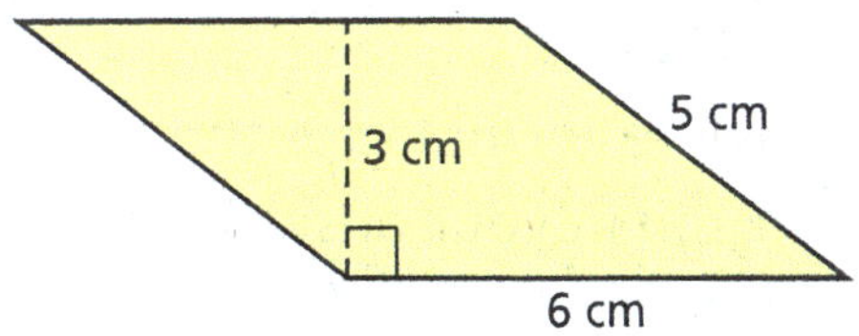

2a. To calculate the area of the parallelogram, you need the two side lengths, 5 cm and 6 cm.

○ True ○ False

2b. To calculate the perimeter of the parallelogram, you need the base and height, 6 cm and 3 cm.

○ True ○ False

2c. To calculate the area of the parallelogram, you need the base and height, 6 cm and 3 cm.

○ True ○ False

2d. To calculate the perimeter of the parallelogram, you need the two side lengths, 5 cm and 6 cm.

○ True ○ False

Name ______________________________

3 The area of any triangle is one-half the area of its related parallelogram.

Part A

Draw a diagram on the grid below to show why the statement above is true. On your diagram, label the base *b* and the height *h*.

Part B

Explain how the formulas for the area of a parallelogram and the area of a triangle relate to your drawing.

Part C

Is the formula for the area of a triangle true for any triangle? Explain your answer.

4 For rectangle *ABCD*, use subtraction to find the length of side *BC*. Explain how you found the length.

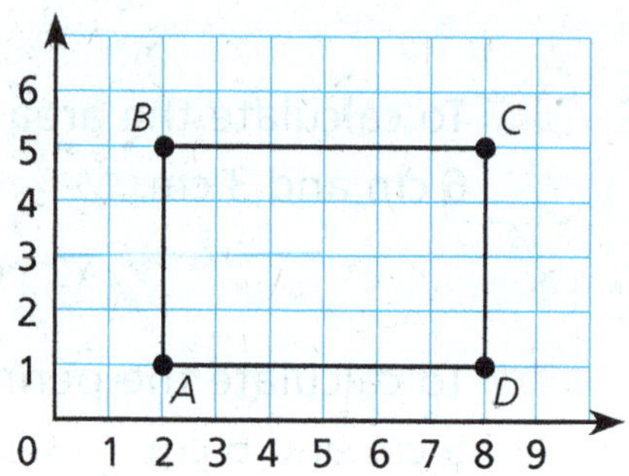

__________ units

Name ______________________________

Choose a number from the number tiles to show each unknown side length. Then write and label your answer.

5
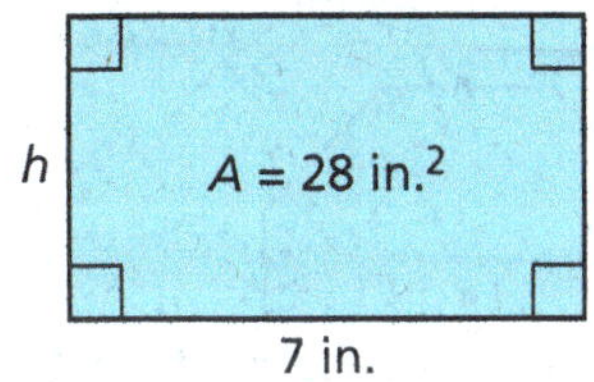

h = ____________

6
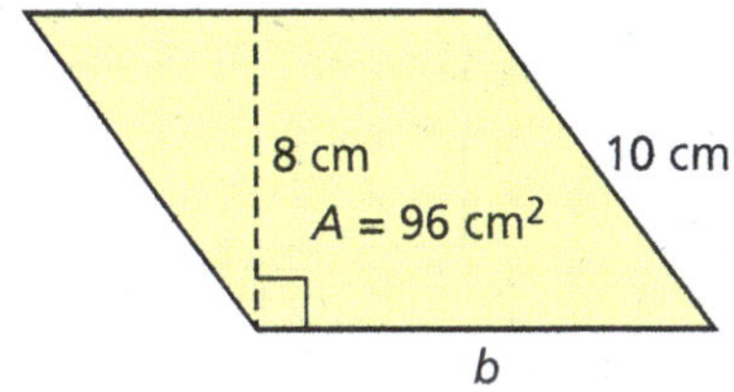

b = ____________

2 4 6 9 10 12 16

Find the perimeter and area of each figure.

7
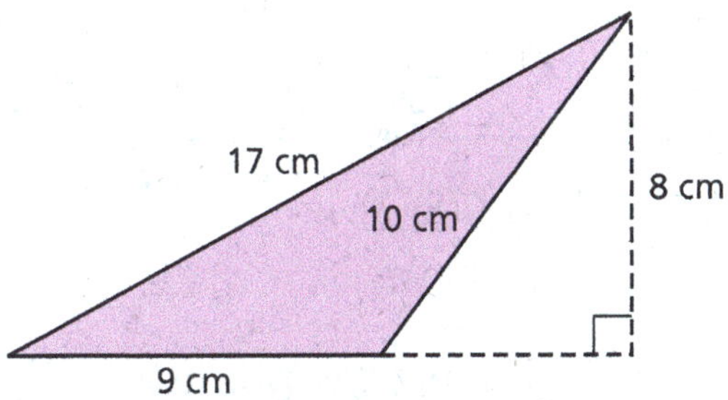

Perimeter	Area
○ 27 cm	○ 36 cm^2
○ 35 cm	○ 45 cm^2
○ 36 cm	○ 68 cm^2
○ 44 cm	○ 72 cm^2

8
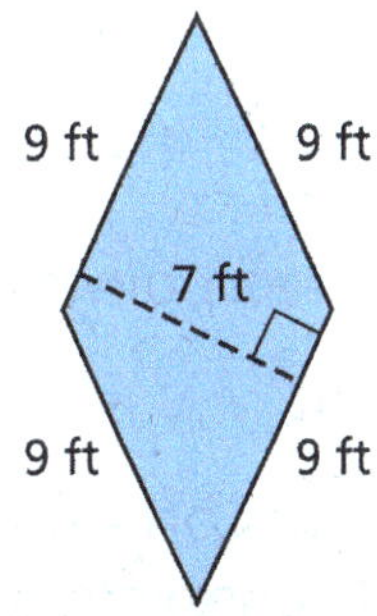

Perimeter	Area
○ 25 ft	○ 31.5 ft^2
○ 36 ft	○ 40.5 ft^2
○ 34 ft	○ 63 ft^2
○ 43 ft	○ 81 ft^2

9 The floor of Hanh's room is in the shape of a parallelogram that has a base of 4 yards and a height of 3 yards. She wants to cover the floor with carpeting that costs \$10 a square yard. How much will the carpeting cost? Show your work.

\$ ____________

Name ______________________

Find the perimeter and area of each figure.

10

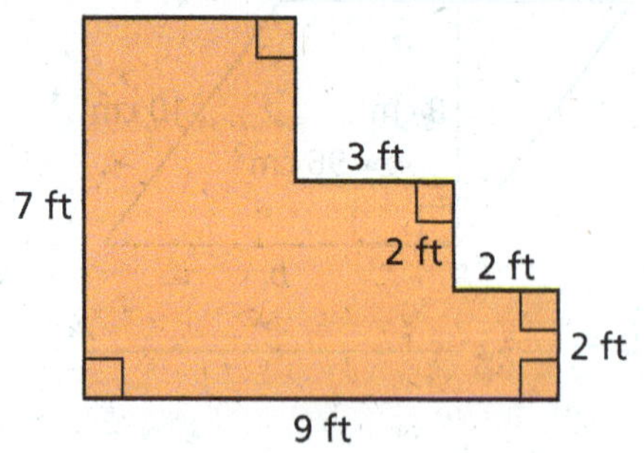

$P =$ ______________

$A =$ ______________

11

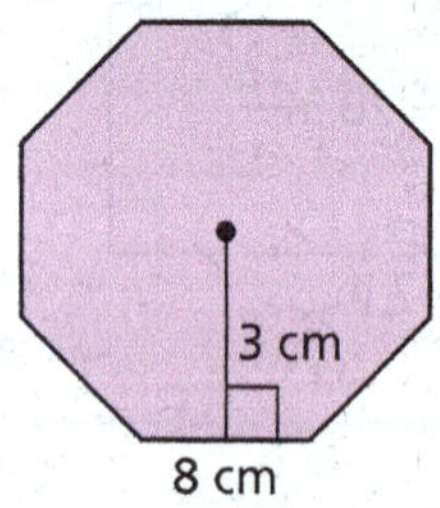

$P =$ ______________

$A =$ ______________

12 The coordinates of three points are $A(2, 3)$, $B(11, 7)$, and $C(8, 3)$.

Part A

Plot and label the points on grid paper. Using a ruler, connect the points to form polygon *ABC*. Then explain how subtraction can be used to find the length of *AC*.

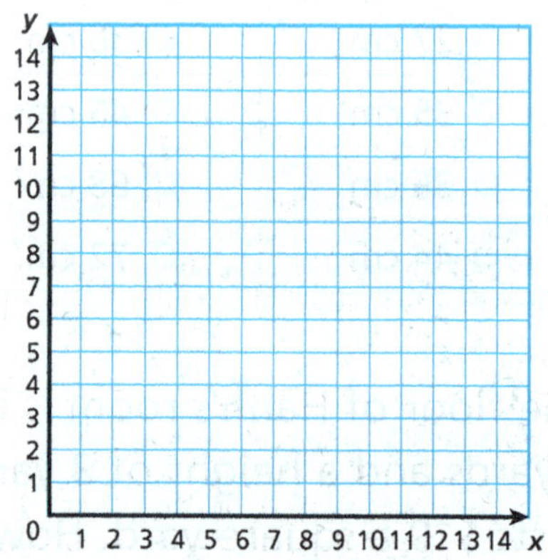

Part B

The length of segment *AB* to the nearest unit is 10 units. The length of segment *BC* is 5 units. Find the perimeter of the triangle to the nearest unit. Find the area of the triangle. Use the correct unit for both measures. Show your work.

$P =$ ______________ $A =$ ______________

Name ______________________

13 A line segment has endpoints (3, 14) and (3, 22). Which of the following statements is true?

Ⓐ The segment has a length of 8 units and is horizontal.

Ⓑ The segment has a length of 8 units and is vertical.

Ⓒ The segment has a length of 18 units and is horizontal.

Ⓓ The segment has a length of 18 units and is vertical.

14 A gazebo in Jamal's yard is in the shape of a regular hexagon. Each side is 5 feet long. The perpendicular distance from each side to the center is 4 feet to the nearest foot. Jamal wants to put a string of lights around the gazebo and outdoor carpeting on the floor.

He wrote the four expressions shown below. Match each expression to the description of what it represents.

$5 + 5 + 5 + 5 + 5 + 5$ •	• the length of the string of lights
$6 \times \frac{1}{2}(5 \times 4)$ •	• area of the floor of the gazebo
60 ft^2 •	• calculation needed to find the perimeter of the gazebo
30 ft •	• calculation to find the amount of carpet to cover the floor

15 Casey is making square posters with perimeters of 8 feet. How many square feet of cardboard will Casey need to make 4 posters? Show your work.

__________ ft^2

Unit 2
Review/Test

Name ______________________

16 Cal's patio is in the shape of a regular pentagon with a perimeter of 60 feet. The perpendicular distance from a side to the center is 8 feet to the nearest whole foot. What is the area of his patio to the nearest square foot? *Show your work.*

______________ ft^2

17 Bonne is planting a flower garden. She will plant sunflowers in the shaded part of the garden.

Bonne's Flower Garden

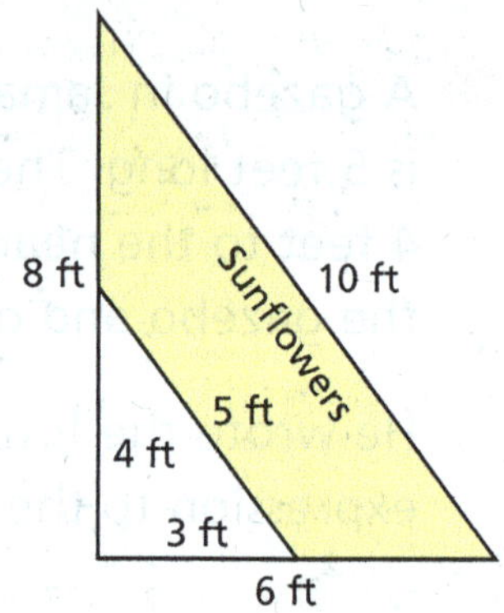

17a. Use the numbers below to write an expression that represents A, the area of the shaded part of the garden.

$\frac{1}{2}$ (3) (8) – (6) $\frac{1}{2}$ (4)

____

17b. Simplify your expression to find A, and explain why your answer represents the area of the shaded part of the garden.

18 The border of a field was marked with posts at these coordinates: $D(0, 2)$, $E(6, 10)$, $F(11, 10)$, and $G(16, 2)$.

18a. Plot the locations of the posts on grid paper. Using a ruler, connect the points to form a four-sided polygon.

18b. What is the area of the field? Explain your answer.

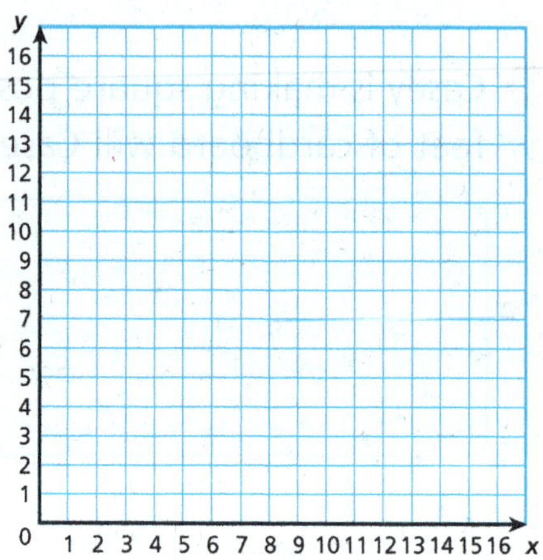

Unit 2
Performance Task

Name ______________________________

Complex Figures

1 For each of the polygons below, write the name of the polygon, find its perimeter, and find its area. Each square on the grid represents 1 cm^2.

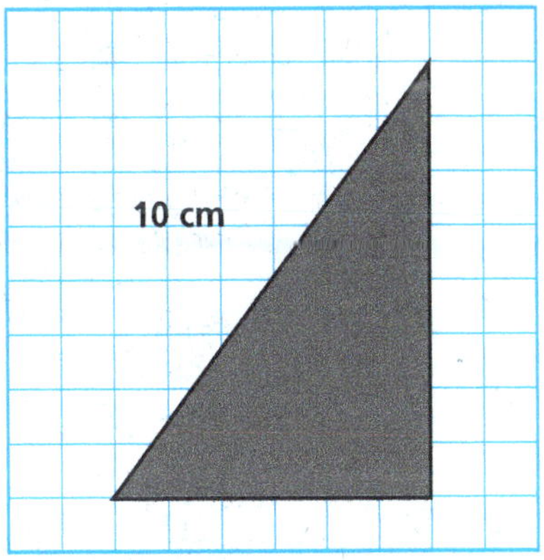

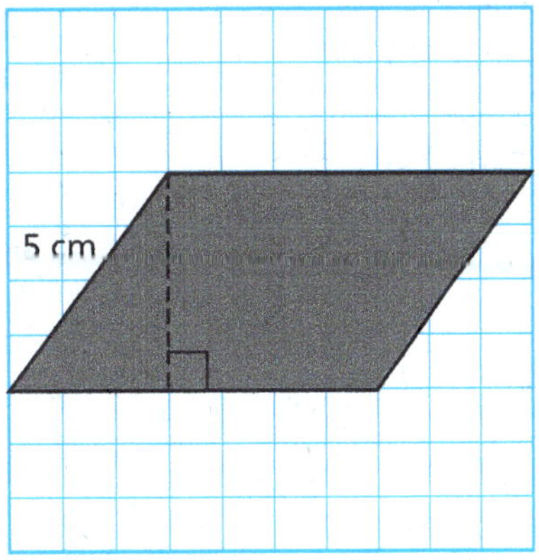

Name ______________________

Perimeter ______________________

Area ______________________

Name ______________________

Perimeter ______________________

Area ______________________

2 On each grid below, draw a polygon that fits the description. Each square on the grid represents 1 cm^2.

Draw a triangle with area 60 cm^2.

Draw a trapezoid with area 80 cm^2.

Name ______________________________

3 A complex figure is composed of different polygons. On the grid below, draw a complex figure that has an area of exactly 200 square units and has

- at least one triangle.
- at least one parallelogram that is not a rectangle or square.
- at least one other polygon.

4 Show or explain how you know the area of the figure you drew is exactly 200 square units.

Dear Family:

In this unit of *Math Expressions*, your child will focus on division of whole numbers and operations with fractions and decimals. Some of the methods used in this unit are shown below.

Addition and Subtraction of Fractions and Decimals

$$\frac{2}{3} + \frac{4}{5} = \frac{10}{15} + \frac{12}{15} = \frac{22}{15} = 1\frac{7}{15}$$

$$\begin{array}{r} \scriptsize{3\ 10} \\ 1.\cancel{4}\cancel{0} \\ -\ 0.25 \\ \hline 1.15 \end{array}$$

Equivalent Fractions

Multiply the numerator and denominator by the same number.

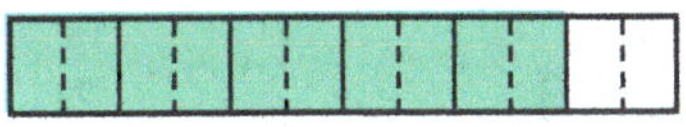

$$\frac{5}{6} = \frac{5 \cdot 2}{6 \cdot 2} = \frac{10}{12}$$

Divide the numerator and denominator by the same number.

$$\frac{10}{12} = \frac{10 \div 2}{12 \div 2} = \frac{5}{6}$$

Multiplication of Fractions and Decimals

Multiply numerators and denominators.

$$\frac{2}{3} \cdot \frac{4}{5} = \frac{2 \cdot 4}{3 \cdot 5} = \frac{8}{15}$$

Count decimal places in the factors to place the decimal point in the product.

$$0.12 \cdot 0.4 = 0.048$$

2 places | 1 place | 3 places

Division of Fractions and Decimals

Multiply by the reciprocal.

$$\frac{2}{5} \div \frac{3}{7} = \frac{2}{5} \cdot \frac{7}{3} = \frac{14}{15}$$

Sometimes you can divide numerators and denominators.

$$\frac{8}{15} \div \frac{2}{3} = \frac{8 \div 2}{15 \div 3} = \frac{4}{5}$$

Make the divisor a whole number by multiplying it and the dividend by the same number.

Here we multiply both by 10.

$$\begin{array}{r} 0.4 \\ 0.2\overline{)0.08} \end{array}$$

Your child will also use estimation strategies, such as rounding and benchmarks, to determine whether answers to whole number, fraction, and decimal problems are reasonable.

If you have any questions or comments, please contact me.

Sincerely,
Your child's teacher

Estimada familia:

En esta unidad de *Expresiones en matemáticas*, su hijo se centrará en la división de números enteros y en operaciones con fracciones y decimales. A continuación se muestran algunos de los métodos usados en esta unidad.

Suma y resta de fracciones y decimales

$$\frac{2}{3} + \frac{4}{5} = \frac{10}{15} + \frac{12}{15} = \frac{22}{15} = 1\frac{7}{15}$$

$$\begin{array}{r} \overset{3\ 10}{1.\cancel{4}\cancel{0}} \\ -\ 0.25 \\ \hline 1.15 \end{array}$$

Fracciones equivalentes

Multiplicar el numerador y el denominador por el mismo número.

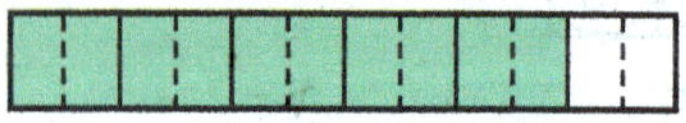

$$\frac{5}{6} = \frac{5 \cdot 2}{6 \cdot 2} = \frac{10}{12}$$

Dividir el numerador y el denominador entre el mismo número.

$$\frac{10}{12} = \frac{10 \div 2}{12 \div 2} = \frac{5}{6}$$

Multiplicación de fracciones y decimales

Multiplicar los numeradores y denominadores.

$$\frac{2}{3} \cdot \frac{4}{5} = \frac{2 \cdot 4}{3 \cdot 5} = \frac{8}{15}$$

Contar los lugares decimales en los factores para colocar el punto decimal en la respuesta.

$$0.12 \cdot 0.4 = 0.048$$

2 lugares | 1 lugar | 3 lugares

División de fracciones y decimales

Multiplicar por el recíproco.

$$\frac{2}{5} \div \frac{3}{7} = \frac{2}{5} \cdot \frac{7}{3} = \frac{14}{15}$$

Algunas veces se pueden dividir los numeradores y denominadores.

$$\frac{8}{15} \div \frac{2}{3} = \frac{8 \div 2}{15 \div 3} = \frac{4}{5}$$

Dividir el divisor y el dividendo entre el mismo número para convertir el divisor en un número entero.

Aquí se multiplican ambos por 10.

$$\begin{array}{r} 0.4 \\ 0.2\overline{)0.08} \end{array}$$

Su hijo también usará estrategias de estimación como el redondeo y los puntos de referencia para determinar si las respuestas a los problemas de números enteros, fracciones y decimales son razonables.

Si tiene preguntas, por favor comuníquese conmigo.

Atentamente,
El maestro de su hijo

benchmark	denominator
common denominator	dividend
common factor	divisor

The number below the bar in a fraction. It indicates the number of unit fractions made by dividing the whole into equal parts.

Example:

In the fraction $\frac{3}{5}$, the denominator is 5.

$\frac{3}{5}$ ← denominator

It represents the 5 unit fractions (the 5 fifths) made by dividing the whole into 5 equal parts.

A point of reference used for comparing and estimating. The numbers 0, $\frac{1}{2}$, and 1 are common fraction benchmarks.

The number that is divided in a division problem.

Example:

$56 \div 8 = 7$ $\qquad$ $8\overline{)56}$ with quotient 7

dividend: 56

A common multiple of two or more denominators.

Example:

15 is a common denominator of $\frac{1}{3}$ and $\frac{2}{5}$.

$\frac{1}{3} = \frac{5}{15}$ $\quad$ $\frac{2}{5} = \frac{6}{15}$

The number that divides in a division problem.

Example:

$56 \div 8 = 7$ $\qquad$ $8\overline{)56}$ with quotient 7

divisor: 8

A factor that two or more numbers share.

Example:

4 is a common factor of 12 and 20.

equivalent fractions	least common multiple
estimate	numerator
inverse operations	quotient

The least number that is a multiple of two or more numbers.

Example:
36 is the least common multiple of 9 and 12.

Fractions that represent the same number.

Example:
$\frac{1}{2}$ and $\frac{3}{6}$ are equivalent fractions.

The number above the bar in a fraction. It indicates the number of unit fractions the fraction represents.

Example:
In the fraction $\frac{3}{5}$, the numerator is 3.

$\frac{3}{5}$ ← numerator

The numerator shows that the fraction represents 3 fifths: $\frac{3}{5} = \frac{1}{5} + \frac{1}{5} + \frac{1}{5}$.

Find *about* how many or *about* how much, often by using rounding, compatible numbers, or benchmark numbers.

The result of a division.

Example: quotient

$56 \div 8 = 7$ $\qquad$ $8\overline{)56}$ with quotient 7

Operations that undo each other. Addition and subtraction are inverse operations. Multiplication and division are inverse operations.

Examples:
$5 + 9 = 14$, so $14 - 9 = 5$.
$7 \cdot 9 = 63$, so $63 \div 9 = 7$.

reciprocal

remainder

The product of a number and its reciprocal is 1. The reciprocal of the fraction $\frac{a}{b}$ is $\frac{b}{a}$.

Example:

$\frac{4}{3}$ is the reciprocal of $\frac{3}{4}$.

$\frac{3}{4} \cdot \frac{4}{3} = 1$ and $\frac{4}{3} \cdot \frac{3}{4} = 1$

The number left over after dividing a number that is not evenly divisible by the divisor.

Example:

$32 \div 6 = 5$ R2

The remainder is 2.

Name ____________________

Decimal and Whole Number Secret Code Cards

Card (small label)	Card (large digits)
2,000	2,000
0.1	0.1
300	300
0.03	0.03
30	30
1	1
0.01	0.01
2	2
9	9
0.4	0.4
	.00
60	60
0.002	0.002
70	70
0.6	0.6

Name ______________________________

Decimal and Whole Number Secret Code Cards

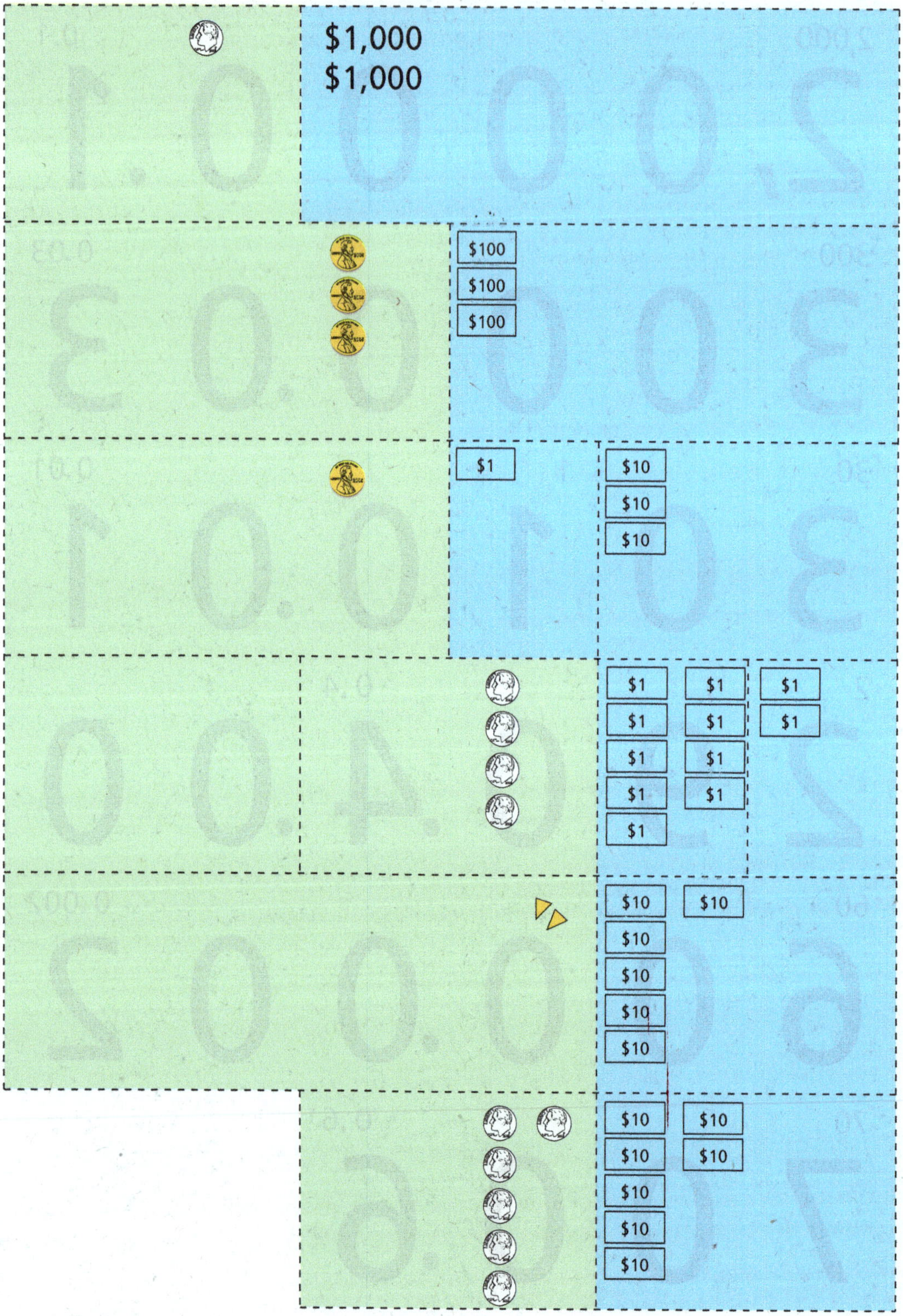

Name ______________________________

Discuss and Summarize

Fill in the blanks and discuss how the parts of each problem are related.

Place Value

× 10 (larger) ⟵⟶ ÷ 10 (smaller)

Thousands	Hundreds	Tens	ONES	Tenths	Hundredths	Thousandths
1,000.	100.	10.	1.	0.1	0.01	0.001
$\frac{1,000}{1}$	$\frac{100}{1}$	$\frac{10}{1}$	$\frac{1}{1}$	$\frac{1}{10}$	$\frac{1}{100}$	$\frac{1}{1,000}$
$1,000.00	$100.00	$10.00	$1.00	$0.10	$0.01	$0.001

1 a.

b.

c. 2,361.632 = 2,000 + ____ + ____ + ____ + ____ + ____ + 0.002

2 a. 0 .6 3 2

b. $+ \frac{\quad}{10} + \frac{\quad}{100} + \frac{\quad}{1,000}$

c. $+ \frac{\quad}{1,000} + \frac{\quad}{1,000} + \frac{\quad}{1,000}$

d.

	0	.6	0	0
+	0	.0	3	0
+	0	.0	0	2
	0	.6	3	2

Name

What's the Error?

Dear Math Students,

I solved the problem 5,619 ÷ 27 on my math homework. I got 28 R3. I know this can't be right because 27 × 28 is approximately equal to 30 • 30, which is 900. That's not even close to 5,619! Will you look at my work and help me figure out what I did wrong?

Your friend,
Puzzled Penguin

$$\begin{array}{r} 28 \\ 27\overline{)5{,}619} \\ \underline{54} \\ 219 \\ \underline{216} \\ 3 \end{array}$$

4 Write an answer to Puzzled Penguin.

PATH to FLUENCY Practice Division

Write each answer as a quotient with a remainder.

5 $23\overline{)3{,}272}$

6 $18\overline{)7{,}342}$

7 $19\overline{)3{,}812}$

Name ______________________________

What's the Error?

Dear Math Students,

I am really having trouble with my math homework today. I had to solve 3,005 ÷ 15. I started, but I got stuck. I know the answer can't be 2, but I don't know what to do next. Can you help me finish the solution?

Your friend,
Puzzled Penguin

$$\begin{array}{r} 2 \\ 15\overline{)3{,}005} \\ \underline{30} \\ 0 \end{array}$$

8 Write an answer to Puzzled Penguin.

Solve.

9 Twelve friends earned $4,250 for painting a house. They want to split the money equally. How much will each friend get? How many cents will be left over?

Check Understanding

Explain how you can check that a quotient is reasonable.

Name ____________________

Summarize Multiplying by 0.1 and 0.01

Multiplying by 0.1 is the same as dividing by 10.

$0.1 \cdot 32.4 = 32.4 \div 10 = 3.24$

Multiplying a number by 0.1 divides it into 10 parts and takes 1 part. It gives a smaller number. Each digit moves one place right.

You can use this idea to multiply any number of tenths.

Fill in the blanks.

1. a. To find 0.2 • \$32.40, divide \$32.40 into 10 parts and take ________ of those parts.

   $0.2 \cdot \$32.40 = (\$32.40 \div 10) \cdot$ ________

   b. To find 6.2 • \$32.40, divide \$32.40 into ________ parts and take ________ of those parts.

   $6.2 \cdot \$32.40 = (\$32.40 \div$ ________ $) \cdot$ ________

Multiplying by 0.01 is the same as dividing by 100.

$0.01 \cdot 32.4 = 32.4 \div 100 = 0.324$

Multiplying a number by 0.01 divides it into 100 parts and takes 1 part. It gives an even smaller number. Each digit moves two places right.

You can use this idea to multiply any number of hundredths.

2. a. To find 0.02 • \$32.40, divide \$32.40 into ________ parts and take ________ of those parts.

   $0.02 \cdot \$32.40 = (\$32.40 \div 100) \cdot$ ________

   b. To find 0.62 • \$32.40, divide \$32.40 into ________ parts and take ________ of those parts.

   $0.62 \cdot \$32.40 = (\$32.40 \div$ ________ $) \cdot$ ________

Name ______________________________

Rule About Multiplying Decimals

Rule: Ignore the decimal points and multiply. Then place the decimal point so the number of decimal places in the product is equal to the total number of decimal places in the factors.

Example
0.4 • 0.02
Ignore the decimal point and multiply: 4 • 2 = 8
Place decimal point so there are three decimal places:
0.4 • 0.02 = 0.008
(1 place) (2 places) (3 places)

3 Find each product in two ways. 1) Use the rule. 2) Use the method of dividing into 10 or 100 parts and then multiplying by the number of tenths or hundredths. Show or explain your work.

	Use the Rule	Divide into Parts and Multiply
a. 0.2 • 0.3	0.06; two decimal places	(0.3 ÷ 10) • 2 = 0.03 • 2 = 0.06
b. 0.02 • 0.3		
c. 0.2 • 3		
d. 0.02 • 3		
e. 0.2 • 3.3		
f. 0.02 • 3.3		

4 Explain why the two methods give the same result.

____
____
____
____
____

Use either method to solve these problems.

5 0.04 • 2 = ______ 6 0.4 • 2 = ______ 7 0.3 • 0.3 = ______ 8 3 • 0.3 = ______

9 0.04 • 6 = ______ 10 0.5 • 7 = ______ 11 0.3 • 0.8 = ______ 12 7 • 0.6 = ______

Check Understanding
Explain how you solved Exercise 11.

Name ____________________

Greater, Equal, or Less

1. Explore what happens when you multiply 4 by different numbers.

Case 1: Multiply 4 by a number greater than 1.

$4 \cdot \mathbf{1.5} =$ ______

4 units
1.5 units | ? sq. units

Is the product less than, greater than, or equal to 4?

______

Case 2: Multiply 4 by 1.

$4 \cdot \mathbf{1} =$ ______

4 units
1 unit | ? sq. units

Is the product less than, greater than, or equal to 4?

______

Case 3: Multiply 4 by a number less than 1.

$4 \cdot \mathbf{0.5} =$ ______

4 units
0.5 units | ? sq. units

Is the product less than, greater than, or equal to 4?

______

2. Multiply 10 by 1, a number greater than 1, and a number less than 1. Tell how each product compares to 10.

____

____

3. Explore what happens when you divide 3 by different numbers.

Case 1: Divide 3 by a number greater than 1.

$3 \div \mathbf{1.5} =$ ______

? units
1.5 units | 3 sq. units

Is the quotient less than, greater than, or equal to 3?

______

Case 2: Divide 3 by 1.

$3 \div \mathbf{1} =$ ______

? units
1 unit | 3 sq. units

Is the quotient less than, greater than, or equal to 3?

______

Case 3: Divide 3 by a number less than 1.

$3 \div \mathbf{0.5} =$ ______

? units
0.5 units | 3 sq. units

Is the quotient less than, greater than, or equal to 3?

______

4. Divide 12 by 1, a number greater than 1, and a number less than 1. Tell how each quotient compares to 12.

____

____

Unit 3
Quick Quiz 1

Name ______________________________

Multiply or divide.

1. $16\overline{)4,940}$

2. $0.6\overline{)33.54}$

3.
$$\begin{array}{r} 7.15 \\ \times \quad 2.4 \\ \hline \end{array}$$

Solve.

Show your work.

4. There are 30 students going on a field trip. If each car can take 4 students, how many cars do they need?

____

5. Sophia works 24 hours each week as a lifeguard. She earns $9.75 per hour. How much does she earn per week?

____

Fluency Check 1

Name ______________________________

PATH to FLUENCY

1. $\begin{array}{r} 0.42 \\ \times\ 15 \\ \hline \end{array}$

2. $\begin{array}{r} 0.73 \\ \times\ 52 \\ \hline \end{array}$

3. $\begin{array}{r} 0.17 \\ \times\ 23 \\ \hline \end{array}$

4. $\begin{array}{r} 0.68 \\ \times\ 11 \\ \hline \end{array}$

5. $\begin{array}{r} 0.35 \\ \times\ 62 \\ \hline \end{array}$

6. $\begin{array}{r} 0.92 \\ \times\ 21 \\ \hline \end{array}$

7. $\begin{array}{r} 0.24 \\ \times\ 64 \\ \hline \end{array}$

8. $\begin{array}{r} 0.87 \\ \times\ 29 \\ \hline \end{array}$

9. $\begin{array}{r} 0.48 \\ \times\ 33 \\ \hline \end{array}$

10. $\begin{array}{r} 0.39 \\ \times\ 24 \\ \hline \end{array}$

11. $\begin{array}{r} 0.41 \\ \times\ 35 \\ \hline \end{array}$

12. $\begin{array}{r} 0.46 \\ \times\ 14 \\ \hline \end{array}$

13. $\begin{array}{r} 0.65 \\ \times\ 28 \\ \hline \end{array}$

14. $\begin{array}{r} 0.28 \\ \times\ 32 \\ \hline \end{array}$

15. $\begin{array}{r} 0.57 \\ \times\ 19 \\ \hline \end{array}$

Name ______________________________

What's the Error?

Dear Math Students,

My friend Wendy had a pizza party. After the party, she had $\frac{1}{3}$ of a cheese pizza left. She also had $\frac{1}{6}$ of a pepperoni pizza. I told Wendy that together she has $\frac{2}{9}$ of a whole pizza left. She says that can't be right.

Can you help me figure out my mistake? How much of a whole pizza does Wendy have?

Your friend,
Puzzled Penguin

11 Write an answer to Puzzled Penguin.

____

____

____

____

____

____

Check Understanding

Complete the sentence.
To rewrite a fraction as an equivalent fraction,

you can ______________ or ______________ the numerator and denominator by the same number.

Name ____________________

Strategies for Comparing

Look for patterns in the fractions and decimals below.

$1 = \frac{2}{2} = \frac{4}{4} = \frac{8}{8}$ — 1.000 = 1.0

0.9

$\frac{7}{8}$ — 0.875

$0.83 \approx \frac{5}{6}$

$0.8 = \frac{4}{5}$

$\frac{3}{4} = \frac{6}{8}$ — 0.750 = 0.75

0.7

$0.67 \approx \frac{4}{6} = \frac{2}{3}$

$\frac{5}{8}$ — 0.625

$0.6 = \frac{3}{5}$

$\frac{1}{2} = \frac{2}{4} = \frac{4}{8}$ — 0.500 = 0.50 = 0.5 = $\frac{3}{6}$

$0.4 = \frac{2}{5}$

$\frac{3}{8}$ — 0.375

$0.33 \approx \frac{2}{6} = \frac{1}{3}$

0.3

$\frac{1}{4} = \frac{2}{8}$ — 0.250 = 0.25

$0.2 = \frac{1}{5}$

$0.17 \approx \frac{1}{6}$

$\frac{1}{8}$ — 0.125

0.1

$\frac{0}{2} = \frac{0}{4} = \frac{0}{8}$ — 0.000

General Cases for Comparing

Case 1: Same denominator or number of places

Fraction with greater numerator is greater. Ignore decimal point. Greater number is greater.

$\frac{3}{5}$ ◯ $\frac{4}{5}$

0.7 > 0.5

Case 2: Same numerator or digits

Fraction with lesser denominator is greater. Decimal with leftmost non-zero digit is greater.

$\frac{6}{9}$ ◯ $\frac{6}{8}$

0.3 ◯ 0.03

Case 3: Different denominators

Find equivalent fractions with a common denominator to change fractions to Case 1.

$\frac{3}{4}$ ◯ $\frac{2}{3}$

Case 4: Mixed numbers

Number with greater whole number is greater. If whole numbers are the same, compare fractions using Cases 1–3.

$5\frac{1}{8}$ ◯ $2\frac{9}{10}$

4.7 > 4.07

Special Cases for Fractions

Case 5: Denominators are factors of 10 or 100.

Compare the decimal equivalents.

$\frac{3}{5}$ ◯ $\frac{4}{10}$

Case 6: One fraction > $\frac{1}{2}$. One fraction < $\frac{1}{2}$.

Fraction > $\frac{1}{2}$ is greater.

$\frac{5}{8}$ ◯ $\frac{3}{7}$

Use strategies to compare.

26. 0.76 ◯ 0.67
27. $\frac{2}{3}$ ◯ $\frac{7}{12}$
28. $1\frac{1}{2}$ ◯ $1\frac{2}{5}$
29. $\frac{5}{8}$ ◯ $\frac{5}{6}$
30. 0.09 ◯ 0.1
31. $\frac{4}{9}$ ◯ $\frac{3}{5}$

Check Understanding

Complete the sentence. To add, subtract, or compare fractions with different denominators, start by finding a ____________ denominator.

Unit 3
Quick Quiz 2

Name ______________________

Add or subtract.

1. $\frac{4}{5} - \frac{3}{10} =$ ____________

2. $\frac{2}{3} + \frac{1}{4} =$ ____________

3. $6.7 - 0.85 =$ ____________

4. $9\frac{5}{6} + 3\frac{5}{6} =$ ____________

Solve.

Show your work.

5. On Thursday, $\frac{3}{4}$ of the students in Mario's class wore sneakers to school. On Friday, $\frac{7}{10}$ of the students wore sneakers. On which day did more students wear sneakers? Explain.

____

____

____

____

____

____

Fluency Check 2

Name ____________________

PATH to FLUENCY

1. $\begin{array}{r} 3.8 \\ \times\ 8.2 \\ \hline \end{array}$

2. $\begin{array}{r} 5.3 \\ \times\ 7.2 \\ \hline \end{array}$

3. $\begin{array}{r} 7.3 \\ \times\ 4.3 \\ \hline \end{array}$

4. $\begin{array}{r} 6.8 \\ \times\ 1.9 \\ \hline \end{array}$

5. $\begin{array}{r} 8.1 \\ \times\ 4.4 \\ \hline \end{array}$

6. $\begin{array}{r} 3.9 \\ \times\ 1.6 \\ \hline \end{array}$

7. $\begin{array}{r} 6.4 \\ \times\ 3.9 \\ \hline \end{array}$

8. $\begin{array}{r} 9.8 \\ \times\ 2.5 \\ \hline \end{array}$

9. $\begin{array}{r} 8.3 \\ \times\ 7.4 \\ \hline \end{array}$

10. $\begin{array}{r} 4.8 \\ \times\ 1.3 \\ \hline \end{array}$

11. $\begin{array}{r} 6.6 \\ \times\ 2.8 \\ \hline \end{array}$

12. $\begin{array}{r} 9.1 \\ \times\ 5.4 \\ \hline \end{array}$

13. $\begin{array}{r} 9.3 \\ \times\ 8.7 \\ \hline \end{array}$

14. $\begin{array}{r} 8.9 \\ \times\ 6.1 \\ \hline \end{array}$

15. $\begin{array}{r} 7.2 \\ \times\ 5.6 \\ \hline \end{array}$

Name ______________________

What's the Error?

Dear Math Students,

I am planting a flower garden! The space I have to plant in is $3\frac{1}{2}$ feet wide and $4\frac{1}{2}$ feet long. I told my friend that the area of my flower garden is $12\frac{1}{4}$ square feet. She says I've made a mistake! Can you help me find my mistake and the correct area?

Your friend,
Puzzled Penguin

14 Use this drawing to explain Puzzled Penguin's error. Then find the correct area.

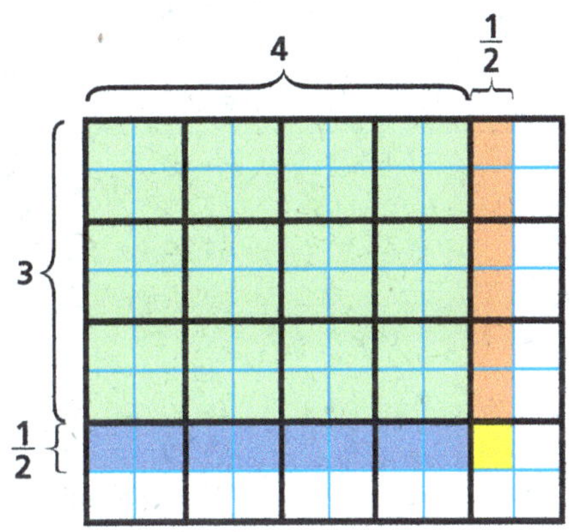

Check Understanding

Make a drawing to show the product $\frac{2}{3} \cdot \frac{1}{4}$.

Name

Solve Word Problems

34 Greenie the grasshopper hopped 3 meters in the length of time it took Tiny the ant to crawl $\frac{1}{5}$ meter. Greenie hopped how many times as far as Tiny crawled? Explain your answer.

35 Tiny crawled how many times as far as Greenie hopped? Explain your answer.

What's the Error?

Dear Math Students,

The problem below was marked wrong on my math quiz.

$$\frac{1}{3} \div 4 = \frac{3}{1} \cdot 4 = \frac{3}{1} \cdot \frac{4}{1} = \frac{12}{1} = 12$$

Can you describe my mistake and explain how I can find the correct quotient? Thank you.

Your friend,
Puzzled Penguin

36

Check Understanding

Draw a model to show $6 \div \frac{1}{2}$.

Unit 3
Quick Quiz 3

Name ______________________________

Multiply or divide.

1. $6 \div \frac{1}{10} =$ ______________

2. $\frac{2}{3} \cdot \frac{3}{4} =$ ______________

3. $\frac{1}{2} \div 10 =$ ______________

Solve.

Show your work.

4. A block of cheese weighing $\frac{7}{8}$ of a pound is cut into 4 equal parts. What is the weight in pounds of each part?

____

5. At a sleepover, three friends ate $\frac{5}{8}$ of a pizza. For a snack the next day, the friends ate $\frac{1}{2}$ of the leftover pizza. What fraction of the whole pizza was not eaten?

____

Fluency Check 3

Name ____________________

PATH to FLUENCY

1. $\begin{array}{r} 0.25 \\ \times\ 1.3 \\ \hline \end{array}$

2. $\begin{array}{r} 0.63 \\ \times\ 5.2 \\ \hline \end{array}$

3. $\begin{array}{r} 0.37 \\ \times\ 4.3 \\ \hline \end{array}$

4. $\begin{array}{r} 0.77 \\ \times\ 4.3 \\ \hline \end{array}$

5. $\begin{array}{r} 0.63 \\ \times\ 4.1 \\ \hline \end{array}$

6. $\begin{array}{r} 0.49 \\ \times\ 1.8 \\ \hline \end{array}$

7. $\begin{array}{r} 0.24 \\ \times\ 1.1 \\ \hline \end{array}$

8. $\begin{array}{r} 0.63 \\ \times\ 2.5 \\ \hline \end{array}$

9. $\begin{array}{r} 0.81 \\ \times\ 2.7 \\ \hline \end{array}$

10. $\begin{array}{r} 0.23 \\ \times\ 8.7 \\ \hline \end{array}$

11. $\begin{array}{r} 0.17 \\ \times\ 3.6 \\ \hline \end{array}$

12. $\begin{array}{r} 0.52 \\ \times\ 8.3 \\ \hline \end{array}$

13. $\begin{array}{r} 0.16 \\ \times\ 1.4 \\ \hline \end{array}$

14. $\begin{array}{r} 0.11 \\ \times\ 8.6 \\ \hline \end{array}$

15. $\begin{array}{r} 0.93 \\ \times\ 4.7 \\ \hline \end{array}$

 Name ____________

Relating Multiplication and Division

VOCABULARY
inverse operations

Find the unknown factor in each multiplication equation. Then rewrite the multiplication as a division equation.

Multiplication Equation	Related Division Equation
3 $\frac{2}{3} \cdot \frac{\square}{\square} = \frac{8}{15}$	$\frac{8}{15} \div \frac{2}{3} = \frac{\square}{\square}$
4 $\frac{5}{7} \cdot \frac{\square}{\square} = \frac{15}{56}$	$\frac{15}{56} \div \frac{5}{7} = \frac{\square}{\square}$
5 $\frac{5}{8} \cdot \frac{\square}{\square} = \frac{20}{72}$	
6 $\frac{2}{5} \cdot \frac{\square}{\square} = \frac{6}{20}$	

Multiplication and division are **inverse operations** for all whole numbers, decimals, and fractions. One operation undoes the other.

$$\frac{2}{5} \cdot \frac{1}{5} \div \frac{1}{5} = \frac{2}{5}$$

7 You solved each division equation in the table by using the unknown factor from a multiplication equation. Another way to solve a division equation is to divide the numerators and divide the ____________.

Divide by dividing numerators and dividing denominators.

8 $\frac{9}{20} \div \frac{3}{5} =$ ______ 9 $\frac{16}{45} \div \frac{2}{9} =$ ______ 10 $\frac{6}{45} \div \frac{2}{9} =$ ______

11 a. For Exercise 6, simplify the product by dividing the numerator and denominator by 2. $\frac{6}{20} = \frac{6 \div 2}{20 \div 2} =$

b. Can you use the method of dividing numerators and denominators? Why or why not? $\frac{3}{10} \div \frac{2}{5} = \frac{\square}{\square}$

____

____

Check Understanding

Explain how a multiplication problem with an unknown factor is related to a division problem.

Name ______________________________

Unsimplify to Divide

$\frac{2}{3} \div \frac{5}{7} = ?$

We cannot divide the numerator of $\frac{2}{3}$ by 5 or the denominator by 7.

To be able to divide, we need to unsimplify $\frac{2}{3}$. To unsimplify we rewrite it as an equivalent fraction so the numerators and denominators divide evenly.

Step 1 $\quad \frac{2}{3} \div \frac{5}{7} = (\frac{2}{3} \cdot \frac{5}{5} \cdot \frac{7}{7}) \div \frac{5}{7}$

(above the bracket: $\frac{2}{3} \cdot 1 \cdot 1$; below the bracket: $\frac{2}{3}$ unsimplified)

Step 2 $\quad = \frac{2 \cdot 5 \cdot 7}{3 \cdot 5 \cdot 7} \div \frac{5}{7}$

($5 \div 5 = 1$; $7 \div 7 = 1$)

Step 3 $\quad = \frac{2 \cdot 7}{3 \cdot 5}$

Step 4 $\quad = \frac{2}{3} \cdot \frac{7}{5}$

1 How is the number you divide $\frac{2}{3}$ by in the original division problem related to the number you multiply $\frac{2}{3}$ by in the final multiplication problem?

____

____

---

2 Complete.

Step 1 $\quad \frac{3}{8} \div \frac{2}{5} = (\frac{3}{8} \cdot \frac{2}{2} \cdot \frac{5}{5}) \div \frac{2}{5}$

(above the bracket: $\frac{3}{8} \cdot 1 \cdot 1$; below the bracket: $\frac{3}{8}$ unsimplified)

Step 2 $\quad = \frac{3 \cdot 2 \cdot 5}{8 \cdot 2 \cdot 5} \div \frac{2}{5}$

($2 \div 2 =$ ____; $5 \div 5 =$ ____)

Step 3 $\quad = \frac{3 \cdot 5}{8 \cdot 2}$

Step 4 $\quad = \frac{3}{8} \cdot \frac{\square}{\square}$

3 Complete.

Step 1 $\quad \frac{4}{9} \div \frac{3}{8} = (\frac{4}{9} \cdot \frac{3}{3} \cdot \frac{8}{8}) \div \frac{3}{8}$

(above the bracket: $\frac{4}{9} \cdot 1 \cdot 1$; below the bracket: $\frac{4}{9}$ unsimplified)

Step 2 $\quad = \frac{4 \cdot 3 \cdot 8}{9 \cdot 3 \cdot 8} \div \frac{3}{8}$

($3 \div 3 =$ ____; $8 \div 8 =$ ____)

Step 3 $\quad = \frac{4 \cdot 8}{9 \cdot 3}$

Step 4 $\quad = \frac{4}{9} \cdot \frac{\square}{\square}$

Summary: When dividing fractions, unsimplifying the dividend and then dividing numerators and denominators is the same as multiplying by the reciprocal of the divisor. For example, $\frac{2}{3} \div \frac{5}{7} = \frac{2}{3} \cdot \frac{7}{5}$.

Name ______________________________

Fraction Mixed Review

Solve.

Show your work.

13 The table at the right uses fractions and mixed numbers to represent the weights and costs of peaches that can be purchased at a roadside fruit stand.

Complete the table.

Weight (pounds)	Cost (dollars)
$\frac{3}{4}$	
1	$3\frac{3}{5}$
	$4\frac{1}{2}$
$1\frac{5}{8}$	

14 A triangle has a base measure of $5\frac{1}{2}$ centimeters and a height of $2\frac{1}{2}$ centimeters. What is the area of the triangle? Use a mixed number in your answer.

____

15 Quinn knows that the area of a triangle is $\frac{1}{18}$ square yard and its base measures $\frac{1}{9}$ yard. What is the height of the triangle?

____

Simplify before multiplying. If the product is equal to or greater than 1, write the answer as a whole or mixed number.

16 $\frac{14}{8} \cdot \frac{32}{42} =$ ______

17 $\frac{44}{36} \cdot \frac{72}{33} =$ ______

18 $\frac{16}{24} \cdot \frac{15}{28} =$ ______

19 $\frac{14}{25} \cdot \frac{27}{32} \cdot \frac{35}{21} \cdot \frac{64}{8} =$ ______

20 $\frac{32}{18} \cdot \frac{21}{20} \cdot \frac{15}{32} \cdot \frac{8}{49} =$ ______

Name ______________________________

What's the Error?

Dear Math Students,

To find the product at the right, I followed the steps below.

$2\frac{1}{3} \cdot 1\frac{3}{7}$

Step 1: Multiply the whole numbers. $2 \cdot 1 = 2$

Step 2: Multiply the fractions. $\frac{1}{\cancel{3}_{1}} \cdot \frac{\cancel{3}^{1}}{7} = \frac{1}{7}$

Step 3: Add the results from Step 1 and Step 2. $2 + \frac{1}{7} = 2\frac{1}{7}$ X

Please explain my mistake and tell me how I can find the correct product.

Your friend,
Puzzled Penguin

21 ______________________________

____

____

Dear Math Students,

To find the quotient at the right, I followed the steps below.

$3\frac{3}{4} \div 1\frac{1}{3}$

Step 1: Change the mixed numbers to fractions. $3\frac{3}{4} = \frac{15}{4}$ and $1\frac{1}{3} = \frac{4}{3}$

Step 2: Multiply the fractions. $\frac{\cancel{15}^{5}}{\cancel{4}_{1}} \cdot \frac{\cancel{4}^{1}}{\cancel{3}_{1}} = \frac{5}{1} = 5$ X

Please explain my mistake and tell me how I can find the correct quotient.

Your friend,
Puzzled Penguin

22 ______________________________

____

____

Check Understanding

Complete the sentences. Multiplying $\frac{a}{b}$ by a fraction less than 1 gives a product that is ______________ than $\frac{a}{b}$. Dividing $\frac{a}{b}$ by a fraction less than 1 gives a quotient that is ______________ than $\frac{a}{b}$.

Name ______________________

What's the Error?

Dear Math Students,

I got the two answers below marked wrong on my math test.

$2\frac{1}{4} - 1\frac{3}{8} = 1\frac{7}{8}$ $\qquad$ $\frac{7}{8} + \frac{2}{5} = \frac{9}{13}$

My friend got 100% on the test. She said she always uses estimation to make sure her answers are reasonable.

Can you explain how I could have used estimation to check my answers?

Your Friend,
Puzzled Penguin

24 Write a response to Puzzled Penguin.

Is the Answer Reasonable?

Is the answer reasonable or unreasonable? Explain.

25 $\frac{7}{8} - \frac{4}{7} = 1\frac{3}{8}$

26 $3\frac{4}{5} + 7\frac{1}{6} = 9\frac{29}{30}$

27 $\frac{9}{10} - \frac{7}{8} = \frac{1}{40}$

28 $6\frac{5}{6} + 2\frac{3}{4} = 6\frac{1}{12}$

Unit 3
Quick Quiz 4

Name ____________________

Divide.

1. $\frac{5}{6} \div \frac{1}{6} =$

______

2. $\frac{7}{12} \div \frac{3}{4} =$

______

3. $\frac{1}{4} \div \frac{1}{2} =$

______

Solve.

Show your work.

4. A block of cheese weighing $\frac{3}{4}$ of a pound is cut into identical pieces each weighing $\frac{1}{8}$ of a pound. Into how many pieces is the block of cheese cut?

______

5. A gear that is spinning completes a full turn, or revolution, every $\frac{1}{10}$ of a second. How many revolutions will the gear complete in $\frac{1}{2}$ of a second?

______

Fluency Check 4

Name ____________________

PATH to FLUENCY

1. $\begin{array}{r} 0.46 \\ \times \quad 18 \\ \hline \end{array}$

2. $\begin{array}{r} 2.9 \\ \times \quad 6.4 \\ \hline \end{array}$

3. $\begin{array}{r} 0.45 \\ \times \quad 6.6 \\ \hline \end{array}$

4. $\begin{array}{r} 4.8 \\ \times \quad 2.1 \\ \hline \end{array}$

5. $\begin{array}{r} 0.15 \\ \times \quad 19 \\ \hline \end{array}$

6. $\begin{array}{r} 0.87 \\ \times \quad 4.1 \\ \hline \end{array}$

7. $\begin{array}{r} 0.16 \\ \times \quad 7.7 \\ \hline \end{array}$

8. $\begin{array}{r} 9.4 \\ \times \quad 9.6 \\ \hline \end{array}$

9. $\begin{array}{r} 0.79 \\ \times \quad 26 \\ \hline \end{array}$

10. $\begin{array}{r} 0.38 \\ \times \quad 6.3 \\ \hline \end{array}$

11. $\begin{array}{r} 0.57 \\ \times \quad 13 \\ \hline \end{array}$

12. $\begin{array}{r} 5.8 \\ \times \quad 4.9 \\ \hline \end{array}$

13. $\begin{array}{r} 0.63 \\ \times \quad 88 \\ \hline \end{array}$

14. $\begin{array}{r} 8.4 \\ \times \quad 5.6 \\ \hline \end{array}$

15. $\begin{array}{r} 0.97 \\ \times \quad 8.2 \\ \hline \end{array}$

Name ___

Select all that apply.

1. $2\overline{)629}$

   Ⓐ 213

   Ⓑ 314 R1

   Ⓒ 314.5

   Ⓓ 345

2. $25\overline{)2,515}$

   Ⓐ 55

   Ⓑ 95.6

   Ⓒ 100.6

   Ⓓ 100 R15

3. Is the problem below a multiplication or a division problem? Explain your answer.

   The rectangular floor of a playpen has an area of 14 square feet. One measure of the floor is $3\frac{1}{2}$ feet. What is the other measure?

4. Select True or False for each statement.

4a. $0.9 \div 7.5 = 0.12$	○ True	○ False
4b. $63.2 \div 8 = 7.8$	○ True	○ False
4c. $72.8 \div 5.2 = 1.4$	○ True	○ False
4d. $7 \div 0.35 = 20$	○ True	○ False

Name ____________________

5 Without doing any computation, predict if the quotient $73 \div 0.42$ will be greater than or less than the product $0.42 \cdot 73$. Explain your reasoning in terms of the size of 0.42.

Use the numbers and the decimal point (if needed) to write the product. Each tile may be used more than once.

0	1	2	4
6	7	8	.

6 $\begin{array}{r} 0.4 \\ \times 0.3 \\ \hline \end{array}$ ______

7 $\begin{array}{r} 0.06 \\ \times 12 \\ \hline \end{array}$ ______

8 The fraction pairs in the table are not equivalent. Find the LCM for each fraction pair. Rewrite each pair as an equivalent fraction pair using the LCM as the denominator.

Fraction Pair	$\frac{2}{7}, \frac{1}{3}$	$\frac{5}{12}, \frac{3}{4}$	$\frac{7}{10}, \frac{4}{15}$
LCM			
Equivalent Fraction Pair	______	______	______

Multiply. Write the product.

9 $\begin{array}{r} 5.8 \\ \times 2.5 \\ \hline \end{array}$

Product: ______

10 $\begin{array}{r} 2.9 \\ \times 0.81 \\ \hline \end{array}$

Product: ______

Unit 3 Review/Test

Name ______________________________

Find the sum or difference. Select one number from each column to make the equation true.

11 $\frac{3}{8} + \frac{7}{8} = $ ■

whole number	fraction
○ 0	○ $\frac{5}{8}$
○ 1	○ $\frac{4}{5}$
○ 2	○ $\frac{1}{4}$
○ 3	○ $\frac{3}{4}$

12 $\frac{7}{9} + \frac{5}{6} = $ ■

whole number	fraction
○ 0	○ $\frac{3}{7}$
○ 1	○ $\frac{7}{9}$
○ 2	○ $\frac{11}{13}$
○ 3	○ $\frac{11}{18}$

Write a number in the box to make the equation true.

13 $3\frac{2}{5} - \square = 1\frac{1}{2}$

14 $\square - 1.78 = 0.82$

15 George calculated a sum of $\frac{15}{24}$.

Which fractions are equivalent to $\frac{15}{24}$? Choose all that apply.

Ⓐ $\frac{10}{16}$

Ⓑ $\frac{5}{6}$

Ⓒ $\frac{7}{12}$

Ⓓ $\frac{5}{8}$

Ⓔ $\frac{3}{8}$

Ⓕ $\frac{30}{48}$

Name ____________________

16 Read the division problem below. Then select True or False for each statement.

$\frac{3}{4} \div 7 = \blacksquare$

16a. To find the quotient, first find a common denominator. ○ True ○ False

16b. The quotient will be less than $\frac{3}{4}$. ○ True ○ False

16c. You can simplify the quotient. ○ True ○ False

Draw a line to match each missing numerator or denominator to its value. You will not use all of the choices.

17 $\frac{3}{5} \cdot \frac{\square}{\square} = \frac{6}{35}$

18 $\frac{1}{4} \cdot \frac{\square}{\square} = \frac{3}{20}$

2	3	4	5	6	7

Choose the expressions that make the equation true. Select all that apply.

19 $\frac{8}{15} \div \frac{4}{5} = \blacksquare$

Ⓐ $\frac{1}{3}$

Ⓑ $\frac{2}{3}$

Ⓒ $\frac{20}{60}$

Ⓓ $\frac{40}{60}$

20 $1\frac{5}{8} \div 1\frac{1}{2} = \blacksquare$

Ⓐ $2\frac{7}{16}$

Ⓑ $\frac{39}{16}$

Ⓒ $\frac{26}{24}$

Ⓓ $1\frac{1}{12}$

Name ____________________

21 Seth wrote an expression that simplifies to 0.36.

Choose Yes or No to indicate if the expression has a value of 0.36.

21a. $36 \cdot 0.01$	○ Yes	○ No
21b. $3.6 \cdot 0.1$	○ Yes	○ No
21c. $3.6 \div 0.1$	○ Yes	○ No
21d. $0.036 \div 0.01$	○ Yes	○ No

22 Darnell has two scraps of cloth. The first scrap is 3.75 cm in length. The second scrap is $\frac{1}{5}$ as long as the length of the first.

Part A

What is the total length of the scraps? Give your answer in decimal form. Show your work.

_______ cm

Part B

Answer the following question without making a calculation. Explain how you know the answer.

If Darnell's second scrap was $\frac{1}{3}$ as long as the first, would the total length of the scraps be greater than or less than the answer you found in Part A?

 Name ____________________

23 Lydia has $8\frac{1}{2}$ cups of juice to serve.

Part A

If each serving is $\frac{3}{4}$ cup, how many full servings can she make? What amount of juice, if any, will be left over? Show your work.

______ servings

______ left over

Part B

If she needs 15 servings, how much more juice does she need?

Ⓐ $2\frac{1}{4}$ cups Ⓑ 3 cups Ⓒ $2\frac{3}{4}$ cups Ⓓ 4 cups

Part C

Lydia decides to make each serving of juice $\frac{5}{8}$ cup. Without calculating, predict if she can make more full servings or fewer full servings using the $8\frac{1}{2}$ cups of juice. Explain your choice. Then confirm your prediction.

Predict:

Confirm:

24 Dana's dog Skippy weighs 20.4 pounds. In comparison, her cat Bruiser weighs 0.75 as much as Skippy.

a. Does Bruiser weigh more or less than Skippy? Explain.

b. How much does Bruiser weigh?

______ pounds

Name ______________________________

Recipes from Around the World

One day each spring, the home economics students at Eisenhower School gather recipes from around the world and make foods for other students to taste.

Parts of two recipes that were used in this year's event are shown below.

Dal Makhani: India
(serves 4)

150 g whole lentils

1.5 L water

75 g kidney beans

1.25 cm piece ginger

Oeufs à la Florentine: France
(serves 6)

$\frac{3}{4}$ teaspoon chicken bouillon

$1\frac{1}{8}$ cup half and half

$1\frac{1}{2}$ lb frozen chopped spinach

Solve.

1. The students focused first on the Dal Makhani recipe.

   - If the students doubled the amount of each ingredient in the Dal Makhani recipe, would they make at least 10 servings?

   - If they do make at least 10 servings, how many additional servings would there be? If they do not, how many additional servings would they need? Explain and show your work.

   - If the students had a 5 centimeter piece of ginger, what is the maximum number of servings of Dal Makhani that they could make? Explain and show your work.

Name ________________________________

2 The students next turned their attention to the Oeufs (eggs) à la Florentine recipe.

- If the students cut in half the amount of each ingredient in the Oeufs à la Florentine recipe, would they make at least 2 servings?

- If they do make at least 2 servings, how many additional servings would there be? If they do not, how many additional servings would they need? Explain and show your work.

- If the students had 3 pounds of frozen chopped spinach, what is the maximum number of servings of oeufs à la florentine that they could make? Explain and show your work.

3 For the event, the students made 10 servings of Dal Makhani and 2 servings of Oeufs à la Florentine. Calculate the amount of each ingredient that was used.

- Dal Makhani

_______________ g whole lentils

_______________ L water

_______________ g kidney beans

_______________ cm piece ginger

- Oeufs à la Florentine

_______________ tsp chicken bouillon

_______________ c half and half

_______________ lb frozen chopped spinach

Dear Family:

In this unit, students are studying the surface area of prisms and pyramids. **Surface area** is the sum of the areas of all the faces of a geometric figure. Your child will make nets to visualize the parts that make up the surface area of a prism or pyramid and learn a systematic approach to finding the total surface area of the solid figure.

Rectangular Prism Net

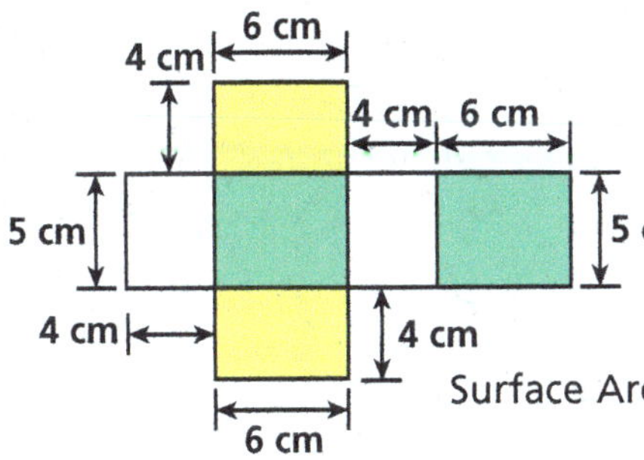

Rectangular Prism

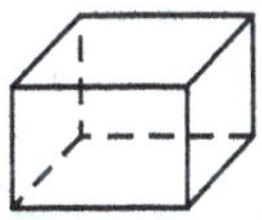

Surface Area $= 2(6 \times 5) + 2(4 \times 5) + 2(6 \times 4)$
$= 60 + 40 + 48 = 148$

Surface Area is 148 cm²

The types of prisms and pyramids that students will be calculating the surface areas for are shown below.

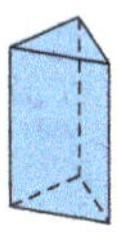
triangular prism

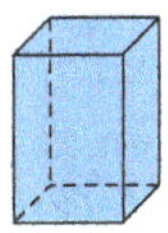
rectangular prism

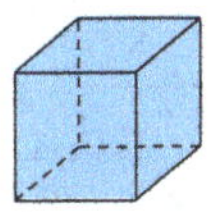
cube

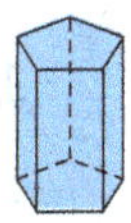
pentagonal prism

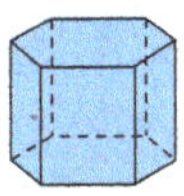
hexagonal prism

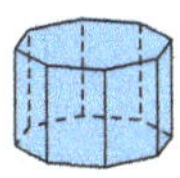
octagonal prism

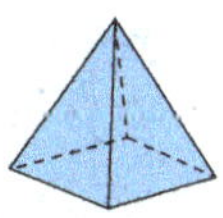
square pyramid

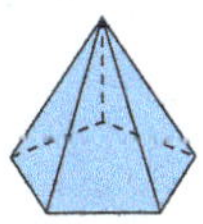
pentagonal pyramid

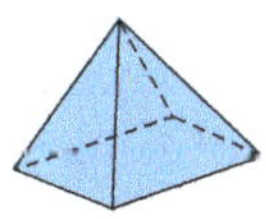
rectangular pyramid

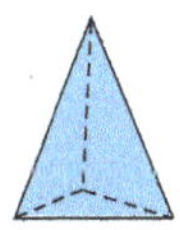
triangular pyramid

Students will also explore real-life applications of surface area.

If you need practice materials or if you have any questions, please contact me.

Sincerely,
Your child's teacher

Estimada familia:

En esta unidad, los estudiantes aprenderán a calcular el área total de los prismas y las pirámides. El **área total** es la suma de las áreas de las caras de una figura geométrica. Su hijo hará plantillas para visualizar las partes que forman el área total de un prisma o una pirámide y aprenderán un método para hallar la superficie total del cuerpo geométrico.

Plantilla de prisma rectangular

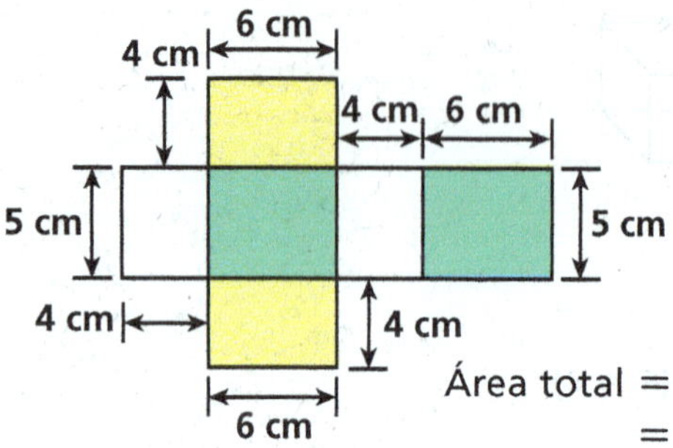

Prisma Rectangular

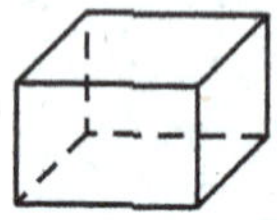

$$\text{Área total} = 2(6 \times 5) + 2(4 \times 5) + 2(6 \times 4)$$
$$= 60 + 40 + 48 = 148$$

El área total es 148 cm^2

Los estudiantes calcularán el área total de los tipos de prismas y pirámides que se muestran abajo.

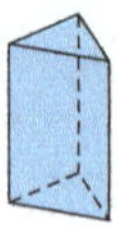

prisma triangular

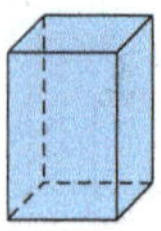

prisma rectangular

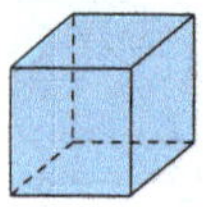

cubo

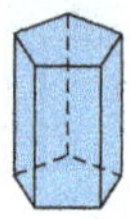

prisma pentagonal

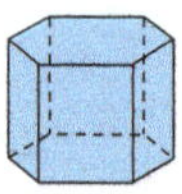

prisma hexagonal

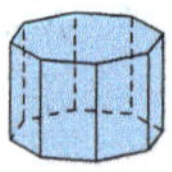

prisma octagonal

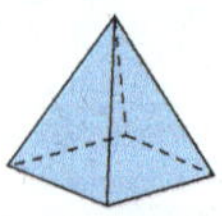

pirámide cuadrangular

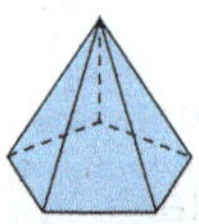

pirámide pentagonal

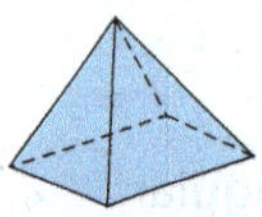

pirámide rectangular

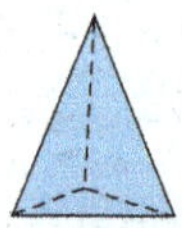

pirámide triangular

Los estudiantes también explorarán situaciones de la vida real en las que se aplica lo que han aprendido acerca del área total.

Si necesita materiales para practicar o si tiene preguntas, por favor comuníquese conmigo.

Sinceramente,
El maestro de su hijo

base of a prism	edge
base of a pyramid	face of a prism
cube	face of a pyramid

The line segment where two faces meet in a three-dimensional figure.

Examples:

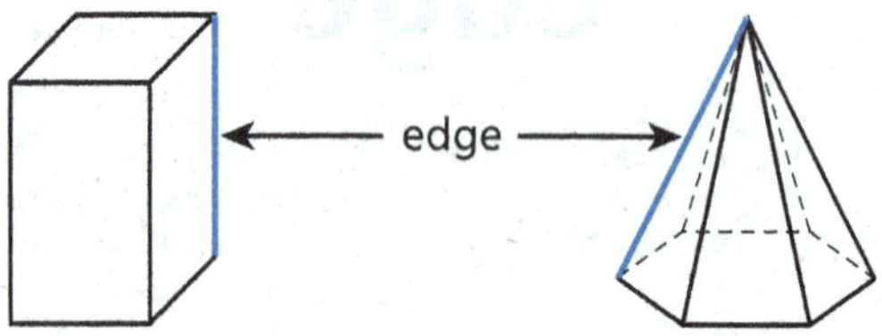

A base is one of the congruent parallel faces.

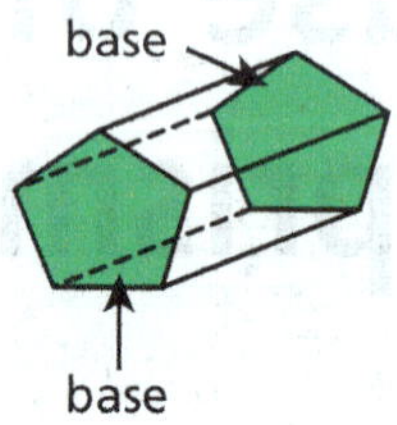

Any of the flat surfaces of a prism.

Example:

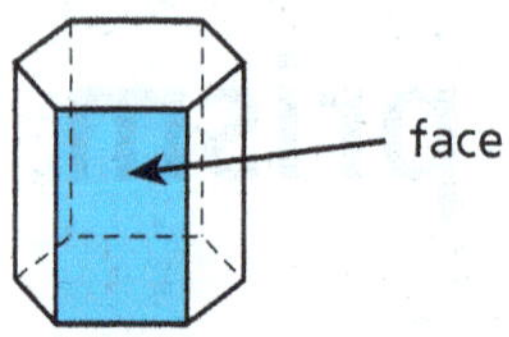

The base is the face that does not touch the vertex of the pyramid.

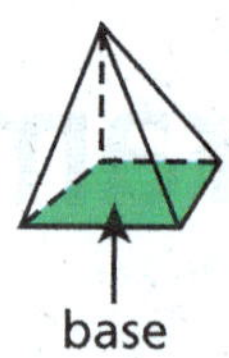

Any of the flat surfaces of a pyramid.

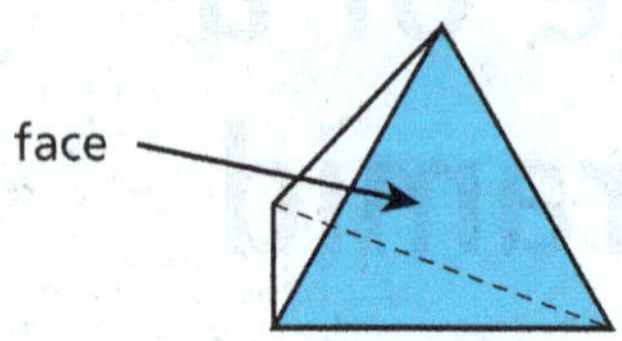

A rectangular prism with six congruent square faces.

lateral face	pyramid
net	rectangular prism
prism	slant height

A solid with a polygon for a base whose vertices are all joined to a single point.

Examples:

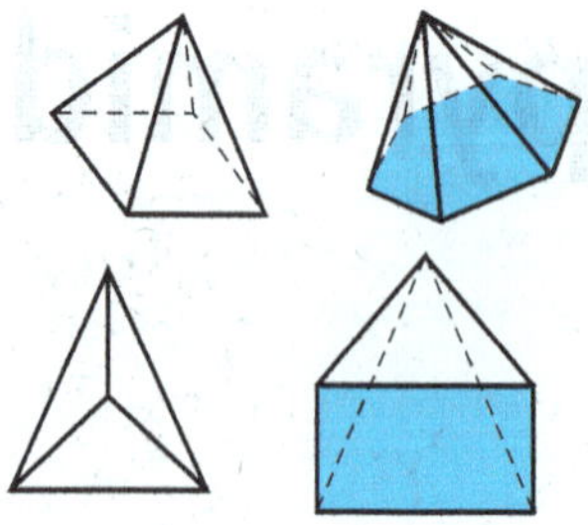

A face that is not a base. Prisms have rectangular lateral faces and pyramids have triangular lateral faces.

Examples:

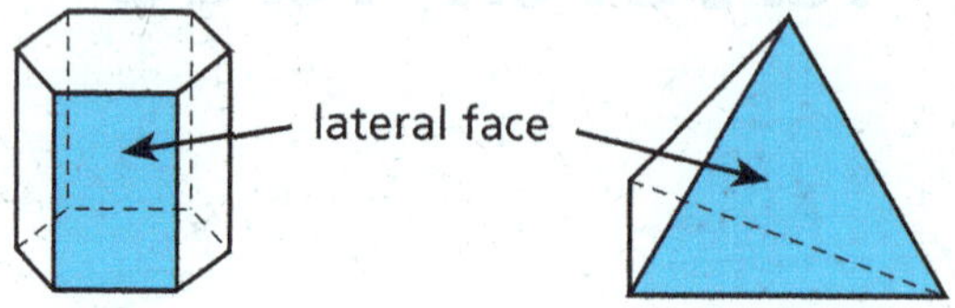

A solid figure with two rectangular bases that are congruent and parallel.

Example:

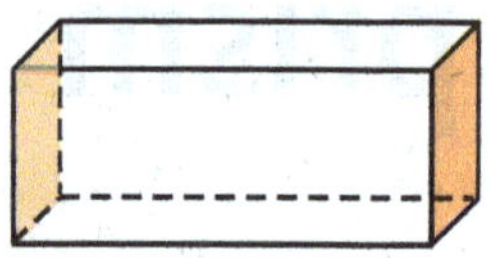

A two-dimensional flat pattern that can be folded into a three-dimensional figure.

Example:

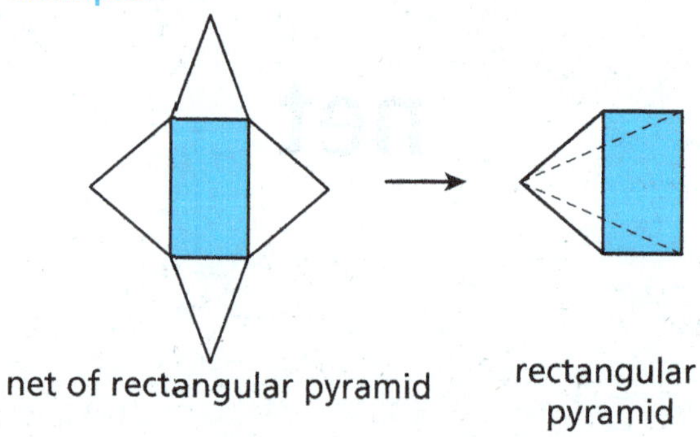

The height of a triangular face of a pyramid.

Example:

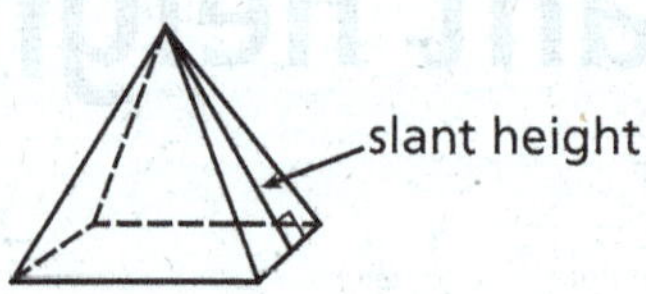

A solid figure with two congruent parallel bases.

Examples:

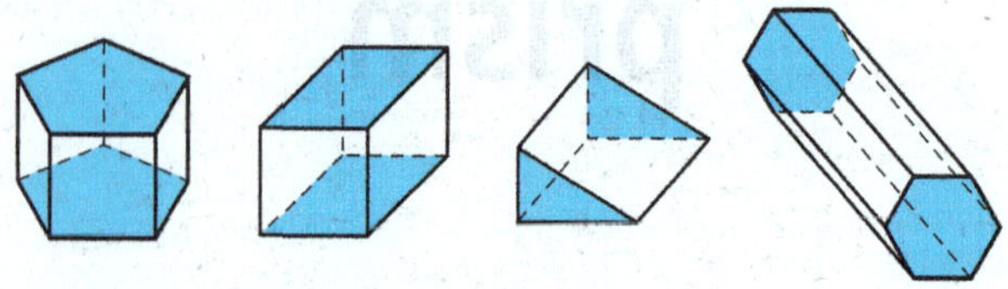

solid figure

surface area

A solid figure is a three-dimensional figure; it is not flat.

Examples:

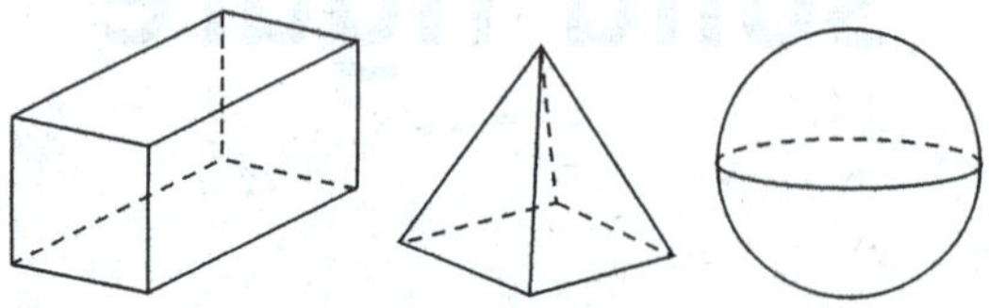

The total area of all the faces of a solid figure.

Name ____________________

VOCABULARY
net
solid figure

Rectangular Prism Net

A **net** is a two-dimensional flat pattern that can be folded into a three-dimensional figure.

Cut out the net and form the solid figure.

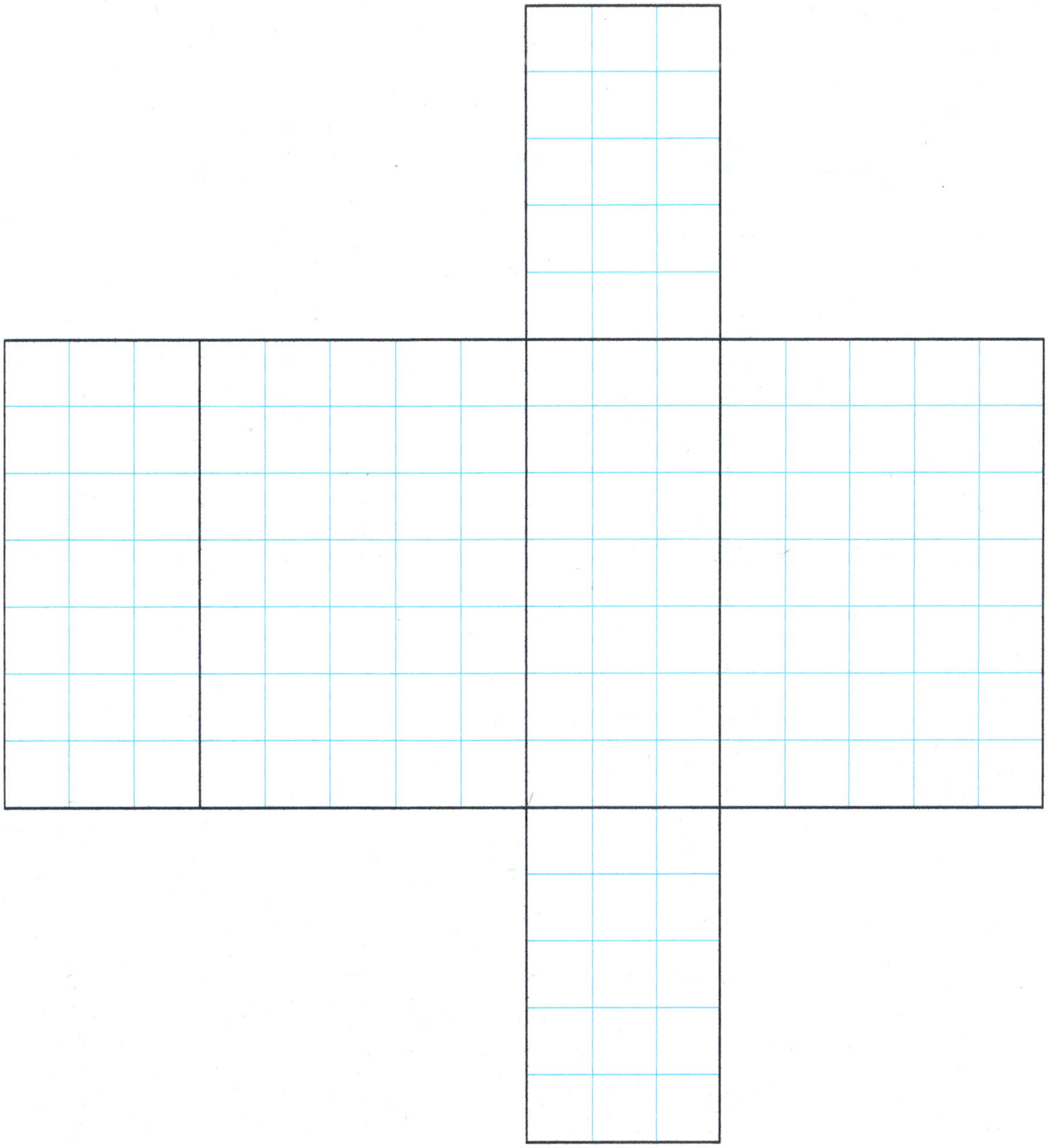

Name

Rectangular Prism Net (continued)

Name ______________________________

Make a Rectangular Prism from a Net

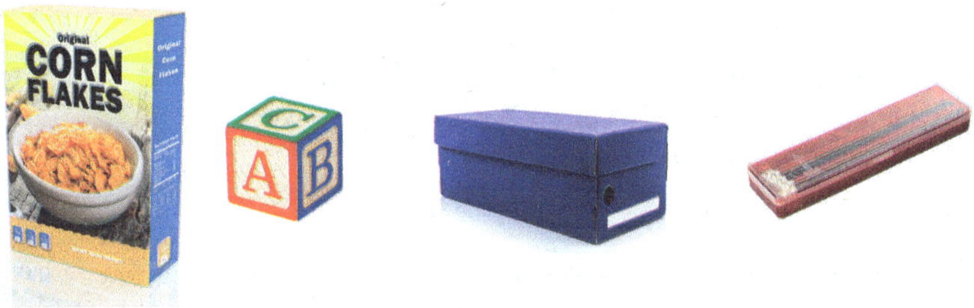

VOCABULARY
prism
face of a prism
rectangular prism
base of a prism
lateral face
edge

1. The flat rectangular sides of a **prism** are called **faces**. The line segment where two faces meet is called an **edge**.

   a. How many faces does a **rectangular prism** have? ____________

   b. How many edges does a **rectangular prism** have? ____________

2. Two parallel faces of a prism are called **bases**. What shape are the bases of a rectangular prism? ____________

3. The faces that are not bases are called **lateral faces**.

   What shape are the lateral faces? ____________

Place your rectangular prism in the same position as shown in the picture below on the right.

Use your rectangular prism to answer questions 4–6.

4. What are the dimensions of the bases of your rectangular prism?

   ____

5. What are the dimensions of the lateral faces?

   ____

   ____

6. Record the dimensions of the prism you made on the picture at the right.

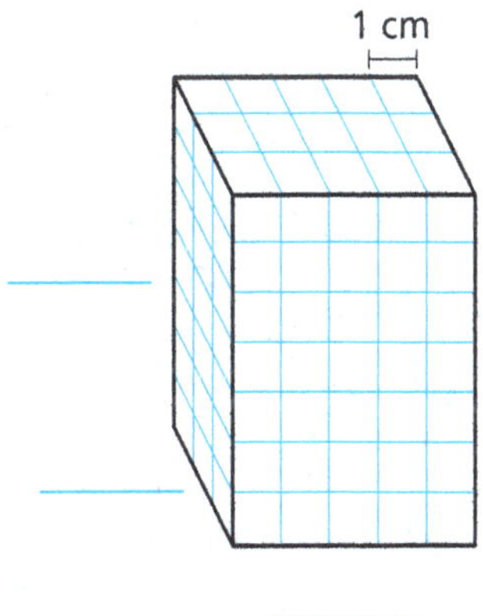

Name ______________________________

What's the Error?

Dear Math Students,

Today I made this net for a rectangular prism. Before I trace this net on cardboard, can you tell me if the net will form a rectangular prism? If not, can you tell me what I did wrong?

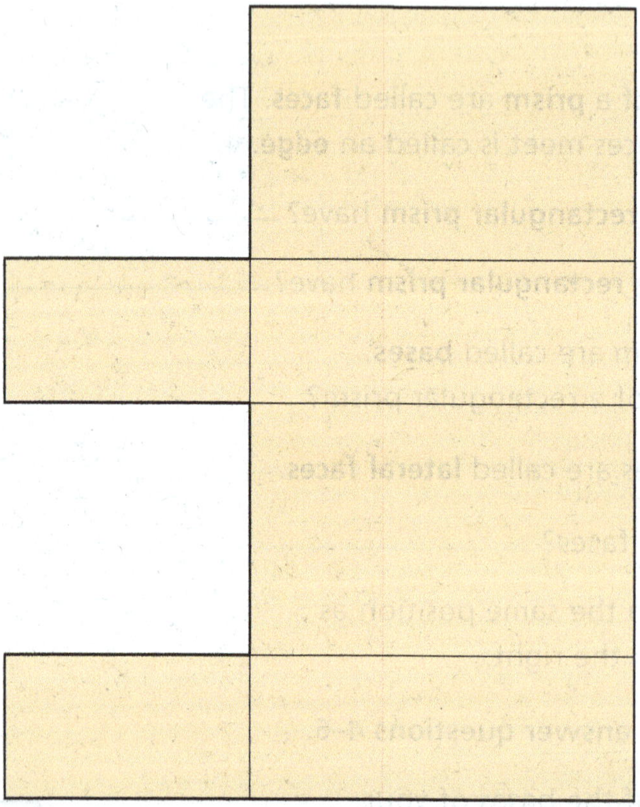

Your friend,
Puzzled Penguin

7 Write a response to the Puzzled Penguin.

____

____

____

____

Name ______________________________

Draw a Net for a Rectangular Prism

Draw a net for a rectangular prism. Then cut out the net and form a rectangular prism.

Name

Draw a Net for a Rectangular Prism (continued)

Name ______________________________

Find Surface Area Using Nets

VOCABULARY
surface area

The net on the left forms the rectangular prism on the right. Fill in the missing dimensions. Then find the **surface area** of each rectangular prism.

8

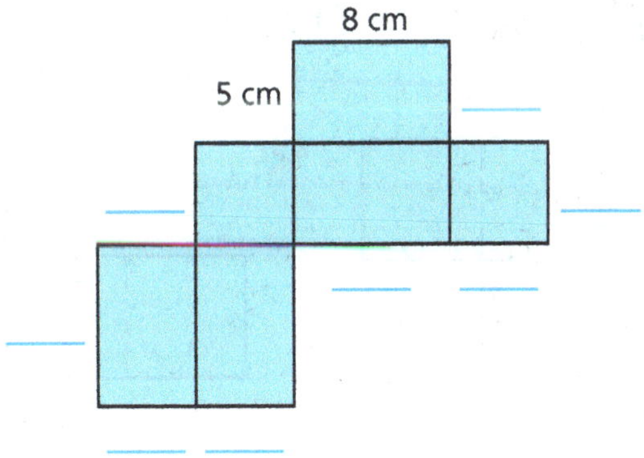

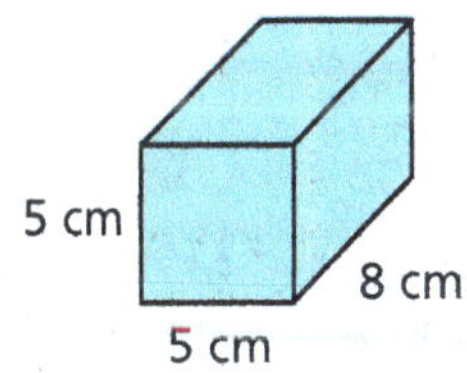

Area of a square base: __________ Area of a rectangular face: __________

Surface area: __________

9

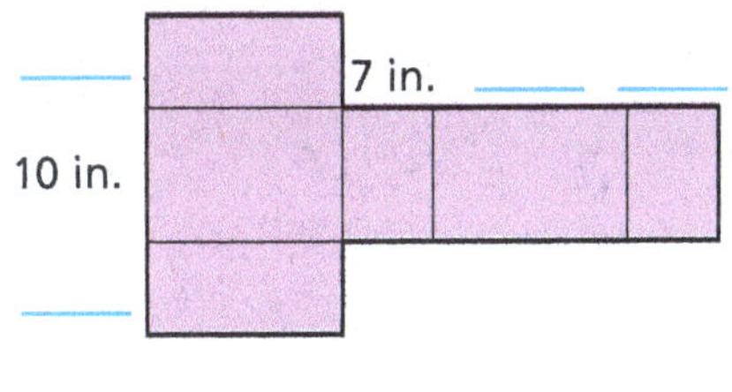

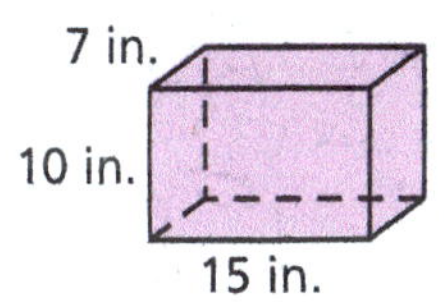

Area of top rectangular face: __________

Area of side rectangular face: __________

Area of front rectangular face: __________

Surface area: __________

10 How can you find the surface area of any rectangular prism?

____

____

11 Use the rectangular prism at the right to write an expression to show how you can find the surface area of any rectangular prism.

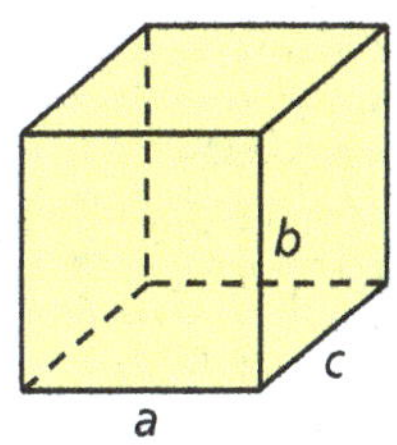

____

Name ______________________________

Identify Cube Nets

VOCABULARY
cube

A **cube** is a rectangular prism that has six congruent square faces.

Put a check mark next to each net that will form a cube. Fix the other nets so they will form a cube.

20 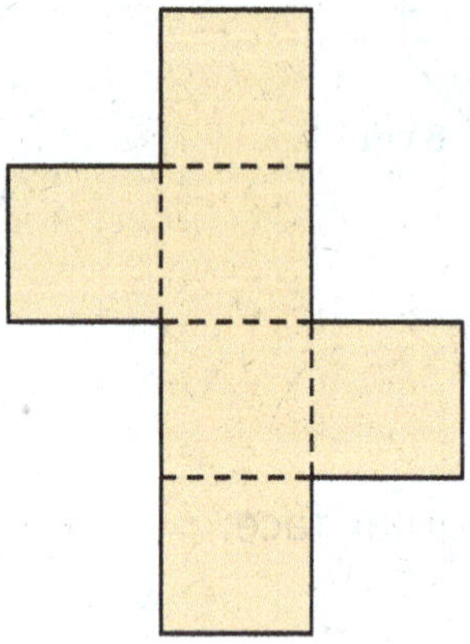

21 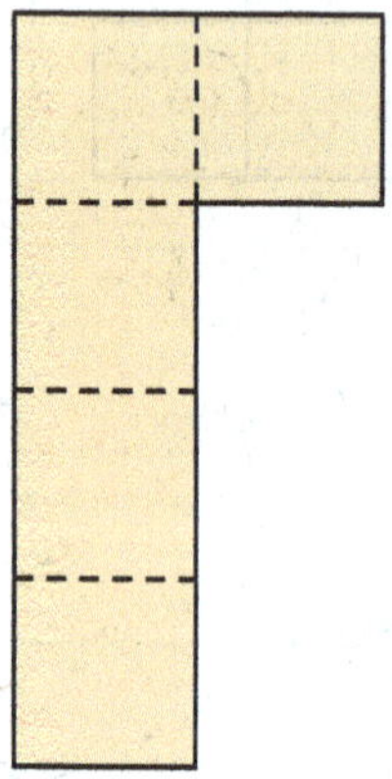

22 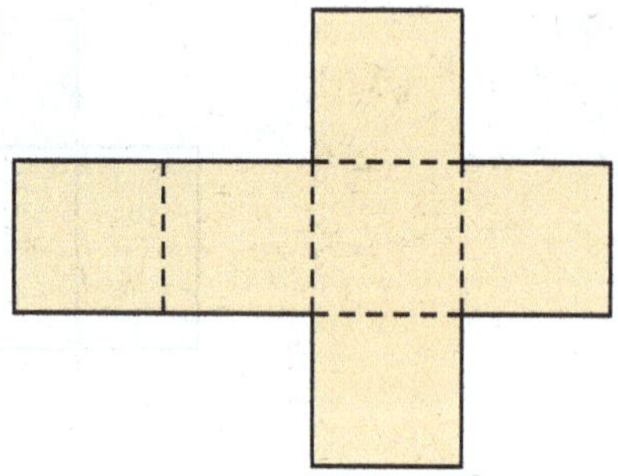

23 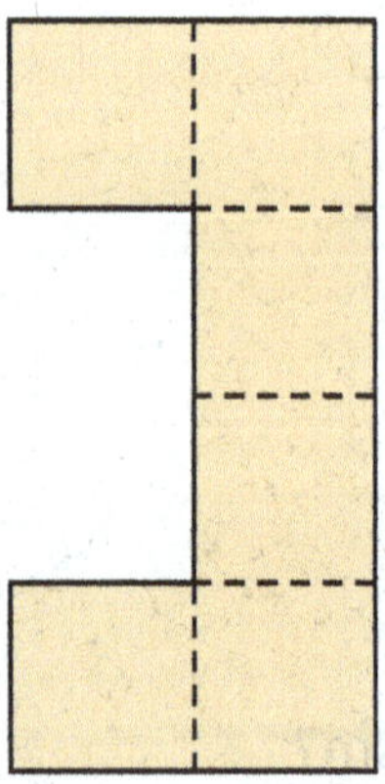

24 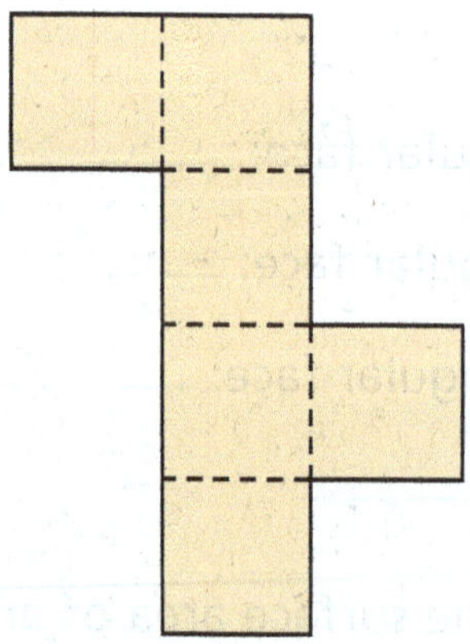

25 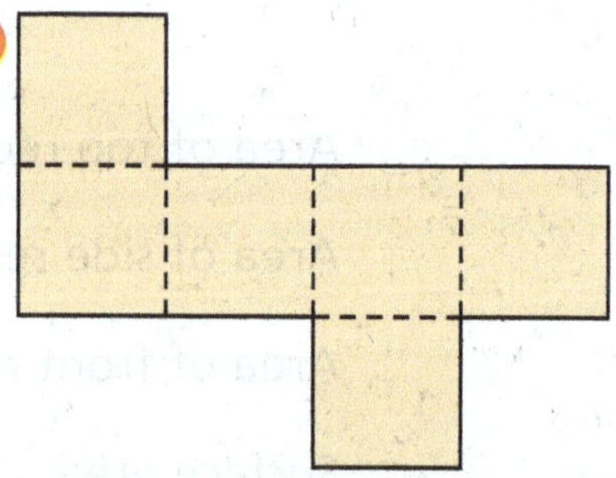

Name ______________________

Fractional Edge Lengths

The net can be used to form a cube. Fill in the missing dimensions. Then find the area of a face and the surface area. Use mixed numbers in your answers.

26

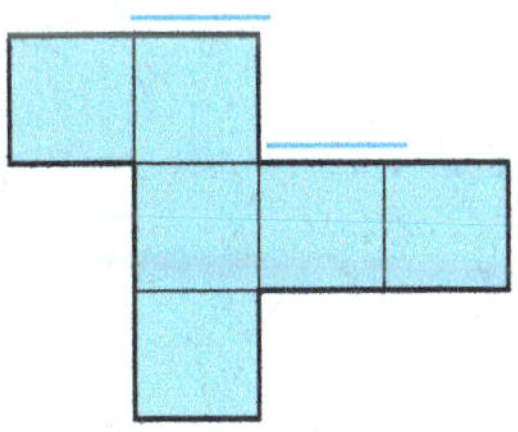

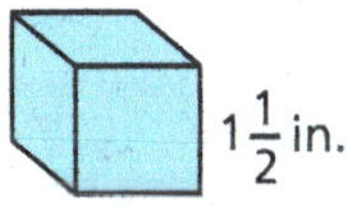

Area of a face: ______________ Surface area: ______________

27

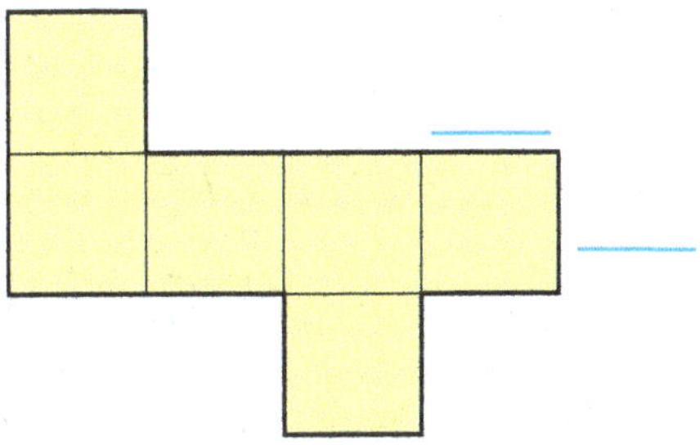

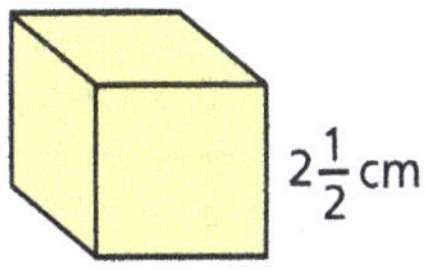

Area of a face: ______________ Surface area: ______________

Find the surface area. Draw a net if you need to.

28

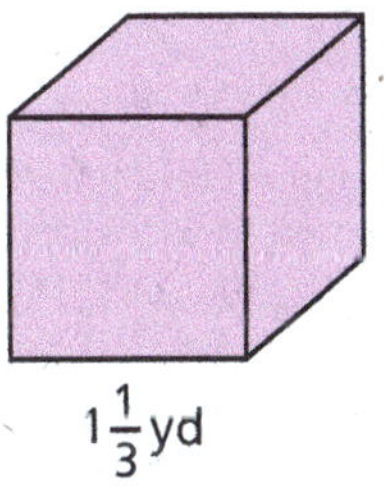

Surface area: ______________

29

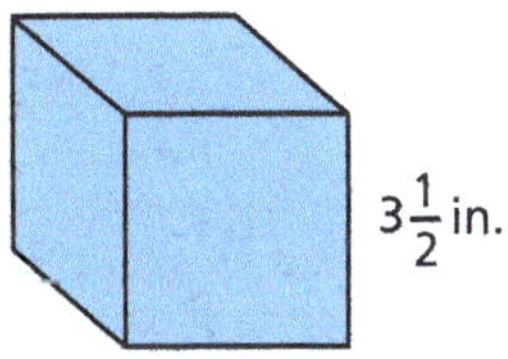

Surface area: ______________

30 Use the cube at the right to write an expression to show how you can find the surface area of any cube.

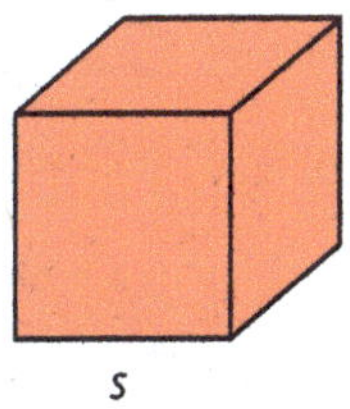

____

Check Understanding

Draw a net for a cube with edge length 2 cm.
Write an expression for its surface area. ______________

Name ______________________________

Make Nonrectangular Prisms

Cut out the polygons from this page and the rectangles from the next page to make nonrectangular prisms.

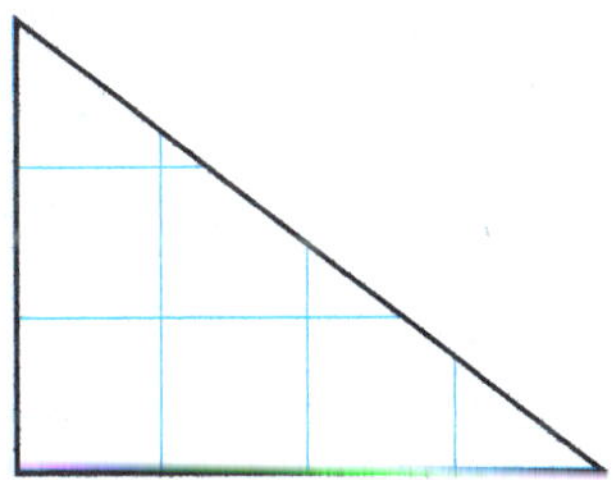

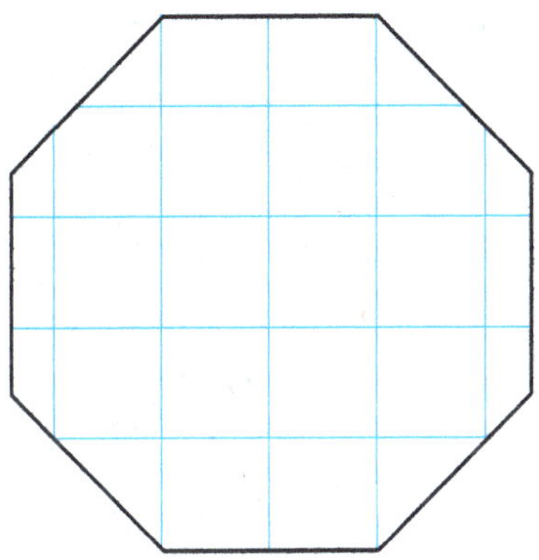

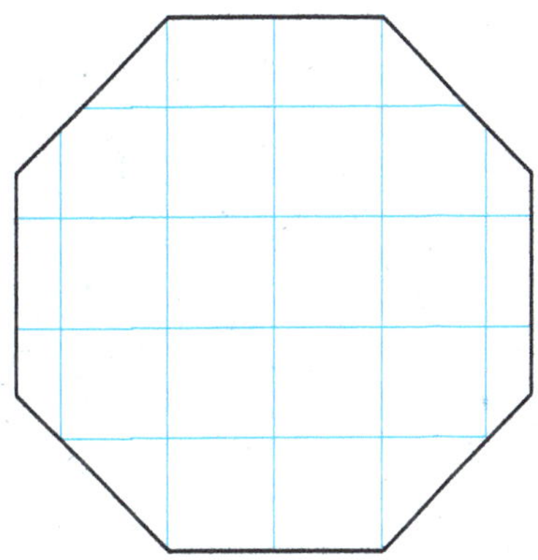

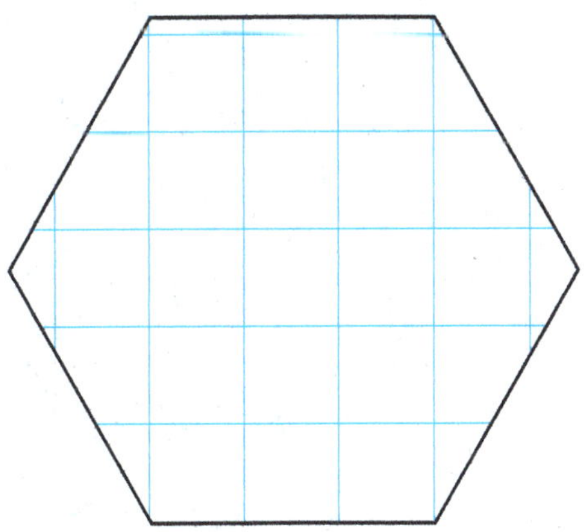

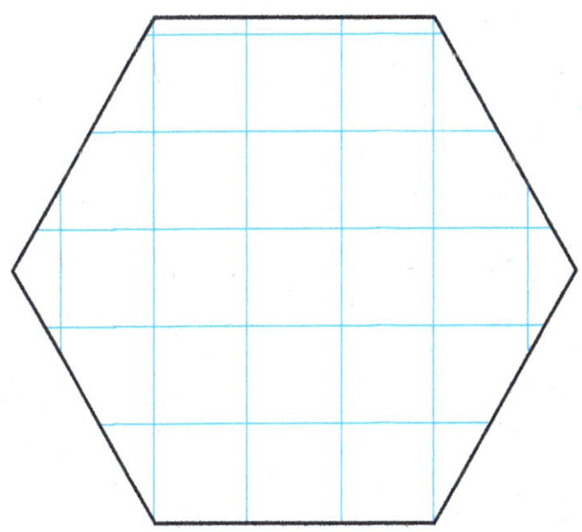

Name ____________________

Make Nonrectangular Prisms (continued)

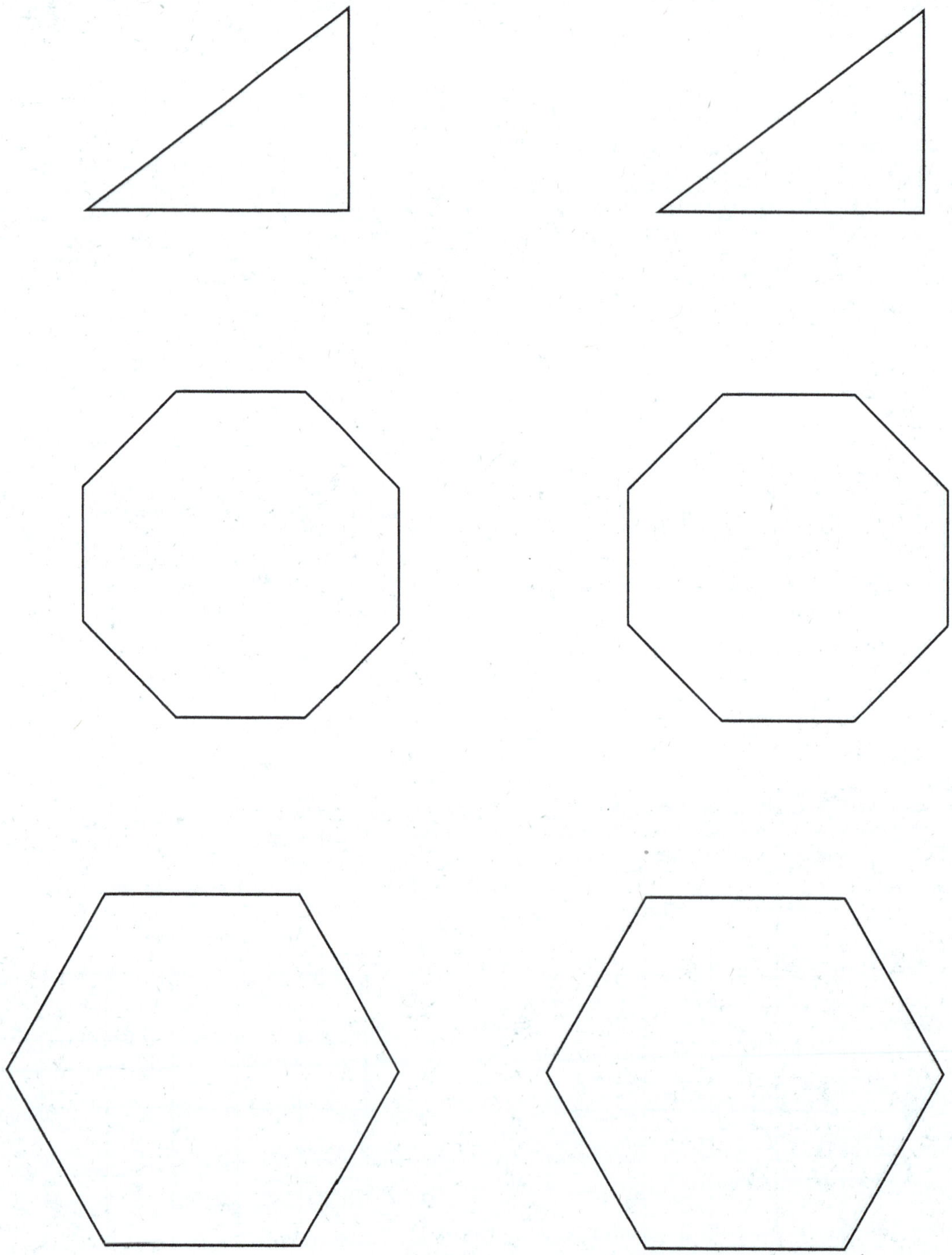

Name ____________________

Make Nonrectangular Prisms (continued)

Cut out each rectangle.
Fold on the dashed rules.
Tape the ends together to form the lateral faces of the prism.

For triangular prism

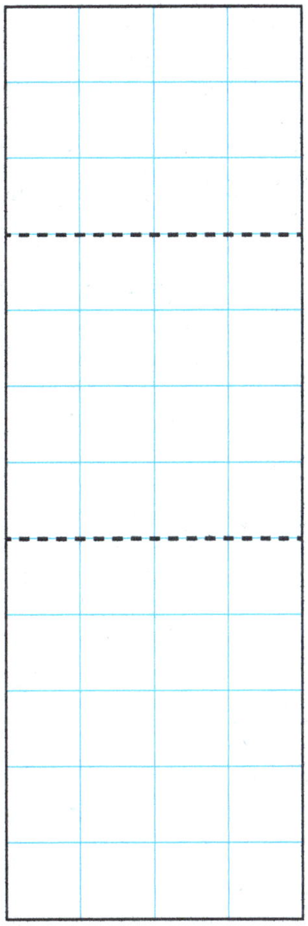

For octagonal prism

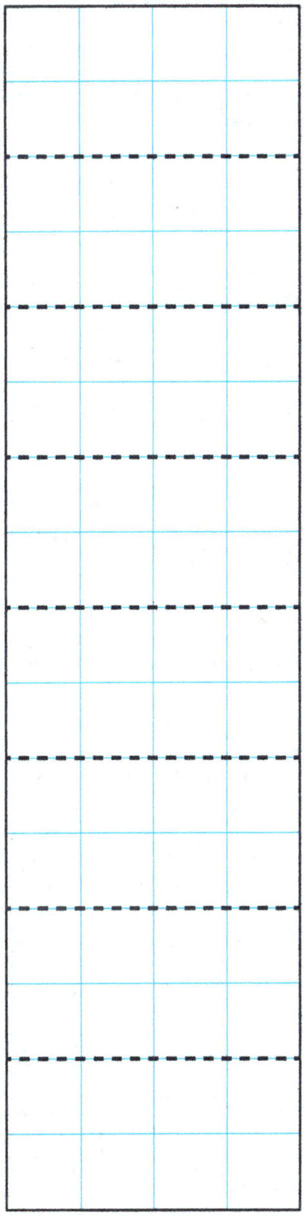

For hexagonal prism

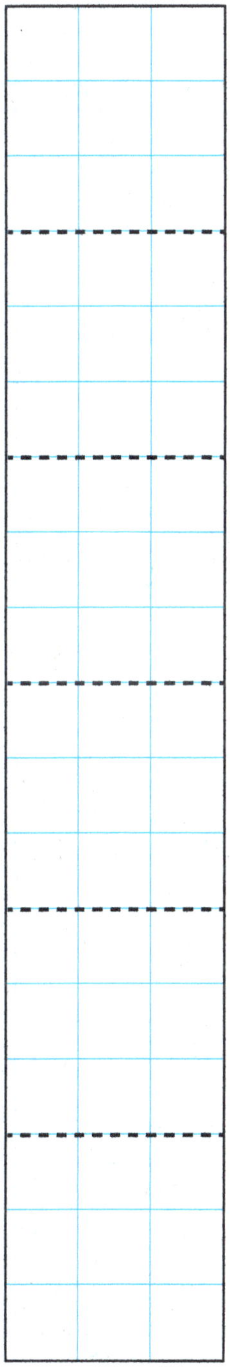

Name ____________________

Make Nonrectangular Prisms (continued)

Name

Draw a Net for a Nonrectangular Prism

Draw a net for a nonrectangular prism. Then cut out the net and form a nonrectangular prism.

Name ____________________

Draw a Net for a Nonrectangular Prism (continued)

Name ____________________

What's the Error?

Dear Math Students,

I designed some shipping boxes with no overlapping cardboard. I found that it takes 444 in.^{2} to make this box. Is my answer correct? If not, can you tell me what I did wrong?

Your friend,
Puzzled Penguin

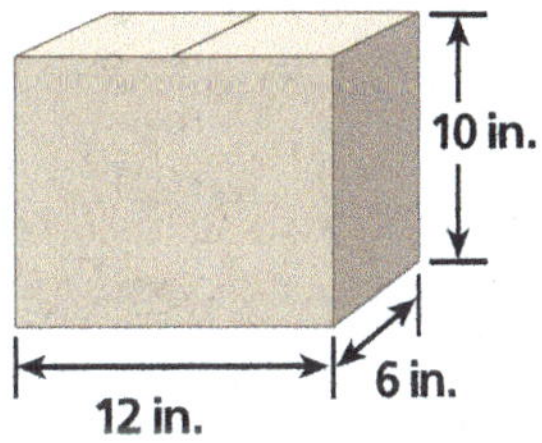

1. Write a response to the Puzzled Penguin.

____

____

____

Dear Math Students,

Here is another shipping box I invented with no overlapping cardboard. I found that it takes 240 in.^{2} to make this box. Is my answer correct? If not, can you tell me what I did wrong?

Your friend,
Puzzled Penguin

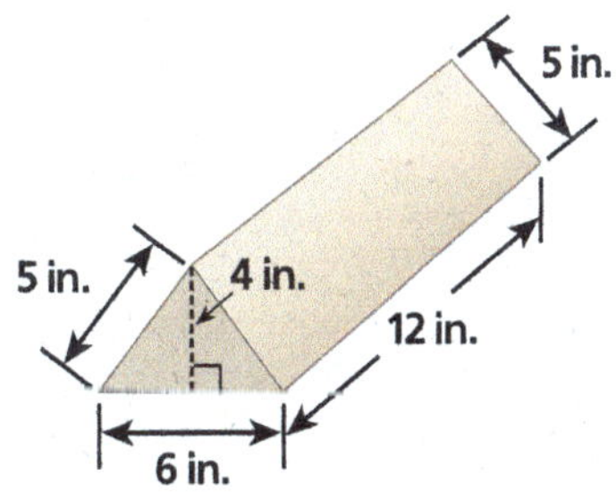

2. Write a response to the Puzzled Penguin.

____

____

____

Unit 4
Quick Quiz 1

Name ______________________

Name the solid each net will form.

1 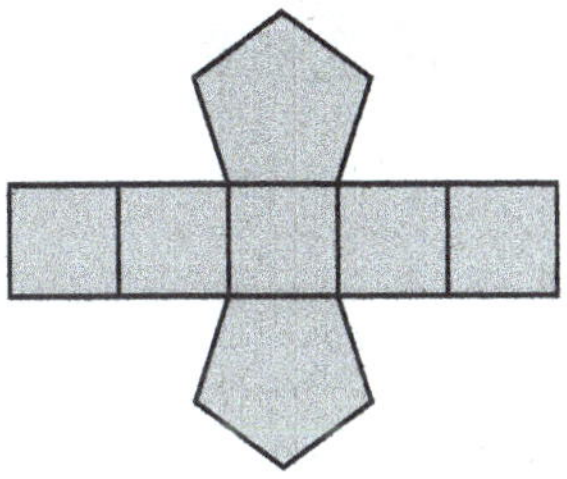

____

2 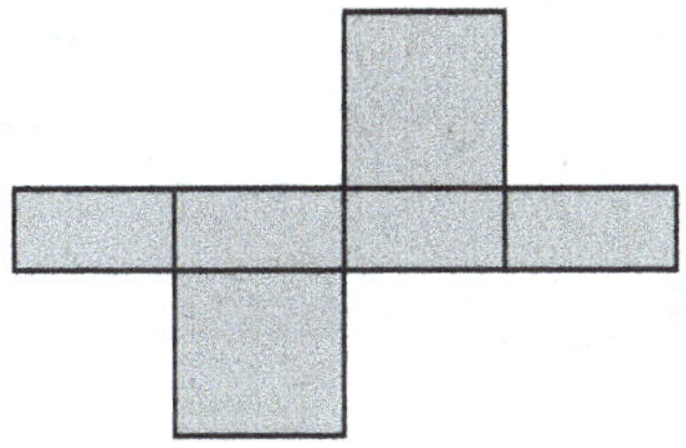

____

Find the surface area.

3 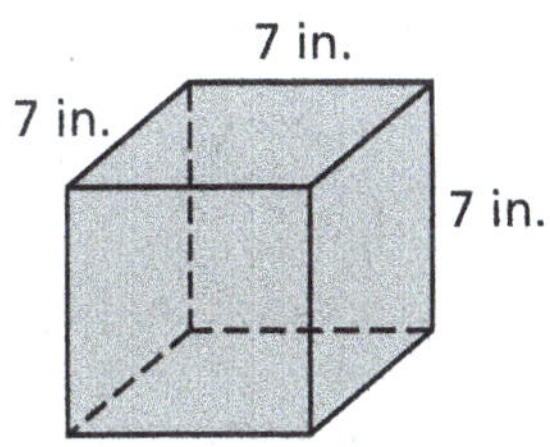

____

4 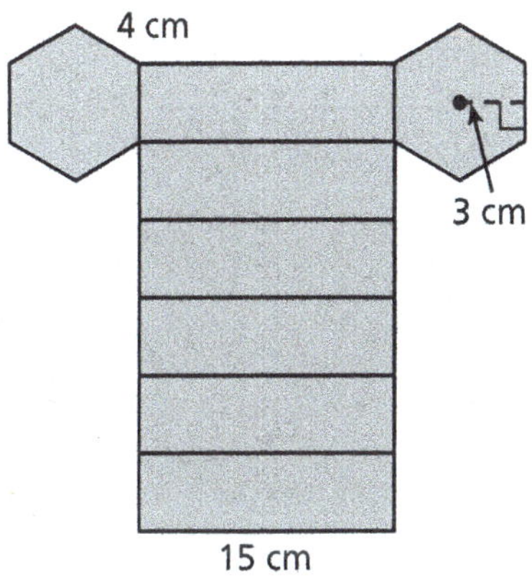

____

Solve.

5 A gift box is shaped like a rectangular prism. The length of the box is 16 cm, the width is 6 cm, and the height is 6 cm. Is a sheet of wrapping paper measuring 20 cm by 20 cm enough paper to wrap the box? Explain.

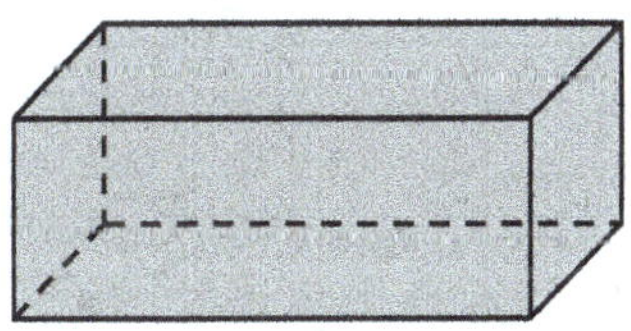

____

____

____

____

____

Fluency Check 5

Name ______________________

PATH to FLUENCY

1. $23\overline{)2{,}645}$
2. $44\overline{)6{,}812}$
3. $52\overline{)8{,}496}$
4. $35\overline{)7{,}807}$
5. $67\overline{)3{,}417}$
6. $19\overline{)1{,}627}$
7. $54\overline{)7{,}157}$
8. $71\overline{)1{,}195}$
9. $41\overline{)3{,}567}$
10. $72\overline{)2{,}016}$
11. $30\overline{)2{,}861}$
12. $28\overline{)3{,}839}$
13. $64\overline{)5{,}321}$
14. $17\overline{)1{,}632}$
15. $14\overline{)9{,}426}$

Name ______________________________

Make a Pyramid

Cut out the net and form the solid figure.

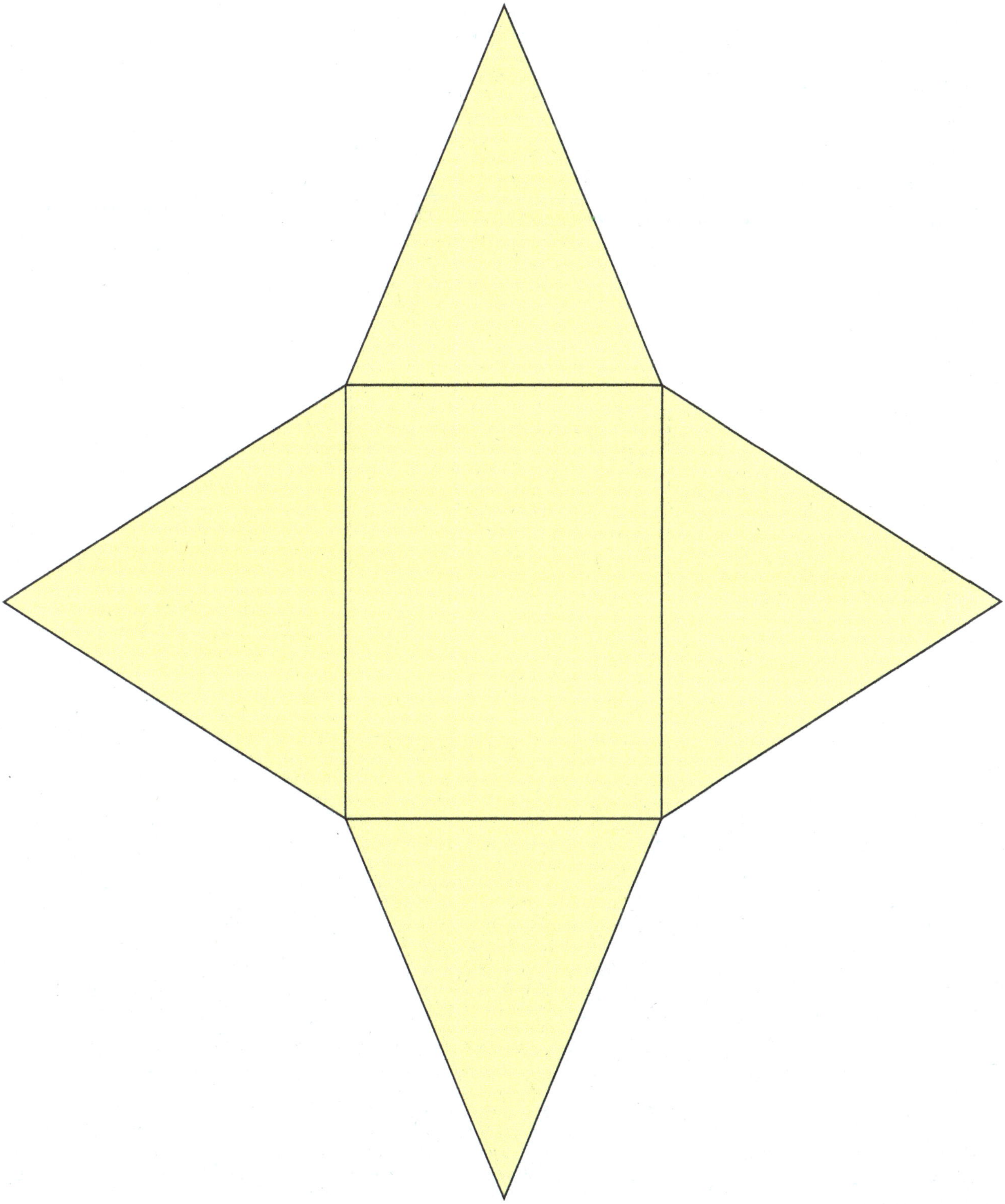

Name ______________________________

Make a Pyramid (continued)

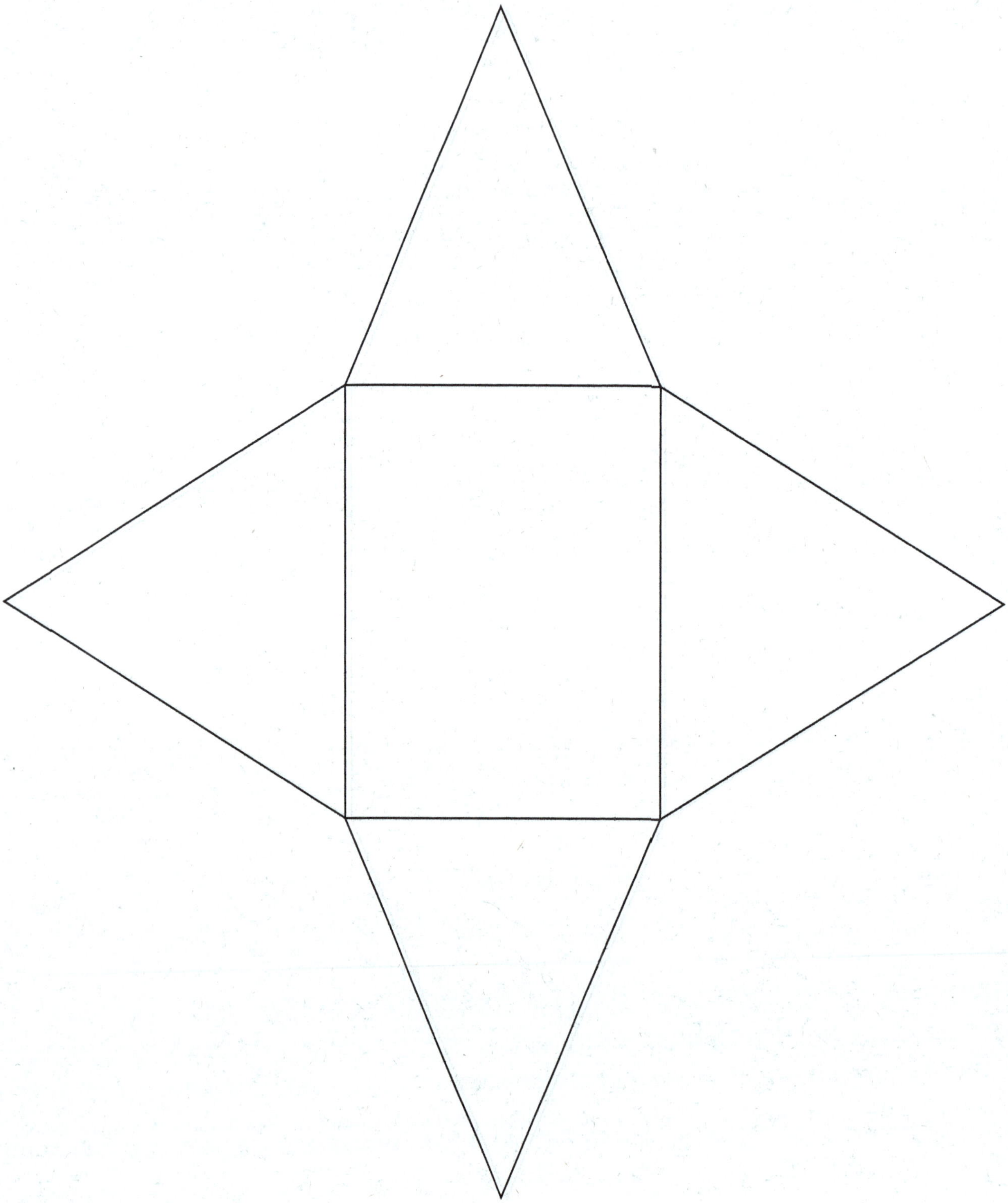

Name ______________________

Make Another Pyramid

Cut out the net and form the solid figure.

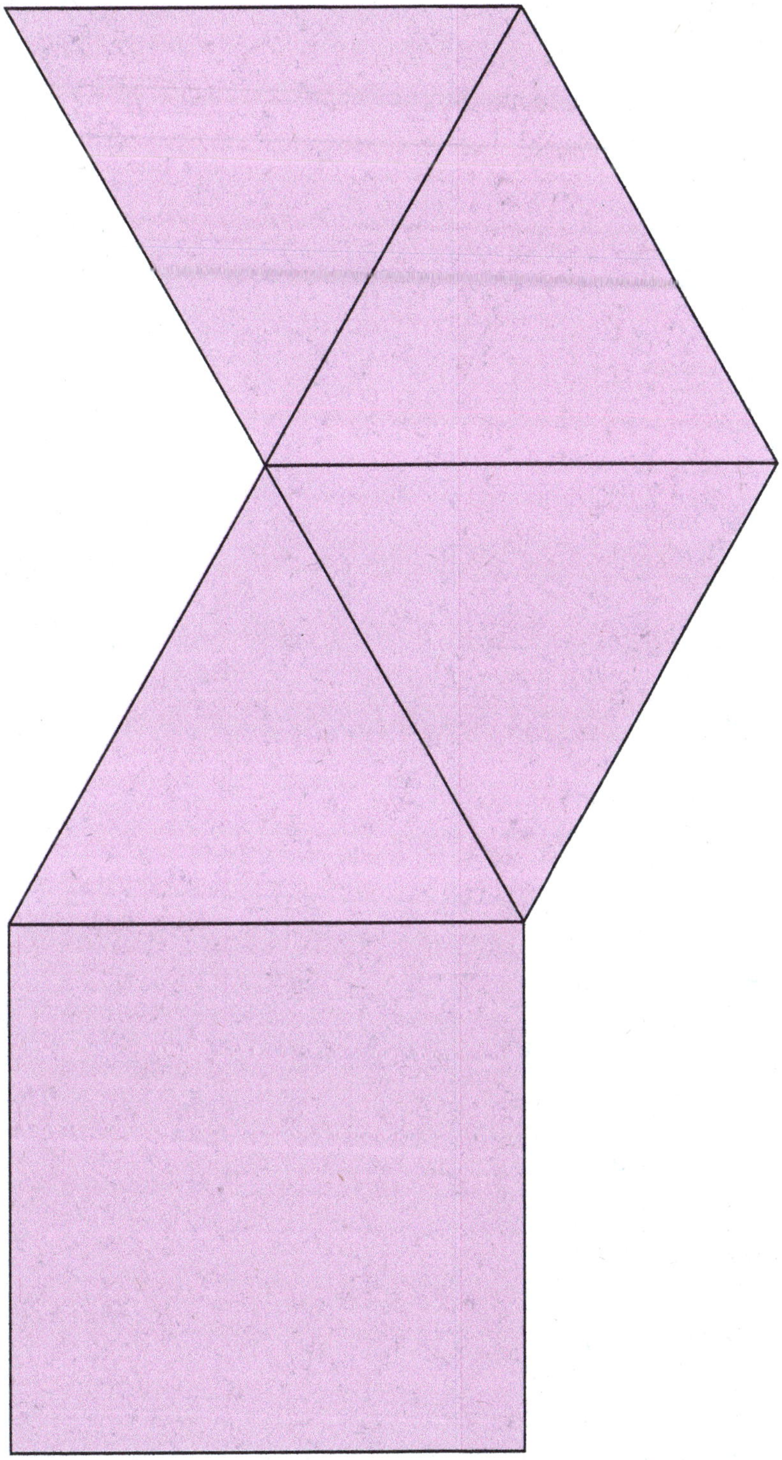

Name ______________________________

Make Another Pyramid (continued)

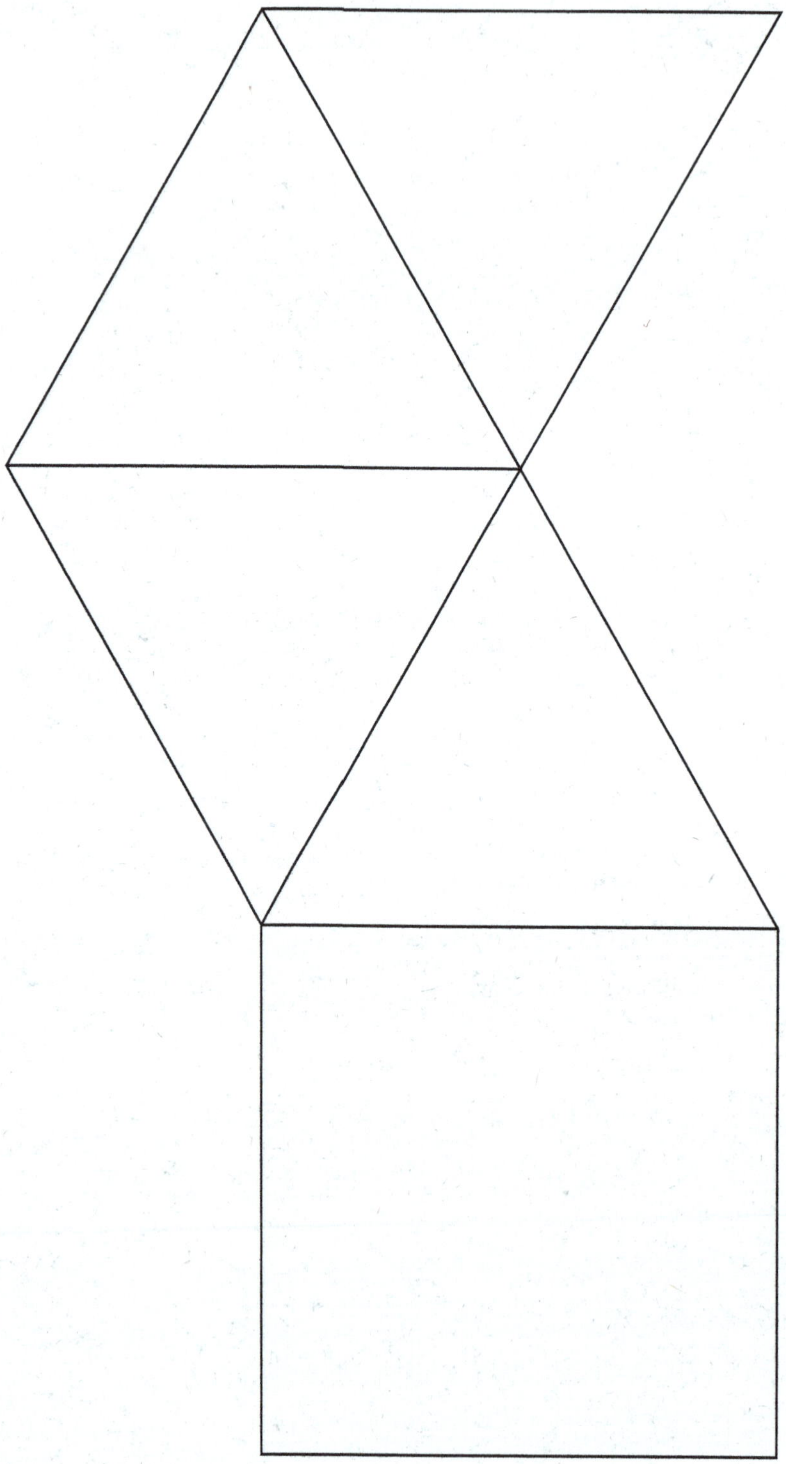

Name ______________________________

Draw a Net for a Square Pyramid

Draw a net for a pyramid with a square base. Then cut out the net and form the pyramid.

Name ______________________________

Draw a Net for a Pyramid (continued)

Name ______________________________

Make Pyramids with Other Bases

Cut out the polygons from this page and the triangles from the next page to form pyramids.

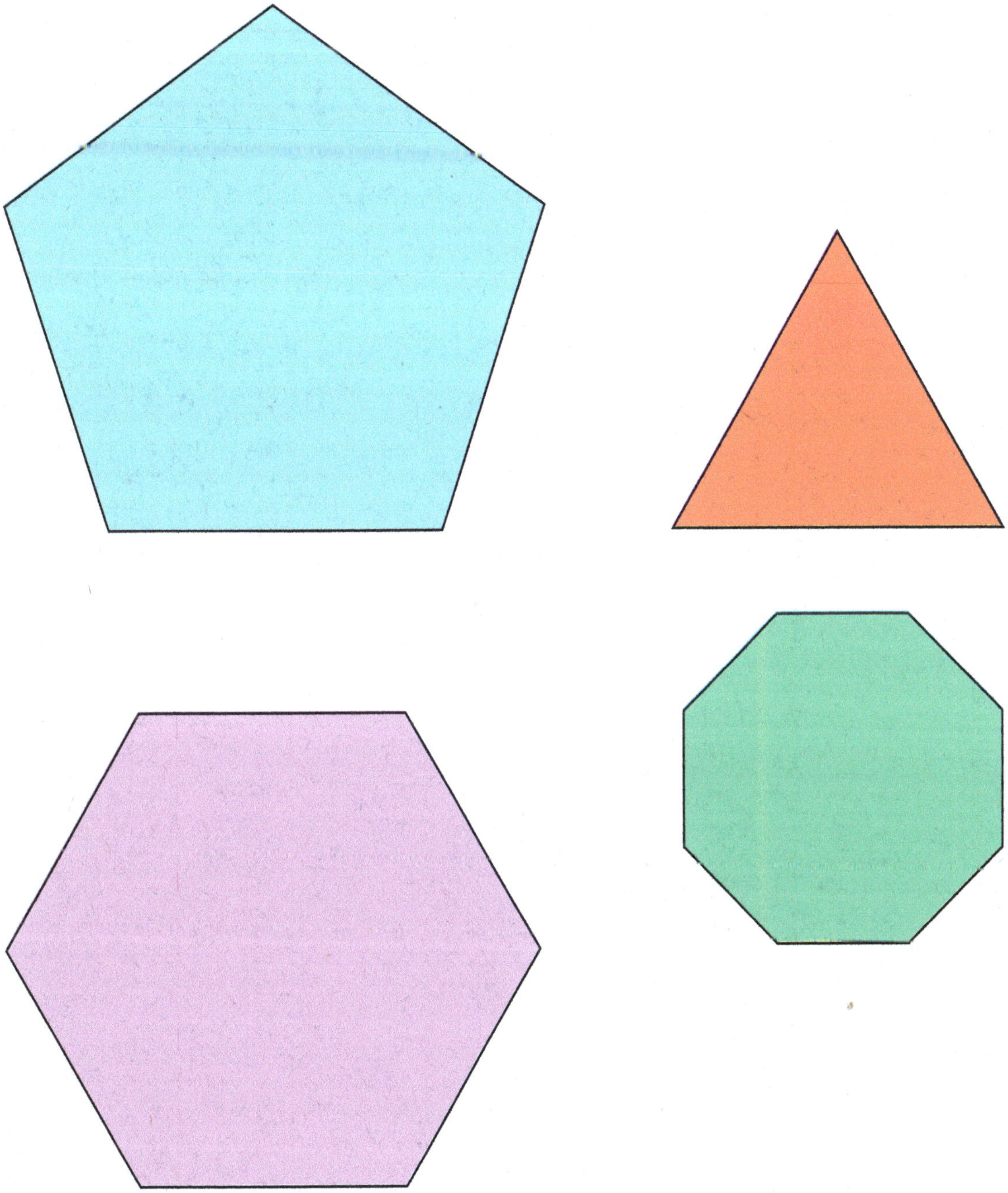

Name ______________________________

Make Pyramids with Other Bases (continued)

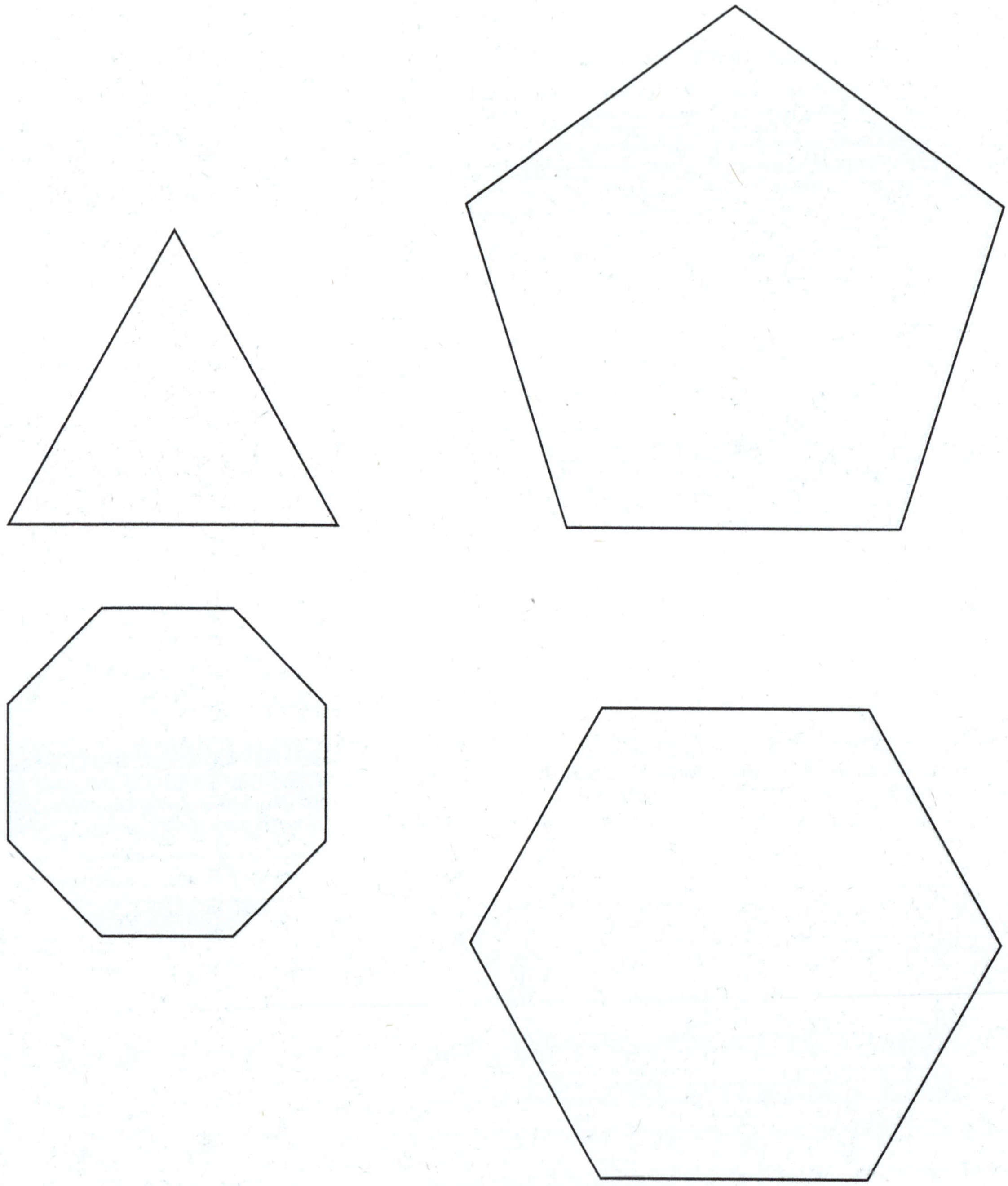

Name ______________________________

Make Pyramids with Other Bases (continued)

VOCABULARY
slant height

Name ____________________

Make Pyramids with Other Bases (continued)

Unit 4
Quick Quiz 2

Name ________________________________

Name the solid each net will form.

1 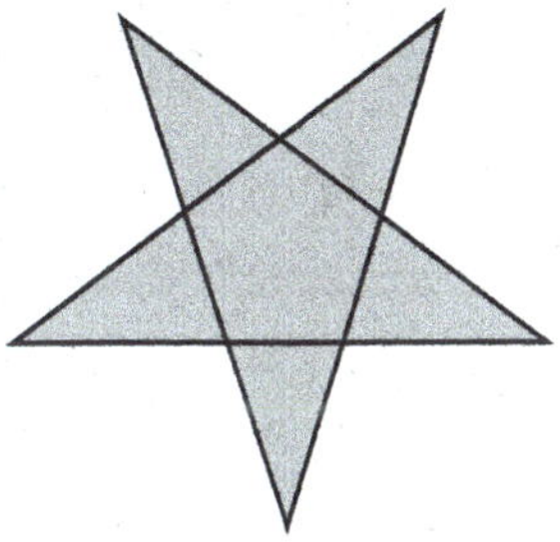

____

2 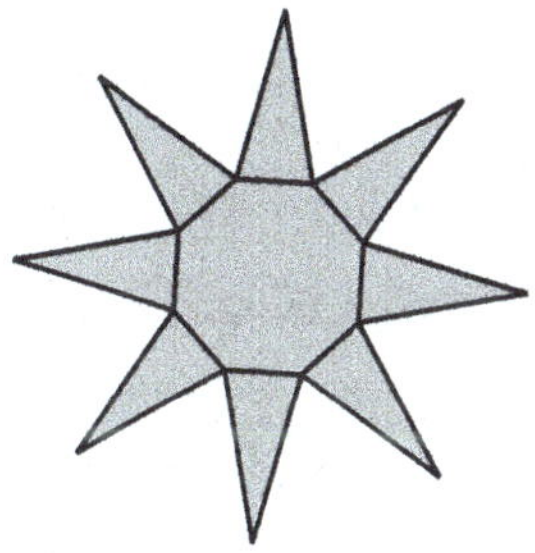

____

Find the surface area.

3 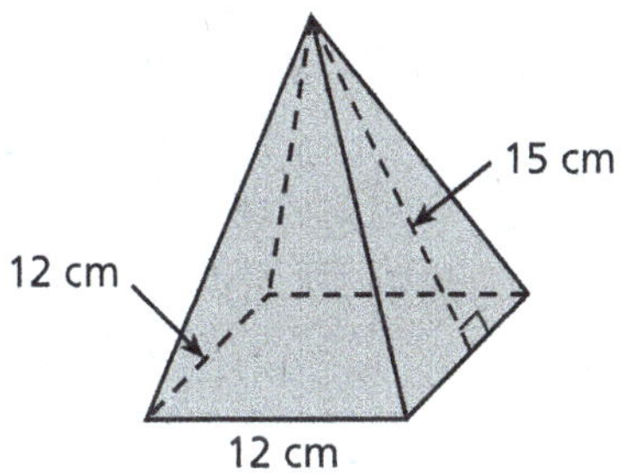

____

4 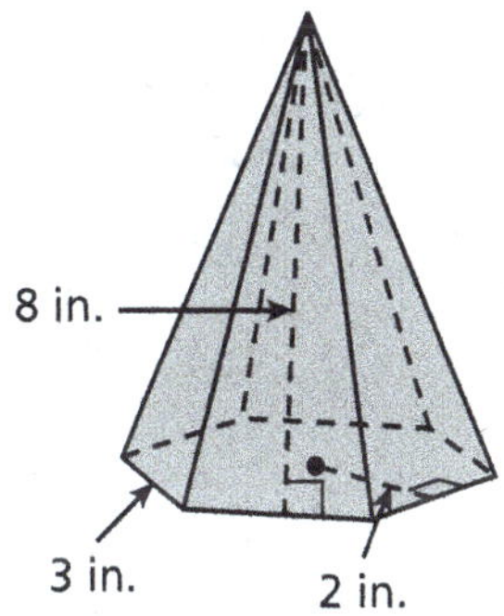

____

Solve.

5 A decorative cut and polished stone is shaped like an octagonal pyramid. Each triangular face of the stone has a base of 1.5 inches and a height of 4 inches. The perpendicular distance from an edge of the base to its center is 4 inches. When the stone is placed on its base on a pedestal for display, what is the area of its visible faces?

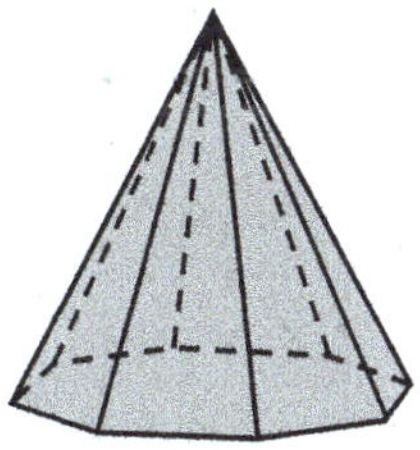

____

Fluency Check 6

Name ____________________

PATH to FLUENCY

1. $17\overline{)20.91}$
2. $61\overline{)25.62}$
3. $58\overline{)19.72}$
4. $76\overline{)85.88}$
5. $31\overline{)47.74}$
6. $12\overline{)43.32}$
7. $22\overline{)91.96}$
8. $49\overline{)41.16}$
9. $35\overline{)27.30}$
10. $72\overline{)88.56}$
11. $21\overline{)51.45}$
12. $91\overline{)88.27}$
13. $26\overline{)62.14}$
14. $18\overline{)92.52}$
15. $36\overline{)23.40}$

Unit 4 Review/Test

Name ____________________

1 Identify the units in which surface area can be measured. Select all that apply.

Ⓐ inches

Ⓑ square feet

Ⓒ square inches

Ⓓ feet

Ⓔ square yards

Ⓕ yards

2 Are the lateral faces of a right rectangular prism always rectangles? Explain.

3 For 3a–3d, choose Yes or No to indicate if the solid figure has triangular lateral faces.

3a.	rectangular prism	○ Yes	○ No
3b.	rectangular pyramid	○ Yes	○ No
3c.	triangular prism	○ Yes	○ No
3d.	triangular pyramid	○ Yes	○ No

4 How do you know the number of rectangular faces a right nonrectangular prism will have? Explain.

Name ______________________________

5 Mark the minimum number of different surface areas you need to find to calculate the surface area of a rectangular prism that is not a cube or square prism.

Ⓐ 3

Ⓑ 4

Ⓒ 5

Ⓓ 6

6 The net below is a net of a rectangular prism. The bases are marked B.

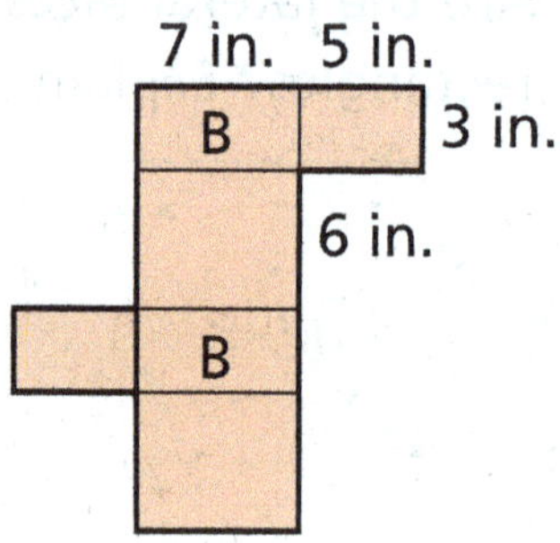

Part A

Mark the pairs of congruent lateral faces using the labels L1 and L2.

Part B

Describe how can you use B, L1, and L2 to calculate the total surface area of the prism with a *minimum* number of computations.

Part C

Use the method you described above to find the surface area (*SA*) of the prism. Label your answer.

SA = ______________

Name ______

7 For 7a–7c, choose Yes or No to indicate if the net will form a solid figure.

7a. 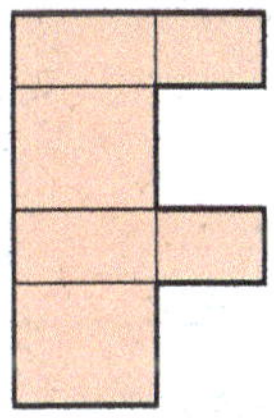 ○ Yes ○ No

7b. 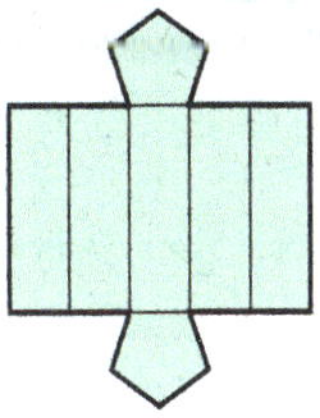 ○ Yes ○ No

7c.  ○ Yes ○ No

7d. If you answered No for any net above, correct the net so it forms a solid figure.

7e. Choose the word that makes the sentence true.

Figure 7a will form a [pentagonal prism / square prism / rectangular prism].

Figure 7b will form a(n) [pentagonal prism / octagonal prism].

Figure 7c will form a(n) [pentagonal prism / square prism / octagonal pyramid].

Name ______________________________

For Exercises 8 and 9, use the net to find the total surface area of the solid figure it represents. Show your work.
(Some of the given measurements are rounded to simplify the computation.)

8 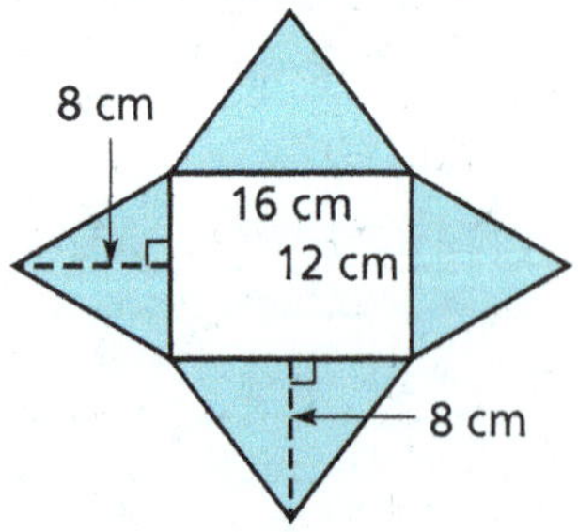

______________ cm^2

9 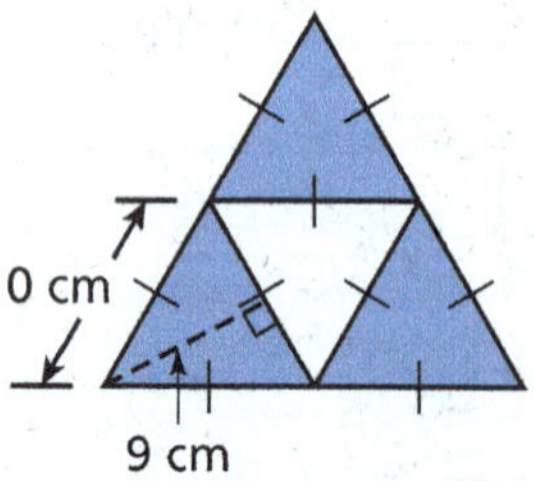

______________ cm^2

10 Are the lateral faces of a pyramid always triangles? Explain your answer.

11 Janice calculated the surface area of this prism as 200 in.^{2}. Review her method and decide if her calculation is correct. Explain your answer.

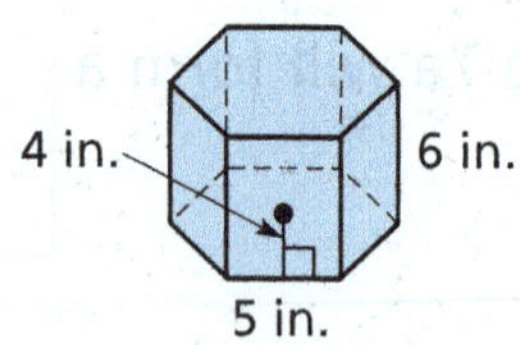

Lateral area: $6(5 \cdot 6) = 6 \cdot 30 = 180$

Base area: $\frac{1}{2}(5 \cdot 4) = \frac{1}{2}(20) = 10$

SA $= 180 + 2(10) = 200$ in.^{2}

Name ______________________________

12 A prism has 8 rectangular sides.

12a. The name of this solid figure is a(n) ____________ prism.

12b. On the grid below, sketch a net that could be a net of the prism. Think: Is it best to draw the lateral sides or the bases first?

13 Draw a line to match each solid figure with its net.

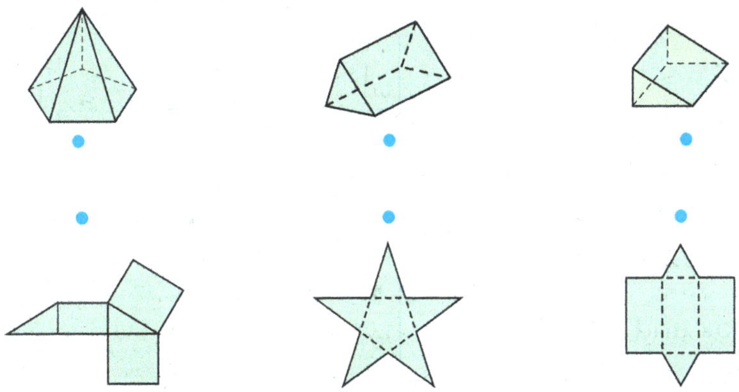

For Exercises 14–16, use the numbers from the number tiles to represent the surface area of each figure. You may use each number more than once.

65	100	456	480	528	700	800	1,500

14

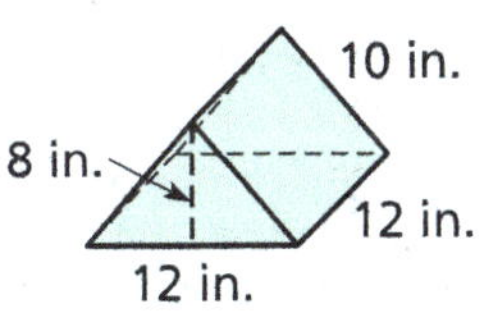

☐ in.²

15

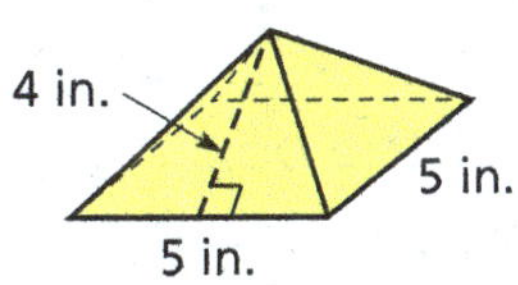

☐ in.²

16

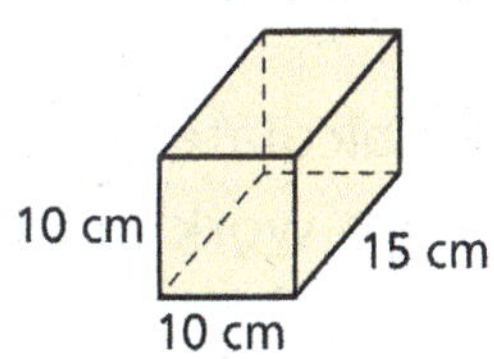

☐ cm²

Name ______________________

17 In a math class, students are making hexagonal pyramids out of cardboard. How much cardboard did it take to make this hexagonal pyramid? Show your work.

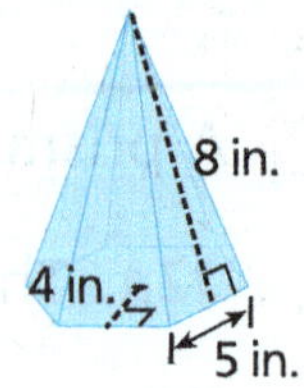

______ in.^{2}

18 Ray covered a box with purple paper. The figure shows the dimensions of the box.

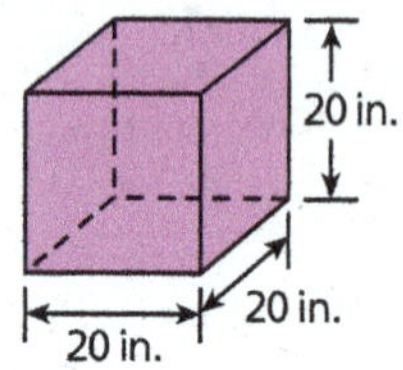

Use the numbers and symbols below to write an equation that shows how much paper he used. Ignore any overlap. You will not need all of the numbers and symbols.

20	20	4	6	×	÷	×	=	2,600	2,400

______ in.^{2}

19 An unopened box of raisins in the shape of a rectangular prism has a top that measures 4 inches by $1\frac{3}{4}$ inches. The back of the box measures 6 inches by 4 inches.

Part A: Draw a picture of the box and label the sides with the measurements provided.

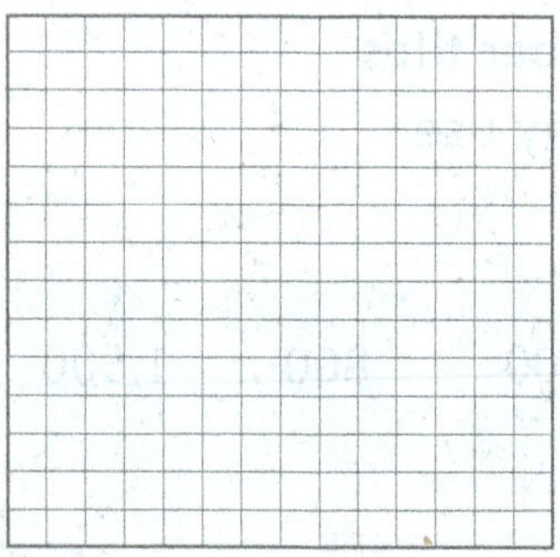

Part B: Calculate the surface area of the box. Show your work in the space below.

______ in.^{2}

Name ________________________________

Surface Area of Prisms and Pyramids

Andy is going to buy a new digital clock for his brother as a gift. There are two clocks in the store that he will choose from. Clock 1 is shaped like an equilateral triangular prism, and Clock 2 is shaped like a square pyramid. The dimensions of both clocks are shown below.

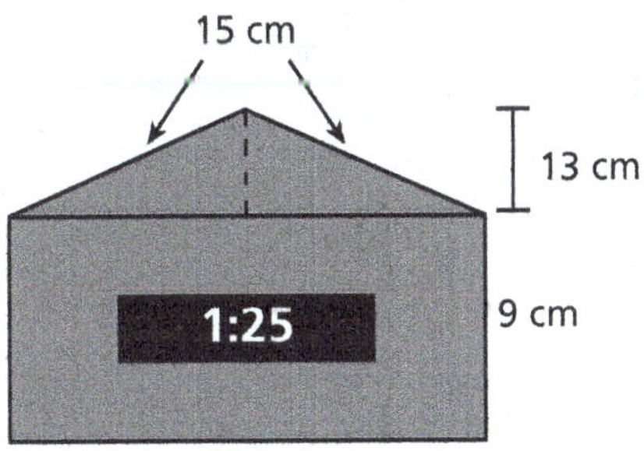

Clock 1

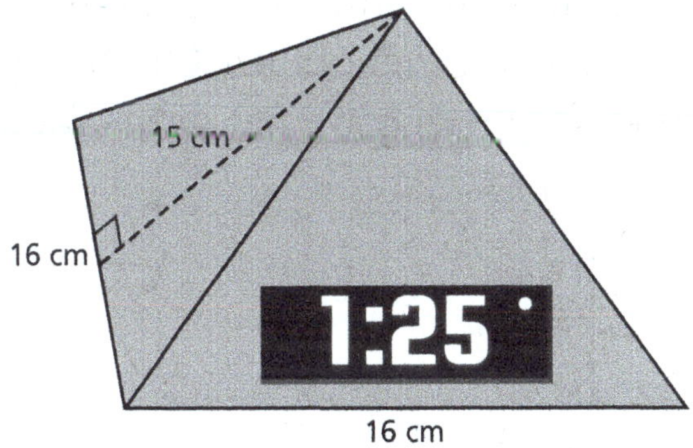

Clock 2

1. What is the total surface area of each clock? Show or explain the steps that you took to find your answers.

   Clock 1: ____________ Clock 2: ____________

2. The time display on each clock is a rectangle that is 8 cm long and 3 cm high. What is the area of the time display? Show your work.

Name ______________________________

3 Andy can have either of the clocks gold plated. The gold plate will cover the entire clock, except the time display. For each of the clocks, what is the surface area that can be gold plated?

Clock 1: ____________ Clock 2: ____________

4 Andy is going to make a box that covers the clock that he buys, either the prism or the pyramid. When open, the box will look like a net of the clock. Draw a picture of a net of the triangular prism and a net of the square pyramid.

5 Andy has a square piece of wrapping paper with a side length of 25 centimeters. Is this enough to cover either clock? Explain.

6 Andy notices that another clock in the store has the same shape as the square pyramid clock, except that all of its dimensions are doubled. What is the surface area of the larger square pyramid clock? How is this related to the surface area of the smaller square pyramid clock? Show or explain how you got your answer.

Dear Family:

In our math class, we are studying algebra. We will study:

- algebraic expressions,
- how quantities vary together,
- solving equations,
- solving inequalities,
- writing the prime factorization of a number, and
- finding the greatest common factor and least common multiple of two numbers.

An *algebraic expression* summarizes a calculation in a concise way. For example, we can write the calculation "subtract 3 from a number and then multiply the result by 5" with the algebraic expression $(s - 3) \cdot 5$. The letter s is a *variable* that stands for "a number." We can substitute any number for s and evaluate the expression to get a value.

To help students interpret numerical and algebraic expressions, we relate them to math diagrams that indicate quantities.

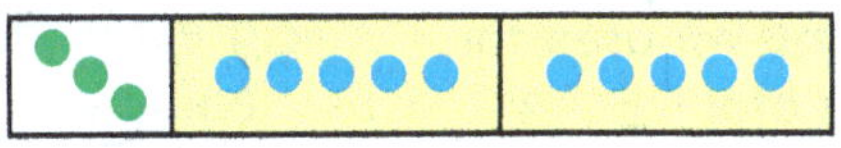

$3 + 2 \cdot 5$

$3 + 2 \cdot d$

In this unit, we will study quantities that *vary together*.
For example:

- The weight of potato salad and its cost vary together.
- The distance a person has walked and the time that has elapsed since the person started walking vary together.

To show how quantities vary together, we will use double number lines, tables, graphs, diagrams, and equations. Here is a double number line that shows distance and time varying together for a person walking at a constant rate of 3 feet per second.

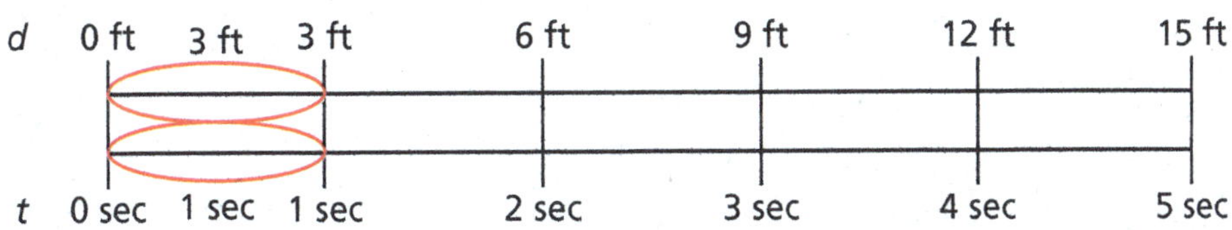

In this unit, your child will also study solving equations. To *solve an equation* means to find the numbers that make the left side of the equation equal to the right side. Students find solutions of equations in several ways.

- They check numbers to see if they make the sides of the equation equal. For example, $x = 12$ is a solution of $7x - 1 = 83$ because $7(12) - 1 = 84 - 1 = 83$.
- They reason about what number makes the two sides of an equation equal. For example, both sides of $14 + 72 = 72 + x$ have an addend of 72. Therefore, the other addends must also be equal. So, $x = 14$.
- They use the inverse operation to write a related equation that is easier to solve. For the addition equation $32 + x = 51$, we can write the related subtraction equation $x = 51 - 32$. Now it is easy to see that $x = 19$.
- They apply the same operation to both sides of an equation to get an equivalent equation with the variable alone on one side. For example, multiplying both sides of $\frac{1}{2}x = 5$ by 2 gives the equation $x = 10$.

Our work with equations will lead to a study of *inequalities*. An inequality is a statement that compares two expressions using one of the symbols shown at the right.

Inequality Symbols

$>$ greater than

$\geq$ greater than or equal to

$<$ less than

$\leq$ less than or equal to

$\neq$ not equal to

We will solve inequalities using methods similar to those we used for solving equations. For instance, adding 2 to both sides of $x - 2 > 3$ gives the result $x > 5$. This means that any number greater than 5 will make a true statement when it is substituted for x in $x - 2 > 3$. Since it is impossible to list all these solutions, we picture them using an arrow on a number line, as shown below. The open dot at 5 shows that 5 is *not* a solution.

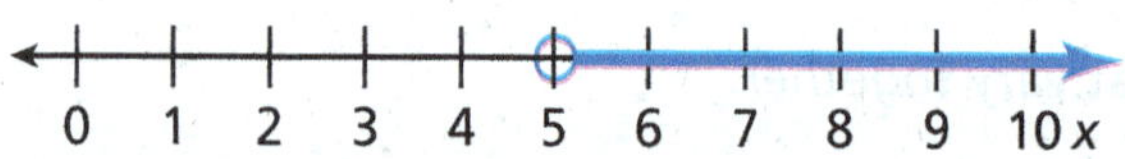

This unit concludes with a study of two types of numbers.

- A *prime number* is a whole number greater than 1 that can be divided evenly only by itself and 1. Examples of prime numbers: 2, 5, 7, 11, 19
- Numbers greater than 1 that are not prime are *composite numbers*. Examples of composite numbers: 4, 9, 12, 15, 21

If you have any questions or comments, please contact me.

Sincerely,
Your child's teacher

Estimada familia:

En la clase de matemáticas estamos estudiando álgebra. Aprenderemos acerca de:

- las expresiones algebraicas,
- cómo algunas cantidades varían juntas,
- resolver ecuaciones,
- resolver desigualdades,
- escribir el factor primo de un número, y
- hallar el máximo común divisor y el mínimo común múltiplo de dos números.

Una *expresión algebraica* resume un cálculo de una manera concisa. Por ejemplo, podemos escribir el cálculo "restar 3 de un número y luego, multiplicar el resultado por 5" usando la expresión algebraica $(s - 3) \cdot 5$. La letra s es una *variable* que representa "un número". Podemos sustituir s con cualquier número y resolver la expresión para obtener un valor.

Para ayudar a los estudiantes a interpretar expresiones numéricas y algebraicas, las relacionaremos con diagramas matemáticos.

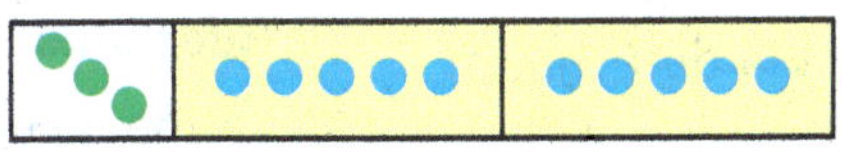

$3 + 2 \cdot 5$

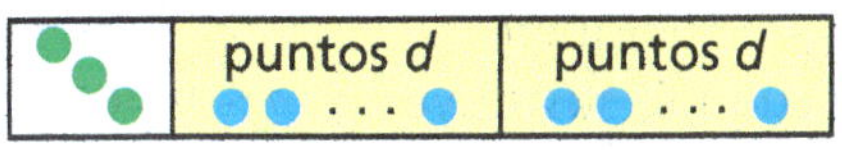

$3 + 2 \cdot d$

En esta unidad, estudiaremos cantidades que *varían juntas*.
Por ejemplo:

- El peso de una ensalada de papas y su costo varían juntos.
- La distancia que una persona camina y el tiempo que transcurre desde que comienza a caminar varían juntos.

Para mostrar cómo varían juntas algunas cantidades, usaremos rectas numéricas dobles, tablas, gráficas, diagramas y ecuaciones. La siguiente es una recta numérica doble que muestra cómo varían juntos la distancia y el tiempo cuando una persona camina a una velocidad constante de 3 pies por segundo.

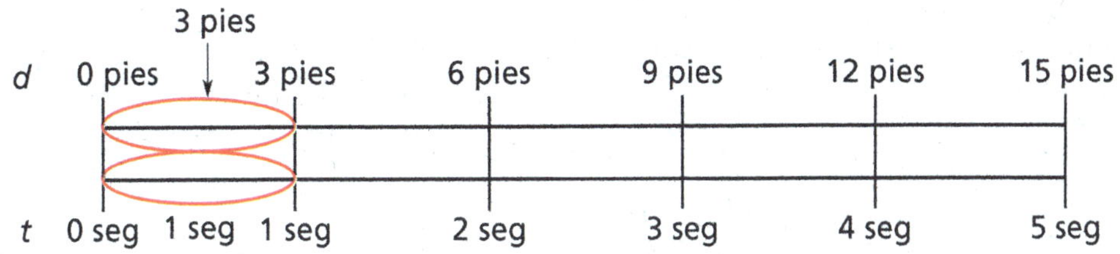

En esta unidad su hijo también aprenderá cómo resolver ecuaciones. *Resolver una ecuación* significa hallar los números que igualan el lado izquierdo con el lado derecho de la ecuación. Los estudiantes pueden hallar soluciones para las ecuaciones de diferentes maneras:

- Probando números para ver cuáles igualan ambos lados de la ecuación. Por ejemplo, $x = 12$ es una solución para $7x - 1 = 83$ porque $7(12) - 1 = 84 - 1 = 83$.
- Razonando para determinar cuál número puede usarse para igualar ambos lados de una ecuación. Por ejemplo, ambos lados de $14 + 72 = 72 + x$ tienen 72 como un sumando. Por lo tanto, los otros sumandos, también deben ser iguales. Entonces, $x = 14$.
- Usando la operación inversa para escribir una ecuación relacionada que sea más fácil de resolver. Para la ecuación de suma $32 + x = 51$, podemos escribir la ecuación relacionada de resta $x = 51 - 32$. Ahora es fácil ver que $x = 19$.
- Aplicando la misma operación a ambos lados de una ecuación para obtener una ecuación equivalente que tenga la variable sola en un lado. Por ejemplo, al multiplicar ambos lados de $\frac{1}{2}x = 5$ por 2 se obtiene la ecuación $x = 10$.

Nuestro trabajo con ecuaciones conducirá a un estudio de las *desigualdades*. Una desigualdad es un enunciado que compara dos expresiones usando uno de los símbolos mostrados a la derecha.

Símbolos de desigualdad

$>$ mayor que

$\geq$ mayor que o es igual a

$<$ menor que

$\leq$ menor que o es igual a

$\neq$ no es igual a

Resolveremos las desigualdades usando métodos similares a los que usamos para resolver ecuaciones. Por ejemplo, sumar 2 a ambos lados de $x - 2 > 3$ da el resultado de $x > 5$. Esto significa que cualquier número mayor que 5 hará un enunciado verdadero cuando sustituye x por $x - 2 > 3$. Dado que es imposible enumerar todas estas soluciones, las imaginamos usando una flecha en una recta numérica como se muestra a continuación. El punto abierto en 5 muestra que 5 *no* es una solución.

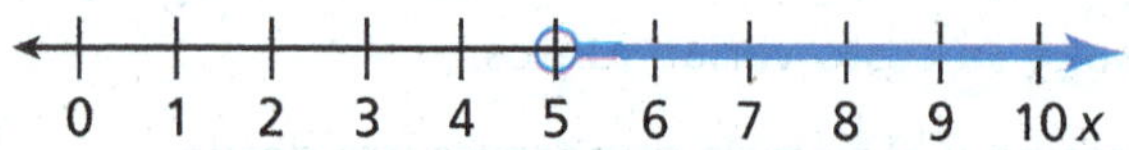

Esta unidad concluye con un estudio de dos tipos de números.

- Un *número primo* es un número entero mayor que 1 que puede ser dividido en partes iguales solo por sí mismo y 1. Ejemplos de números primos: 2, 5, 7, 11, 19
- Los números mayores que 1 que no son primos son números compuestos. Ejemplos de números compuestos: 4, 9, 12, 15, 21

Si tiene alguna pregunta, por favor comuníquese conmigo.

Atentamente,
El maestro de su hijo

algebraic expression	base of a power
Associative Property of Addition	coefficient
Associative Property of Multiplication	Commutative Property of Addition

The number, variable, or expression that is the repeated factor in a power.

Example:

4 is the base in the power 4^3.
a is the base in the power a^7.

An expression that includes one or more variables.

Example:

$10(b + a)$
$7n$
$5x^2 - x$

The number part of a term when the term is a number times a variable or a number times a product of variables.

Example:

In $5x + 2xy$, 5 is the coefficient of the term $5x$ and 2 is the coefficient of the term $2xy$.

The property that states that changing the grouping of addends does not change their sum. For any numbers a, b, and c, $(a + b) + c = a + (b + c)$.

Example:

$(7 + 8) + 2 = 7 + (8 + 2)$

The property that states that changing the order of addends does not change their sum. For any numbers a and b, $a + b = b + a$.

Example:

$18 + 21 = 21 + 18$

The property that states that changing the grouping of factors does not change their product. For any numbers a, b, and c, $(a \cdot b) \cdot c = a \cdot (b \cdot c)$.

Example:

$(9 \cdot 15) \cdot 20 = 9 \cdot (15 \cdot 20)$

Commutative Property of Multiplication	Distributive Property
composite number	double number line
dependent variable	equivalent expressions

The property that allows us to distribute a factor to the terms of a sum or difference or to pull out a common factor from the terms of a sum or difference. For any numbers *a*, *b*, and *c*, $a(b + c) = ab + ac$.

Examples:

Distribute a factor:

$6(x - 2) = 6 \cdot x - 6 \cdot 2 = 6x - 12$

Pull out a factor:

$4y + 8 = 4 \cdot y + 4 \cdot 2 = 4(y + 2)$

The property that states that changing the order of factors does not change their product. For any numbers *a* and *b*, $a \cdot b = b \cdot a$.

Example:

$36 \cdot \frac{3}{4} = \frac{3}{4} \cdot 36$

A diagram with two number lines that shows how two quantities relate.

Example:

This double number line shows how distance and time are related for walking at a rate of 3 feet per second.

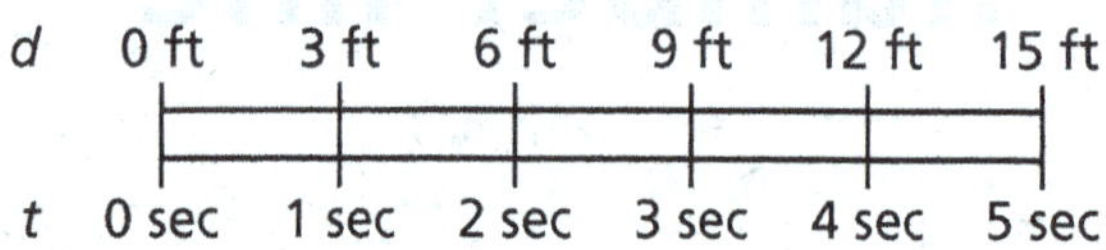

A whole number greater than 1 that has factors other than 1 and itself.

Example:

8 is a composite number because its factors are 1, 2, 4, and 8.

Expressions that always have the same value.

Example:

$b + b + b$ and $3b$ are equivalent expressions.

In a relationship between two variables, the variable whose value depends on the value of the other variable.

Example:

The cost of gas, *c*, depends on the number of gallons purchased, *g*. The cost, *c*, is the dependent variable.

evaluate an algebraic expression	factor tree
exponent	greatest common factor (GCF)
expression	independent variable

A way of writing the factors of a number to find its prime factorization.

Example:

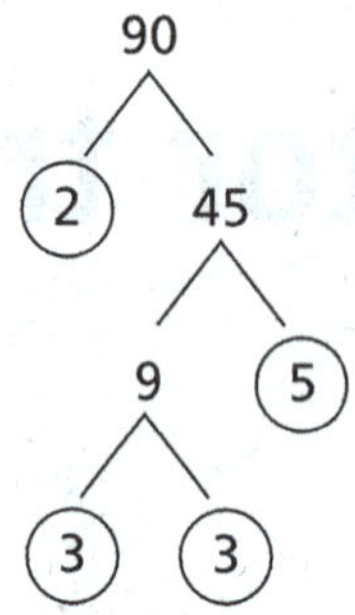

Substitute values for the variables in an expression and then simplify the resulting numerical expression.

Example:

Evaluate $10(b + a)$ when $b = 3$ and $a = 4$.

$10(b + a) = 10(3 + 4) = 10 \cdot 7 = 70$

The greatest factor that two or more numbers share.

Example:

15 is the GCF of 30 and 45.

In a power, the small, raised number that indicates how many times the base is used as a factor.

Example:

3 is the exponent in the power 4^3.

$4^3 = 4 \cdot 4 \cdot 4 = 64$

In a relationship between two variables, the variable whose values influence the values of the other variable.

Example:

The cost of gas, *c*, depends on the number of gallons purchased, *g*. The number of gallons purchased, *g*, is the independent variable.

A number, variable, or a combination of numbers and variables with one or more operations. An expression does not include an equals sign.

Examples:

n $\quad$ $5 \cdot 2^2$

$x - 9$ $\quad$ $\frac{1}{2}bh$

inequality	like terms
infinite	multiplicative inverse
inverse operations	numerical expression

Terms with the same variables raised to the same powers. Number terms are like terms, even though they do not have variables.

Example:
In $6 + 2x + 1 + x$,
6 and 1 are like terms and
$2x$ and x are like terms.

A statement that compares two expressions using one of these symbols: $>$ (greater than), $<$ (less than), $\geq$ (greater than or equal to), $\leq$ (less than or equal to), $\neq$ (not equal to).

Examples:
$4 + 7 > 10$
$x - 2 \leq 8$

The product of a number and its multiplicative inverse is 1.

Example:
6 is the multiplicative inverse of $\frac{1}{6}$.
$6 \cdot \frac{1}{6} = 1$ and $\frac{1}{6} \cdot 6 = 1$.

Unlimited. An infinite set of numbers cannot be shown in a list.

Example:
$x > 3$ has an infinite number of solutions.

An expression that includes only numbers.

Examples:
$36 - (2 + 9) \cdot 3$
$20 - 8 \div 2$

Operations that undo each other. Addition and subtraction are inverse operations. Multiplication and division are inverse operations.

Examples:
$5 + 9 = 14$, so $14 - 9 = 5$.
$7 \cdot 9 = 63$, so $63 \div 9 = 7$.

Order of Operations

prime number

power

relatively prime

prime factorization

simplify an expression

A whole number greater than 1 whose only factors are 1 and itself.

Example:
2, 11, and 53 are prime numbers.

A rule that states the order in which the operations in an expression should be done:

1. Perform operations in parentheses.
2. Simplify powers.
3. Multiply and divide from left to right.
4. Add and subtract from left to right.

Two numbers are relatively prime if their greatest common factor (GCF) is 1.

Example:
6 and 35 are relatively prime.

An expression that includes an exponent and represents a repeated multiplication.

Example:
4^3 (read "four raised to the third power") means $4 \cdot 4 \cdot 4$.

Combine all like terms in the expression.

Example:
Simplify $3x + 5 + x + 2$.
$3x + 5 + x + 2 = 4x + 7$

The expression of a number as the product of prime numbers.

Example:
The prime factorization of 90 is $2 \cdot 3 \cdot 3 \cdot 5$.

solution of an equation	solve
solution of an inequality	term
solution set of an inequality	variable

Find the solution(s) of an equation or inequality.

In an equation with one variable, a number that can be substituted for the variable to make a true statement.

Example:

$x = 4$ is a solution of $3x + 1 = 13$ because $3(4) + 1 = 13$ is true.

Terms are parts of an expression that are added or subtracted.

Example:

4, $3b$, and b^2 are terms of the expression $4 + 3b + b^2$.

In an inequality with one variable, a number that can be substituted for the variable to make a true statement.

Example:

$x = 10$ is a solution of $x + 3 < 20$ because $10 + 3 < 20$ is true.

A letter or symbol used to represent an unknown number or a quantity that varies.

Example:

$y = 2x$

x and y are variables.

The set of all solutions of an inequality.

Examples:

This graph shows the solution set for $x > 3$.

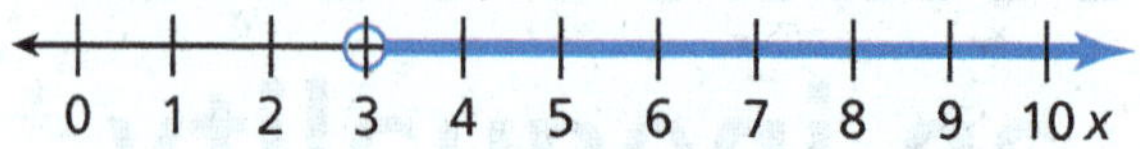

This graph shows the solution set for $x \geq 3$.

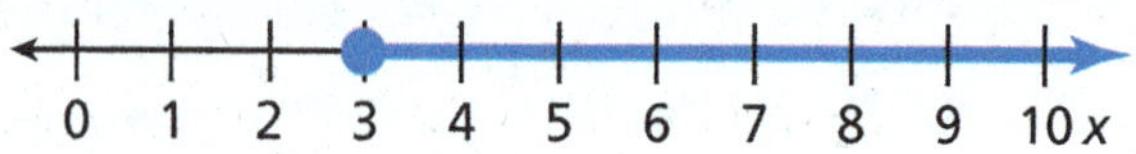

Name ____________________

Exponents and the Order of Operations

In the Order of Operations, powers are simplified after operations inside parentheses and before multiplication and division.

Order of Operations

1. Perform all operations inside parentheses.
2. Simplify powers.
3. Multiply and divide from left to right.
4. Add and subtract from left to right.

Simplify. Follow the Order of Operations.

11 $4 + 3^2 =$ ________ 12 $5 + 5 \cdot 2^3 =$ ________ 13 $4 \div 2^2 + 1 =$ ________

14 $(7 - 2)^2 =$ ________ 15 $1 + 6^2 \cdot 2 =$ ________ 16 $3^2 + 3^3 =$ ________

Evaluate each expression for $a = 5$ and $b = 8$.

17 $3 \cdot a^3$ ________ 18 $9^2 \cdot (b + 1)$ ________ 19 $(b - a)^2$ ________

What's the Error?

Dear Math Students,

My friend said I did not simplify the three expressions shown below correctly.

$2^6 = 12$ $10^4 = 40$ $5^2 \cdot 2^3 = 60$

What error did I make? Please help me understand how to find the number that each expression represents.

Your Friend,
Puzzled Penguin

20 Write an answer to Puzzled Penguin.

Name ______

Squares and Cubes

Solve.

21 Write a power to represent the area of a 5 meter by 5 meter square.

area = ______ m^2

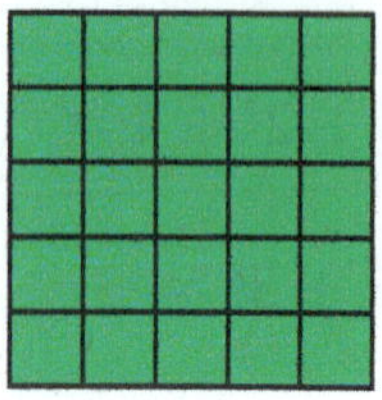

22 Write a power to represent the volume of a 5 cm by 5 cm by 5 cm cube.

volume = ______ cm^3

Solve.

23 On the grid at the right, use a straightedge to draw a ten by ten square.

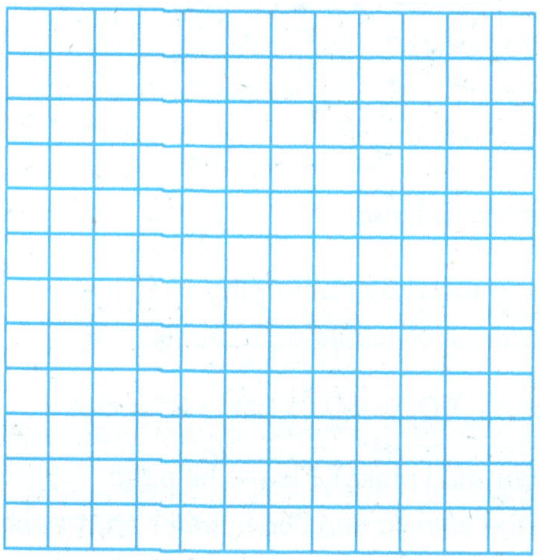

a. What repeated multiplication represents the area of the square?

______

b. What power represents the area of the square?

______

c. What is the area of the square?

______

24 The answer for Exercise 21 is often read as "five squared," and the answer for Exercise 22 is often read as "five cubed." Explain why it makes sense to read the answers in this way.

______

______

Name ___________________

Matching Parts of Expressions and Figures

Match the terms of each expression to parts of the figure. Then simplify the expression to find the total number of dots or cubes.

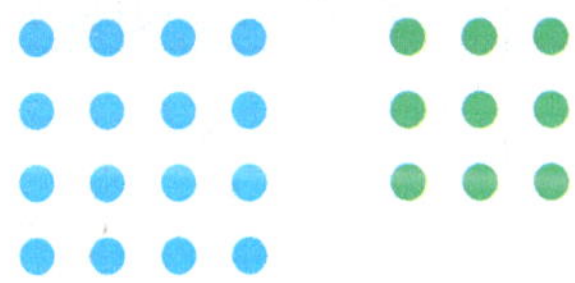

$4^2 + 3^2$ dots

25 total: ______ dots

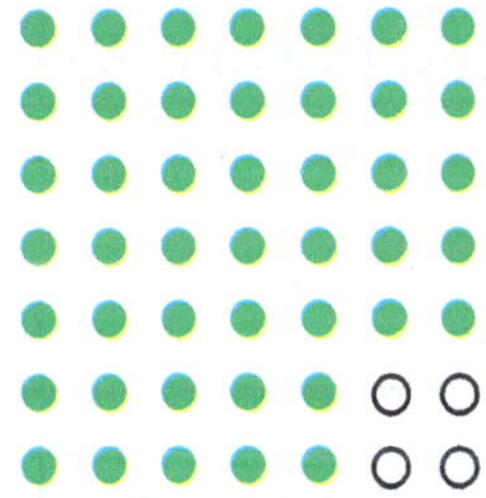

$7^2 - 2^2$ dots

26 total: ______ dots

$2^3 + 4^3$ cubes

27 total: ______ cubes

$3 + 3^2 + 3^3$ cubes

28 total: ______ cubes

Write an expression to represent the shaded area of each figure. Then match terms of the expression to parts of the figure.

29

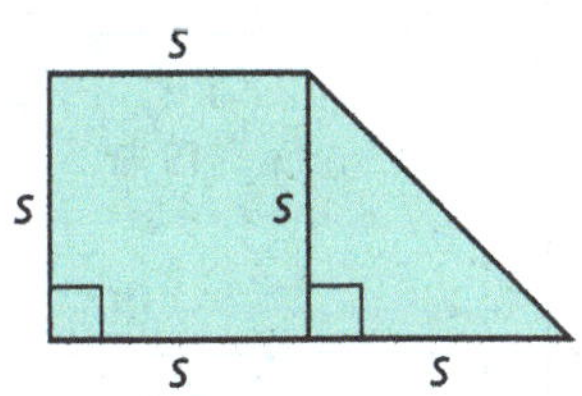

______ + ______ square units

30

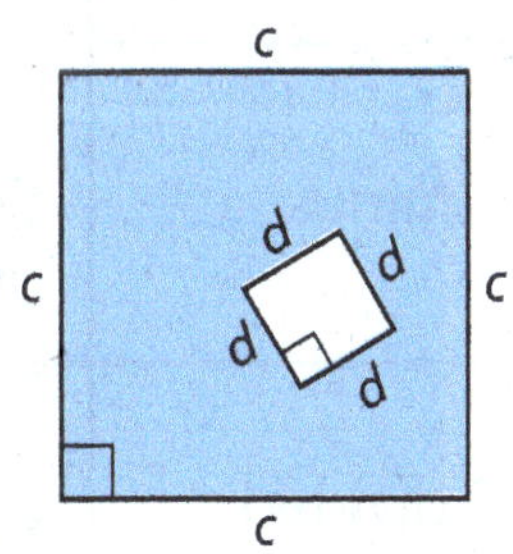

______ − ______ square units

Check Understanding

Use an exponent to write $5 \times 5 \times 5 \times 5 \times 5 \times 5$. ______

Name ________________________________

Language of Expressions

Complete the table.

	Algebraic Expression	Plus, Minus, Times, Divided By	Add, Subtract, Multiply, Divide	Sum, Difference, Product, Quotient
1	$5 - y$	5 minus y	Subtract ___ from ___.	$5 - y$ is a ________.
2	$12 \cdot a$	12 ________ a	Multiply ___ and ___.	$12 \cdot a$ is the ________ of ___ and ___.
3	$c \div 3$	___ divided by ___	Divide ___ by ___.	$c \div 3$ is a ________.
4	________	b plus 2.3	Add ___ and ___.	________ is the ___ of ___ and ___.
5	________	d times $\frac{5}{6}$	Multiply ___ and ___.	________ is the ________ of ___ and ___.
6	________	___ minus ___.	Subtract $\frac{2}{3}$ from e.	________ is a ________.
7	________	___ divided by ___	Divide $\frac{3}{4}$ by f.	________ is a ________.
8	________	14.2 minus g	____________________	________ is a ________.

Name ______________________________

Analyze and Describe (continued)

9 Follow the steps to analyze $18 \div 2 + 4 \cdot p^2$.

$18 \div 2 + 4 \cdot p^2$

Step 1: Look for parts of the expression in **parentheses.** Circle them.

Step 2: Look for **powers**. Circle them.

Step 3: Look for **multiplications** and **divisions,** from left to right. Circle them.

Step 4: Look for **additions** and **subtractions,** from left to right. Circle any terms that are not already circled.

10 Below is a diagram for $18 \div 2 + 4 \cdot p^2$. Discuss how it matches the expression in Exercise 9.

Analyze the expression. Then match the expression with the diagram that describes it.

11 $12 - 4 \cdot (c + 1)$ ____________

A.
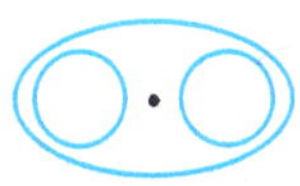

12 $7 \cdot 8 - 5 \cdot d$ ____________

B.
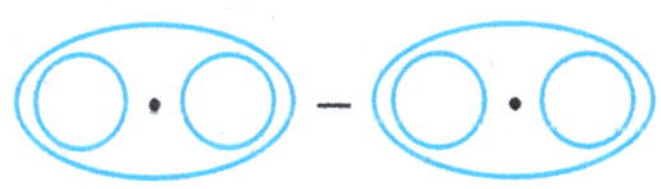

13 $2 \cdot (e - 3 + 9)$ ____________

C.
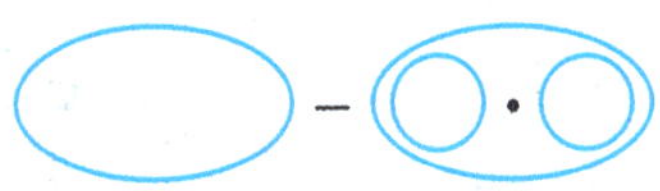

Name ______________________

Analyze and Describe (continued)

Analyze each expression. Then make a diagram to describe it.

14 $7 + 2 \cdot (a - 3)$

15 $b^2 + 5 \cdot b + 6$

16 $(c - 3) \div 4 + \frac{1}{2} \cdot c^2$

17 $m \cdot (4 + m)$

What's the Error?

Dear Math Students,

Here's how I analyzed $m \cdot (4 + m)$. Did I do it right? If not, help me understand what I did wrong.

Step 1: I circled the part in parentheses. $m \cdot (4 + m)$

Step 2: There are no powers, so I didn't do anything. $m \cdot (4 + m)$

Step 3: I circled the multiplication. $m \cdot (4 + m)$

Step 4: I looked for addition and subtraction and circled the terms. $m \cdot (4 + m)$

Your friend,
Puzzled Penguin

18 Write an answer to Puzzled Penguin.

____

____

Check Understanding

Draw a diagram on your MathBoard to describe the following expression. $(n - 5) \cdot 12 + n^2$

Name ______________________________

Relate Expressions and Models

Analyze each expression. (That is, follow the Order of Operations to circle the parts.) Then match the terms of the expression with parts of the dot diagram.

1. $3 + 2 \cdot 5$

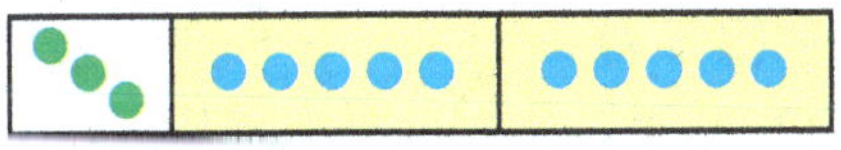

2. $3 + 2 \cdot d$

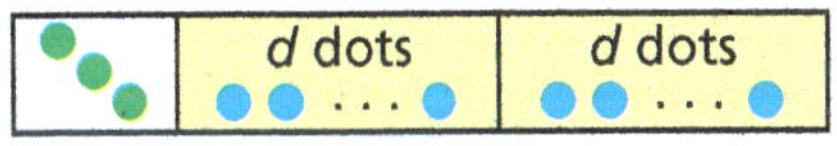

3. $4 \cdot 5 - 2$

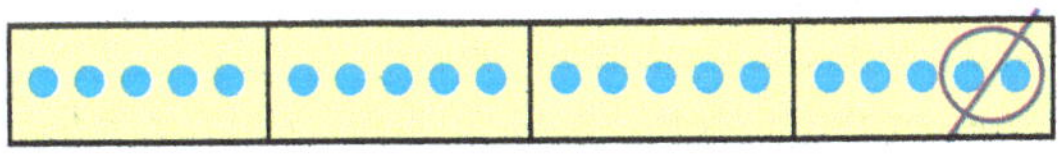

4. $4 \cdot c - 2$

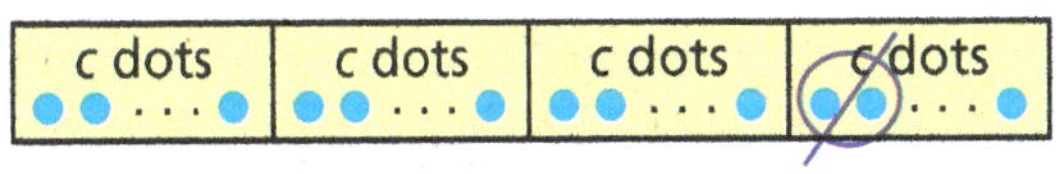

5. $3 \cdot 5 + 3 + 5 \cdot 2$

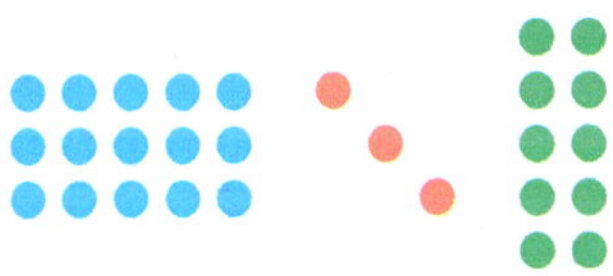

6. $3 + 3 \cdot (4 + 4)$

Simplify Expressions

To simply an expression, first analyze it. Then perform the operations for each term from the *inside out*. Finally, combine the terms. For example, here is how you would simplify the expression in Exercise 6.

$3 + 3 \cdot (4 + 4) =$	Analyze the expression.
$3 + 3 \cdot 8 =$	Compute the inside part of the second term.
$3 + 24 =$	Compute the outside part of the second term.
27	Combine terms.

You analyzed the expressions below in Exercises 1 and 5. Use your analysis to help you simplify each expression. Compare your answer to the numbers of dots in Exercises 1 and 5.

7. $3 + 2 \cdot 5 =$ ______________

8. $3 \cdot 5 + 3 + 5 \cdot 2 =$ ______________

Name ______________________________

Match Models to Expressions

Put a check next to the expressions that tell the number of dots in the diagram. Look for more than one expression for each dot diagram.

9

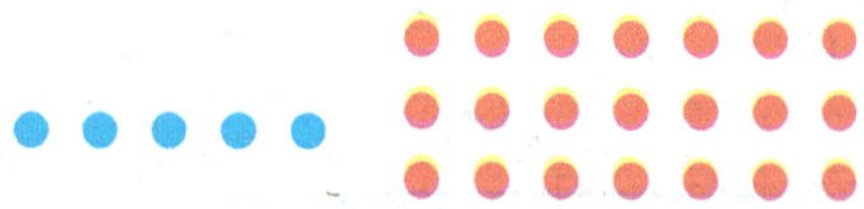

$(5 + 3) \cdot 7$

$5 + (3 \cdot 7)$

$3 \cdot (7 + 5)$

$5 + 3 \cdot 7$

10

$3 \cdot (5 + 6)$

$3 \cdot 5 + 6$

$3 \cdot 5 + 3 \cdot 6$

$(3 \cdot 5) + 6$

11

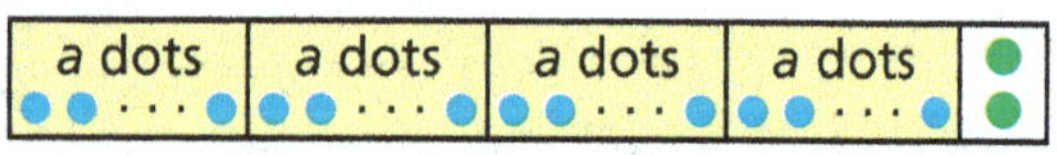

$4 + a + 2$

$a + a + a + a + 2$

$4 \cdot a + 2$

12

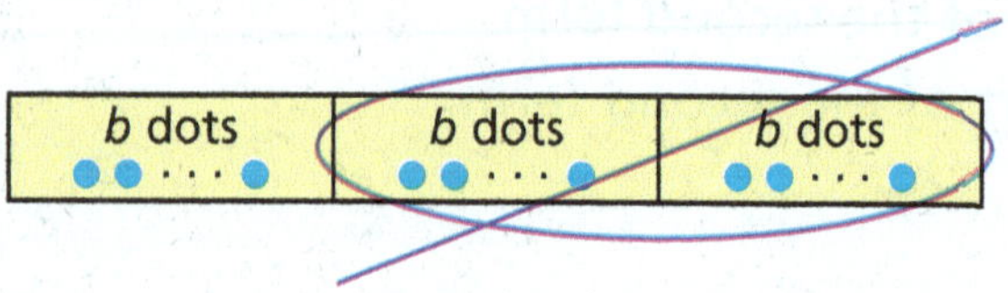

$3 \cdot b - 2$

$3 \cdot b - 2 \cdot b$

$b + b + b - b - b$

Name ______________________

Write and Evaluate Expressions

17

Write an expression and analyze it.

____

____

Evaluate the expression for $d = 7$. ________

18

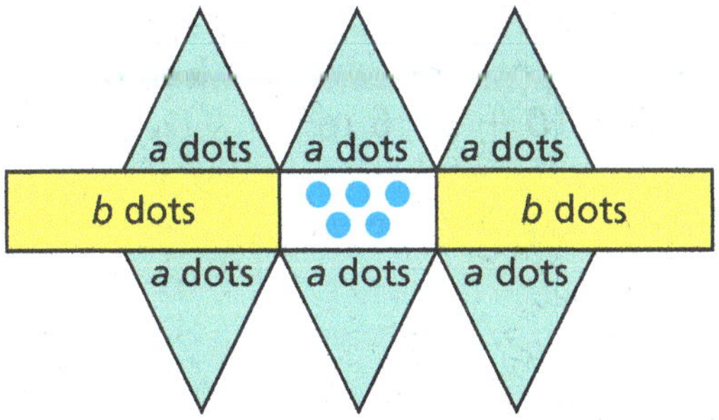

Write an expression and analyze it.

____

____

Evaluate the expression for $a = 2$ and $b = 7$. ________

What's the Error?

Dear Math Students,

I tried to simplify $3 + 4 \cdot 5$. I added $3 + 4$ and got 7. Then I multiplied that by 5 and got 35. My teacher said this is not correct. What did I do wrong?

Please make a dot diagram to help me understand how to simplify the expression $3 + 4 \cdot 5$.

Your Friend,
Puzzled Penguin

19 Write a response to Puzzled Penguin.

____

____

____

Check Understanding

Draw a diagram to represent the expression $3 + 4 \cdot d$, where *d* stands for *d* dots.

Name ______________________

Area of a Floor Plan

The figures below show a floor plan for a room. Keiko, Alex, and DeShun each found a different expression for the area of the room.

Analyze the expressions. Then discuss with your partner how the student might have thought about the area. Describe how the parts of the expression relate to the diagram.

1. 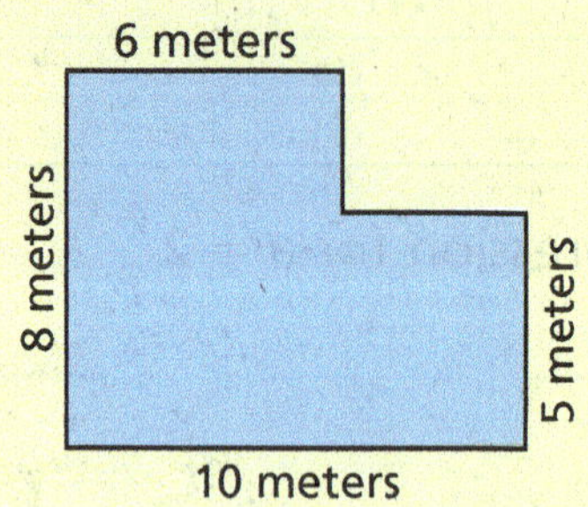

Keiko's expression: $5 \cdot 10 + 3 \cdot 6 \text{ m}^2$

____

____

____

____

2. 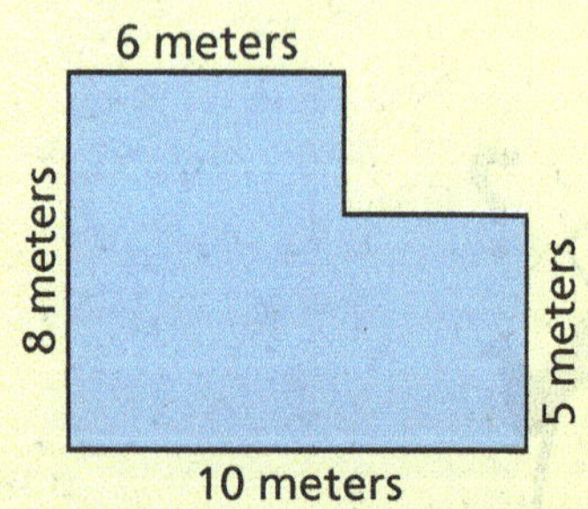

Alex's expression: $8 \cdot 6 + 4 \cdot 5 \text{ m}^2$

____

____

____

____

3. 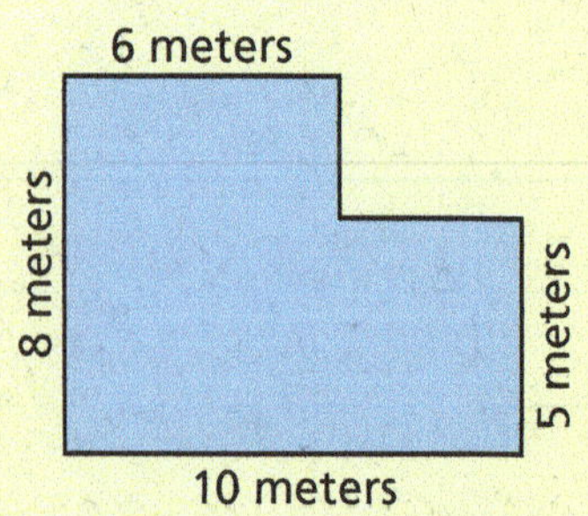

DeShun's expression: $8 \cdot 10 - 3 \cdot 4 \text{ m}^2$

____

____

____

____

Unit 5
Quick Quiz 1

Name ____________________

Simplify. Follow the Order of Operations.

Show your work.

1 $2 \cdot 6 - 9 \div 3 =$ __________

2 $24 - 6 \div 2 + 4^2 =$ __________

Solve.

3 Evaluate the expression for $b = 3$ and $c = 2$.

$b^2 + 2 \cdot 3 - 5c =$ __________

4 Circle the terms in the expression. Then explain how you know your answer is correct.

$a^2 - 4 \cdot b + 1$

____

____

____

5 Circle the expression or expressions at the right that represent the number of dots in the model below.

$2 \cdot 4 + 5$

$2 \cdot (4 + 5)$

$(2 + 4) \cdot (2 + 5)$

$(2 \cdot 4) + (2 \cdot 5)$

Fluency Check 7

Name ____________________

PATH to FLUENCY

1. $5.12\overline{)230.4}$
2. $8.1\overline{)267.3}$
3. $2.6\overline{)14.3}$
4. $4.8\overline{)139.2}$
5. $1.25\overline{)77.5}$
6. $2.14\overline{)160.5}$
7. $3.4\overline{)66.3}$
8. $9.3\overline{)753.3}$
9. $8.72\overline{)261.6}$
10. $7.2\overline{)223.2}$
11. $2.1\overline{)178.5}$
12. $6.15\overline{)196.8}$
13. $3.9\overline{)370.5}$
14. $7.06\overline{)988.4}$
15. $8.5\overline{)35.7}$

Name ______________________

VOCABULARY
equivalent expressions

Introduce Equivalent Expressions

Equivalent expressions always have the same value.

$a + 2 + 3$ and $a + 5$ are equivalent expressions because $a + 2 + 3 = a + 5$ for all values of a.

$a + 5$ and $3 + 4$ are *not* equivalent expressions because $a + 5 = 3 + 4$ *only* when a is 2.

As you learned in Unit 2, the multiplication symbol can be dropped as long as it is not between two numbers.

$3c$ means $3 \cdot c$ $\quad$ ab means $a \cdot b$ $\quad$ $4(p + 6)$ means $4 \cdot (p + 6)$

Complete the table.

	Situation and Diagram	With +		With •		Without •
	Example A Three identical packages weigh $\frac{1}{5}$ gram each. $\frac{1}{5}$ | $\frac{1}{5}$ | $\frac{1}{5}$	$\frac{1}{5} + \frac{1}{5} + \frac{1}{5}$	=	$3 \cdot \frac{1}{5}$	=	$\frac{3}{5}$
	Example B Three identical packages weigh a grams each. a | a | a	$a + a + a$	=	$3 \cdot a$	=	$3a$
1	Two boxes hold b books each. b | b		=		=	
2	Four bags hold c peaches each.		=	$4 \cdot c$	=	
3	______________________	$d + d + d + d + d$	=		=	

Name ______________________

Use Diagrams to Model Expressions

Drawing diagrams and thinking about real world situations can help you find equivalent expressions and understand why expressions are *not* equivalent.

Example 1

Consider the expression $3a - 3$.

Situation: Three boxes each contain *a* apples. William takes three of the apples.

Diagram

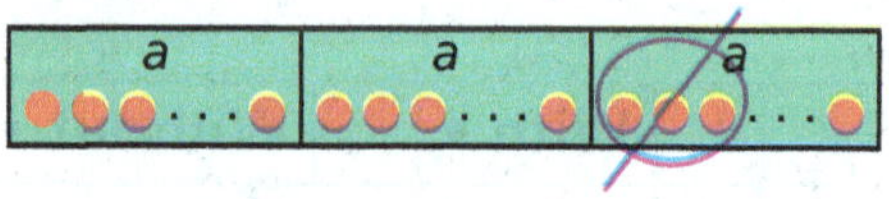

Equivalent expressions:

$$3a - 3 = 2a + (a - 3)$$
$$= a + a + a - 3$$

Non-equivalent expression:
$3a - 3$ is *not* equivalent to *a*.

Example 2

Consider the expression $4b - b$.

Situation: Hannah has four stamp albums with *b* stamps each. She gives one album away.

Diagram

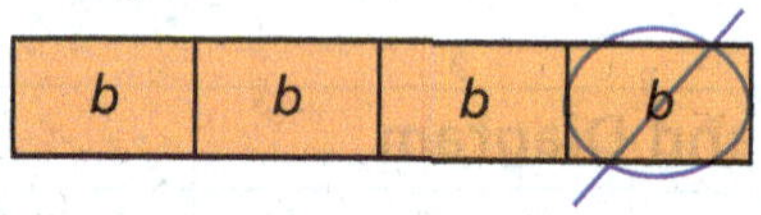

Equivalent expressions:

$$4b - b = b + b + b + b - b$$
$$= 4b - 1b$$
$$= 3b$$

Non-equivalent expression:
$4b - b$ is *not* equivalent to 4.

For each expression, describe a situation and make a diagram. Then circle the expression(s) that are equivalent to the original expression.

12 $4 + 3d$

Situation: ______________________

Diagram

Circle the equivalent expression(s).

$7d$ $4 + 2d + d$ $4 + d + d + d$

13 $2e + e$

Situation: ______________________

Diagram

Circle the equivalent expression(s).

$(e + e) + e$ $2 + e + e$ $3e$

Name ___________________________

Use Diagrams to Model Expressions (continued)

For each expression, describe a situation and make a diagram. Then circle the expression(s) that are equivalent to the original expression.

14 $5 + 1 + 2c$

Situation: ___________________________

____

____

____

Diagram

Circle the equivalent expression(s).

$6 + (2 \cdot c)$ $\quad$ $8c$

$6 + c + c$ $\quad$ $6 + 2c$

15 $3g + 3 + 3$

Situation: ___________________________

____

____

____

Diagram

Circle the equivalent expression(s):

$9g$ $\quad$ $3g + 6$ $\quad$ $g + g + g + 6$

Think about how the situation and diagram model the expression. Then circle the expression(s) that are equivalent to the original expression.

16 $\frac{1}{3}f$

Situation: One third of the f students at a school take Spanish.

Diagram

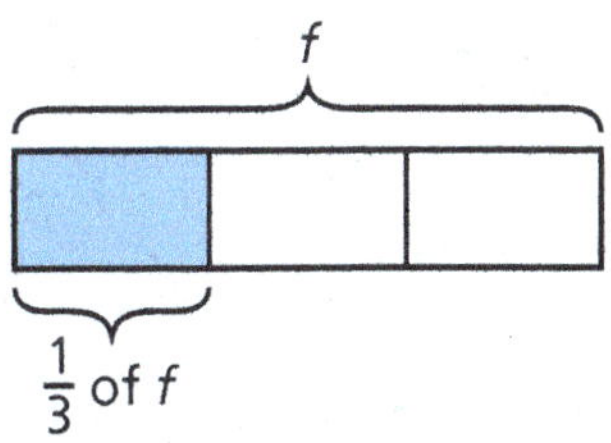

Circle the equivalent expression(s).

$\frac{f}{3}$ $\quad$ $3f$ $\quad$ $f \div 3$

17 $2f + 2 + 1$

Situation: Rachel bought two boxes of golf balls, each containing f golf balls. She also found 2 golf balls in her car and 1 in her golf bag.

Diagram

Circle the equivalent expression(s).

$5f$ $\quad$ $2f + 3$ $\quad$ $f + f + 3$

Name ______________________

What's the Error?

Dear Math Students,

I just had a math quiz about equivalent expressions. Here are two problems I got wrong:

$4x + 3 = 7x$ $\quad\quad$ $7x - x = 7$

Can you explain why my answers are not right and help me find correct equivalent expressions?

It might help me understand if you use a model or make up a situation.

Your Friend,
Puzzled Penguin

21 Write a response to Puzzled Penguin.

Show your work.

____

____

____

____

____

Practice

Write an equivalent expression with fewer terms if possible. Make quick drawings or use tiles if you need to.

22 $6m - m =$ ____________

23 $8 + 3t =$ ____________

24 $7w - 5 =$ ____________

25 $4s + 4s =$ ____________

Check Understanding

Make a diagram and write two equivalent expressions to represent the expression $6m + 3 + 2$.

Name ______________________

Combine Terms with Algebra Tiles

Model each expression with algebra tiles. Then rearrange the tiles to model an equivalent expression with fewer terms. Write the new expressions. Make quick drawings to record your work.

1. $6 + 2x + 1 + x =$ ______________

Model of Original Expression

Model of Rearranged Expression

2. $3x + 1 + 1 + 2x =$ ______________

Model of Original Expression

Model of Rearranged Expression

3. $x + 2 + x + 4 + x =$ ______________

Model of Original Expression

Model of Rearranged Expression

Name ______________________

Simplify Expressions

You can use all the properties you have learned in this lesson to simplify expressions. Simplifying an expression can include writing the terms with the coefficients in front, combining like terms, and doing all possible computations.

Example

Simplify $2(3x) + 4 + (5x)4 + 1$.

$2(3x) + 4 + (5x)4 + 1 = 6x + 4 + 20x + 1$	Rewrite terms with coefficients in front.
$= 6x + 20x + 4 + 1$	Put like terms together.
$= 26x + 5$	Combine like terms.

Simplify each expression.

15 $2x + 5(6x) + 1 =$ ______________

16 $2(8x) + 3 + 4(2x) + 4 =$ ______________

What's the Error?

Dear Math Students,

I had to simplify this expression on my homework.

$$5 + 3(2x) + 4x(2) + 2^2$$

I didn't see any like terms, so I just left this like it is. I got the problem marked wrong. Please help me understand what to do.

Your friend,
Puzzled Penguin

17 Write a response to Puzzled Penguin.

____

____

____

Check Understanding

Simplify the expression $4x + 5 + x + 3$. Then make quick drawings of the original expression and the simplified expression.

Name ______________________

Two Ways to Use the Distributive Property

VOCABULARY
Distributive Property

The **Distributive Property** gives us two opposite ways to transform expressions into equivalent expressions.

- We can distribute a factor to the terms of a sum or difference.

  $(5 + 2)c = 5c + 2c$ c is distributed to 5 and 2.

- We can pull out a common factor from the terms of a sum or difference.

  $5c + 2c = (5 + 2)c$ c is pulled out of $5c$ and $2c$.

Use the completed rows as a guide to help you fill in the blanks. Draw arrows to show how a factor is pulled out or distributed.

	Distributing	Pulling Out a Common Factor
2	$(a + b)c = ac + bc$	$ac + bc = (a + b)c$
3	$(2 + 3)x =$	$2x + 3x =$
4	$(y + 2)x =$	$yx + 2x =$
5	$(a - b)c = ac - bc$	$ac - bc = (a - b)c$
6	$(x - 3) \cdot 7 =$	$x \cdot 7 - 3 \cdot 7 =$
7	$(7 - 2)x =$	$7x - 2x =$
8	$d(e + f) = de + df$	$de + df =$
9	$5(x + 2) =$	$5x + 5 \cdot 2 =$
10	$6(3 + y) =$	$6 \cdot 3 + 6y =$
11	$d(e - f) = de - df$	$de - df =$
12	$x(y - 4) =$	$xy - x \cdot 4 =$
13	$4(x - y) =$	$4x - 4y =$

Name

Connect Expressions, Diagrams, and Situations

For each expression, describe a situation and make a diagram. Then circle the equivalent expression(s).

15 $4x + 2$

Situation: ______________________

____

____

____

Diagram

Circle the equivalent expression(s).

$6x$ $x + x + x + x + 2$ $6 + x$

16 $2m - 1$

Situation: ______________________

____

____

____

Diagram

Circle the equivalent expression(s).

$m + m - 1$ m $2(m - 1)$

17 At a restaurant, Maria and Sam both ordered the same thing and each paid *d* dollars for their food, and each left \$3 for the tip.

Draw a diagram to represent the total amount Maria and Sam paid.

Write three different, equivalent expressions to represent this situation.

____

____

____

Name ______________________________

1. Josie has \$62 in her savings account now. She deposits \$8 each week. Write an expression for the number of dollars she will have in her account w weeks from now.

   ____

   Evaluate your expression when $w = 10$.

   ____________ dollars

Solve.

2. Apply the Distributive Property and then combine like terms to write an equivalent expression.

   $x + 7(x + 1) =$ ________

3. Write the sum as a product by using the Distributive Property to pull out the greatest common factor (GCF).

   $48 + 40 =$ ______ $\cdot$ ______ $+$ ______ $\cdot$ ______ $=$ ________ $=$ ________

4. Circle all of the expressions the model at the right represents.

$2x + 10$	$5x + 5x$	$x + 5 + x + 5$	$10x$
$2x + 5$	$2(x + 5)$	$x + 10$	

5. Explain how the diagram at the right shows that $3(x + 4) = 3x + 12$.

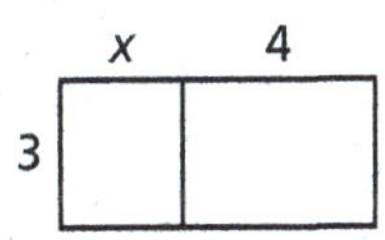

   ____

   ____

   ____

   ____

   ____

Fluency Check 8

Name ____________________

PATH to FLUENCY

1. $38\overline{)\$807.50}$

2. $35\overline{)\$1,134.00}$

3. $55\overline{)\$949.30}$

4. $28\overline{)\$225.40}$

5. $16\overline{)\$72.96}$

6. $57\overline{)\$638.40}$

7. $62\overline{)\$1,643.00}$

8. $39\overline{)\$982.80}$

9. $43\overline{)\$924.50}$

10. $32\overline{)\$33.92}$

11. $18\overline{)\$62.28}$

12. $32\overline{)\$196.80}$

13. $52\overline{)\$421.20}$

14. $76\overline{)\$250.80}$

15. $85\overline{)\$207.40}$

Name ______________________________

Define Variables

At a filling station, a gasoline pump fills the fuel tank of a car at a rate of 1 pint per second.

There are two quantities in this situation. The two quantities vary together—as one changes, the other changes too.

4 What two quantities vary together in this situation?

____

____

5 What units could you use for these two quantities?

____

____

6 Define two variables for your quantities in Exercise 4.

Let ______________ represent ______________________________.

Let ______________ represent ______________________________.

7 Label this double number line to show how the quantities vary together.

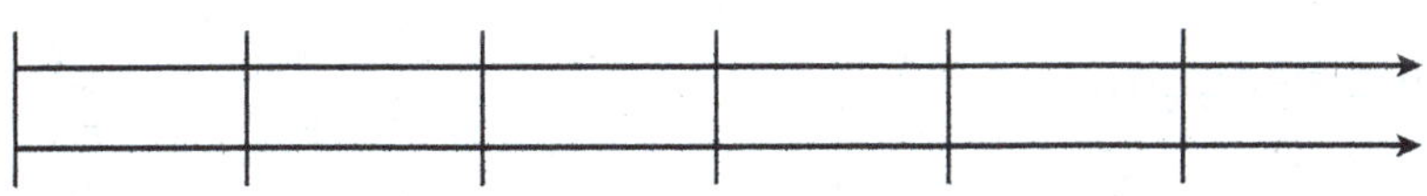

Name ______________________

Three Ways to Represent a Relationship

Mr. Prieto makes his own salad dressing by mixing vegetable oil and vinegar in the ratio of 5 ounces of vegetable oil to 1 ounce of vinegar. The amount of vegetable oil and vinegar vary together.

8. Define the variable x for the amount of vegetable oil, and define the variable y for the amount of vinegar in Mr. Prieto's salad dressing.

   Let x be the number of ______________________.

   Let y be the number of ______________________.

9. Complete the table. Then discuss how the table, the diagram, and the equations are related.

Table

y	x

Diagram

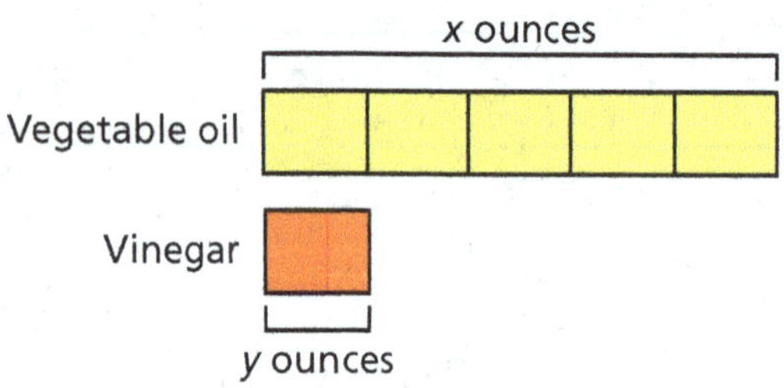

Equations

$x = y + y + y + y + y$

$x = 5y$

$y = x \div 5$

$y = \frac{1}{5}x$

What's the Error?

Dear Math Students,

I thought that because Mr. Prieto's ratio of vegetable oil to vinegar was 5: 1, I could write the equation $5x = y$. My teacher said my equation was not correct. Please help me understand why.

Your Friend,
Puzzled Penguin

10. Write a response to Puzzled Penguin.

____

____

____

Name ______________________________

Write Equations for a Relationship

An electronics store offers a payment plan for purchases over \$200. Customers can make a \$100 down payment and then pay the remainder in three equal payments.

Let *t* be the total amount of a customer's purchase in dollars.

Let *p* be the amount of each of the three equal payments in dollars.

11 Write the missing amounts in the table. Use the diagram and the table to help you find equations that relate *t* and *p*.

Table

t	*p*
	150
1,000	
	250
475	

Diagram

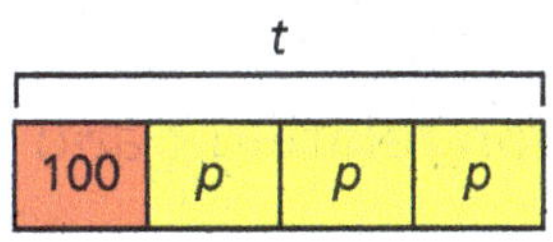

Equations

$t =$ ______________

$p =$ ______________

In a bread dough recipe, the ratio of cups of flour to cups of water is 2 to 1.

f	*w*
	1
4	
	5
16	

12 Define variables for the amounts of flour and water.

Let *f* represent ______________________________.

Let *w* represent ______________________________.

13 Complete the table of values at the right for *f* and *w*.

14 Make a diagram for *f* and *w*.

15 Write equations relating *f* and *w*.

$f =$ __________ $w =$ __________

Check Understanding

Name two quantities that vary together. Then explain why it is important to specify a unit of measure when defining a variable.

Name ____________________

Tables and Equations for Constant Speed

2 Complete each table for the students mentioned on the previous page.

Student 1

Elapsed Time in Seconds (t)	Distance Walked in Feet (d)
0	
1	
2	
3	
4	
5	

Student 2

Elapsed Time in Seconds (t)	Distance Walked in Feet (d)
0	
1	
2	
3	
4	
5	

3 For each student, write an equation relating t and d.

Student 1 equation: ____________________

Student 2 equation: ____________________

4 How is each student's walking rate related to the equation?

____

Graphs for Constant Speed

5 a. On the grids on the next page, graph the data in the tables from Exercise 2.

b. Does it make sense to connect the points on the graphs? If so, connect them.

c. Draw two unit rate triangles on each graph.

d. How is each student's walking rate related to the graph?

____

____

Name

Graphs for Constant Speed (continued)

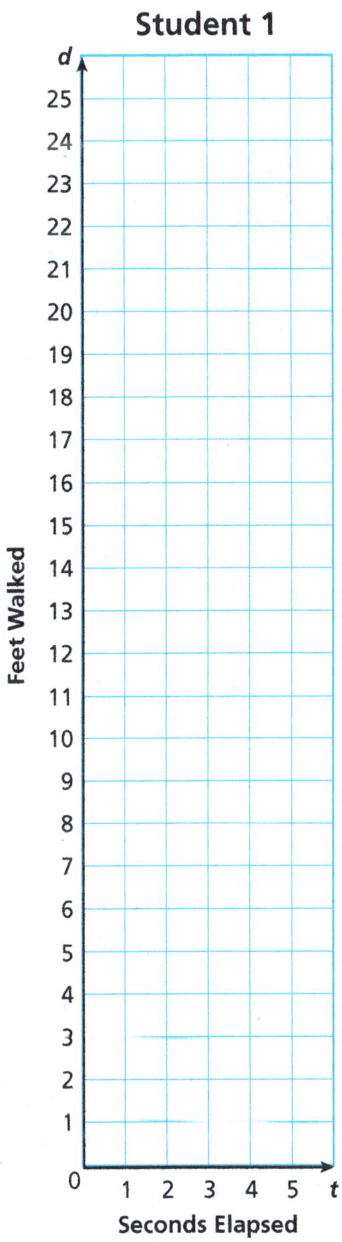

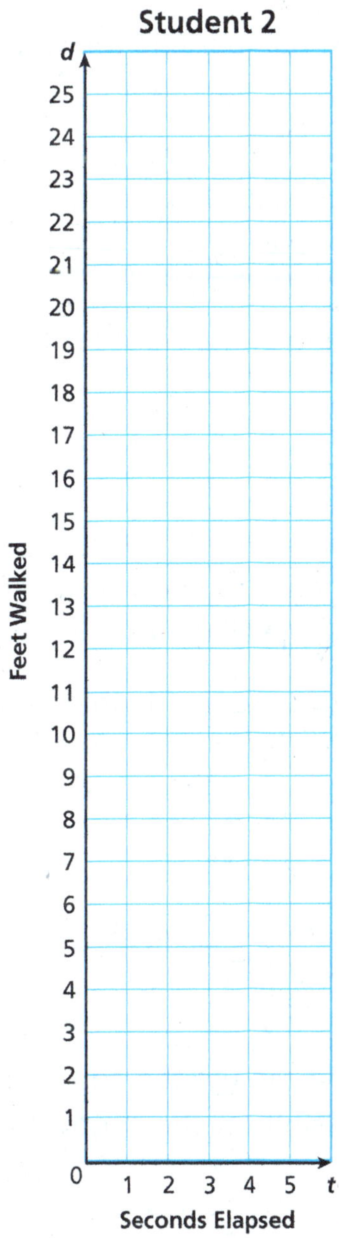

Name ______________________________

Double Number Line for Constant Speed

Suppose Student 3 walks at a constant rate of 4 feet per second.

6 Label this double number line for Student 3.

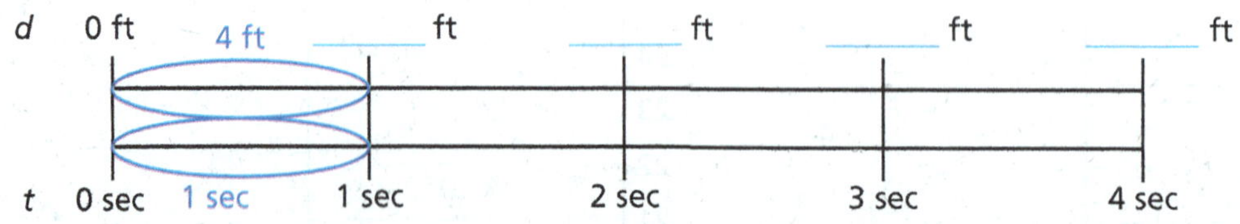

7 Complete the table at the right for Student 3.

Student 3

Elapsed Time in Seconds (t)	Distance Walked in Feet (d)
0	
1	
2	
3	
4	
5	

8 Write an equation relating d and t for Student 3.

____

9 Seth and Kinsey want to know how far Student 3 will have walked after $2\frac{1}{2}$ seconds.

a. Seth says he can use the double number line to find the distance. Explain how he might do this.

____

____

____

b. Kinsey says she can use the equation to find the distance. Explain how she might do this.

____

____

Calculate how far Student 3 walks in the given length of time.

10 $3\frac{1}{4}$ seconds ______________

11 $2\frac{5}{8}$ seconds ______________

Name ______________________________

Find the Unit Rate

Suppose Student 4 walks at a constant rate of 7 feet every 2 seconds. In the exercises below, if the answer is greater than 1, write the answer as a whole or mixed number.

12 Label this double line graph for Student 4.

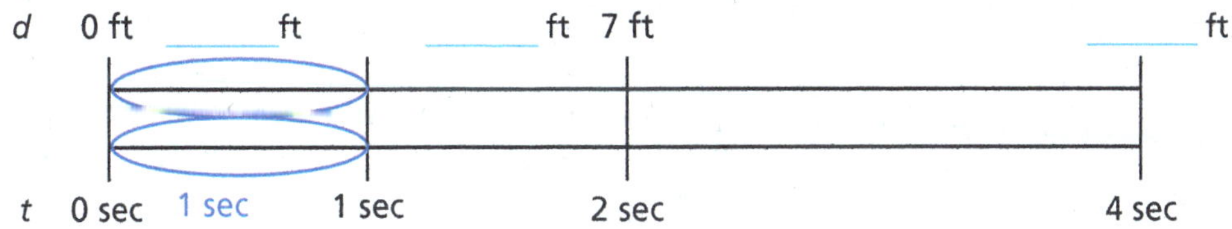

13 Complete the table below for Student 4.

Student 4

Elapsed Time in Seconds (t)	Distance Walked in Feet (d)
0	
1	
2	
3	
4	
5	

14 What is the unit rate for Student 4?

____

15 Write an equation relating d and t for Student 4.

____

Calculate how far Student 4 walks in the given length of time.

16 3 seconds ____________

17 $2\frac{1}{2}$ seconds ____________

Name ______________________________

Find the Unit Rate (continued)

Suppose Student 5 walks at a constant rate of 11 feet every 3 seconds. If the answer is greater than 1, write the answer as a whole or mixed number.

18 Write an equation relating d and t for Student 5. ____________

Calculate how far Student 5 walks in the given length of time.

19 6 seconds ____________

20 $7\frac{1}{2}$ seconds ____________

Summarize Walking at a Constant Speed

21 Suppose a student walks at a constant rate of r feet per second. Label the double number line below for the student and discuss why the equation $d = rt$ relates the distance, rate, and elapsed time for this situation.

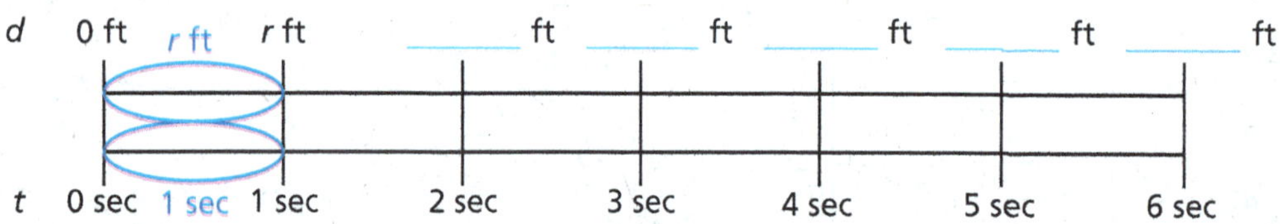

22 Summarize what you learned today about how distance, rate, and elapsed time are related for motion at a constant rate.

____

____

Check Understanding

Suppose Student 6 walks at a constant rate of 14 feet every 4 seconds. How far would Student 6 walk in 24 seconds? ____________

Explain how you found your answer.

Name ______________________________

Three Ways to Represent Motion at a Constant Speed

Suppose a high-speed train travels at a constant rate between Greenville and Orange Lake.

Let *t* be the number of minutes elapsed.

Let *d* be the number of miles the train has traveled.

The variables *d* and *t* vary together. Their relationship is represented by the equation $d = 2.5t$.

Let *t* be the independent variable. Let *d* be the dependent variable.

1. Complete the table.

Minutes Elapsed (*t*)	Miles Traveled (*d*)
0	
1	
2	
3	
4	
5	
6	

2. Graph the points from the table.

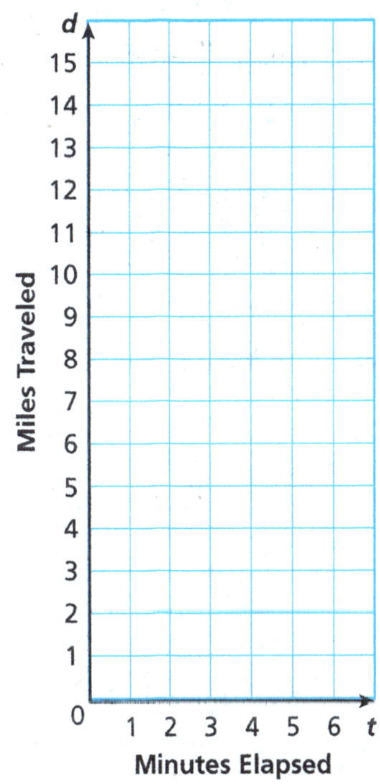

3. Does it make sense to connect the points on the graph? If so, connect them.

____

4. Draw a unit rate triangle on your graph.

5. What is the speed of the train in miles per minute (that is, what is the unit rate)?

____

6. With your class, discuss how *t* and *d* are related in the equation, in the table, and on the graph.

Name

Is the Change Constant?

SuperHero Supplies, Inc. produces different Superpower Soups. In the factory, each type of soup flows into a different vat.

Let t be the number of seconds elapsed.

Let v be the number of liters of soup in the vat.

For each vat, v and t vary together and are related by an equation.

Vat 1
(Super Strength)
$v = t^2$

Vat 2
(x-ray Vision)
$v = 5t$

Vat 3
(Flying)
$v = 5t + 3$

Vat 4
(Lightning Speed)
$v = 2t + 10$

Vat 5
(Invisibility)
$v = 3t + 10$

7 Complete the table for Vat 1.

Vat 1: $v = t^2$

Seconds Elapsed (t)	Liters in Vat (v)
0	
1	
2	
3	
4	
5	
6	

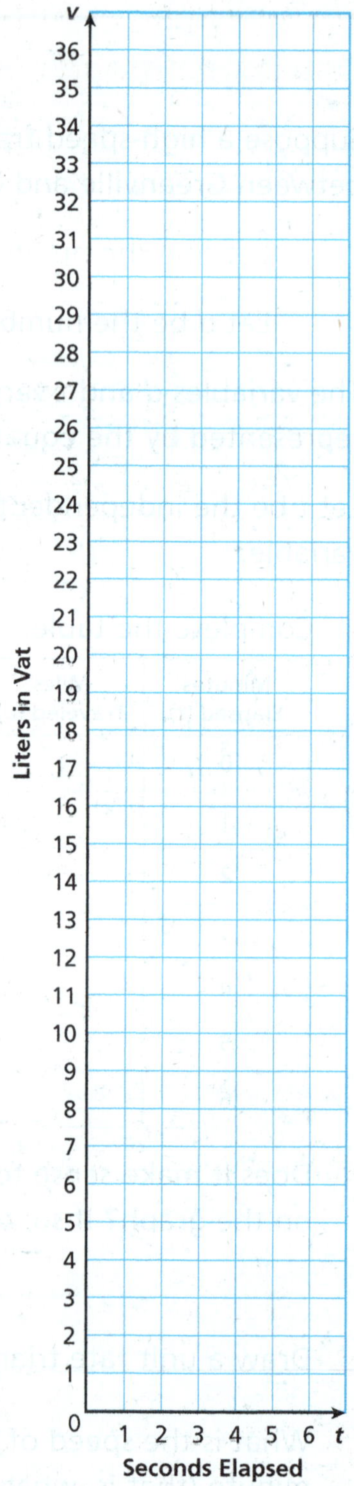

8 Plot the points for Vat 1. Connect the points if it makes sense to.

9 Is the soup flowing into Vat 1 at a constant rate?

____

Name ______________________

Compare Change

10 Complete the tables for Vats 2 and 3.

Vat 2: $v = 5t$

Seconds Elapsed (t)	Liters in Vat (v)
0	
1	
2	
3	
4	
5	
6	

Vat 3: $v = 5t + 3$

Seconds Elapsed (t)	Liters in Vat (v)
0	
1	
2	
3	
4	
5	
6	

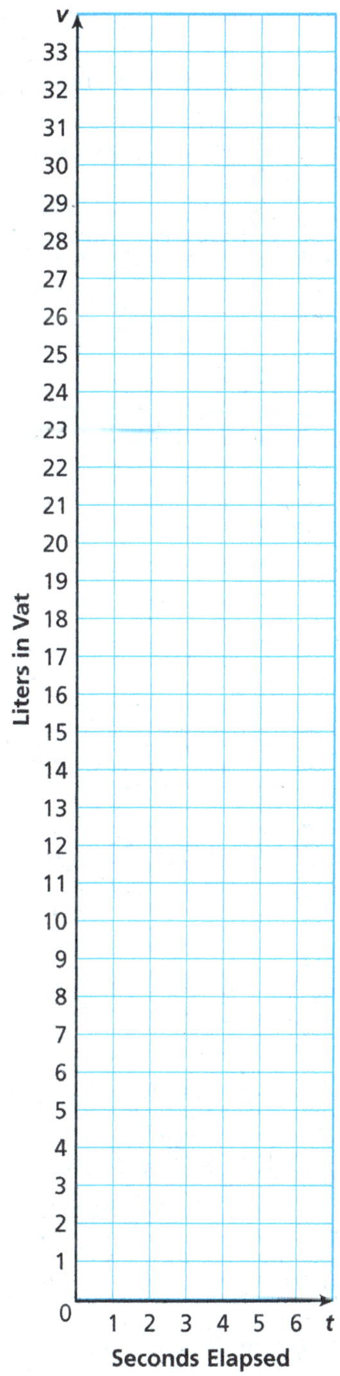

11 Plot the points for Vat 2 on the grid. Connect the points if it makes sense to.

12 Use a different color to plot the points for Vat 3 on the same grid. Connect the points if it makes sense to.

13 Tell whether soup is flowing into the vat at a constant rate.

Vat 2 ____________ Vat 3 ____________

14 What does the 5 in $v = 5t$ tell you?

____

15 What does the 5 in $v = 5t + 3$ tell you? What does the 3 tell you?

____

____

____

Name ____________________

Compare Change (continued)

16 Complete the tables for Vats 4 and 5.

Vat 4: $v = 2t + 10$

Seconds Elapsed (t)	Liters in Vat (v)
0	
1	
2	
3	
4	
5	
6	

Vat 5: $v = 3t + 10$

Seconds Elapsed (t)	Liters in Vat (v)
0	
1	
2	
3	
4	
5	
6	

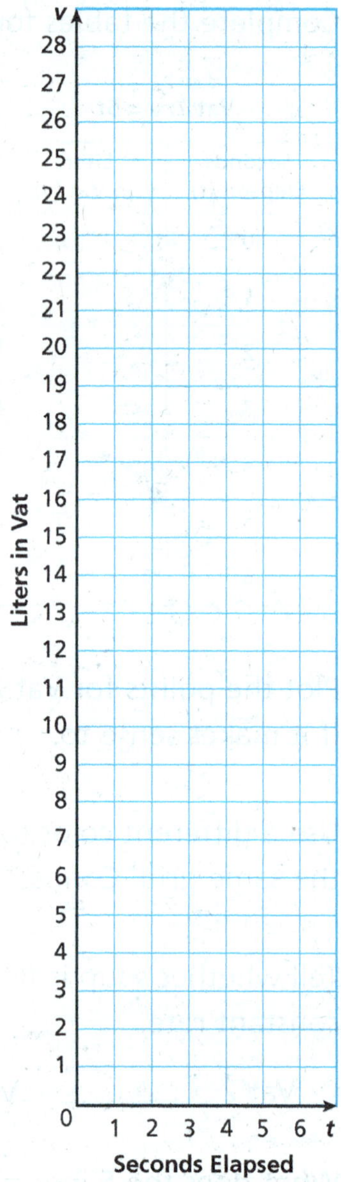

17 Plot the points for Vat 4 on the grid. Connect the points if it makes sense to.

18 Use a different color to plot the points for Vat 5 on the same grid. Connect the points if it makes sense to.

19 Tell whether soup is flowing into the vat at a constant rate.

Vat 4 __________ Vat 5 __________

20 What do the 2 in $v = 2t + 10$ and the 3 in $v = 3t + 10$ tell you?

____

21 What does the 10 in $v = 2t + 10$ and in $v = 3t + 10$ tell you?

____

Check Understanding

The equation for Vat 6 is $v = 4t + 3$. Make a table for Vat 6. Then plot the points for Vat 6 on the same grid as Vats 4 and 5.

Name ______________________________

Compare Costs

Seward Elementary School plans to sell friendship bracelets. The bracelets can be purchased from three companies.

Company A charges \$30 for 24 bracelets, plus a flat rate of \$4 for shipping any number of bracelets.

Company B charges \$13 for 10 bracelets and does not charge for shipping.

Company C charges \$18 for 15 bracelets, plus a flat rate of \$10 for shipping any number of bracelets.

Let n be a number of bracelets, and let c be the total cost in dollars.

1 Complete this table for Company A. In the shaded cells, write expressions, rather than the final values.

Number of Bracelets (n)	Cost in Dollars	Shipping Cost in Dollars	Total Cost (c) in Dollars
24	30	4	34
12			
6			
2			
1	1.25	4	$1 \bullet 1.25 + 4$
5			
17			
33			
n			

2 Write an equation that describes the total cost c of purchasing n friendship bracelets from Company A.

Company A: $c =$ ______________________

3 Tell what the numbers in your equation represent.

____

____

Name ______________________

Compare Costs (continued)

4 Now consider Company B. Write an equation for the total cost in dollars c in terms of the number of friendship bracelets n. Show your work.

Company B: $c =$ ______________

5 For Company C, write an equation for the total cost in dollars c in terms of the number of friendship bracelets n. Show your work.

Company C: $c =$ ______________

6 In the first row of the table below, write your equations from Exercises 2, 4, and 5. Then complete the table to find the costs of buying different quantities of bracelets from each company.

Number of Bracelets (n)	Company A Cost $c =$ ______	Company B Cost $c =$ ______	Company C Cost $c =$ ______	Lowest Total Cost?
25				
100				
150				
250				

Check Understanding

For Company D, the equation $c = 1.40n + 5$ represents the total cost in dollars c in terms of the number of friendship bracelets n. Find the total cost of 100 bracelets. ______________

Name ______________________________

Suppose an online retailer offers pocket calculators for $4 each, plus a fixed shipping charge of $2 for any number of calculators.

1. Complete the table.

Calculators Purchased, *n*	Cost of Purchase ($)	Shipping Charge ($)	Total Cost ($), *c*
1		2	
2		2	
3	12	2	14
4		2	
n		2	

2. On the grid at the right, plot the values in the table for *n* and *c*. Draw a dashed line through the points. Only points that represent a whole number of calculators make sense, so a solid line should not be used.

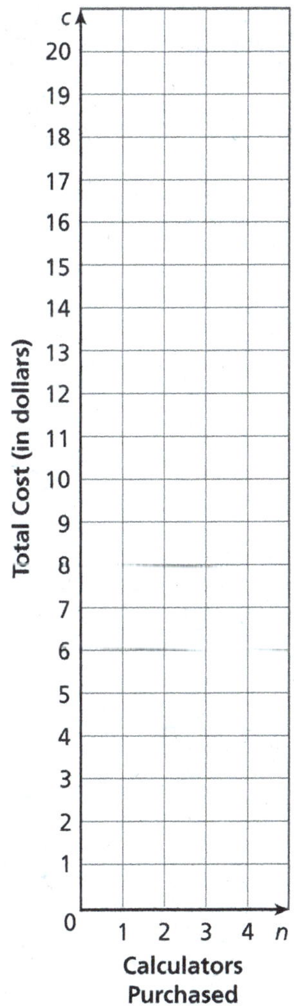

3. Write an equation to represent the total cost in dollars *c* for *n* calculators.

____

4. Explain how the table, the graph, and the equation represent the cost of each calculator.

____

____

____

____

5. Explain how the graph and the equation represent the shipping charge.

____

____

____

Fluency Check 9

Name ______________________

PATH to FLUENCY

1. 0.45×28

2. 0.32×63

3. 8.4×2.7

4. 6.9×7.1

5. 0.38×0.7

6. 0.15×0.6

7. $14\overline{)41.58}$

8. $21\overline{)26.88}$

9. $34\overline{)19.04}$

10. $47\overline{)36.66}$

11. $7.3\overline{)1{,}752}$

12. $1.09\overline{)87.2}$

13. $6.18\overline{)154.5}$

14. $25\overline{)\$762.00}$

15. $88\overline{)\$1{,}386.00}$

Name ______________________________

Graphing Solutions (> and <)

VOCABULARY
infinite
solution set of an inequality

Most inequalities have an **infinite** number of solutions. This means it is not possible to show all of the solutions in a list. However, it is possible to show all of the solutions in a graph on a number line.

The **solution set of an inequality** is the set of all of its solutions. The graph of a solution set of an inequality is often a ray. When you graph the ray, you graph an open dot if the endpoint is *not* a solution. You graph a filled-in dot if the endpoint *is* a solution.

Example 1

This graph shows the solutions of $x > 3$.

The open dot at 3 shows that 3 is *not* a solution. The blue arrow shows that all the numbers to the right of 3 (greater than 3) are solutions.

Example 2

This graph shows the solutions of $x < 6$.

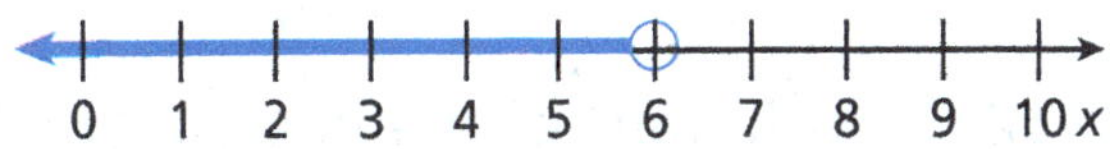

The open dot at 6 shows that 6 is *not* a solution. The blue arrow shows that all the numbers to the left of 6 (less than 6) are solutions.

Graph all the solutions of the inequality.

24 $m > 7$

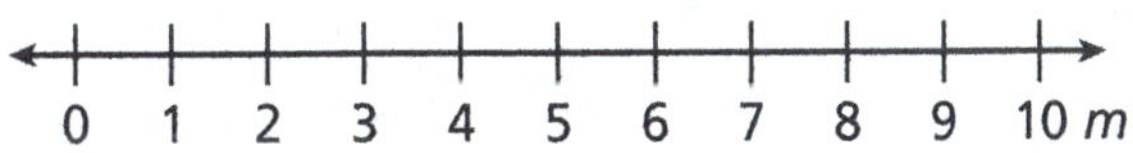

25 $t < 5$

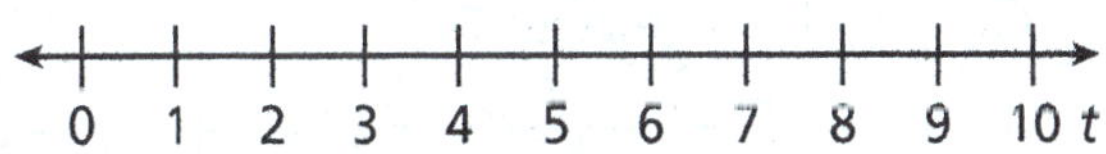

26 A shipping company charges an extra fee for boxes that weigh more than 200 pounds. Let w represent the weight in pounds of a box for which an extra fee was charged. Write an inequality for the possible values of w. ______________

Graph the inequality.

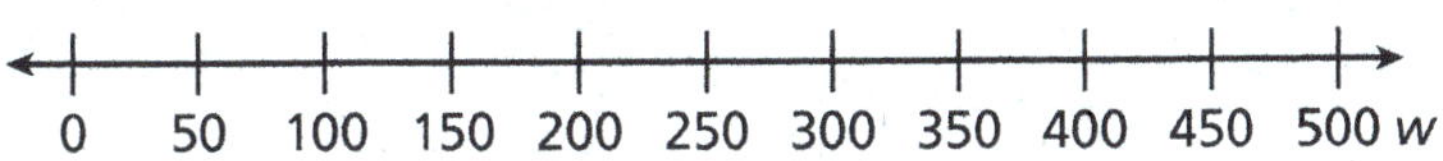

Name ____________________

Graphing Solutions (≥ and ≤)

When you graph a solution set on a number line, you use a filled-in dot to show that the endpoint is included in the set of solutions.

Example 1

This graph shows the solutions of $x \geq 3$.

The filled-in dot at 3 shows that 3 is a solution. The blue arrow shows that all the numbers to the right of 3 are also solutions.

Example 2

This graph shows the solutions of $x \leq 6$.

The filled-in dot at 6 shows that 6 is a solution. The blue arrow shows that all the numbers to the left of 6 are also solutions.

Graph all the solutions of the inequality.

27 $m \geq 7$

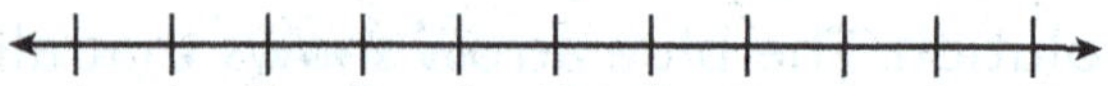

28 $t \leq 5$

29 The weather reporter said temperatures would not rise above 3°F all week. Let t represent the temperatures in degrees Fahrenheit for the week. Write an inequality to represent the possible values of t. ____________________

Graph the inequality.

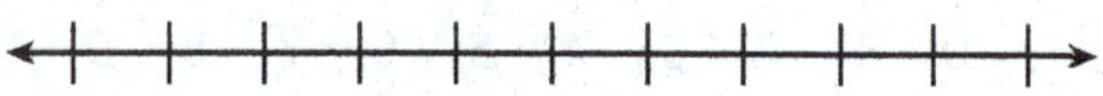

30 Describe a real world situation that can be represented by an inequality. Write an inequality to represent the situation, and then graph it on a number line.

____

____

____

Check Understanding

Explain how you knew to choose a filled-in or open dot for the graph in Exercise 29 above.

Name ______________________________

What's the Error?

Dear Math Students,

On my homework, I am supposed to find a solution of the inequality shown at the right.

I think $x = 7$ is a solution because when x is 7, both sides of the inequality are equal to 10.

Is my thinking correct?

Your Friend,
Puzzled Penguin

$x + 3 > 10$

16 Write a response to Puzzled Penguin.

____

____

____

Dear Math Students,

Another problem on my homework asks me to find the solution of the equation shown at the right.

I know that both sides of any equation represent the same number. So, since 2^5 on the right side of the equation is $2 \cdot 5$, or 10, I think x should be 11.

Is $x = 11$ the solution of the equation $x - 1 = 2^5$?

Your Friend,
Puzzled Penguin

$x - 1 = 2^5$

17 Write a response to Puzzled Penguin.

____

____

____

Check Understanding

Solve the equation $7x - 2x = 55$ by thinking about what value of x will make the sides of the equation equal. __________

Name ______________________

VOCABULARY
inverse operations

Use Inverse Operations

Use an inverse operation to write a related equation. Then solve the equation for x.

1. $x + 9 = 20$ ______
2. $x - 3 = 2$ ______
3. $x - 7 = 10$ ______
4. $x + 12 = 25$ ______
5. $x + 32 = 40$ ______
6. $x - 14 = 34$ ______

Solve with Algebra Tiles

Write and solve the equation each model represents. Circle the tiles you remove from both sides.

7. 

______

8. 

______

9. 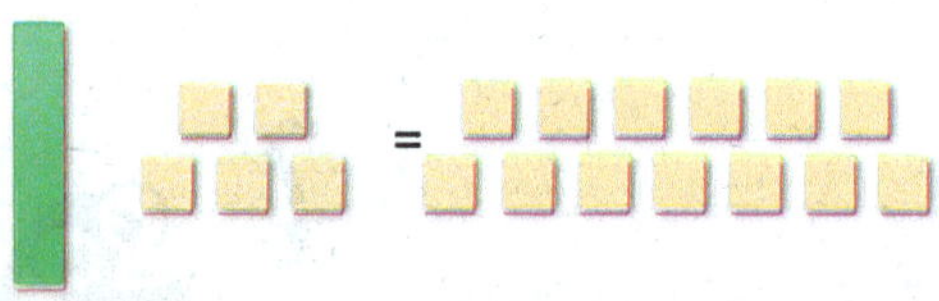

______

10. 

______

Use your algebra tiles to model each equation. Make a quick drawing of your model. Then solve the equation and check your answer using substitution.

11. $x + 2 = 6$ $x =$ ______
12. $x + 5 = 16$ $x =$ ______
13. $x + 8 = 10$ $x =$ ______
14. $x + 3 = 12$ $x =$ ______

Name ______________________________

What's the Error?

Dear Math Students,

The problem shown below was part of my homework assignment.

To get ready for a social studies test, Vera studied 35 more minutes than she studied for a language arts test. If Vera studied 45 minutes for her social studies test, how many minutes did she study for her language arts test?

Here are the steps I followed to solve the problem:

Step 1: I read the problem twice, like I always do. Then I chose m to represent the number of minutes Vera studied for her language arts test.

Step 2: I decided that the phrase more minutes suggests addition.

Step 3: The numbers in the problem are 35 minutes and 45 minutes, so I wrote the equation shown below.

$$45 + 35 = m$$

Step 4: I solved the equation by adding 45 and 35. For my answer, I wrote that Vera studied 80 minutes, or 1 hour and 20 minutes, for her language arts test.

When my homework assignment was graded, my answer was marked wrong! Can you help me understand what I did wrong, and explain how to find the correct answer?

Your Friend,
Puzzled Penguin

30 Write a response to the Puzzled Penguin.

Name ______________________________

What's the Error?

Dear Math Students,

An exercise on my homework assignment asked me to solve the equation shown below.

$$\frac{1}{2}x = 62$$

I know that one way to solve the equation is to use the multiplicative inverse of the coefficient.

The coefficient is $\frac{1}{2}$, and its multiplicative inverse is $\frac{2}{1}$. So, I multiplied the coefficient by $\frac{2}{1}$.

$$\frac{2}{1} \cdot \frac{1}{2}x = 62$$

The left side of the equation simplified to x.

$$\frac{\overset{1}{\cancel{2}}}{1} \cdot \frac{1}{\underset{1}{\cancel{2}}}x = 62$$

So, I concluded that $x = 62$, but my answer was marked wrong. Can you help me identify my error, and explain how to solve the equation correctly?

Your Friend,
Puzzled Penguin

34 Write a response to Puzzled Penguin.

____

____

____

____

____

____

____

Name ______________________________

Discuss Modes of Transportation

The rate you are charged to ride in a taxi cab varies from city to city. Most rates include a fixed initial charge, and a fixed cost for every fraction of a mile traveled.

The table below illustrates the cost of a taxi ride for various distances. The total cost includes a fixed $3 fee upon entry, and a cost for every one-fifth of a mile traveled.

Cost of a Taxi Ride

Distance in Miles (*d*)	Mileage Cost in Dollars	Initial Charge in Dollars	Total cost in Dollars (*t*)
$\frac{1}{5}$	2	3	5
$\frac{3}{5}$		3	
1			
$1\frac{2}{5}$		3	
2		3	

1. Complete the table.

2. Which three quantities vary, and which two quantities are constant?

____

____

3. Graph the data for distance and total cost. Describe your graph.

____

____

____

4. Write an equation that can be used to find the total cost in dollars (*t*) of a ride for any distance in miles (*d*). ______________

5. Use your graph to predict the cost of a $1\frac{4}{5}$ mile ride. Use your equation to check your prediction. ______________

Name

Broken-Line Graphs

Have you ever had a ride in a hot air balloon, or wondered what riding in one would be like?

The table below shows some flight data about the first few minutes of a hot air balloon ride.

Flight Data of a Hot Air Balloon

Elapsed Time in Minutes	Height above Ground in Feet
1	100
2	300
3	650
4	700
5	550

6 Graph the data.

7 **Discuss** Compare your graph with the taxi-ride graph on the previous page. How are the graphs alike and how are they different?

8 **Discuss** Why is one of the graphs a straight line and the other graph a broken line?

9 Which type of graph can be extended and used to make a precise prediction? Give an example to support your answer.

Unit 5
Quick Quiz 4

Name ______________________

Solve.

1. A bank charges a fee if a customer's balance falls below $200. Quinn was charged a fee.

   Let *b* represent the balance in Quinn's account when he is charged a fee. Write an inequality for all possible values of *b*. ______________

   Graph the inequality.

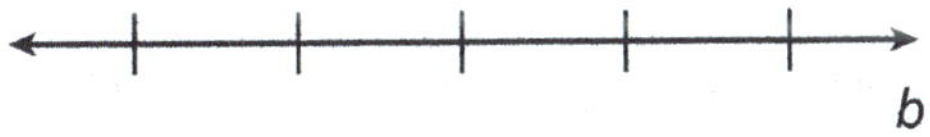

2. When the temperature is 80°F or more, Javier wears sandals to the beach.

   Let *t* represent a temperature in degrees Fahrenheit for which Javier wears sandals. Write an inequality for all possible values of *t*. ______________

   Graph the inequality.

Write an equation or inequality to represent the problem. Then use the equation or inequality to solve the problem.

Show your work.

3. Twelve students in a sixth grade class are members of a school athletic team. Those students represent $\frac{2}{3}$ of the class. How many students are in the class?

   ____

4. While vacationing on Friday, Karl's family drove 58 miles in the morning and 12 miles in the afternoon. By the end of the day, they had driven 136 miles. How many miles had they driven that evening?

   ____

5. After depositing $19.75 in her savings account, Hua's account balance was more than $112.40. What inequality shows Hua's possible account balances before the deposit?

   ____

Fluency Check 10

Name ______________________

PATH to FLUENCY

1. $\begin{array}{r} 42.79 \\ +\ 6.53 \\ \hline \end{array}$

2. $\begin{array}{r} 28.34 \\ +\ 3.88 \\ \hline \end{array}$

3. $\begin{array}{r} 60.62 \\ +\ 7.18 \\ \hline \end{array}$

4. $\begin{array}{r} 36.17 \\ +\ 12.74 \\ \hline \end{array}$

5. $\begin{array}{r} 73.28 \\ +\ 23.05 \\ \hline \end{array}$

6. $\begin{array}{r} 54.56 \\ +\ 29.7 \\ \hline \end{array}$

7. $\begin{array}{r} 317.24 \\ +\ 38.7 \\ \hline \end{array}$

8. $\begin{array}{r} 409.07 \\ +\ 62.5 \\ \hline \end{array}$

9. $\begin{array}{r} 641.29 \\ +\ 73.9 \\ \hline \end{array}$

10. $\begin{array}{r} 890.05 \\ +\ 77.2 \\ \hline \end{array}$

11. $\begin{array}{r} \$7.62 \\ +\ \$0.59 \\ \hline \end{array}$

12. $\begin{array}{r} \$4.78 \\ +\ \$0.25 \\ \hline \end{array}$

13. $\begin{array}{r} \$6.09 \\ +\ \$0.33 \\ \hline \end{array}$

14. $\begin{array}{r} \$5.85 \\ +\ \$2.47 \\ \hline \end{array}$

15. $\begin{array}{r} \$4.77 \\ +\ \$2.82 \\ \hline \end{array}$

Name ____________________

VOCABULARY
composite number
prime number
prime factorization
factor tree

Factor Trees

Every **composite number** can be written as the product of **prime numbers**. This is called **prime factorization**.

You can use a **factor tree** to find the prime factorization of a number.

1 Discuss Sam and Zoe's factor trees for the number 90.

Sam's Factor Tree

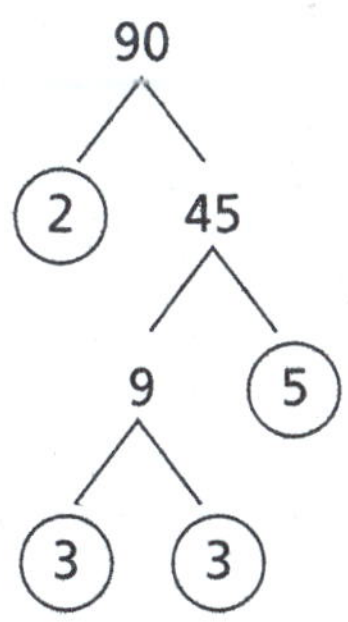

prime factorization of 90:
$2 \cdot 5 \cdot 3 \cdot 3$

Zoe's Factor Tree

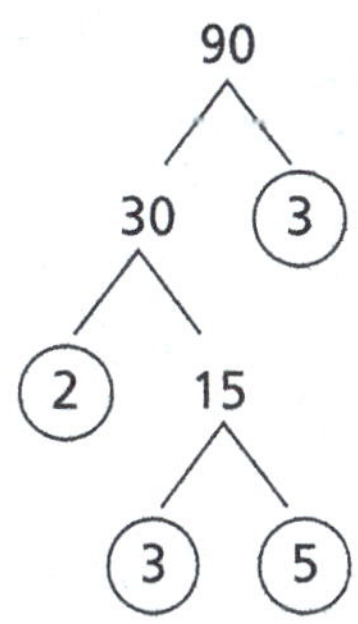

prime factorization of 90:
$3 \cdot 2 \cdot 3 \cdot 5$

Sam wrote the prime factorization of 90 as $2 \cdot 5 \cdot 3 \cdot 3$.
When the factors are listed in order, the prime factorization is $2 \cdot 3 \cdot 3 \cdot 5$.

Zoe wrote the prime factorization of 90 as $3 \cdot 2 \cdot 3 \cdot 5$.
When the factors are listed in order, the prime factorization is $2 \cdot 3 \cdot 3 \cdot 5$.

The prime factorization can also be written using exponents: $2 \cdot 3^2 \cdot 5$.

Both factor trees result in the same prime factorization for 90.

Complete each factor tree. Write the prime factorization, listing the factors in order. Use an exponent whenever possible.

2 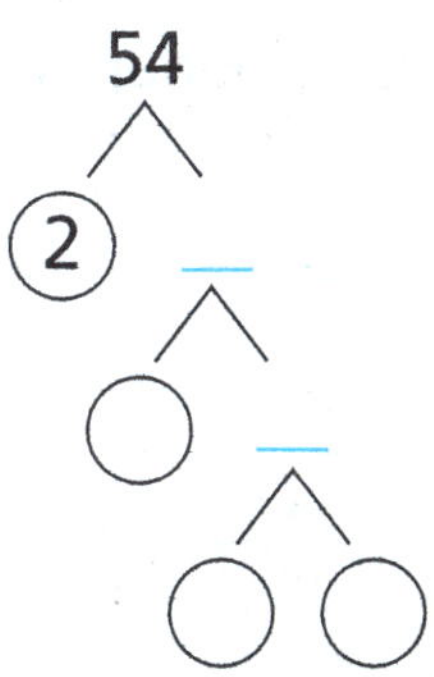

prime factorization of 54: ____________________

3 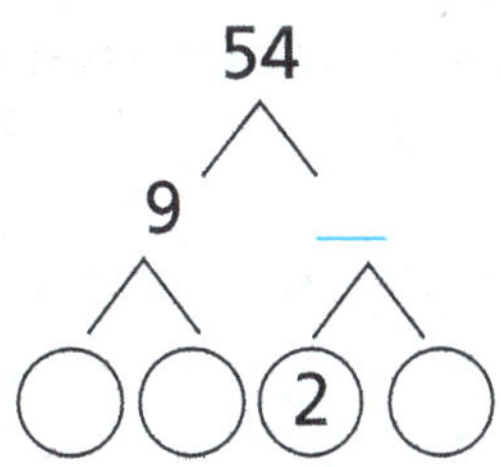

prime factorization of 54: ____________________

4 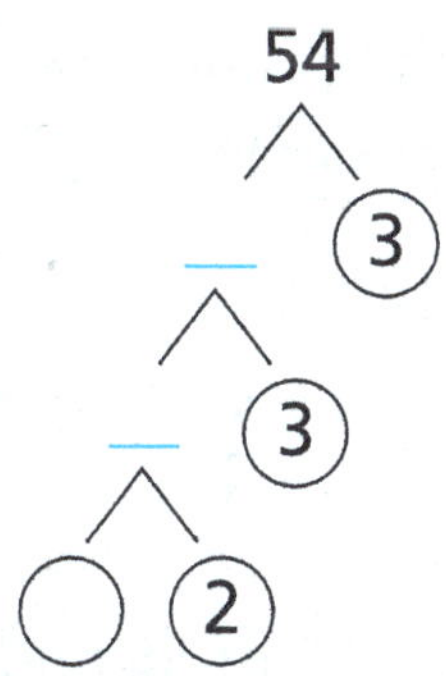

prime factorization of 54: ____________________

Name ________________________________

Prime Factorization and Greatest Common Factor

Solve.

14 Look at the example below and discuss how prime factorization can be used to find the greatest common factor of 24 and 60.

Method 1

$24 = 2 \cdot 2 \cdot 2 \cdot 3$

$60 = 2 \cdot 2 \cdot 3 \cdot 5$

Multiply the common factors:

$2 \cdot 2 \cdot 3 = 12$

Method 2

$24 = 2^3 \cdot 3$

$60 = 2^2 \cdot 3 \cdot 5$

Multiply the common factors:

$2^2 \cdot 3 = 12$

The greatest common factor (GCF) of 24 and 60 is 12.

Use prime factorization to find the GCF of each pair of numbers.

15 30 and 70

$30 = 2 \cdot 3 \cdot 5$

$70 = 2 \cdot 5 \cdot 7$

GCF of 30 and 70 is _______.

16 63 and 42

$63 = 3^2 \cdot 7$

$42 = 2 \cdot 3 \cdot 7$

GCF of 63 and 42 is _______.

Write the prime factorization for each number. Then find the GCF.

17 45 and 75

45 = ____________________

75 = ____________________

GCF of 45 and 75 is _______.

18 70 and 66

70 = ____________________

66 = ____________________

GCF of 70 and 66 is _______.

Write the prime factorization for each number. Then find the GCF. Use exponents when possible.

19 56 and 84

56 = ____________________

84 = ____________________

The GCF of 56 and 84 is _______.

20 360 and 150

360 = ____________________

150 = ____________________

The GCF of 360 and 150 is _______.

Name ______________________________

Prime Factorization and Least Common Multiple

27 Look at the example below and discuss how prime factorization can be used to find the least common multiple of 12 and 30.

$12 = 2 \cdot 2 \cdot 3$ $\qquad 2 \cdot 3 \cdot 2 \cdot 5 = 60$

$30 = 2 \cdot 3 \cdot 5$

The least common multiple (LCM) of 12 and 30 is 60.

Use prime factorization to find the LCM of each pair of numbers.

28 20 and 14

$20 = 2 \cdot 2 \cdot 5$

$14 = 2 \cdot 7$

LCM of 20 and 14 is ________.

29 105 and 45

$105 = 3 \cdot 5 \cdot 7$

$45 = 3 \cdot 3 \cdot 5$

LCM of 105 and 45 is ________.

Write the prime factorization for each number. Then find the LCM.

30 4 and 6

4 = ________

6 = ________

LCM of 4 and 6 is ________.

31 8 and 12

8 = ________

12 = ________

LCM of 8 and 12 is ________.

32 35 and 14

35 = ________

14 = ________

LCM of 35 and 14 is ________.

33 45 and 10

45 = ________

10 = ________

LCM of 45 and 10 is ________.

34 30 and 21

30 = ________

21 = ________

LCM of 30 and 21 is ________.

35 35 and 55

35 = ________

55 = ________

LCM of 35 and 55 is ________.

Name ____________________

What's the Error?

Dear Math Students,

I am trying to find the least common multiple of 20 and 75.

I started by finding the prime factorization of each number.

$20 = 2^2 \cdot 5$

$75 = 3 \cdot 5^2$

So I found the LCM to be $2 \cdot 3 \cdot 5 = 30$.

My friend said that the LCM of 20 and 75 has to be 75 or greater.
Can you help me?

Your friend,
Puzzled Penguin

16 Write a response to Puzzled Penguin.

17 What is the correct LCM of 20 and 75?

Check Understanding

Find the GCF and the LCM for 12 and 16.

GCF = ________ LCM = ________

Unit 5
Quick Quiz 5

Name ____________________

Write the prime factorization for each number. Use exponents whenever possible. Then find the greatest common factor and the least common multiple.

1. 32 and 40

   32 = ____________

   40 = ____________

   The greatest common factor of 32 and 40 is ____________.

   The least common multiple of 32 and 40 is ____________.

2. 25 and 45

   25 = ____________

   45 = ____________

   The greatest common factor of 25 and 45 is ____________.

   The least common multiple of 25 and 45 is ____________.

3. Tell if the greatest common factor or least common multiple is needed to solve the problem. Then solve the problem.

   A red line train arrives at a station every 12 minutes. A blue line train arrives at the station every 15 minutes. Both trains arrived at 1:00 PM. When will they arrive at the same time again?

   ____

4. Tarik wrote the greatest common factor of two numbers using exponents: $2^2 \cdot 3 \cdot 5$. Write two numbers (neither equal to $2^2 \cdot 3 \cdot 5$) that have this greatest common factor.

   ____________ and ____________

Fluency Check 11

Name ___________________________

PATH to FLUENCY

1. $\begin{array}{r} 22.08 \\ +\ 5.97 \\ \hline \end{array}$

2. $\begin{array}{r} 60.17 \\ +\ 9.83 \\ \hline \end{array}$

3. $\begin{array}{r} 75.44 \\ +\ 4.36 \\ \hline \end{array}$

4. $\begin{array}{r} 46.21 \\ +\ 11.88 \\ \hline \end{array}$

5. $\begin{array}{r} 51.29 \\ +\ 13.67 \\ \hline \end{array}$

6. $\begin{array}{r} 29.29 \\ +\ 17.9 \\ \hline \end{array}$

7. $\begin{array}{r} 151.07 \\ +\ 30.8 \\ \hline \end{array}$

8. $\begin{array}{r} 211.67 \\ +\ 97.7 \\ \hline \end{array}$

9. $\begin{array}{r} 663.12 \\ +\ 44.9 \\ \hline \end{array}$

10. $\begin{array}{r} 952.11 \\ +\ 77.3 \\ \hline \end{array}$

11. $\begin{array}{r} \$1.07 \\ +\ \$0.99 \\ \hline \end{array}$

12. $\begin{array}{r} \$4.48 \\ +\ \$0.51 \\ \hline \end{array}$

13. $\begin{array}{r} \$7.34 \\ +\ \$0.79 \\ \hline \end{array}$

14. $\begin{array}{r} \$6.09 \\ +\ \$3.12 \\ \hline \end{array}$

15. $\begin{array}{r} \$3.55 \\ +\ \$3.86 \\ \hline \end{array}$

Name ______________________

For Exercises 1 and 2, use the Order of Operations to simplify each expression.

1. $32 \div 4 \cdot (12 - 8) =$ ______

2. $40 - 2 \cdot 10 + 22 =$ ______

3. Simon wrote the equation $x - 2 = 7$.

   Choose Yes or No to indicate if each equation below has the same solution as $x - 2 = 7$.

   3a. $x - 2 = 7 + 2$ ○ Yes ○ No

   3b. $x - 2 + 2 = 7 + 2$ ○ Yes ○ No

   3c. $x - 2 + 2 = 7$ ○ Yes ○ No

   3d. $x - 2 - 7 = 7 - 7$ ○ Yes ○ No

4. The figure below shows a large rectangle that is made of two smaller rectangles. Use the Distributive Property to write two equivalent expressions that represent the area of the large rectangle. Choose from the numbers and symbols below the figure. Not all choices will be used.

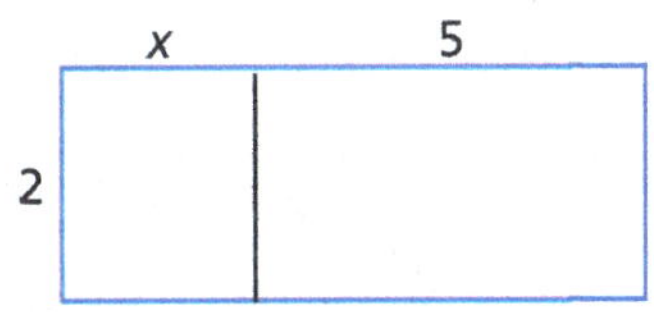

(x+5)	2	−	2x	(2 + 5)	10	+	10	5	=

4a. Represent the area as the sum of exactly two terms.

______

4b. Represent the area as a product in which one factor is a sum.

______

4c. Explain why the expressions are equivalent.

Name ____________________

5 Circle the terms in the expression. Explain how you know they are terms.

$$10a + a^2 - 9 \div 2$$

____

____

____

6 Identify each expression as either Represents or Does Not Represent the surface area of the cube.

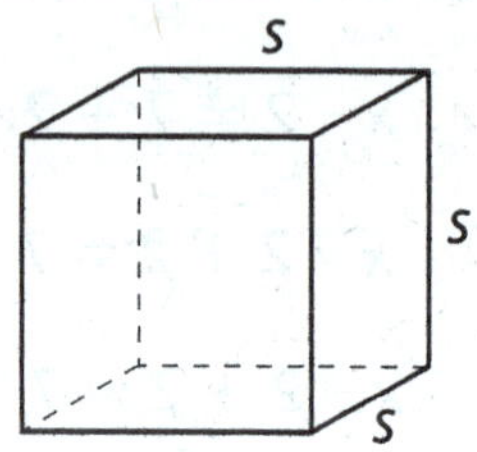

s^3 $6s$ $4s^4$ $6s^2$ $2(s^2) + 4(s^2)$ $s^2 + s^2 + s^2 + s^2 + s^2 + s^2$

Represents	Does Not Represent

For Exercises 7 and 8, solve for x. Show your work and use substitution to check your answer.

7 $x + 49 = 65$

$x =$ ____________________

Check: ____________________

8 $15x = 135$

$x =$ ____________________

Check: ____________________

9 Use the Order of Operations to simplify the expression.

$8x + 6^2 + 2(3x) - 36 =$ ____________________

For Exercises 10 and 11, evaluate each expression for $a = 3$ and $b = 5$.

Show your work.

10 $7 + b^2 - 3a$ ____________________

11 $10 + a \cdot (5 + b)$ ____________________

Name ______________________________

12 Select the expressions the model represents. Mark all that apply.

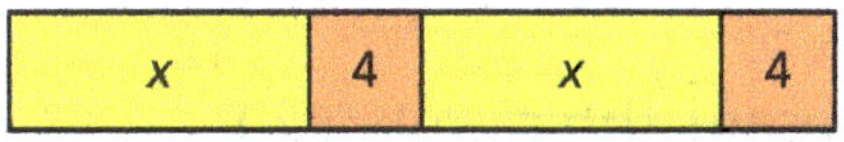

Ⓐ $x + 4 + x + 4$
Ⓑ $4x + 4x$
Ⓒ $2x + 4$
Ⓓ $2(x + 4)$
Ⓔ $2x + 8$
Ⓕ $8x$

13 Rita applied the Distributive Property to part of the expression $x + 4(x + 3)$ to write an equivalent expression. Select the equivalent expression. Mark all that apply.

Ⓐ $x + 4x + 3$
Ⓑ $5x + 12$
Ⓒ $6x + 12$
Ⓓ $x + 4x + 12$

For Exercises 14 and 15, use the given expressions to write each sum as a product by using the Distributive Property to pull out the greatest common factor (GCF).

Example: $24 + 32 = \underline{8 \cdot 3} + \underline{8 \cdot 4} = \underline{8(3 + 4)} = \underline{8 \cdot 7}$

14 $9 \cdot 13$ | $9 \cdot 6$ | $9(7 + 6)$ | $9 \cdot 7$

$63 + 54 =$ ________ $+$ ________ $=$ ________ $=$ ________

15 $6 \cdot 5$ | $6 \cdot 6$ | $6 \cdot 11$ | $6(6 + 5)$

$36 + 30 =$ ________ $+$ ________ $=$ ________ $=$ ________

For Exercises 16 and 17, write a solution for the inequality and equation.

16 $6x - 5 \geq 13$ ______________________________

17 $10 + x = 3x$ ______________________________

Name ______________________

18 Dwayne wants to earn at least $96 by selling cupcakes. He sells each cupcake for $4.

18a. Write and solve an inequality to represent the number of cupcakes Dwayne needs to sell to earn at least $96. Let *c* be the number of cupcakes.

____

18b. List three possible numbers of cupcakes Dwayne could sell.

____

19 Write the prime factorization using exponents for each number. Then find the greatest common factor and the least common multiple.

12 and 16

12 = ________
16 = ________

greatest common factor: ________
least common multiple: ________

20 Bennett's phone plan charges extra if he talks more than 300 minutes in a month. He was charged extra in May.

Part A

Let *m* be the number of minutes Bennett talked on his phone in May. Write an inequality for the possible values of *m*.

____

Part B

Graph the inequality on the number line.

Explain your graph.

Unit 5 Review/Test

Name ______________________

For Exercises 21 and 22, write an equation to represent the problem. Then use the equation to solve the problem.

21 Twelve of the students in science club went on a trip to the planetarium. If this is $\frac{3}{4}$ of the students in the club, what is the total number of students in the club? Let *c* be the number of students in science club.

______ students are in the club.

22 After Janelle deposited \$72.50 in her savings account, her balance was \$323. What was her balance before she made the deposit? Let *b* be the balance in dollars before Janelle made the deposit.

\$ ______

23 When the temperature is 20°F or less, Jenn wears her full-length parka.

Part A

Let *t* be the temperatures in degrees Fahrenheit for which Jenn wears her parka. Write an inequality for the possible values of *t*. ______

Part B

Graph the inequality on the number line.

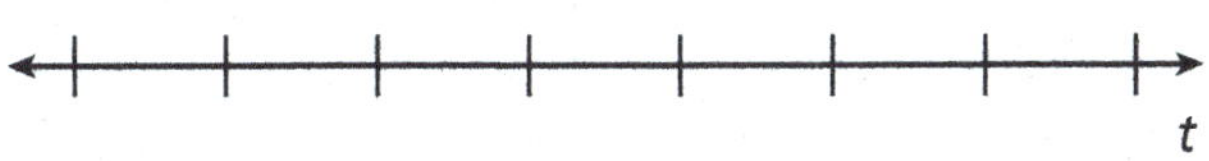

Explain your graph.

Unit 5 Review/Test

Name

24 An online sock store charges \$3 per pair of socks. They charge \$1 for shipping, no matter how many pairs you buy.

Part A

Complete the table.

Pairs Bought, n	Cost of Socks (\$)	Shipping Charge (\$)	Total cost (\$), c
1		1	
2	6	1	7
3		1	
4		1	
5		1	

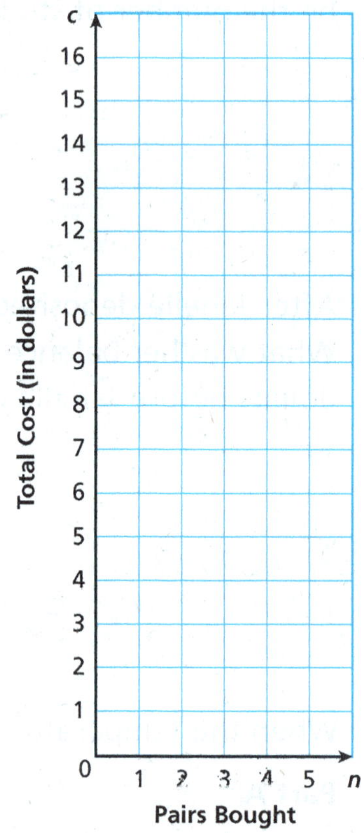

Part B

On the grid at the right, plot the values in the table for n and c. Draw a dashed line through the points. Only points that represent a whole number of pairs make sense, so a solid line should not be used.

Part C

Write an equation for the total cost c for n pairs.

$c =$ ______________________

Part D

- Explain how the cost for each pair of socks is represented in the graph and in the equation.

- Explain how the shipping charge is represented in the graph and in the equation.

Name ________________________________

Expressions and Equations

Remember, simplifying expressions and solving equations involves following the Order of Operations.

1. Explain the difference between an *expression* and an *equation*.

2. Evaluate the expression $5(s + 2) - s^2$ when $s = 4$.
Show your work.

3. Write your own expression that contains the variable n and includes two terms.

____

Write a value for n. Then evaluate your expression.
Show your work.

4. Write your own expression that contains the variable n and includes

- an exponent and
- addition, subtraction, *and* division.

____

Write a value for n. Then evaluate your expression.
Show your work.

Name ______________________________

5 Is $t = 3$ a solution of the equation $5t - 2 = 13$? Show or explain how you know.

6 Solve the equation $2x = 15 - 3$ for x. Show or explain how you got your answer.

7 Write your own equation that contains the variable n and includes two operations.

Show the steps for solving your equation.

8 Write an equation that contains the variable n and

- includes a number times a sum or difference,
- includes an exponent *and* parentheses,
- includes addition *and* subtraction, and
- has a solution of 3.

Show or explain how you know that the solution of your equation is $n = 3$.

An **angle** is formed by two rays with a common endpoint, called the **vertex of the angle.**

Adjacent angles have the same vertex and a common ray and do not overlap.

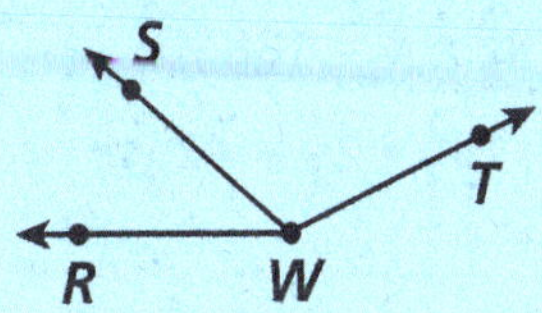

$\angle RWS$ and $\angle TWS$ are adjacent angles.

Vertical angles are opposite angles formed by intersecting lines.

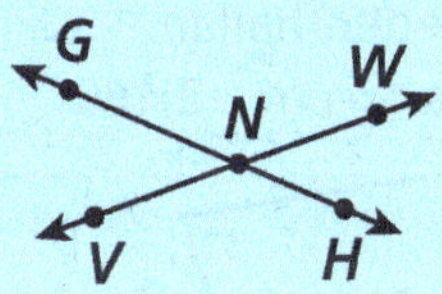

$\angle GNV$ and $\angle WNH$ are vertical angles.
$\angle GNW$ and $\angle VNH$ are vertical angles.

Two angles are **complementary** if the sum of their measures is 90°.

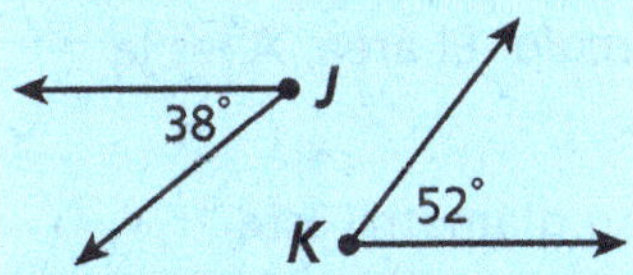

$\angle J$ and $\angle K$ are complementary angles.

Two angles are **supplementary** if the sum of their measures is 180°.

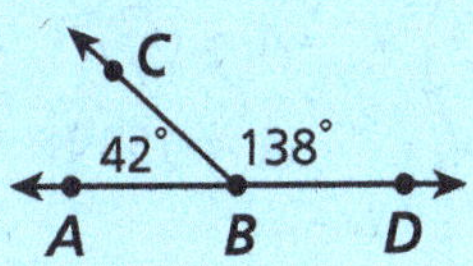

$\angle ABC$ and $\angle CBD$ are supplementary angles.

Dear Family:

In this unit, students are continuing their study of measurement and geometry. They will focus on properties of both solid and plane figures.

Volume of Rectangular Prisms

Volume is the amount of space occupied by a solid figure. For a rectangular prism, the volume V can be found using the formula $V = Bh$. In this formula, B is the area of the rectangular base (length times width, or lw), and h is the height of the prism.

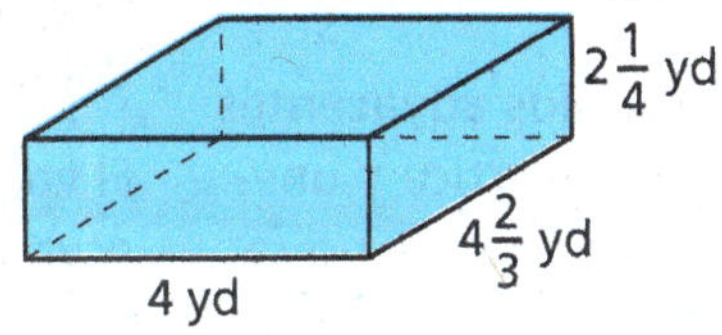

$B = lw = 4\frac{2}{3} \bullet 4 = 18\frac{2}{3}\text{ yd}^2$

$V = Bh = 18\frac{2}{3} \bullet 2\frac{1}{4} = 42\text{ yd}^3$

Angles

Students will study the angle relationships that are shown at the left, and then explore the following facts about the angles of polygons.

The sum of the measures of the interior angles of a triangle is 180°.

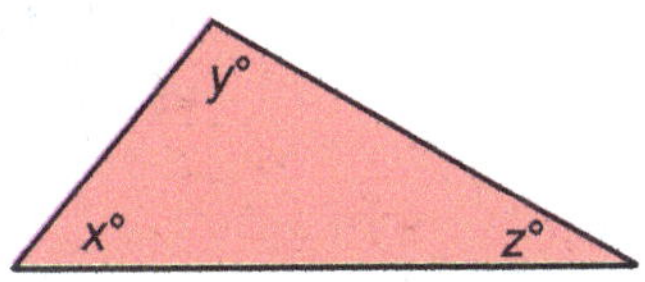

$x° + y° + z° = 180°$

The sum S of the measures of the interior angles of a polygon with n sides can be found using the formula $S = (n - 2)180°$.

$S = p° + q° + r° + s° + t° = (5 - 2)180° = 540°$

Circles

The longest distance across a circle is its **diameter,** d. The **radius,** r, is the distance from the center to any point on a circle. The **circumference,** C, is the distance around a circle. The **area,** A, is the amount of surface a circle encloses.

The ratio of the circumference of a circle to its diameter is represented by the Greek letter **pi** (written π), which is approximated as 3.14 or $\frac{22}{7}$.

The formula $C = \pi d$ can be used to find the circumference of a circle.

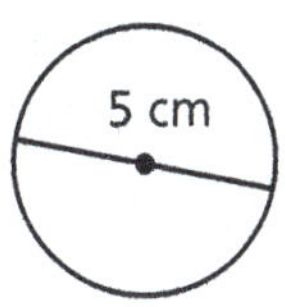

$C = \pi d$

$C \approx (3.14)5$

$C \approx 15.7\text{ cm}$

The formula $A = \pi r^2$ can be used to find the area of a circle.

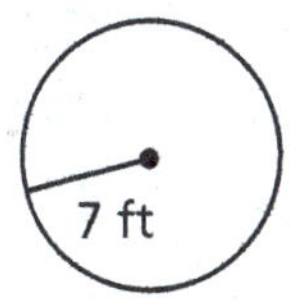

$A = \pi r^2$

$A \approx (\frac{22}{7})7^2$

$A \approx 154\text{ ft}^2$

Sincerely,
Your child's teacher

Un **ángulo** está formado por dos rayos con un extremo común llamado **vértice del ángulo**.

Los **ángulos adyacentes** tienen el vértice y un rayo en común y no se superponen.

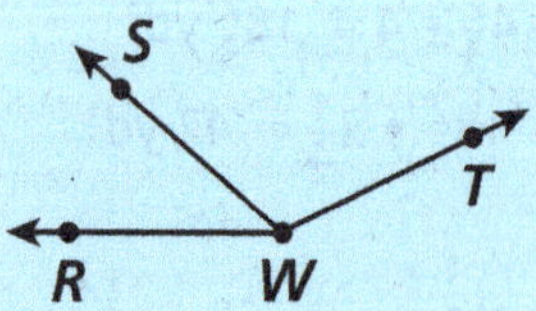

$\angle RWS$ y $\angle TWS$ son ángulos adyacentes.

Los **ángulos verticales** son ángulos opuestos formados por líneas secantes.

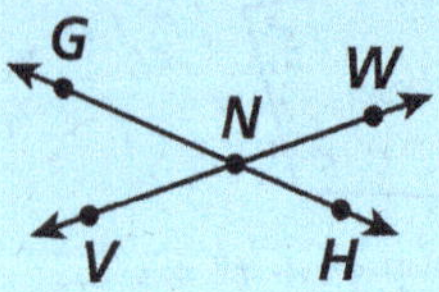

$\angle GNV$ y $\angle WNH$ son ángulos verticales.
$\angle GNW$ y $\angle VNH$ son ángulos verticales.

Dos ángulos son **complementarios** si la suma de sus medidas es 90°.

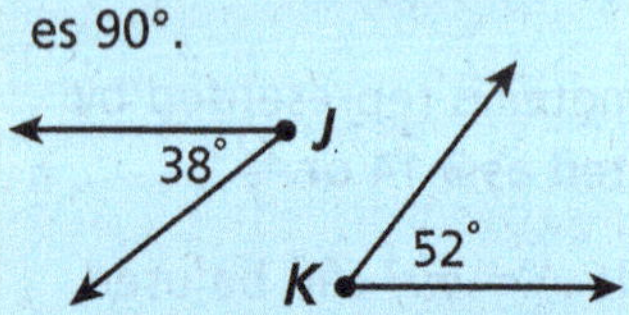

$\angle J$ y $\angle K$ son ángulos complementarios.

Dos ángulos son **suplementarios** si la suma de sus medidas es 180°.

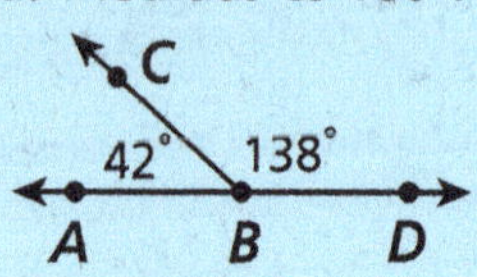

$\angle ABC$ y $\angle CBD$ son ángulos suplementarios.

Estimada familia:

En esta unidad, los estudiantes continúan su estudio de la medición y geometría. Se centrarán en las propiedades de los cuerpos geométricos y figuras planas.

Volumen de prismas rectangulares

El **volumen** es la cantidad de espacio que ocupa un cuerpo geométrico. Para el prisma rectangular, el volumen V se puede hallar usando la fórmula $V = Bh$. En esta fórmula, B es el área de la base rectangular (longitud por ancho, o la), y h es la altura del prisma.

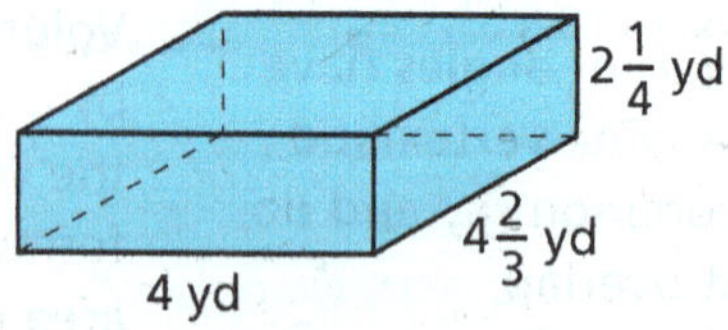

$B = la = 4\frac{2}{3} \cdot 4 = 18\frac{2}{3}\ \text{yd}^2$

$V = Bh = 18\frac{2}{3} \cdot 2\frac{1}{4} = 42\ \text{yd}^3$

Ángulos

Los estudiantes estudiarán las relaciones entre ángulos que se muestran a la izquierda y luego explorarán los siguientes datos sobre los ángulos de polígonos.

La suma de las medidas de los ángulos interiores de un triángulo es 180°.

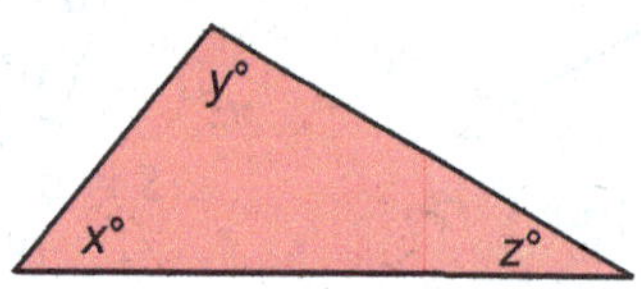

$x° + y° + z° = 180°$

La suma S de las medidas de los ángulos interiores de un polígono con lados n se pueden hallar usando la fórmula $S = (n - 2)180°$.

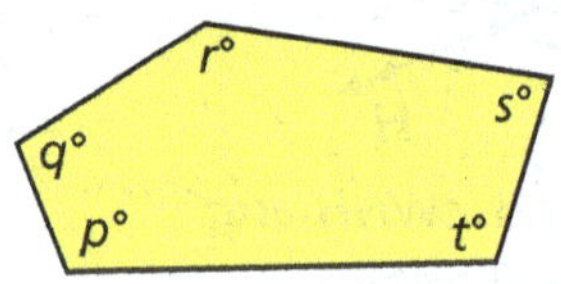

$S = p° + q° + r° + s° + t° = (5 - 2)180° = 540°$

Círculos

La distancia más larga a través de un círculo es su **diámetro**, d. El **radio**, r, es la distancia desde el centro hasta cualquier punto en un círculo. La **circunferencia**, C, es la distancia alrededor de un círculo. El **area**, A, es la cantidad de superficie que rodea un círculo.

The relación entre la circunferencia de un círculo y su diámetro está representada por la letra griega **pi** (escrita π), la cual se aproxima a 3.14 o $\frac{22}{7}$.

La fórmula $C = \pi d$ se puede usar para hallar la circunferencia de un círculo.

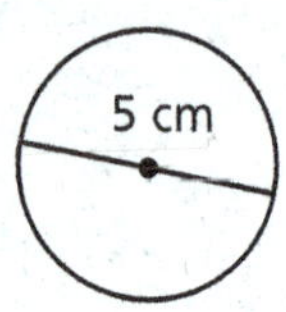

$C = \pi d$

$C \approx (3.14)5$

$C \approx 15.7$ cm

La fórmula $A = \pi r^2$ se puede usar para hallar el área de un círculo.

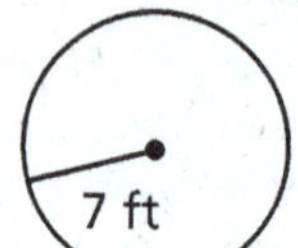

$A = \pi r^2$

$A \approx (\frac{22}{7})7^2$

$A \approx 154\ \text{ft}^2$

Atentamente,
El maestro de su hijo

acute angle	center of a circle
adjacent angles	circumference
angle	complementary angles

The point that is the same distance from all points of the circle.

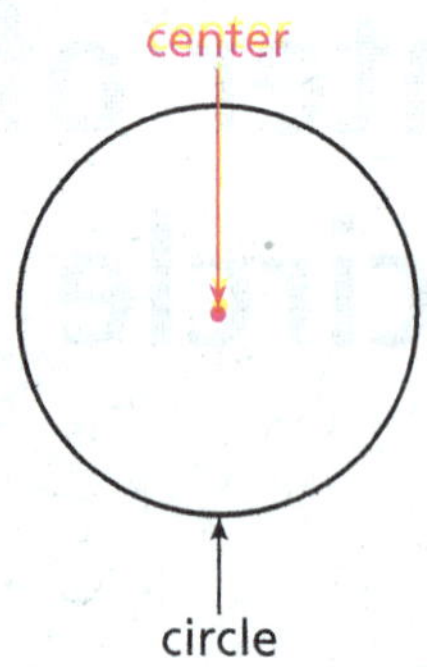

An angle that measures less than 90°.

Examples:

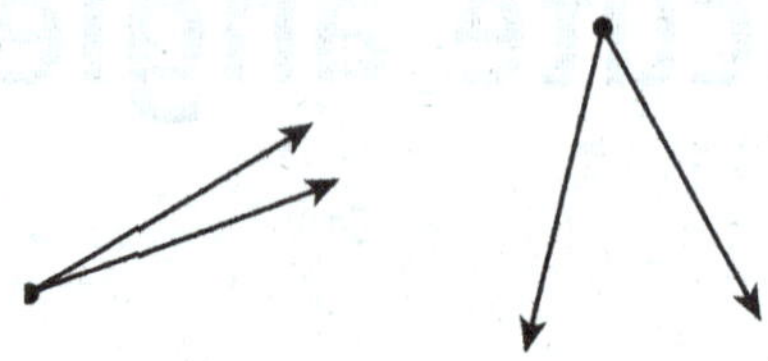

The distance around a circle.

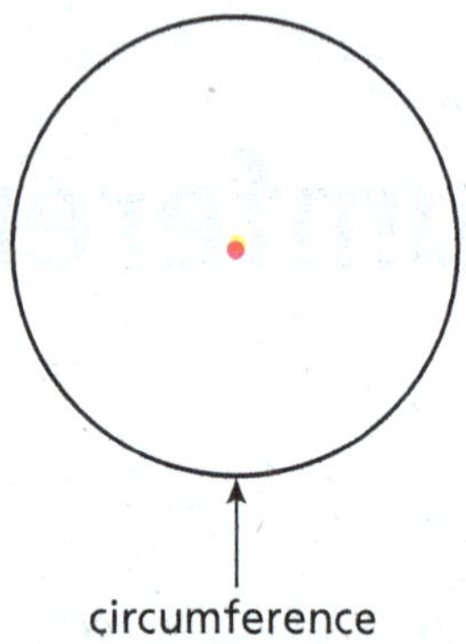

Two angles that have the same vertex and a common ray and do not overlap.

Example:

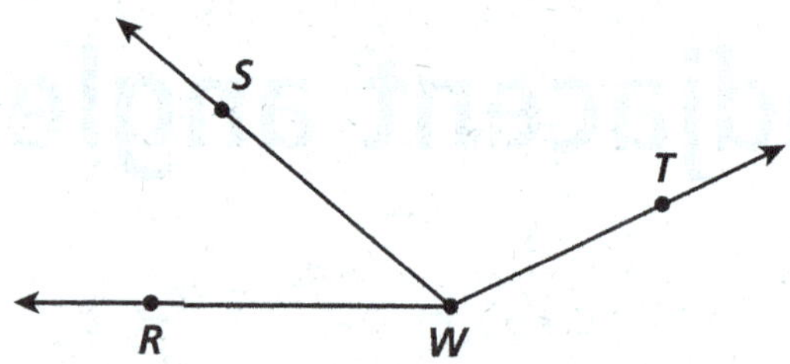

$\angle RWS$ and $\angle SWT$ are adjacent angles.

Two angles for which the sum of their measures is 90°.

Example:

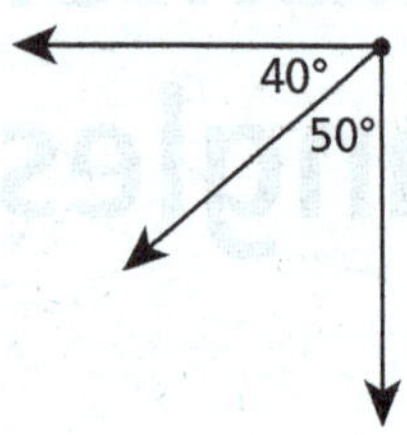

A figure formed by two rays that have the same endpoint.

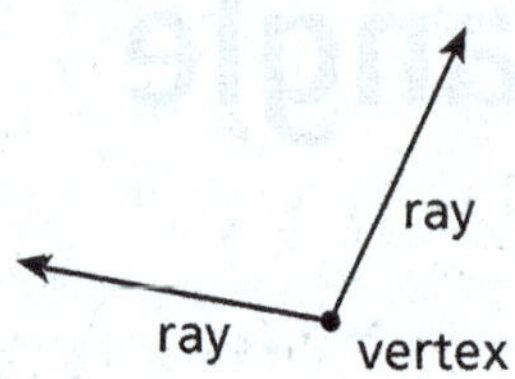

cone	density
cubic unit (unit^3)	diagonal of a polygon
cylinder	diagonal of a quadrilateral

The ratio of the mass of an item to its volume.

density $= \frac{\text{mass}}{\text{volume}}$

A three-dimensional figure that has one base, which is a circle.

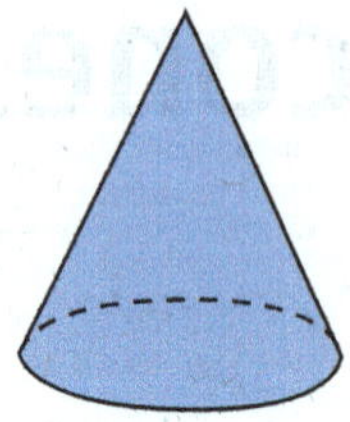

cone

A line segment that connects two vertices of a polygon but is not a side.

Example:

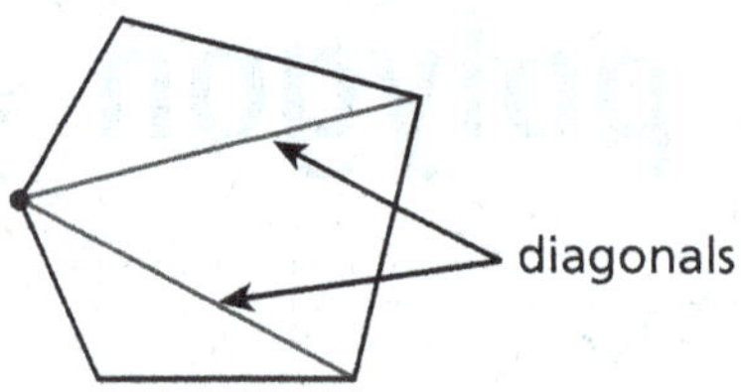

A unit for measuring volume. It is the volume of a cube with each edge 1 unit long.

Example:

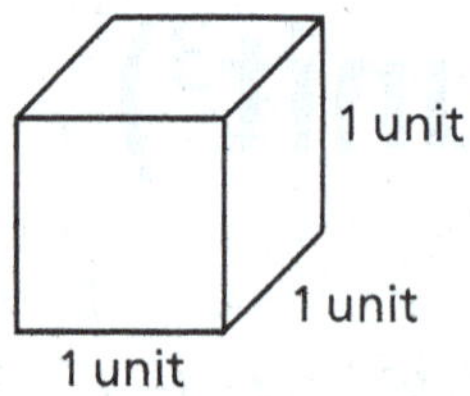

A line segment that connects opposite vertices.

Example:

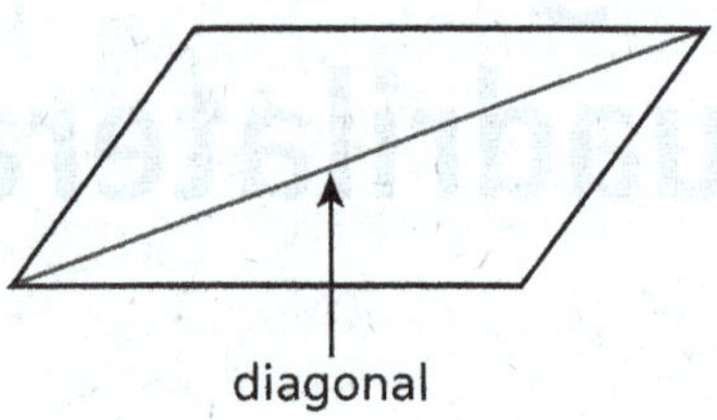

A three-dimensional figure that has two parallel bases that are circles.

Example:

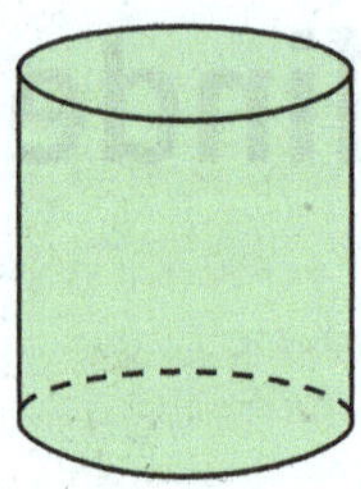

cylinder

diameter	intersecting lines
exterior angle	irrational number
interior angle	obtuse angle

Two lines that meet at a point.

Examples:

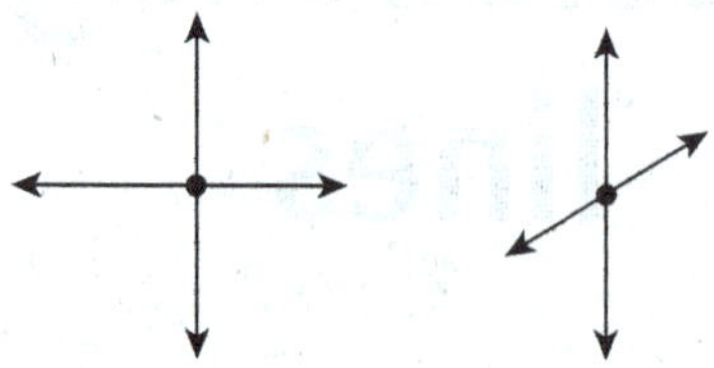

The distance across a circle through its center.

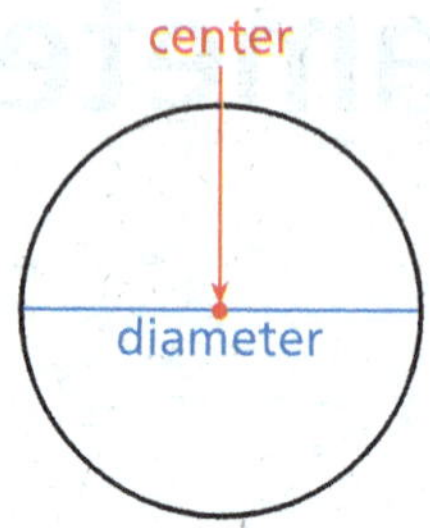

A number that cannot be written as the ratio of two integers.

An angle formed by extending one side of a polygon.

Example:

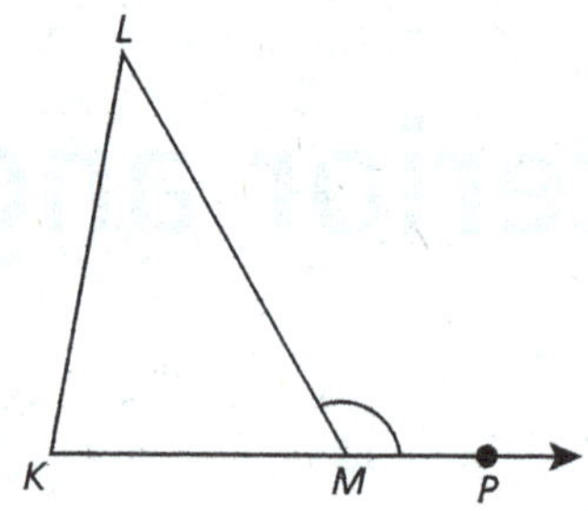

$\angle LMP$ is an exterior angle of triangle KLM.

An angle that measures more than 90° but less than 180°.

Examples:

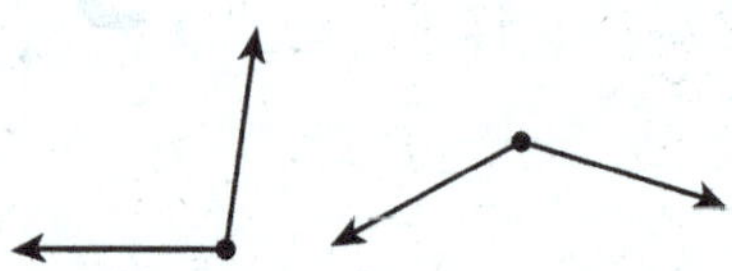

An angle inside a polygon.

Example:

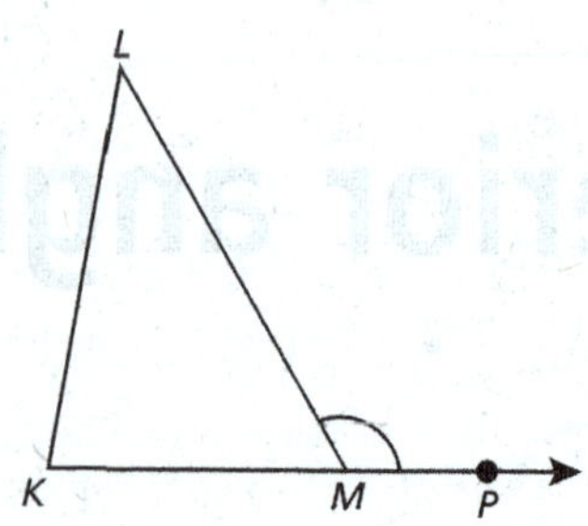

$\angle K$, $\angle L$, and $\angle LMK$ are interior angles.

pi (π)	ray
protractor	right angle
radius	straight angle

A part of a line that starts at one point and goes on forever. The point is called the endpoint of the ray.

Example:

The value of the ratio of a circle's circumference to its diameter. Its approximate value is 3.14 or $\frac{22}{7}$.

An angle that measures 90°.

Examples:

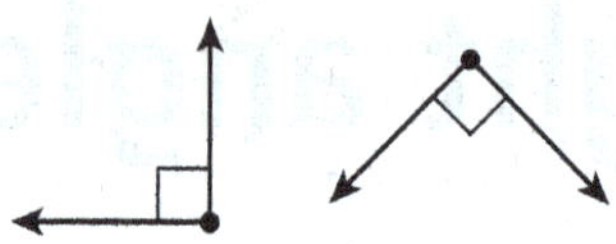

A tool that is used to measure angles.

An angle that measures 180°. It forms a line.

Examples:

The distance from the center of a circle to any point on the circle. The radius of a circle is one half its diameter.

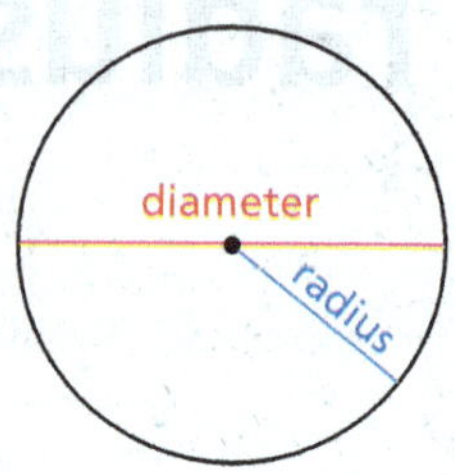

supplementary angles	vertical angles
unit cube	volume
vertex of an angle	

The opposite angles formed by intersecting lines. Vertical angles have the same measure.

Example:

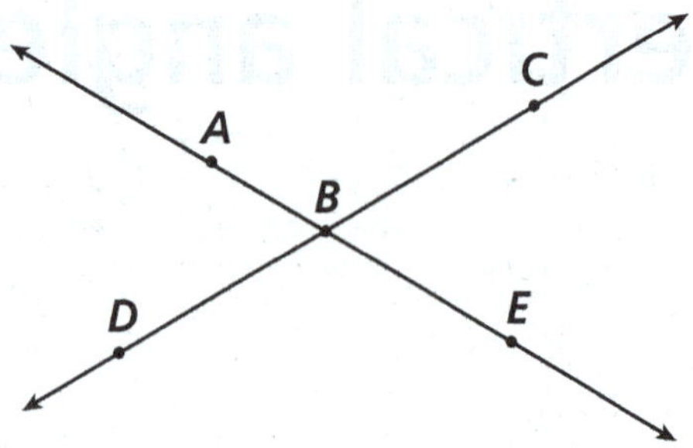

Two angles for which the sum of their measures is 180°.

Example:

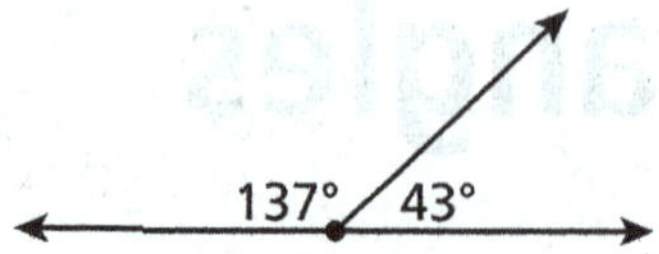

The amount of space occupied by a solid figure. Volume is measured in cubic units.

A cube with one-unit edges.

The shared endpoint of the two rays that form an angle.

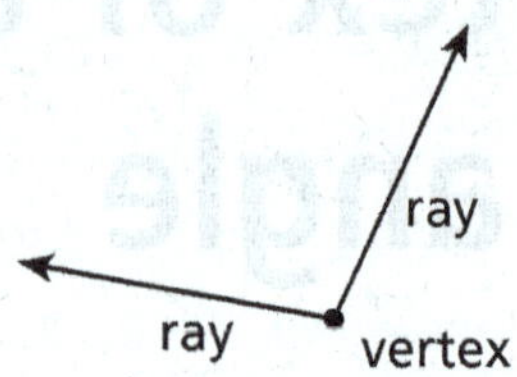

Name ______________________________

Nets for Cubic Units and a Rectangular Prism

Cut out the nets and form the solid figure.

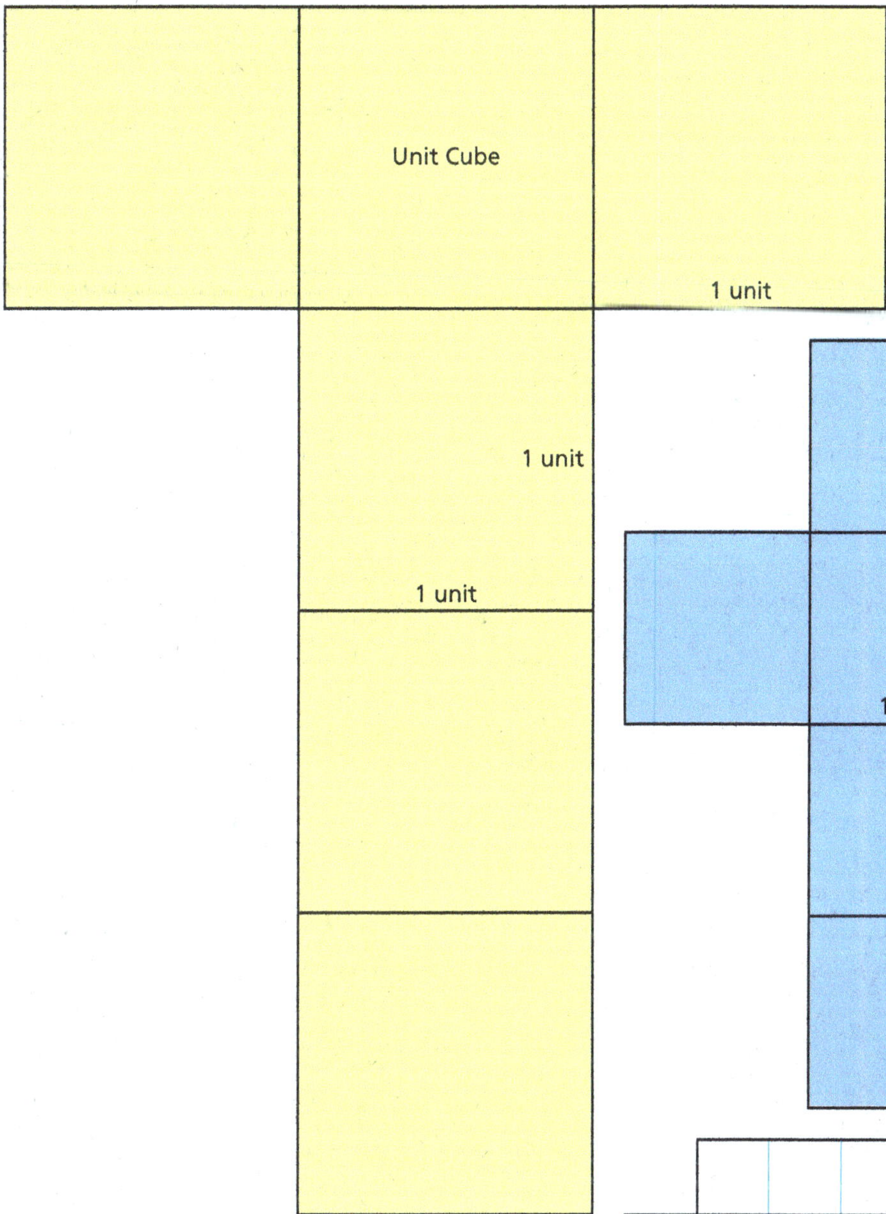

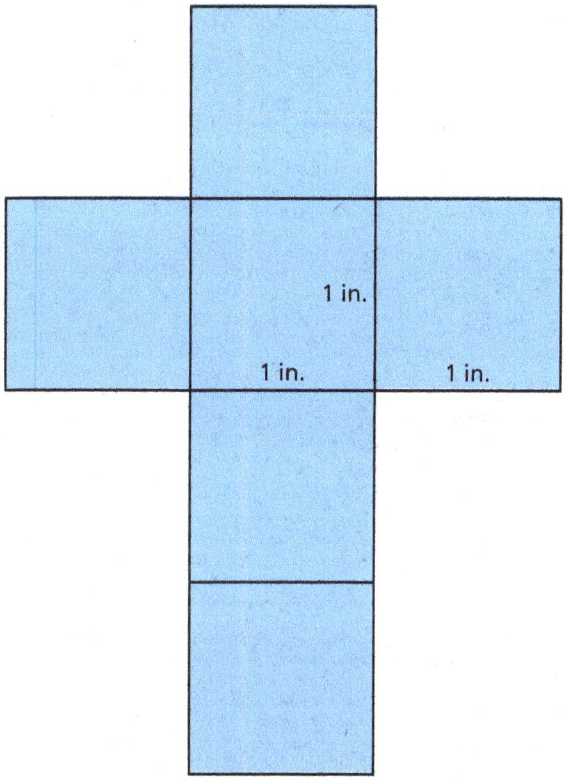

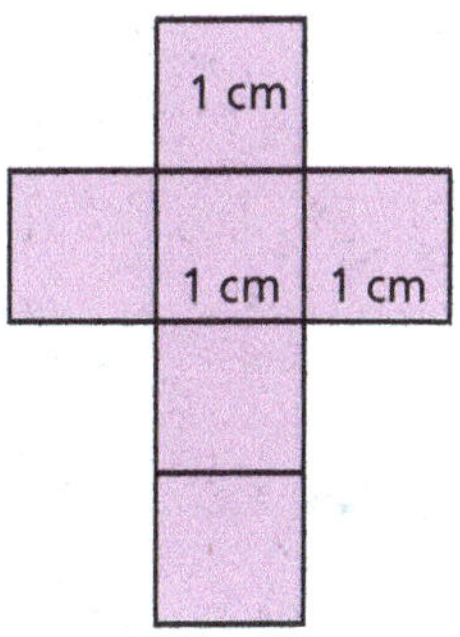

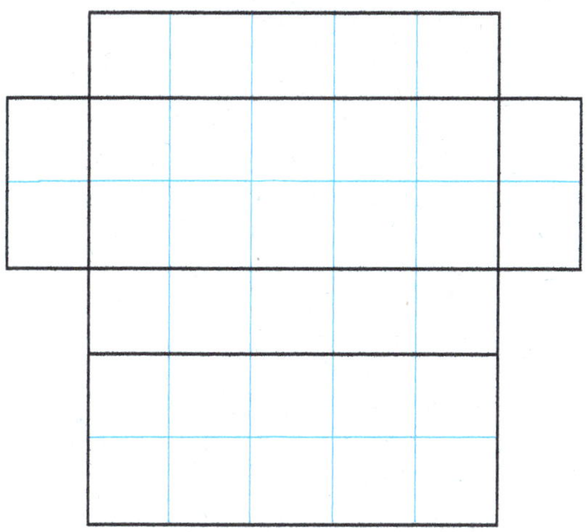

Name ___________________________________

Nets for Cubic Units and a Rectangular Prism (continued)

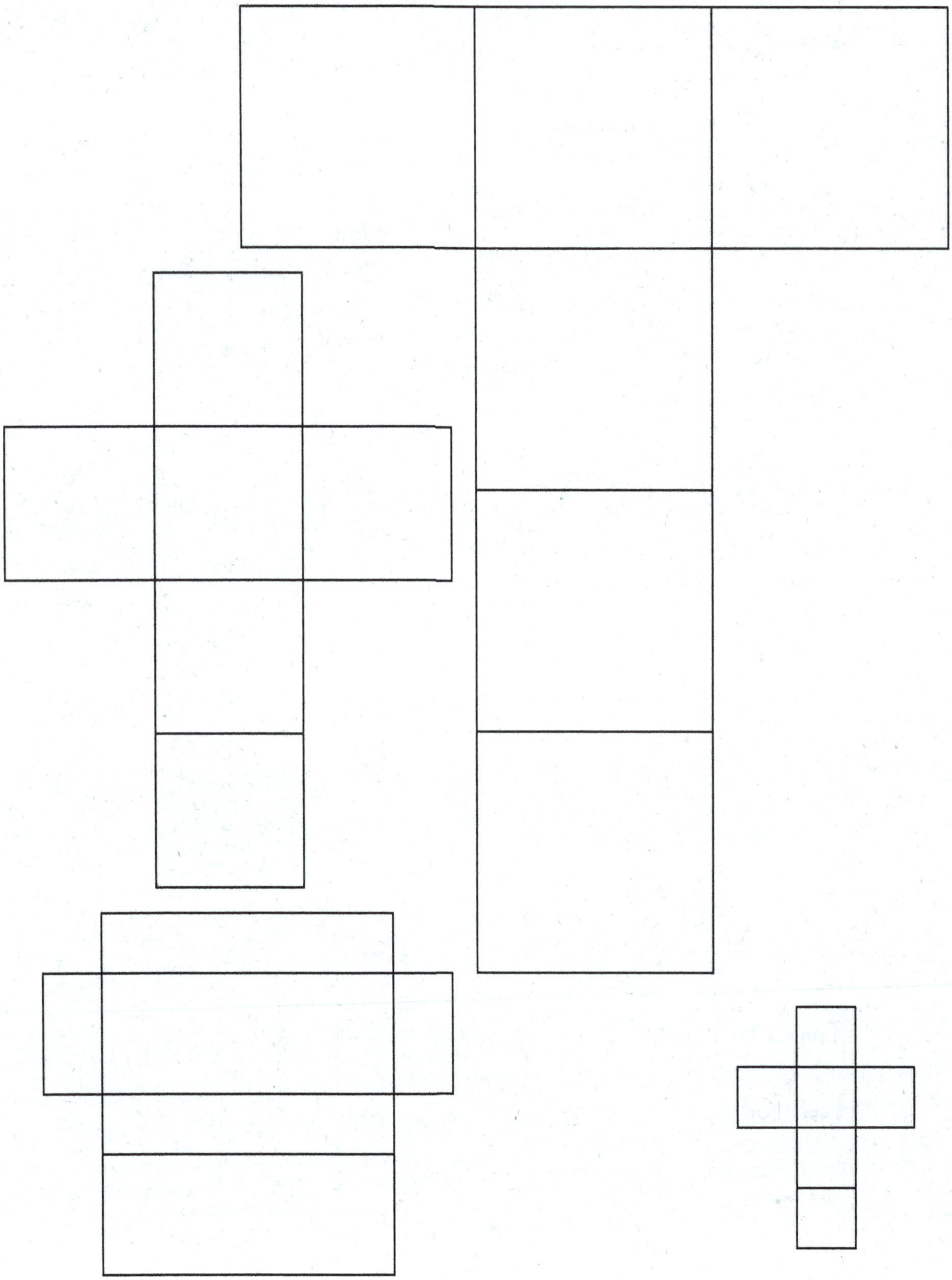

Name ______________________

Cubic Units

VOCABULARY
volume
unit cube
cubic unit (unit³)

The **volume** of a solid figure is the amount of space occupied by the figure. Volume is measured in cubic units.

1. How can you measure the amount of space each of these rectangular prisms takes up? How much space is inside each of the rectangular prisms? How many unit cubes does it take to fill the rectangular prism?

A **unit cube** is a cube with each edge 1 unit long. The volume of a unit cube is 1 cubic unit. It can be written 1 **cubic unit** or 1 unit^3.

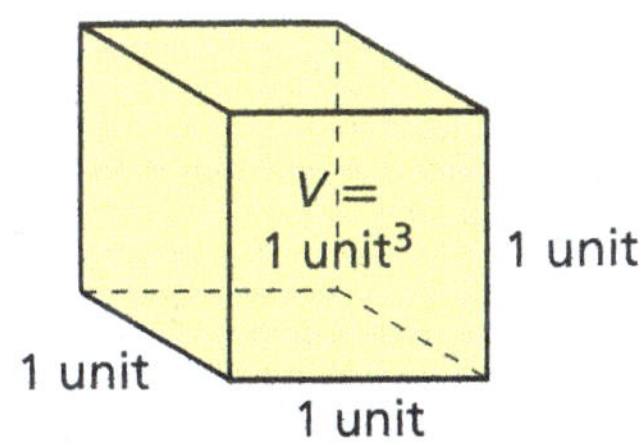

2. Label the length, width, and height of the centimeter cube on the right. Write the volume of a centimeter cube in two ways.

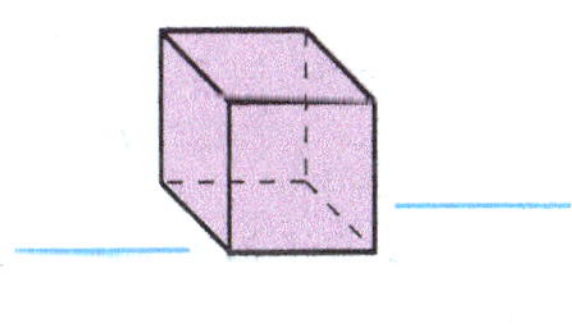

Write the volume of the cube in two ways.

3. inch cube
4. meter cube
5. foot cube
6. yard cube

Name ______________________________

What's the Error?

Dear Math Students,

My assignment was to make a prism with a volume of 4 cm^3. I made the prism at the right. My friend says I have too many cubes in the prism. Who is right? Explain.

Your friend,
Puzzled Penguin

17 Write a response to the Puzzled Penguin.

____

____

____

Dear Math Students,

I found the volume of a cube that is 2 cm by 2 cm by 2 cm to be 6 cm^3, but when I built the cube out of centimeter cubes it took 8 cubes and not 6. What did I do wrong?

Your friend,
Puzzled Penguin

18 Write a response to the Puzzled Penguin.

____

____

____

Name ______________________________

VOCABULARY
density

Relate Mass, Volume, and Density

The ratio of the mass of an item to its volume is called **density**.

density $= \frac{\text{mass}}{\text{volume}}$ $d = \frac{m}{V}$ d = density m = mass V = volume

Density is the mass of one unit of volume.

The table shows the mass, volume, and densities of several pieces of solid metal. Complete the table and use it to solve Problems 31–32.

Metal	Mass (g)	Volume (cm^3)	Density ($\frac{g}{cm^3}$)
27 Lead	1,130 g	100 cm^3	
28 Iron	158 g	20 cm^3	
29 Aluminum	121.5 g		2.7 $\frac{g}{cm^3}$
30 Gold		20 cm^3	19.3 $\frac{g}{cm^3}$

31 Suppose you have a cubic centimeter of lead and a cubic centimeter of aluminum. Which has the greater mass? Why?

____

____

32 Suppose you have a piece of gold and a piece of iron. Each piece has the same mass. Which piece has the greater volume? Why?

____

____

Solve.

33 What is the volume of a piece of silver with a mass of 5,250 grams and a density of 10.5 grams per cubic centimeter?

____

34 What is the mass of a piece of copper with a volume of 50 cubic centimeters and a density of 8.9 grams per cubic centimeter?

____

Name ______________________________

Nets for Part of a Unit Cube

Cut out the nets and form the solid figures.

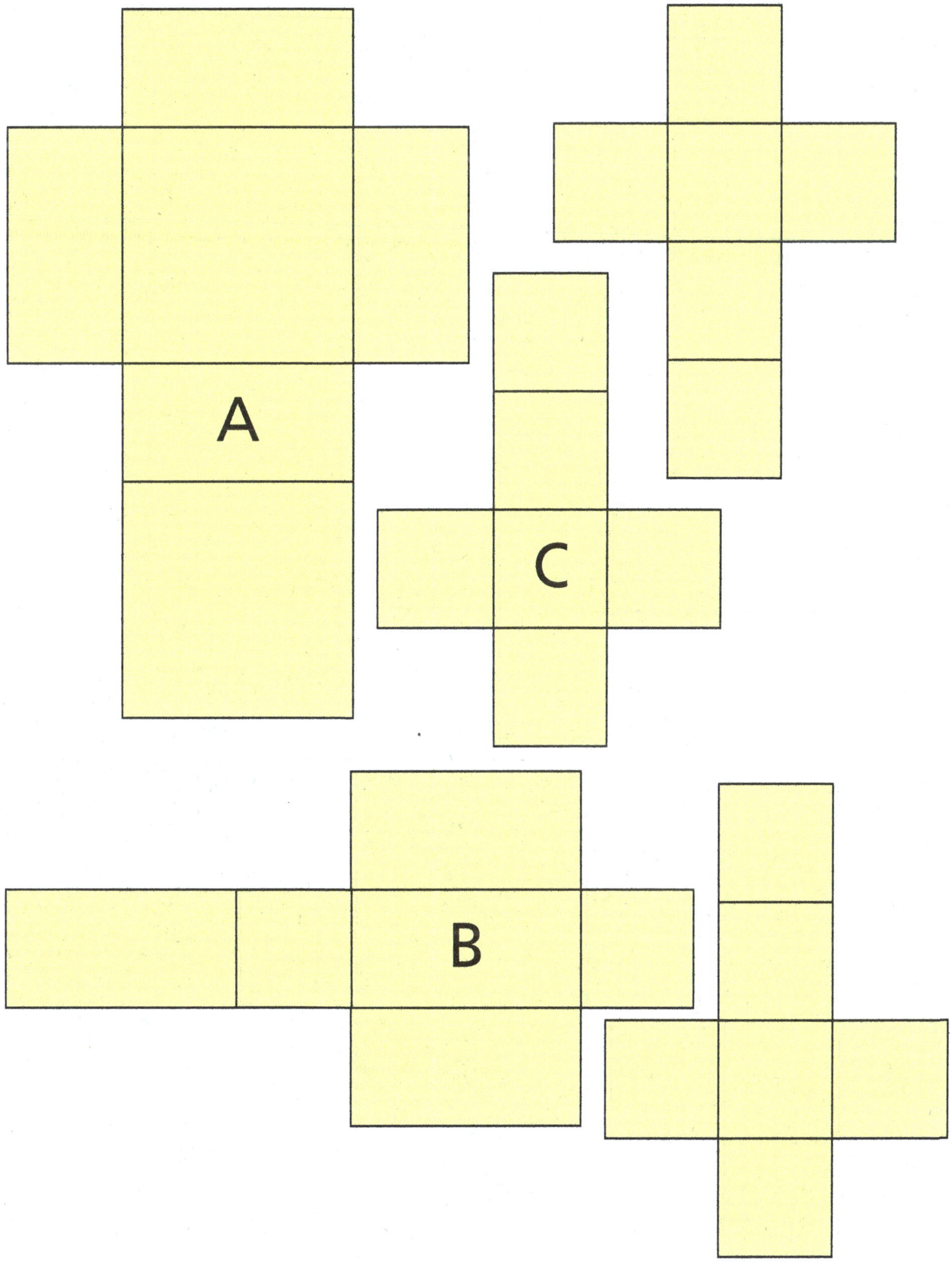

Name ____________________

Nets for Part of a Unit Cube (continued)

Name ______________________

Rectangular Prisms with Volumes Less Than 1 Cubic Unit

Place the cubes on your desk in order from greatest volume to least volume as shown below.

Unit Cube	Prism A	Prism B	Prism C
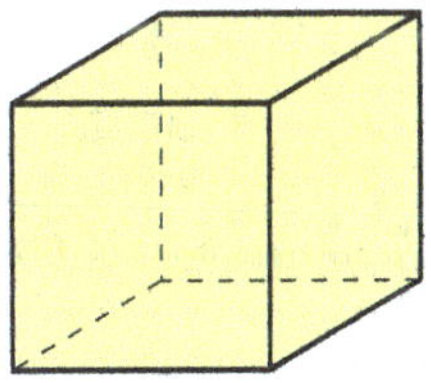	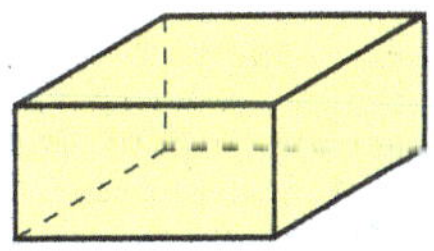	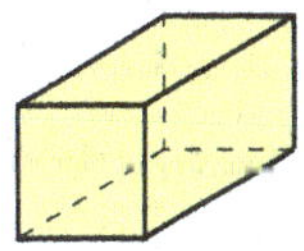	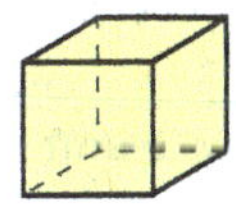
1 cubic unit	$\frac{1}{2}$ cubic unit	______ of Prism A	______ of Prism B

1 How many of each of these prisms does it take to make the Unit Cube?

Prism A: ________ Prism B: ________ Prism C: ________

2 What is the volume of each prism?

Prism A

$V =$ ________

Prism B

$V =$ ________

Prism C

$V =$ ________

Some students found the volume of Prism B by multiplying.

	Volume of Prism B	Volume of Prism C
Terence	$\frac{1}{2}$ of $\frac{1}{2}$ of a unit cube or $\frac{1}{4}$ unit³.	
Serena	$\frac{1}{2} \cdot \frac{1}{2}$ of a cubic unit or $\frac{1}{4}$ unit³.	
Emma	It takes $\frac{1}{4}$ of a unit cube or $\frac{1}{4}$ unit³ to make Prism B.	

3 Why are all 3 descriptions correct?

____

____

____

4 Complete the chart to show how Terence, Serena, and Emma would describe the volume of Prism C.

Name ______________________________

Calculate Volume Less Than 1 Cubic Unit

Complete the table.

	Prism	length (l)	width (w)	height (h)	length × width × height (lwh)	$lwh = V$
5	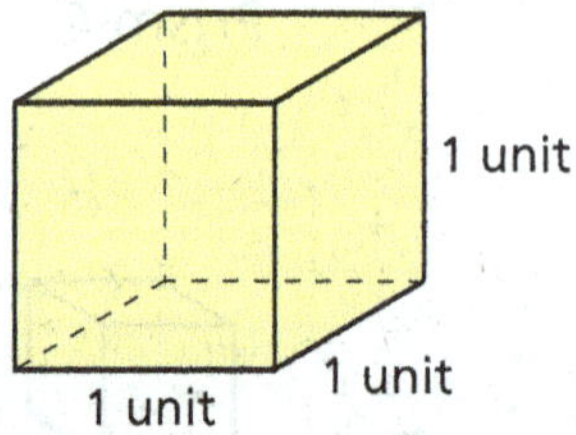	1 unit	1 unit	1 unit	1 • 1 • 1	1 • 1 • 1 = 1 or 1 unit³
6	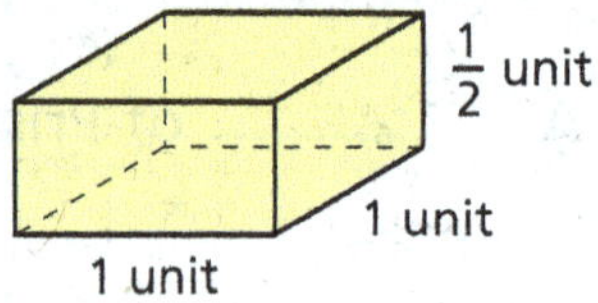					
7	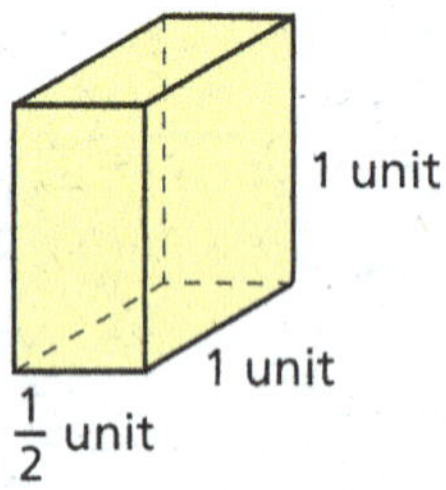					
8	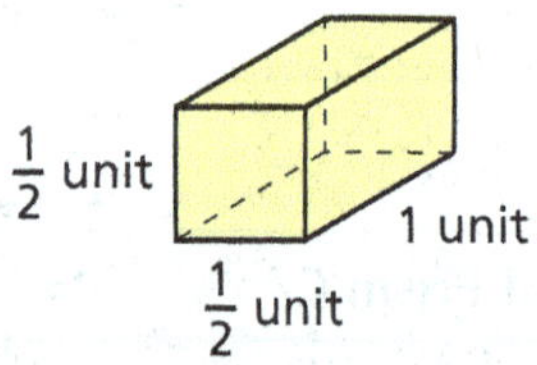					
9	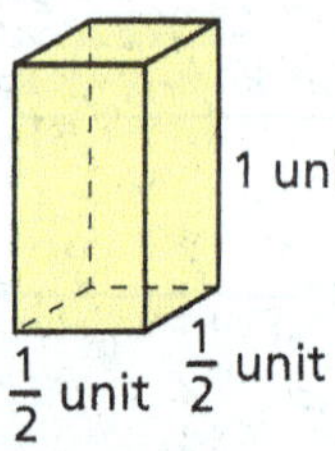					
10	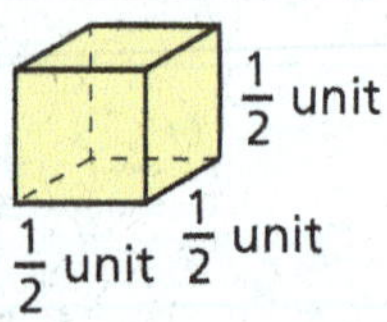					

11 How is the volume of a rectangular prism related to the length, width, and height of the prism? ______________________________

____

Name ______________________________

Find Volume by Packing with Unit Cubes

Solve. If the answer is equal to or greater than 1, write the answer as a whole or mixed number.

12 Model a prism with the base to the right and a height of $\frac{1}{2}$ unit. Use your cubes with $\frac{1}{2}$-unit edge lengths as a unit cube.

13 How many cubes with $\frac{1}{2}$-unit edge lengths did it take to make the prism? ____________

14 What equation can you write to show the volume of 9 of these cubes?

____

15 What other equation can you write to describe the volume of the $\frac{3}{2}$ unit by $\frac{3}{2}$ unit by $\frac{1}{2}$ unit prism?

____

16 Suppose you built a prism on a square base of $\frac{4}{3}$ unit by $\frac{4}{3}$ unit with a height of $\frac{1}{3}$ unit. If you use a cube with $\frac{1}{3}$-unit edge lengths as a unit cube, how many cubes would it take to form the prism?

____

17 What two equations could you write to show the volume of the $\frac{4}{3}$ unit by $\frac{4}{3}$ unit by $\frac{1}{3}$ unit prism?

____

____

18 What equation could you write to show the volume of a $\frac{1}{n}$ by $\frac{1}{n}$ by $\frac{1}{n}$ cube?

____

Name ________________________________

Prism Layers

Cut out the nets and form the solid figures.

Name ______________________________

Prism Layers (continued)

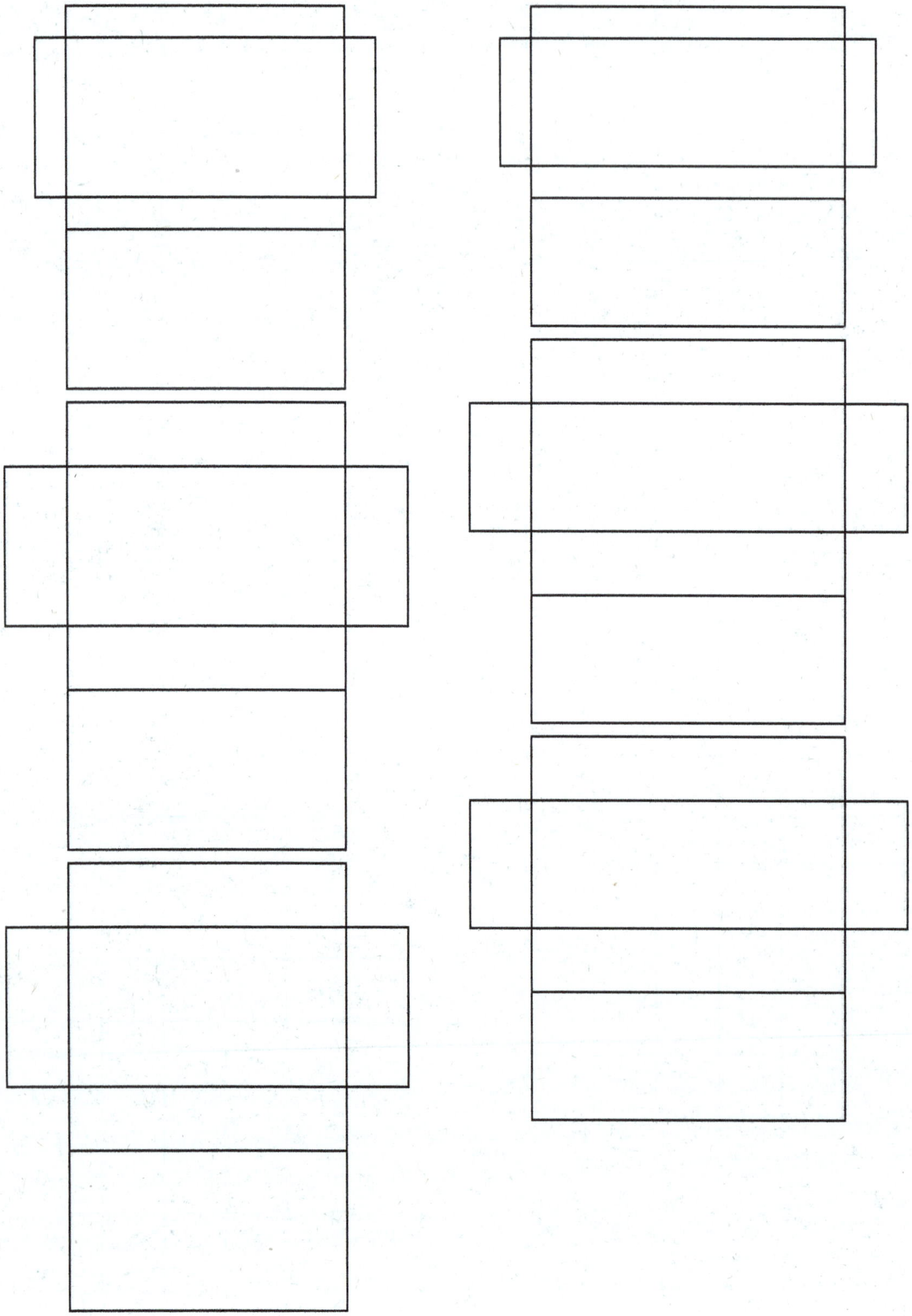

Name ______________________________

Build a Prism with Whole and Half Layers

Here is how to build a prism that has a length of 5 cm, a width of 2 cm, and a height of $2\frac{1}{2}$ cm using whole and half layers.

- Stack two layers of a prism that has a 5 cm by 2 cm base and is 1 cm tall.
- Next stack one layer of a prism that has a 5 cm by 2 cm base and is $\frac{1}{2}$ cm tall.

Build prisms with whole and half layers to complete the table below.

	length (l) (in cm)	width (w) (in cm)	length × width (lw)	Area of Base (B)	height (h)	$V = Bh$
1	5	2	5 • 2	10 10 cm^2	$\frac{1}{2}$ cm	
2	5	2			1 cm	
3	5	2			$1\frac{1}{2}$ cm	
4	5	2			2 cm	
5	5	2			$3\frac{1}{2}$ cm	
6	5	2			4 cm	
7	5	2			$4\frac{1}{2}$ cm	
8	5	2			5 cm	
9	5	2			$5\frac{1}{2}$ cm	

10 Explain the expression you wrote for the volume of the prism with the $3\frac{1}{2}$ cm height in terms of layers of cubes.

____

____

Name ______________________

Build a Prism with Fractional Base Dimensions

Here is how to build a prism that has a length of $4\frac{1}{2}$ cm and a width of $2\frac{1}{2}$ cm and a height of $5\frac{1}{2}$ cm using whole and half layers.

- Stack five layers of a prism that has a $4\frac{1}{2}$ cm by $2\frac{1}{2}$ cm base and is 1 cm tall.
- Next stack one layer of a prism that has a $4\frac{1}{2}$ cm by $2\frac{1}{2}$ cm base and is $\frac{1}{2}$ cm tall.

Use this table to record the volumes of the prisms you build. If the answer is greater than 1, write it as a mixed number.

	length (l) (in cm)	width (w) (in cm)	Area of Base (B)	height (h)	$V = Bh$
11	$4\frac{1}{2}$	$2\frac{1}{2}$	$11\frac{1}{4}$ $11\frac{1}{4}$ cm^2	1 cm	$V = 11\frac{1}{4} \cdot 1 = 11\frac{1}{4}$ $V = 11\frac{1}{4}$ cm^3
12	$4\frac{1}{2}$	$2\frac{1}{2}$		$\frac{1}{2}$ cm	
13	$4\frac{1}{2}$	$2\frac{1}{2}$		$1\frac{1}{2}$ cm	
14	$4\frac{1}{2}$	$2\frac{1}{2}$		$2\frac{1}{2}$ cm	
15	$4\frac{1}{2}$	$2\frac{1}{2}$		$3\frac{1}{2}$ cm	
16	$4\frac{1}{2}$	$2\frac{1}{2}$		4 cm	
17	$4\frac{1}{2}$	$2\frac{1}{2}$		$4\frac{1}{2}$ cm	

18 Explain the expression you wrote for the volume of the prism with a $2\frac{1}{2}$ cm height in terms of layers of cubes.

Name ______________________

Units for *l*, *w*, *h*, *B*, and *V*

If V is the volume of the prism, then we can write these formulas.

$$V = lwh \qquad V = Bh$$

These equations show how the volume of the prism is related to other dimensions of the prism.

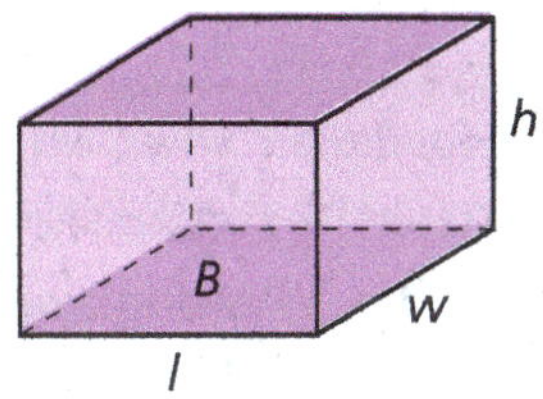

Complete.

1. If the value for h is given in centimeters, what unit should we use for l and w? ______________

2. If the values for l, w, and h are given in centimeters, what unit should we use for B? ______________

3. If the values for l, w, and h are given in centimeters, what unit should we use for V? ______________

What's the Error?

Dear Math Students,

Here is how I found the number of cubic feet of mulch needed on the garden pictured at the right.

$V = lwh$

$V = 10 \cdot 10 \cdot 3 = 300$

The volume is 300 ft^3.

My friend says this is not the correct answer. What did I do wrong?

Your friend,
Puzzled Penguin

4. Write a response to the Puzzled Penguin.

____

____

____

Name ______________________________

What's the Error?

Dear Math Students,

I see in the formula $V = lwh$ that I need to multiply three edge lengths to find the volume. The prism has a lot more edges. Why don't we multiply all the edge lengths to find the volume?

Your friend,
Puzzled Penguin

5 Write a response to the Puzzled Penguin.

____

____

____

____

____

Dear Math Students,

Here is how I found the volume of the prism at the right. Is my answer correct?

$V = 4\frac{1}{2} \times 2 = 9$

The volume is 9 in.^{3}

Your friend,
Puzzled Penguin

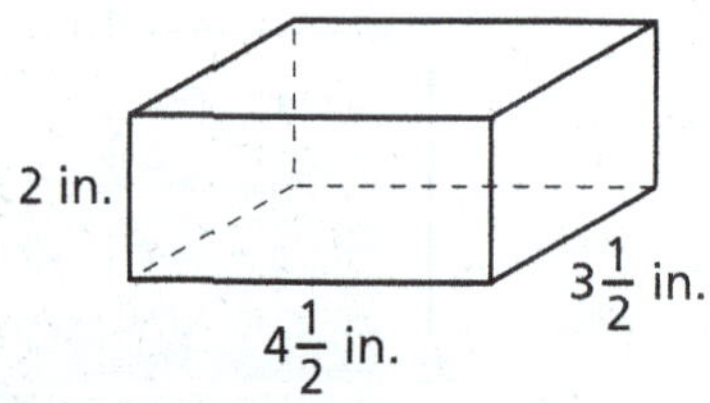

6 Write a response to the Puzzled Penguin.

____

____

____

____

Name ______________________

Math and Construction

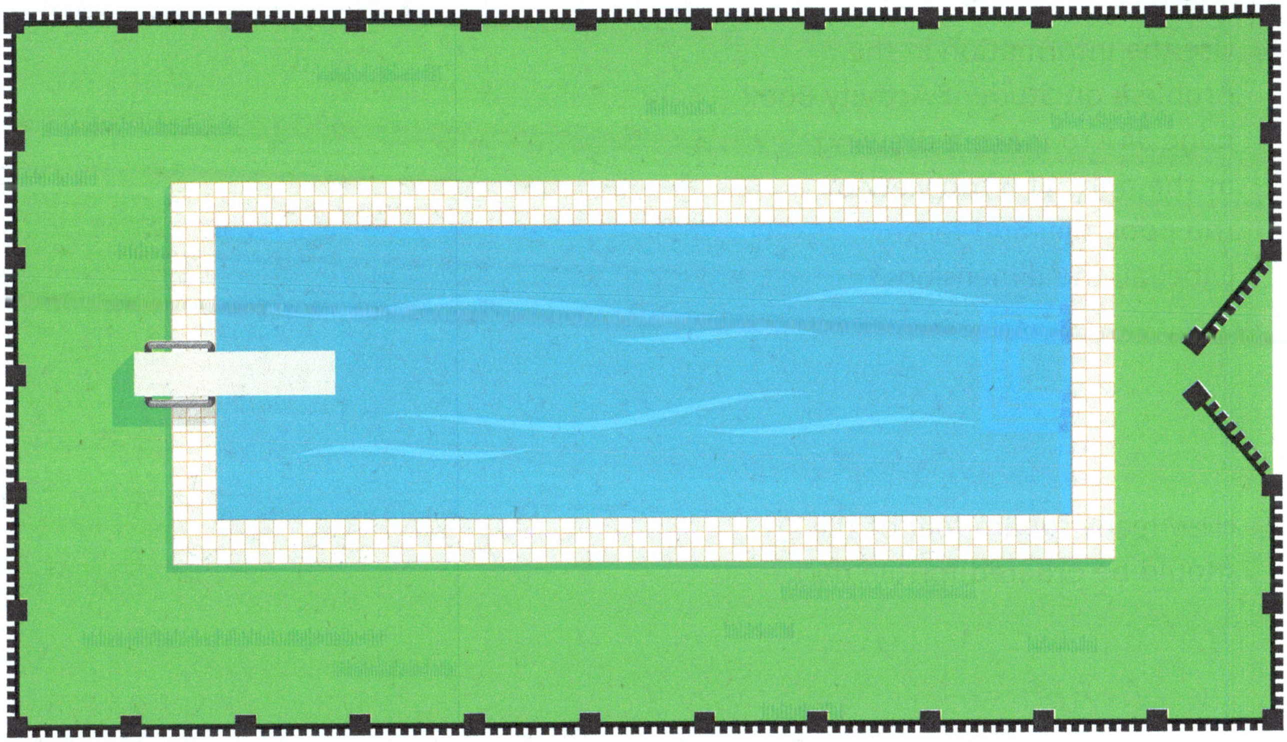

The Best Pool Construction Company is building a community swimming pool. The company has hired you and your associate to find how much tile and fencing needs to be ordered to finish the pool.

The pool is a rectangle 60 ft long and 20 ft wide. One third of the pool is 4 ft deep and the remaining part has a depth of 7 ft. There is to be a 3-ft wide tile deck around the entire pool and a safety fence around the entire area 11 ft from the edge of the tile deck.

1. What strategy will you use to find how much fence and tile is needed to finish the pool?

____

____

____

____

Name ______________________________

Make a Drawing

Complete.

2. Use the information in the problem on Student Activity Book page 347 to make a drawing at the right of a top view of the pool, tile, and fence. Label all the dimensions.

3. How many square feet of tile should be ordered for tile deck?

____

4. Safety fence is sold in 8-ft sections. How many sections should be ordered?

____

5. How many cubic feet of water will it take to fill the pool up to 6 in. below the top?

____

Unit 6
Quick Quiz 1

Name ______________________

Solve.

1. Use the given variables to write a formula for finding the volume (V) of the rectangular prism at the right.

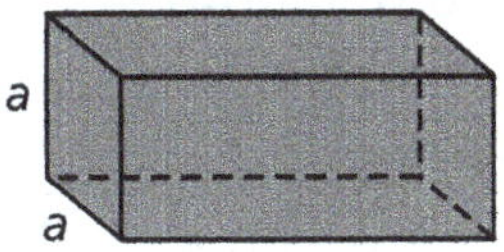

____

Find the volume of each rectangular prism.

2.

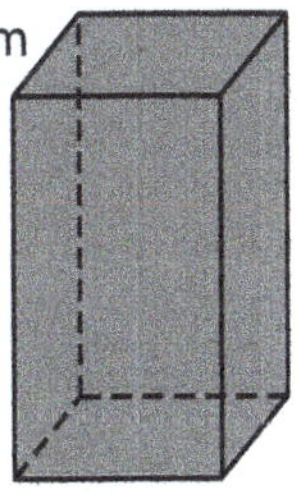

$V =$ ______________

3.

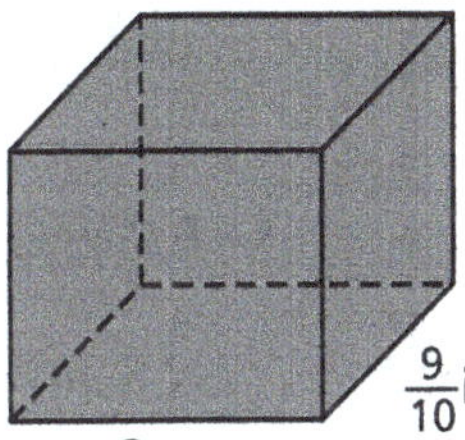

$V =$ ______________

Solve.

Show your work.

4. A shoe box in the shape of a rectangular prism has a volume of 741 cubic inches. What is the width of the box if its length is 13 inches and its height is 6 inches?

____

5. What is the density of a cube of cement with edges of length 5 cm and a mass of 337.5 g?

____

Fluency Check 12

Name ______________________

PATH to FLUENCY

1. $318.6 + 0.46 =$
2. $193.7 + 0.84 =$
3. $562.9 + 0.53 =$
4. $78.8 + 0.75 =$
5. $92.6 + 0.18 =$
6. $0.48 + 0.26 =$
7. $0.64 + 0.34 =$
8. $0.83 + 0.07 =$
9. $1.72 + 0.19 =$
10. $2.09 + 0.75 =$
11. $58 + 0.67 =$
12. $62 + 0.59 =$
13. $70 + 0.88 =$
14. $312 + 0.51 =$
15. $609 + 0.99 =$

Name ______________________________

What's the Error?

Dear Math Students,

Today I found the measure of ∠TYS in the diagram shown at the right. Here is how I found the answer.

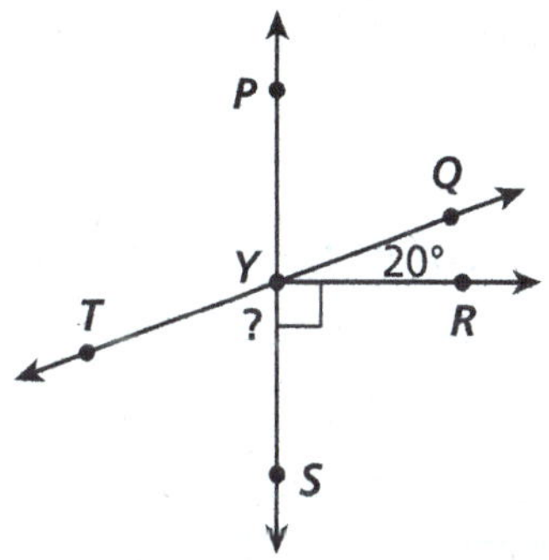

I noticed that ∠TYS and ∠QYR form a pair of vertical angles.
I know that vertical angles have the same measure.

The measure of ∠QYR is 20°.
So the measure of ∠TYS is 20°, too.

Am I correct? If not, please correct my work and explain below.

Your friend,
Puzzled Penguin

31 Write a response to the Puzzled Penguin.

____

____

____

____

____

____

____

____

Check Understanding

Draw a pair of adjacent angles that are supplementary. Explain how you know that the angles are supplementary.

Name ______________________

VOCABULARY
diagonal of a quadrilateral

Interior Angles in a Quadrilateral

1. What is the sum of the measures of the interior angles of each triangle shown at the right?

____

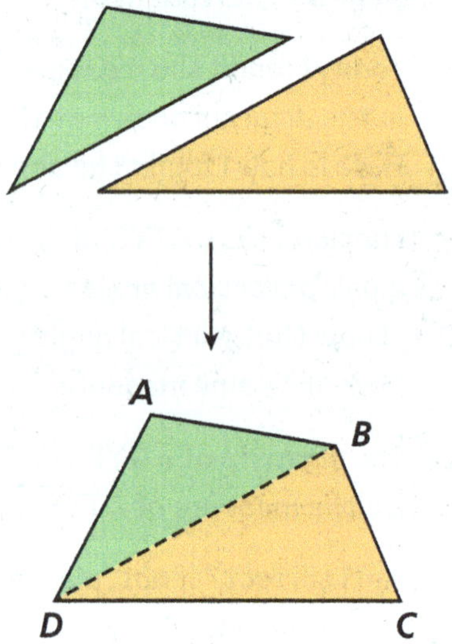

2. Quadrilateral *ABCD* was formed by joining the two triangles. What do you think is the sum of the measures of the interior angles of *ABCD*? Explain your answer.

____

____

____

____

3. A **diagonal of a quadrilateral** is a line segment that connects opposite vertices. Draw one diagonal in each special quadrilateral below.

rectangle

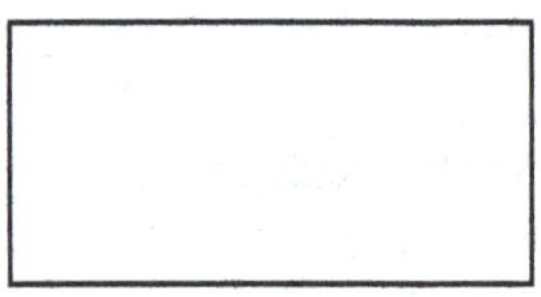

parallelogram

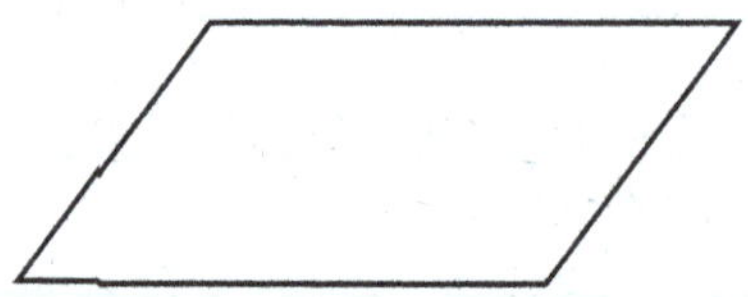

rhombus

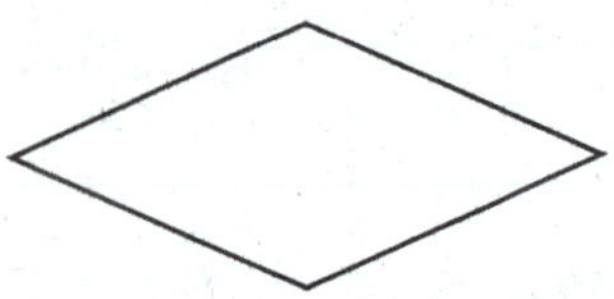

trapezoid

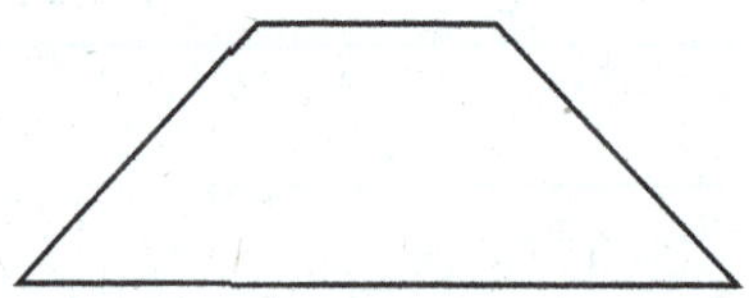

4. What do you think is the sum of the measures of the interior angles of any quadrilateral? Explain your answer.

____

____

____

____

____

____

Name ______________________________

Divide Any Polygon into Triangles

VOCABULARY
diagonal of a polygon

A polygon is formed by line segments, called sides, that meet only at their endpoints. A **diagonal of a polygon** connects two vertices but is not a side.

12 In each polygon, draw all the diagonals from the vertex that is marked with a dot. Count the number of sides in the polygon and the number of triangles formed.

a.

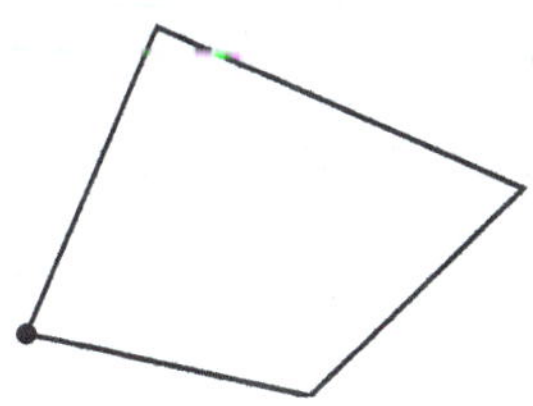

number of sides = ________

number of triangles = ________

b.

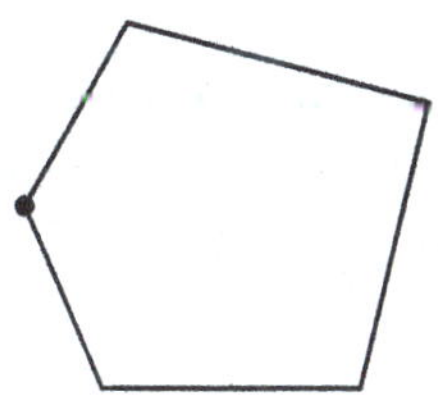

number of sides = ________

number of triangles = ________

c.

number of sides = ________

number of triangles = ________

d.

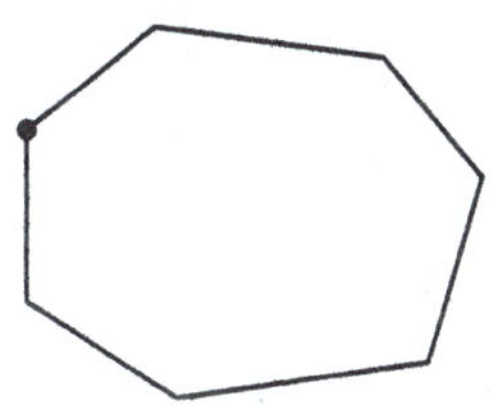

number of sides = ________

number of triangles = ________

Use your answers from Exercise 12 to answer these questions.

13 How does the number of sides compare to the number of triangles?

____

14 How many triangles do you think will be formed in a polygon with 8 sides?

____

15 Write an expression to show how many triangles will be formed in a polygon with *n* sides.

____

Name ______________________________

Interior Angles in Any Polygon

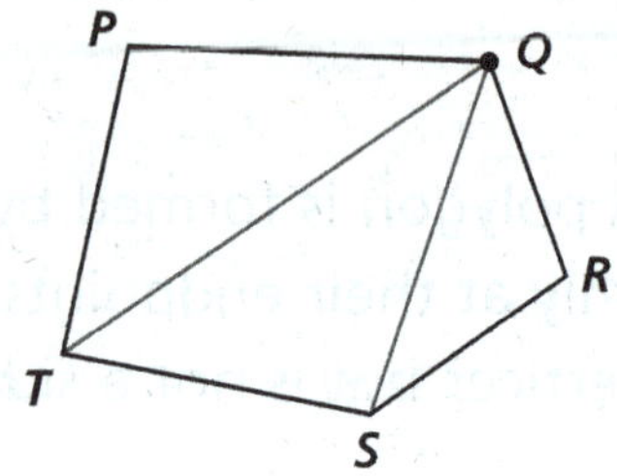

16 The diagonals from one vertex of pentagon *PQRST* form three triangles. How can you use the triangles to find the sum of the interior angles of *PQRST*? What is the sum?

____

____

____

17 a. A hexagon is a polygon with six sides. How many triangles are formed by drawing all the diagonals from one vertex?

____

b. What is the sum of the measures of the interior angles of the hexagon? Explain your answer.

____

____

____

18 Complete the table.

Number of Sides of the Polygon	4	5	6	7	8
Number of Triangles Formed by Drawing All Diagonals from One Vertex	2	3			
Sum of Interior Angles of the Polygon					

19 Answer these questions about a polygon with *n* sides.

a. What expression shows the number of triangles formed by drawing all the diagonals from one vertex? __________

b. Write a formula that you can use to find the sum of the measures of the interior angles.

____

Name ______________________

What's the Error?

Dear Math Students,

I drew some diagonals to help me find the sum of the interior angles of the pentagon shown at the right. The diagonals I drew make five triangles. Here is how I found the sum.

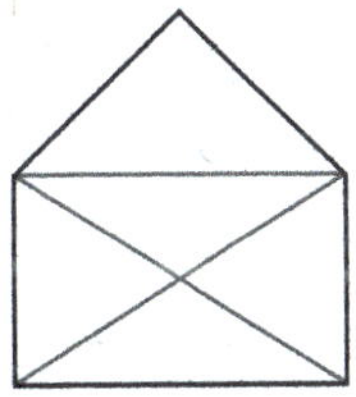

5 triangles × 180° inside each triangle = 900°
So the sum of the measures of the interior angles of the pentagon is 900°.

Am I correct? If not, please correct my work and explain.

Your friend,
Puzzled Penguin

20 Write a response to the Puzzled Penguin.

____

____

____

Dear Math Students,

It looks like I need your help again. I want to find the sum of the interior angles of a polygon with 8 sides. I found the answer using a formula.

$$S = n(180°) = 8 \times 180° = 1{,}440°$$

So I think the sum of the interior angles is 1,440°. But my friend told me I made a mistake. Can you help me figure out what my mistake was?

Your friend,
Puzzled Penguin

21 Write a response to the Puzzled Penguin.

____

____

____

Name ______________________________

Use the diagram to answer Exercises 1 and 2.

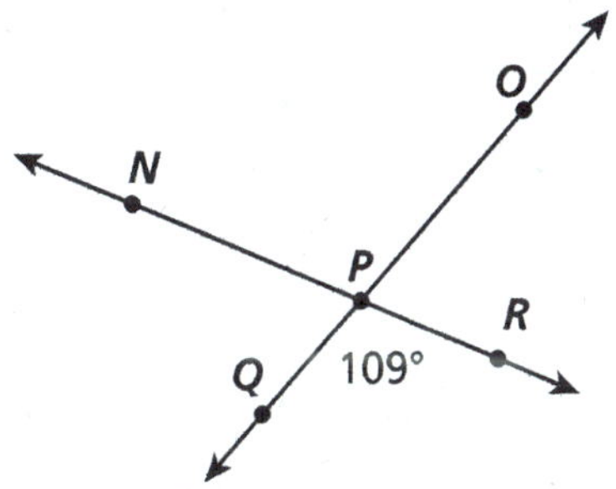

1. Name a pair of supplementary angles in the diagram.

____

2. Write and solve an equation to find the measure of $\angle NPQ$.

____

For exercises 3 and 4, find the value of *x*. Explain your answer.

3. 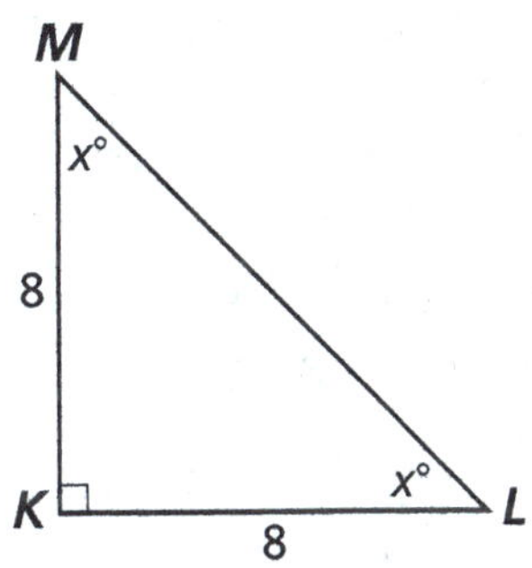

____

____

4. 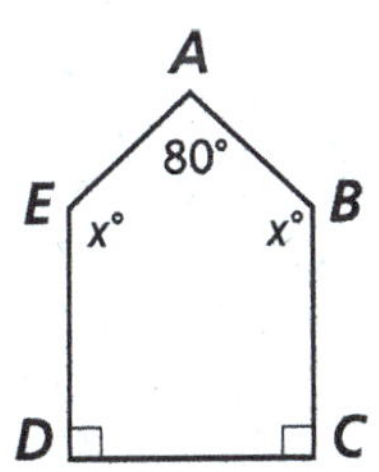

____

____

____

Fluency Check 13

Name ________________

PATH to FLUENCY

1. $226.7 + 0.34 =$

2. $180.2 + 0.91 =$

3. $573.5 + 0.55 =$

4. $26.4 + 0.89 =$

5. $70.7 + 0.43 =$

6. $0.67 + 0.25 =$

7. $0.43 + 0.34 =$

8. $0.99 + 0.05 =$

9. $2.12 + 0.49 =$

10. $1.07 + 0.79 =$

11. $49 + 0.18 =$

12. $96 + 0.63 =$

13. $40 + 0.59 =$

14. $717 + 0.72 =$

15. $202 + 0.22 =$

Name ______________________________

VOCABULARY
diameter
center of a circle
circumference
irrational number
pi (π)

Use the Circumference Formula

The **diameter** of a circle is the distance across the circle through its **center**.

The distance around a circle is the **circumference** of the circle.

The ratio of the circumference of a circle to its diameter is an **irrational number** called **pi**. This number is represented by the symbol **π**.

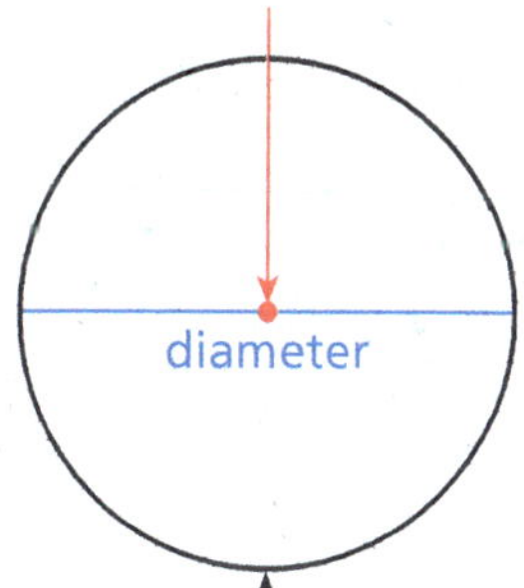

The formula for the circumference of a circle is

$$C = \pi d$$

where C is the circumference and d is the diameter.

You can use 3.14 or $\frac{22}{7}$ as the approximate value of pi, or π.

Complete the table.

Diameter of Circle	Circumference of Circle		
	Use the symbol π.	Use 3.14 for π.	Use $\frac{22}{7}$ for π.
1 21 m			
2 14 cm			
3 2 in.			

Find the circumference of each circle. Use 3.14 or $\frac{22}{7}$ for π.

4 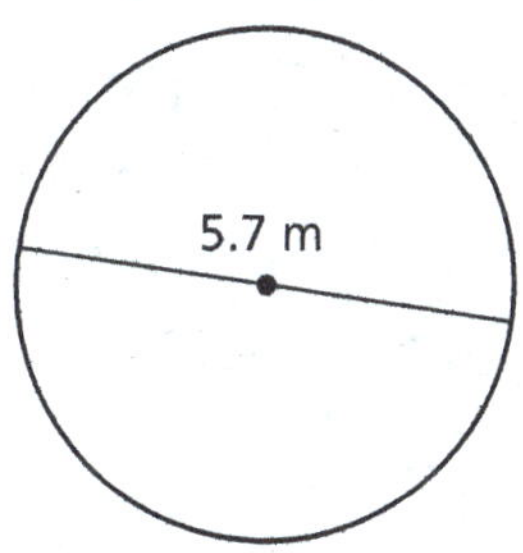

$C \approx$ ____________________

5 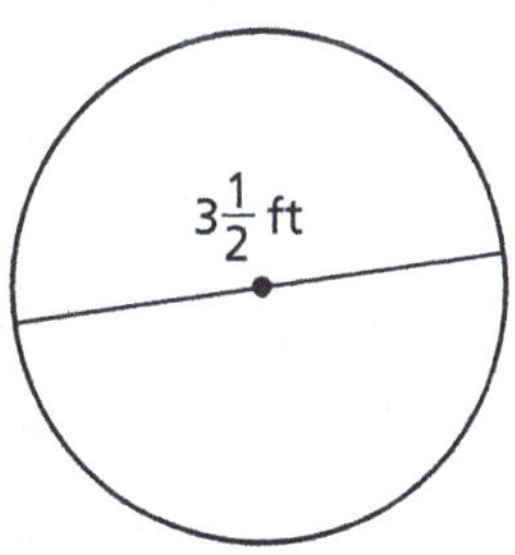

$C \approx$ ____________________

6 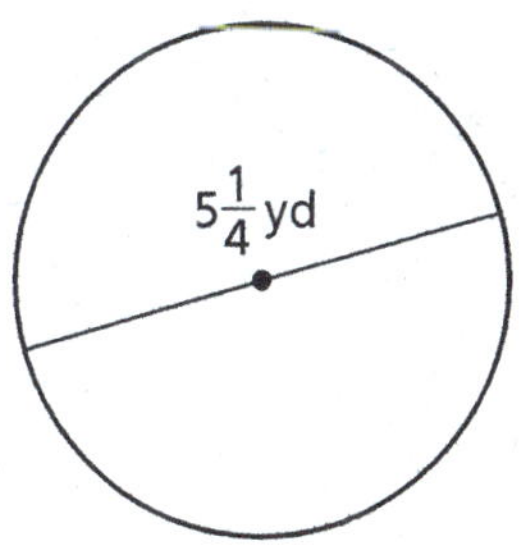

$C \approx$ ____________________

Name

What's the Error?

Dear Math Students,

In my neighborhood, we just built a waddling track. It is not too big since we do not waddle all that fast! This is what our track looks like:

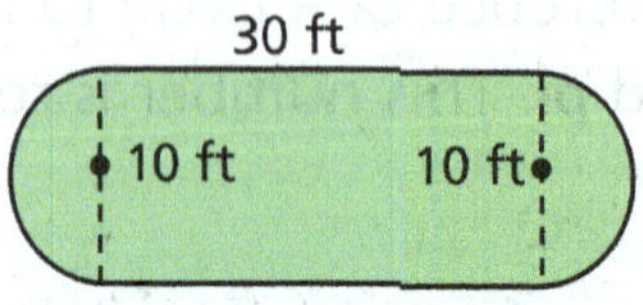

I tried to figure out how far I will have waddled after one lap.

I calculated this way:

For the rectangle, $30 \cdot 10 = 300$.

I estimated the length of the circle formed by the two half-circles at the ends, $3.14 \cdot 5 \cdot 5 = 78.5$.

$300 + 78.5 = 378.5$, so the distance for one lap is about 378.5 ft.

My friends said that this seemed to be an unreasonable distance.

Did I make an error? If so, can you help me to correct it and find the true distance for one lap?

Your friend,
Puzzled Penguin

17 Write a response to Puzzled Penguin.

Check Understanding

Describe how to find the area of a circle if you know its circumference.

Name ______________________________

Use the circle graph for Exercises 1 and 2.

The circle graph shows how the students in Mr. Lopez's class get to school every day.

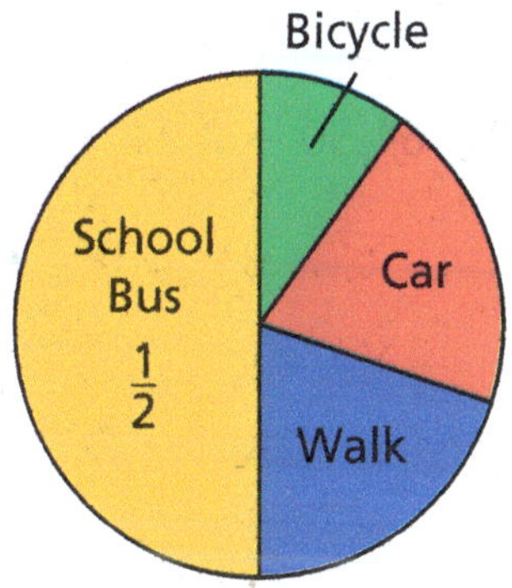

1. There are 30 students in Mr. Lopez's class. How many take the school bus every day?

   ____

2. The number of students who ride in a car is equal to the number of students who walk. The number of students who walk is twice the number that ride a bicycle. How many students ride a bicycle to school? Explain your answer.

   ____

3. What is the area of a circle that has a diameter of 12 inches? Use 3.14 for pi.

   ____

4. A cylinder is 10 centimeters tall. Its circular top has a diameter of 10 centimeters. Draw a net of the cylinder. Label the diameter of the circles, the circumference of the circles, and the length and width of the rectangle. Use 3.14 for pi.

Fluency Check 14

Name ______________________

PATH to FLUENCY

1. 61.50 − 2.21 =

2. 30.76 − 8.19 =

3. 16.02 − 5.67 =

4. 95.33 − 4.94 =

5. 19.91 − 14.6 =

6. 32.07 − 30.2 =

7. 72.55 − 70.6 =

8. 45.21 − 5.29 =

9. 615 − 0.05 =

10. 210 − 0.01 =

11. 1,040 − 0.09 =

12. 4,029 − 0.25 =

13. 2,305 − 0.34 =

14. 5,771 − 5.55 =

15. 1,919 − 5.48 =

Name ________________________________

1 Select True or False for each statement.

1a. Surface area and volume both measure the amount of space occupied by a solid figure. ○ True ○ False

1b. Surface area and volume are measured using the same unit. ○ True ○ False

1c. Surface area and volume are both attributes of solid figures. ○ True ○ False

2 Fill in the bubble next to the unit used to measure volume.

○ square units ○ cubic units ○ linear units

Explain your answer choice in words or with a labeled sketch.

3 The volume of a rectangular prism can be found using the formula $V = Bh$.

Part A Use the tiles to show a different formula you can use to find the volume of a rectangular prism. You will not need to use every tile.

w h B l

$V =$ ____________

Part B Explain how the two formulas are related, and why you can use either formula to find the volume of a rectangular prism.

4 The equation for the volume of the square prism is $V = Mt$. Label the prism.

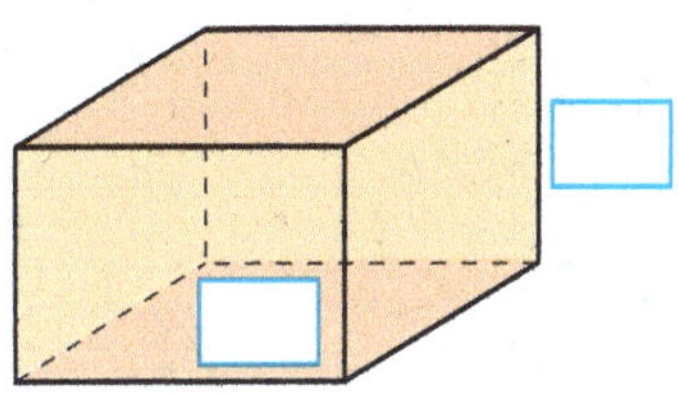

Name ______________________________

5 Choose one value from each column to make the volume of the rectangular prism true.

w	l
○ 3 ft	○ 1 ft
○ 5 ft	○ 2 ft
○ 9 ft	○ 3 ft
○ 10 ft	○ 4 ft

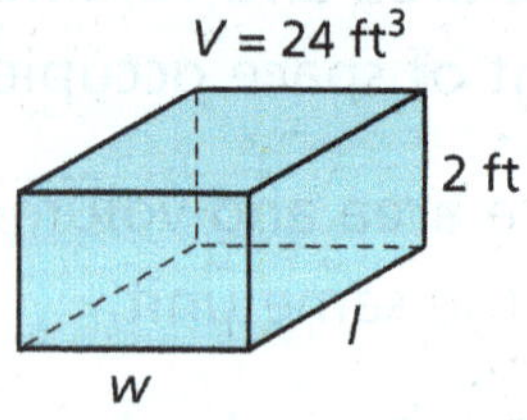

6 Use mental math to find the volume.

$V =$ ______________

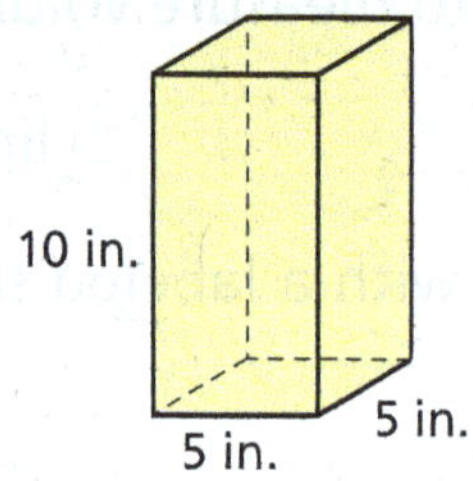

7 The volume of a prism can be found by packing it with unit cubes of the appropriate edge lengths.

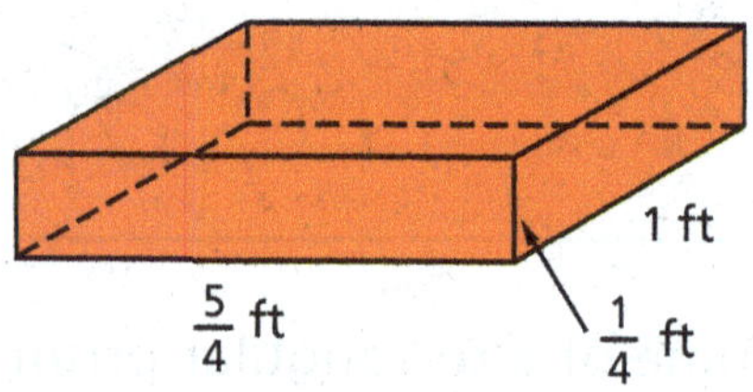

Part A

What is the longest edge length that would be appropriate for the unit cubes? Explain your answer.

______________ edge lengths

Part B

If the longest dimension of the prism was $1\frac{1}{8}$ feet, would the length you chose in Part A be sensible? Explain.

 Name ________________

8 Cecilia used layers to find the volume of the prism below.

Part A Explain how to find the volume using layers.

Part B Use layers to find the volume of the prism.

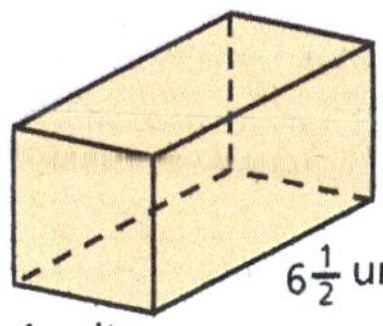

$V =$ ________________ cubic units

9 Find the volume. Show your work.

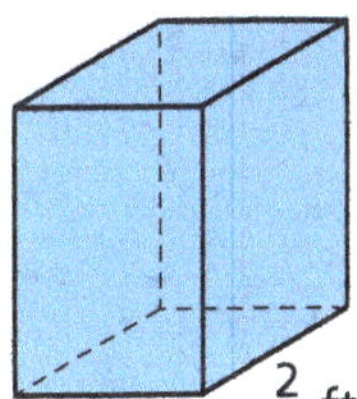

$V =$ ________________

10 Select Yes or No to indicate if the equation represents the volume for the prism with edges of length *e*.

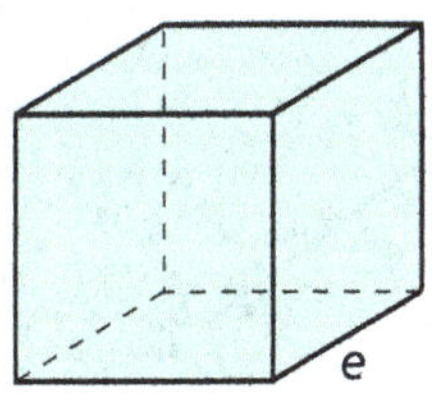

10a. $V = e \cdot e \cdot e$ ○ Yes ○ No

10b. $V = 3e$ ○ Yes ○ No

10c. $V = e^3$ ○ Yes ○ No

Name ______________________

For Exercises 11–14, find the unknown angle measure.

11 $m\angle QNO =$ ______

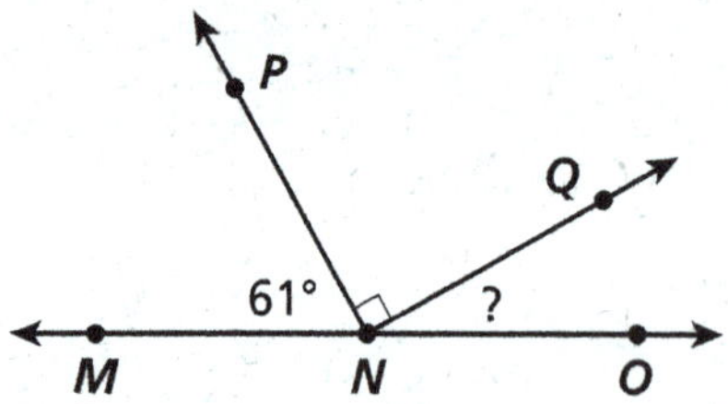

12 $m\angle ACB =$ ______

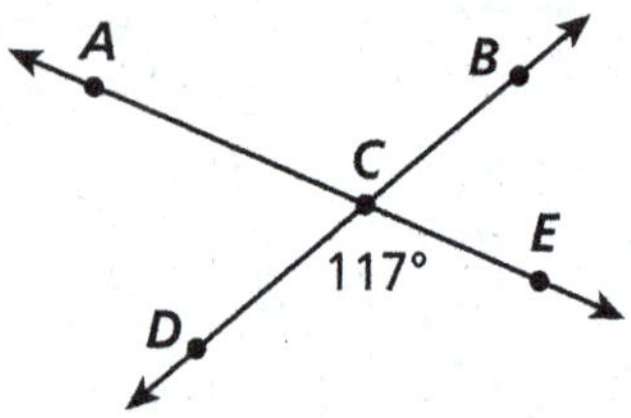

13 $m\angle U =$ ______

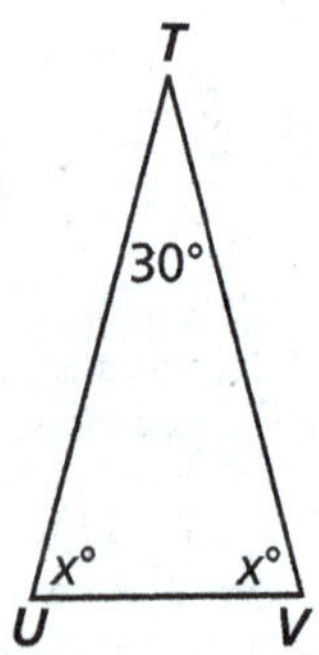

14 $m\angle D =$ ______

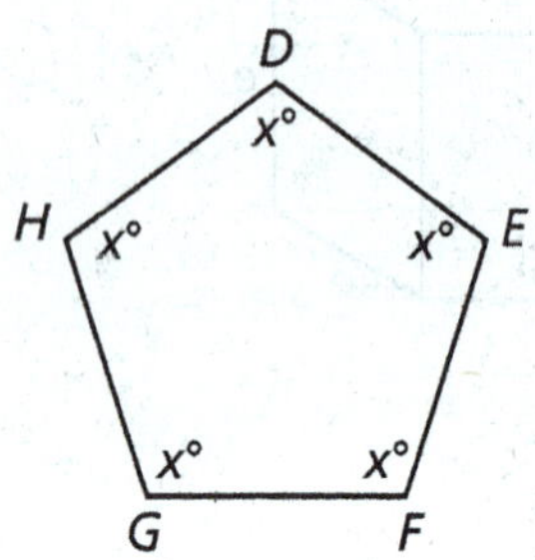

Name ______________________________

Students were asked to name their favorite pizza topping. The results are shown in the circle graph. Use the graph for Exercises 15 and 16.

Favorite Pizza Topping

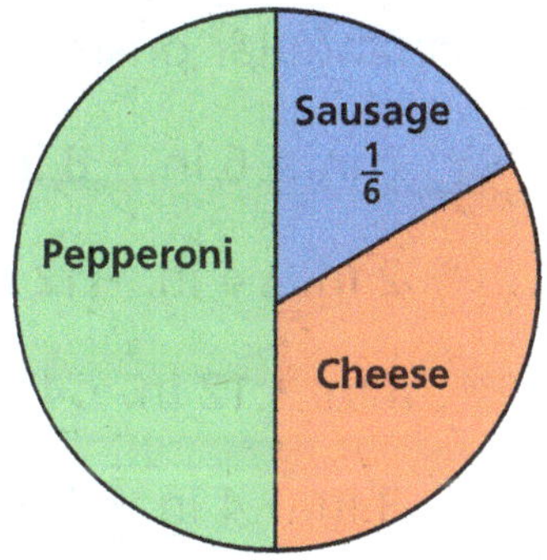

15 A total of 60 students were surveyed. How many students chose sausage?

____

16 Thirty students chose pepperoni. What fraction of the students chose cheese? Explain how you know.

17 A small pool in the shape of a rectangular prism has a length of $6\frac{1}{2}$ ft, a width of 5 ft, and a height of 24 in. Jeb says the volume of the pool is 780 ft^3.

Is Jeb correct? If he is, show how he may have found the volume. If not, explain what he did wrong and give the correct volume.

$V =$ ______________

 Name ________________

18 Choose Yes or No to indicate if the given dimensions represent a rectangular prism with a volume of 96 cubic inches.

18a. 2 in. • 6 in. • 8 in. ○ Yes ○ No

18b. 2 in. • 4 in. • 12 in. ○ Yes ○ No

18c. 4 in. • 12 in. • 4 in. ○ Yes ○ No

18d. 3 in. • 4 in. • 9 in. ○ Yes ○ No

18e. 4 in. • 4 in. • 6 in. ○ Yes ○ No

19 What is the mass of a piece of glass with a volume of 35 cm^3 and a density of 2.4 g/cm^3?

____

20 A circle has a circumference of 31.4 inches. What is the area of the circle? Use 3.14 for π.

____

21 John wants to place a layer of mulch on top of his 12 ft by 24 ft vegetable garden. If a 1.5 ft^3 bag of mulch costs $4, how much will it cost to place a 3-inch layer of mulch on the garden? Show your work.

$ ________________

Name ____________________

Planting Flowers

Olivia is constructing a planter for her tulips that is 3 feet wide, 6 inches long, and 6 inches high. The wood she is using to build the box is 1-inch thick and the planter will have 4 sides and a bottom, but no top. Use this information to answer the questions that follow.

1 Use the grid to sketch a net for the box Olivia is building.

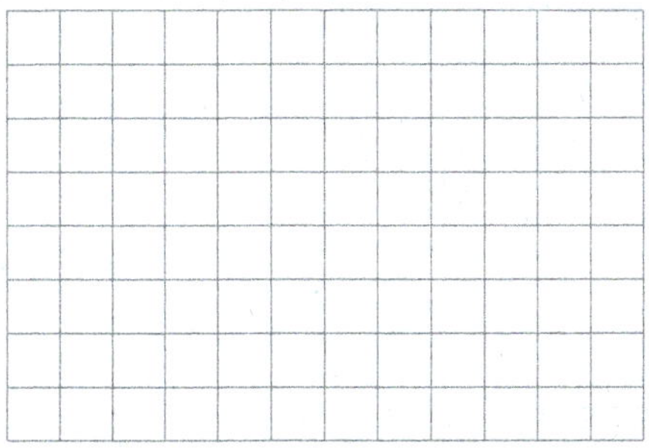

2 Olivia wants to decorate the planter with 1-inch square tiles that cost 4.5¢ ($0.045) each. She will cover the front, back and sides of the planter – but not the bottom. Find how much Olivia will need to spend for the tiles. Show or explain how you got your answer.

3 Olivia wants to know how much space the planter occupies. Find the volume of the planter. Show or explain how you found the volume.

Name ______________________________

4 Olivia made the planter from wood that is 1 inch thick. If the outside dimensions are shown in the diagram, what are the dimensions inside the planter?

☐ inches long ☐ inches wide ☐ inches high

5 Use words or pictures to explain why the dimensions inside the planter are different from the dimensions outside the planter.

6 Soil costs $0.02 per cubic inch. How much will the soil cost to fill the planter? Show or explain how you found your answer.

7 What is the volume of the wood used to build the planter?

8 Suppose Olivia decides to build another planter with the same dimensions, but this time turns the planter on its end so that it is 3 feet tall and the top is open. Explain how the cost of tiles and the cost of soil would change.

Dear Family:

In this unit, your child will work with both metric and customary units of measurement. Benchmarks will help your child estimate using these units. Some benchmarks your child will learn are:

- Eight large trashcans hold about 1 kiloliter.
- A pinch of salt has a mass of about 1 milligram.
- A slice of bread weighs about 1 ounce.

You can use these and other benchmarks at home to estimate measures.

Students will use units of measure as they solve problems about ratios, rates, and percents. The examples below and on the next page show how students will use tables, diagrams, and equations to solve problems.

Purple Berry juice is made from 2 cups of raspberry juice for every 3 cups of blueberry juice. How many cups of blueberry juice are needed for 11 cups of raspberry juice?

Table with Unit Rate

	B	R	
	3	2	
÷ 2	$\frac{3}{2}$	1	÷ 2
· 11	$\frac{33}{2}$	11	· 11

Equation

$\frac{2}{3} = \frac{11}{x}$

$2x = 33$

$x = \frac{33}{2}$

The answer is $\frac{33}{2}$ or $16\frac{1}{2}$ cups of blueberry juice.

A juice company's KiwiBerry juice is made by mixing 2 parts kiwifruit juice with 3 parts strawberry juice. To make 20 liters of KiwiBerry juice, how much kiwifruit juice is needed?

Factor Puzzle

	k	KB
	2	5
1	2	5
4	8	20

Tape Diagram

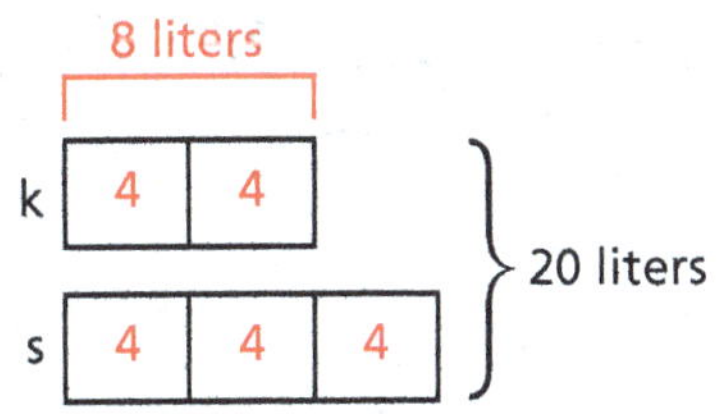

The answer is 8 liters of kiwifruit juice.

If 12 milligrams of niacin is 60% of the recommended daily allowance for niacin, then what is the recommended daily allowance for niacin?

Double Number Line Diagram

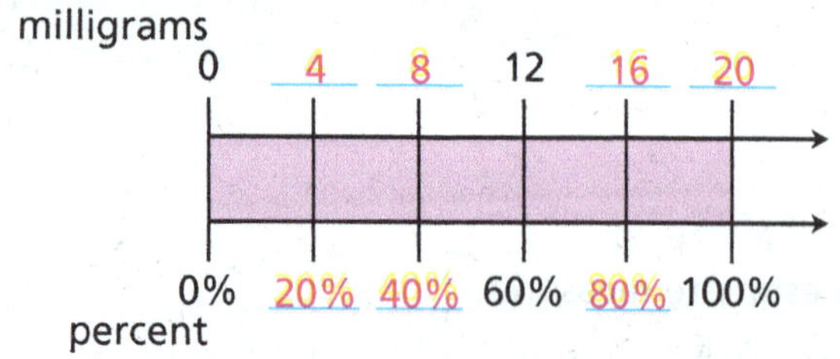

Equation

$$\frac{12}{x} = \frac{60}{100}$$

$$60x = 12 \cdot 100$$

$$x = \frac{12 \cdot 100}{60}$$

$$x = 20$$

The answer is 20 milligrams.

A double number line can be used to convert between centimeters and millimeters. Complete the double number line to show how centimeters and millimeters are related.

Double Number Line Diagram

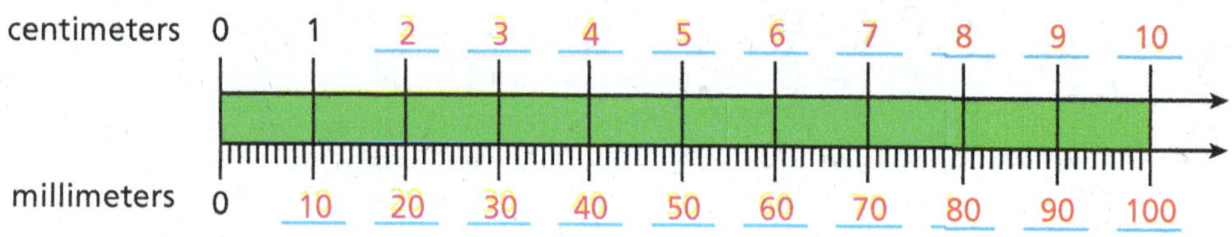

Double number line diagrams can be used to make other conversions, such as feet to inches, milliliters to liters, and kilograms to grams.

Your child will apply the strategies they have learned to also convert units of time, such as seconds to hours, weeks to hours, and hours to years. If you have any questions or comments, please contact me.

Sincerely,
Your child's teacher

Estimada familia:

En esta unidad, su hijo trabajará con unidades métricas y usuales de medida. Los puntos de referencia ayudarán a su hijo a estimar usando estas unidades. Algunos puntos de referencia que su hijo aprenderá son:

- ocho tarros grandes de basura contienen aproximadamente 1 kilolitro
- una pizca de sal tiene una masa de aproximadamente 1 miligramo
- una rebanada de pan pesa aproximadamente 1 onza

Puedes usar estos y otros puntos de referencia en casa para estimar las medidas.

Los estudiantes usarán unidades de medida mientras resuelven problemas de razones, tasas y porcentajes. Los ejemplos abajo y en la siguiente página muestran cómo los estudiantes usarán tablas, diagramas y ecuaciones para resolver problemas.

Para hacer jugo azul se necesitan 2 tazas de jugo de frambuesa por cada 3 tazas de jugo de arándanos. ¿Cuántas tazas de jugo de arándanos se necesitan si se usan 11 tazas de jugo de frambuesa?

Tabla con tasa por unidad

	A	F	
	3	2	
÷ 2	$\frac{3}{2}$	1	÷ 2
· 11	$\frac{33}{2}$	11	· 11

Ecuación

$$\frac{2}{3} = \frac{11}{x}$$
$$2x = 33$$
$$x = \frac{33}{2}$$

La respuesta es $\frac{33}{2}$ o $16\frac{1}{2}$ tazas de jugo de arándanos.

Una compañía hace jugo de kiwi con fresa mezclando 2 partes de jugo de kiwi con 3 partes de jugo de fresa. Para hacer 20 litros, ¿cuánto jugo de kiwi se necesita?

Rompecabezas de factores

	k	KF
	2	5
1	2	5
4	8	20

Diagrama en forma de cinta

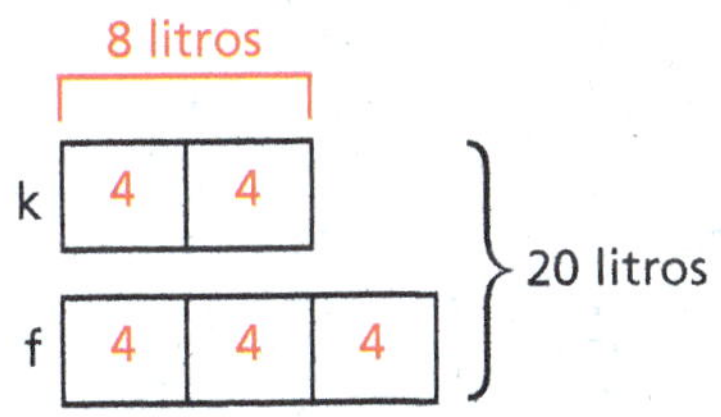

La respuesta es 8 litros de jugo de kiwi.

Si 12 miligramos de niacina equivalen al 60% del consumo diario que se recomienda, entonces, ¿cuál es el consumo diario total de niacina que se recomienda?

Diagrama de recta numérica doble

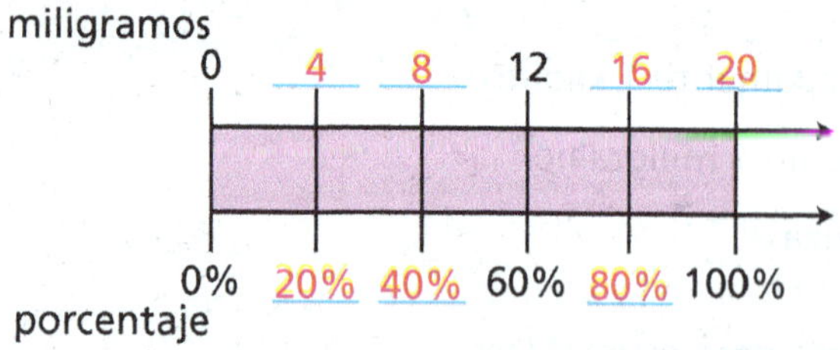

Ecuación

$$\frac{12}{x} = \frac{60}{100}$$
$$60x = 12 \cdot 100$$
$$x = \frac{12 \cdot 100}{60}$$
$$x = 20$$

La respuesta es 20 miligramos.

Se puede usar una recta numérica doble para realizar conversiones entre centímetros y milímetros. Completen la recta numérica doble para mostrar cómo se relacionan los centímetros y los milímetros.

Diagrama de recta numérica doble

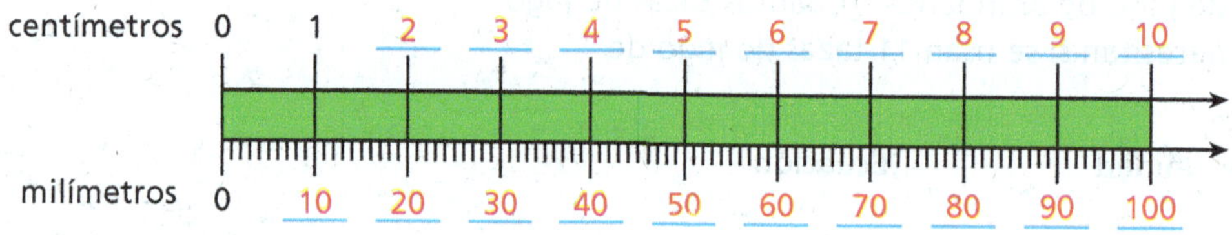

Se pueden usar diagramas de rectas numéricas dobles para realizar otras conversiones como pies a pulgadas, mililitros a litros y kilogramos a gramos.

Su hijo aplicará las estrategias que ha aprendido para también convertir unidades de tiempo como segundos a horas, semanas a horas y horas a años.

Si tiene comentarios o preguntas, por favor comuníquese conmigo.

Atentamente,
El maestro de su hijo

bar graph	cross-multiplication
circle graph	elapsed time
compare ratios	liquid volume

A method used for solving proportions based on the fact that in a proportion, the cross-products are equal.

Example:

$\frac{10}{15} = \frac{18}{27}$ is a proportion.

The cross-products are equal.

$\frac{10}{15} \times \frac{18}{27}$

$18 \cdot 15 = 10 \cdot 27$

A graph that uses the lengths of bars to show data. The bars may be horizontal or vertical.

Example:

The amount of time between a start time and an end time.

A graph used to display data that make up a whole. (Also called a *pie graph* or a *pie chart*.)

Example:

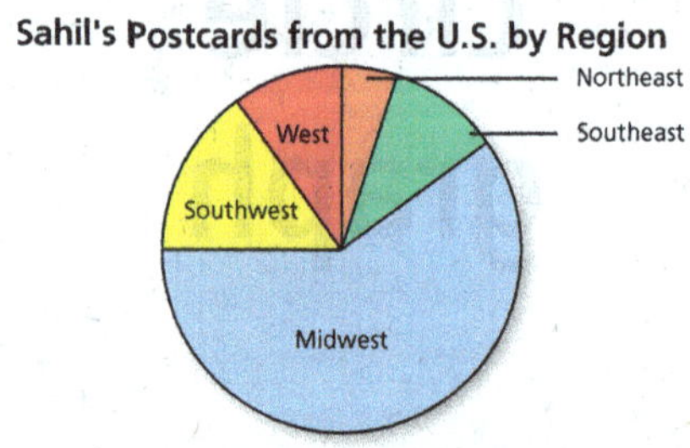

A measure of how much a container can hold. Also called capacity.

For two ratios, to state whether the amount of one quantity in a ratio is less than, greater than, or equal to the same quantity in the other ratio when the value of the other quantity in the ratios is the same.

mass

percent (%)

The amount of matter in an object. Common metric units of mass are kilograms, grams, and milligrams.

An amount out of a hundred or per hundred.

Example:

$34\% = \frac{34}{100}$

$124\% = \frac{124}{100}$

Name ______________________________

Compare Paint Ratios

Grasshopper Green paint has a blue: yellow paint ratio of 2:7. Gorgeous Green paint has a blue: yellow ratio of 4:5.

You can **compare ratios**. You can find out which ratio makes paint that is more blue and which ratio makes paint that is more yellow.

To find out which paint is more blue, make the values for yellow the same. One way to do this is to make the value for yellow be the product of the yellow values in the basic ratios.

1. What is the product of the yellow values in the basic ratios? ______________

2. Complete these ratio tables.

Grasshopper Green	
Blue	Yellow
2	7
	35

Gorgeous Green	
Blue	Yellow
4	5
	35

3. Which paint is more blue? Why?

____

____

____

4. Which paint is less blue? ______________

5. To find out which paint is more yellow, make the values for blue the same. Complete these ratio tables.

Grasshopper Green	
Blue	Yellow
2	7

Gorgeous Green	
Blue	Yellow
4	5

6. Which paint is more yellow? ______________

7. Which paint is less yellow? ______________

Name ______________________

Graph and Compare Paint Ratios

8. Look back at the tables in Exercises 2 and 5 on page 397. Write the three ratios for each paint color in these tables.

Grasshopper Green	
Blue	Yellow

Gorgeous Green	
Blue	Yellow

9. Graph two points from each table. Draw and label a line for *Grasshopper Green* and a line for *Gorgeous Green*.

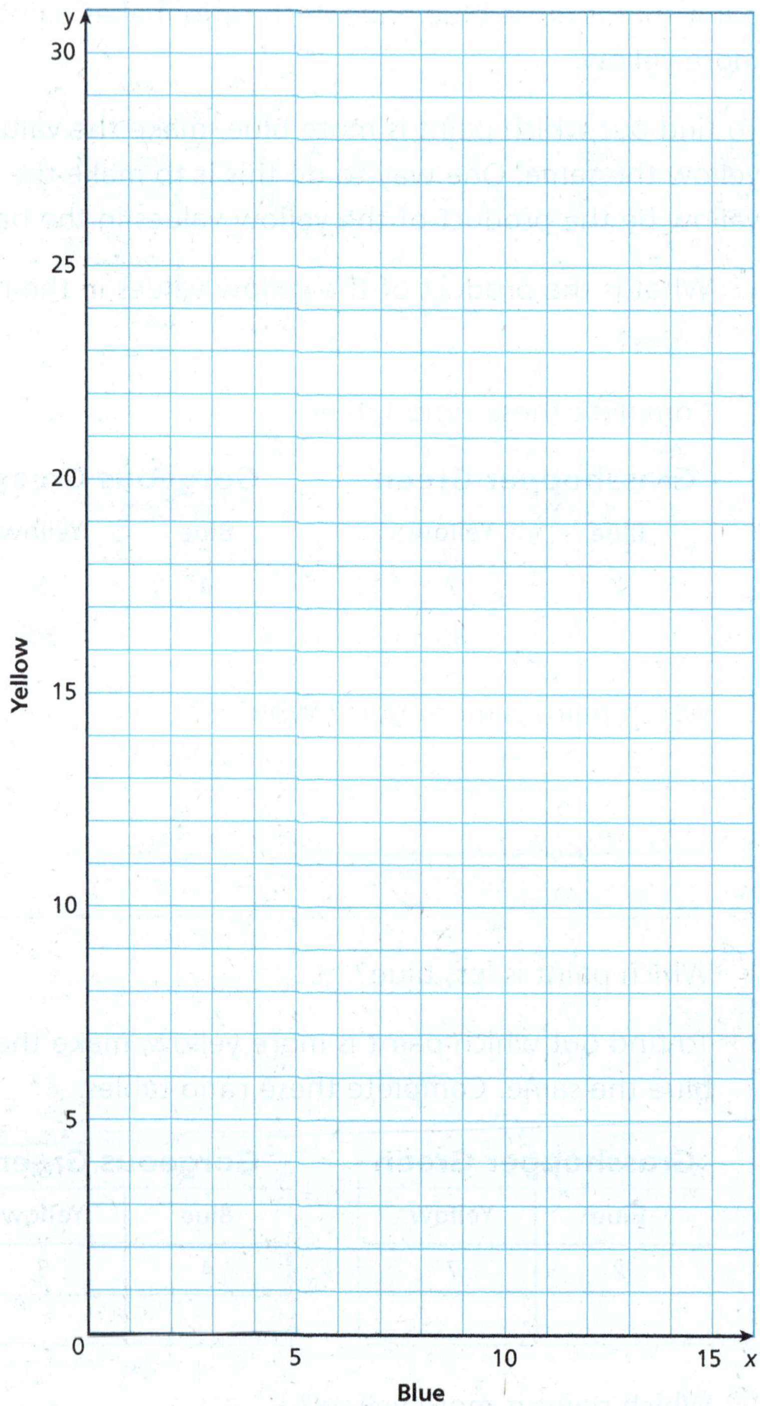

10. Discuss how the graphs can be used to decide which paint is more blue, less blue, more yellow, and less yellow.

Check Understanding

Explain how to compare ratios.

Name ______________________

Ratio as a Quotient

You can use a unit rate to describe *any* ratio. A unit rate for a ratio tells the amount of the first quantity you have for every 1 unit of the second quantity you have.

Look again at Sue's and Ben's drink recipes.

Sue's recipe has 5 cups cherry juice and 4 cups orange juice.

Ben's recipe has 6 cups cherry juice and 5 cups orange juice.

1. Find the amount of cherry juice in each drink for 1 cup of orange juice. Remember that when you divide both quantities in a ratio table by the same number, you get an equivalent ratio.

Sue's Recipe

Cherry	Orange
5	4
$\frac{5}{4}$	1

$\div 4$ (both columns)

$\frac{5}{4}$ is the quotient of $5 \div 4$.

Sue has $\frac{5}{4}$ cups of cherry juice for every cup of orange juice.

The unit rate for the ratio 5:4 is $\frac{5}{4}$.

Ben's Recipe

Cherry	Orange
6	5
$\frac{6}{5}$	1

$\div 5$ (both columns)

________ is the quotient of $6 \div 5$.

Ben has ________ cups of cherry juice for every cup of orange juice.

The unit rate for the ratio ________ is ________.

2. Find the amount of orange juice in each drink for 1 cup of cherry juice. This time use the orange:cherry ratio.

Sue's Recipe

Orange	Cherry
4	5
	1

Sue has ________ cup of orange juice for every cup of cherry juice.

The unit rate for the ratio ________ is ________.

Ben's Recipe

Ben has ________ cup of orange juice for every cup of cherry juice.

The unit rate for the ratio ________ is ________.

Name ____________________

Horizontal Ratio Tables

1. Complete the ratio table.

	Cups of Juice				
Tangerine	◯		1	8		
Cherry	◯	1		6	15	2

a. The basic ratio of $\frac{\text{tangerine}}{\text{cherry}}$ is ________.

b. There are ________ cups of tangerine juice for every cup of cherry juice.

c. The basic ratio of $\frac{\text{cherry}}{\text{tangerine}}$ is ________.

d. There is ________ cup of cherry juice for every cup of tangerine juice.

2. A flower mix has 21 tulips and 14 daffodils.

a. The basic ratio of $\frac{\text{tulips}}{\text{daffodils}}$ is ________.

b. There are ________ tulips for every daffodil.

c. The basic ratio for $\frac{\text{daffodils}}{\text{tulips}}$ is ________.

d. There is ________ daffodil for each tulip.

e. Using the basic ratio, how many tulips would be placed with 6 daffodils?

____

f. Using the basic ratio, how many daffodils would be placed with 6 tulips?

____

Solve.

3. At the farm, the ratios of mothers to baby sheep in each field are equivalent. If there are 20 mothers and 24 babies in the small field, how many babies are with the 45 mothers in the large field?

____

Name ______________________________

Equivalent Fractions and Equivalent Ratios

4 Show how the pattern of equivalent fractions continues.

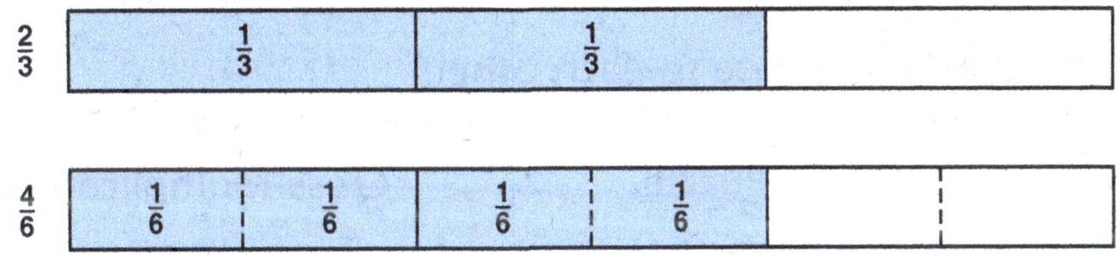

$$\frac{2 \cdot 2}{2 \cdot 3} = \frac{4}{6}$$

a. $\frac{6}{9}$ b. ______________

c. $\frac{8}{12}$ d. ______________

5 Show how the pattern of equivalent ratios continues.

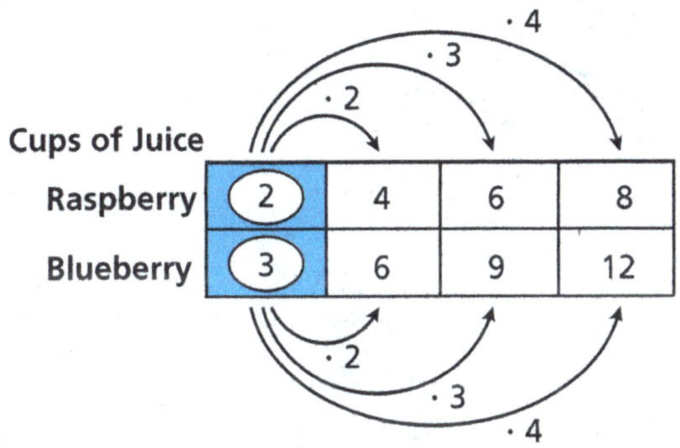

2 cups of raspberry:3 cups of blueberry

4 cups of raspberry:6 cups of blueberry

a. __________ cups of raspberry: __________ cups of blueberry

b. __________ cups of raspberry: __________ cups of blueberry

6 Draw to show the ratio pattern.

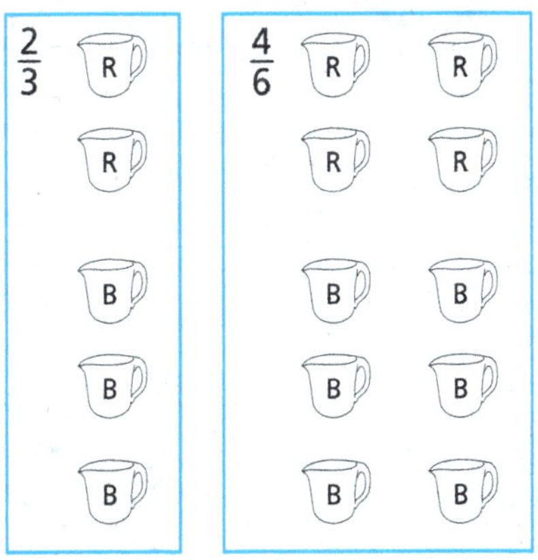

a. $\frac{6}{9}$ b. $\frac{8}{12}$

7 Discuss how equivalent fractions and equivalent ratios are alike and different.

Check Understanding

Draw one picture to represent the fraction $\frac{4}{5}$ and one picture to represent the ratio 4:5.

Name ____________________

Cross-Multiplication and Unit Rates

9 Zander paid \$7 for 5 avocados. How much would 9 avocados cost?

Discuss how these solution strategies relate to each other.

Rate Table

÷ 5 · 9

Dollars	7	$\frac{7}{5}$	$\frac{63}{5}$
Avocados	5	1	9

÷ 5 · 9

Factor Puzzle

		5	9
Dollars	$\frac{7}{5}$	7	$\frac{63}{5}$
Avocados	1	5	9

Cross-Multiplication

$$\frac{7}{5} = \frac{c}{9}$$

$$c \cdot 5 = 7 \cdot 9$$

$$5c = 63$$

$$c = \frac{63}{5}$$

The price for 9 avocados is $\frac{63}{5}$ dollars, or \$12.60.

What's the Error?

Dear Math Students,

It took me 15 minutes to ride my bike 3 miles. I wanted to find out how long it would take me to ride 10 miles. My work can't be right because my answer is only 2 minutes! What did I do wrong?

Thank you.
Puzzled Penguin

$$\frac{15}{3} = \frac{10}{t}$$

$$10 \cdot 3 = 15 \cdot t$$

$$30 = 15t$$

$$2 = t$$

10 Write a response to the Puzzled Penguin.

____

____

____

____

Check Understanding

Write the ratios in the proportion in fraction form.
Then, solve for the unknown. $3:4 = a:16$ ____________

Name ______________________________

Solve.

1 Complete these ratio tables.

Recipe A

Oatmeal (cups)	Flour (cups)
3	4
15	

Recipe B

Oatmeal (cups)	Flour (cups)
5	6
15	

Which recipe contains more flour for the same amount of oatmeal?

____

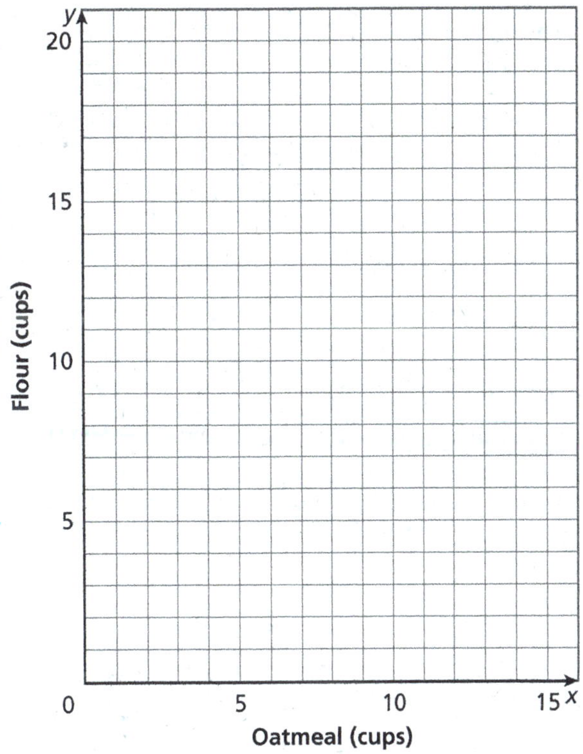

2 Graph the points from each table. Draw and label a line for *Recipe A* and a line for *Recipe B*.

3 Explain how to use the two lines and a straightedge to find which recipe has more oatmeal for the same amount of flour.

____

____

____

____

____

4 A bread recipe requires 7 teaspoons of flax seed for every 2 teaspoons of yeast. What amount of flax seed is required for every teaspoon of yeast?

____

5 A pineapple-orange juice is made by mixing 3 cups of pineapple juice and 5 cups of orange juice. How many cups of orange juice should be mixed with 7 cups of pineapple juice to make a juice that will taste the same as the original?

____

Fluency Check 15

Name ____________________

PATH to FLUENCY

1. 41.38 − 5.27

2. 76.57 − 6.28

3. 34.07 − 8.23

4. 65.14 − 7.73

5. 17.62 − 9.19

6. 28.35 − 24.96

7. 14.08 − 12.79

8. 37.14 − 28.25

9. \$82.17 − \$ 6.45

10. \$19.33 − \$ 6.88

11. \$54.04 − \$ 9.35

12. \$72.56 − \$70.78

13. \$27.11 − \$22.94

14. \$40.68 − \$38.72

15. \$91.60 − \$81.75

Name ______________________________

Using Tape Diagrams to Model Ratios

A juice company's KiwiBerry juice is made by mixing 2 parts kiwifruit juice with 3 parts strawberry juice.

KiwiBerry Juice

2 parts kiwifruit

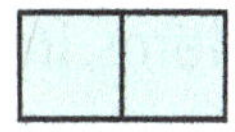

3 parts strawberry

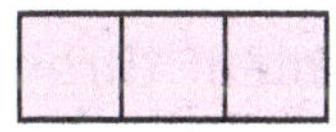

The ratio of parts of kiwifruit juice to parts of strawberry juice can be modeled by using a *tape diagram*.

Solve each problem three ways: using the tape diagram, using a Factor Puzzle, and using cross-multiplication.

1. How many liters of kiwifruit juice should be mixed with 15 liters of strawberry juice to make KiwiBerry juice? ______ liters

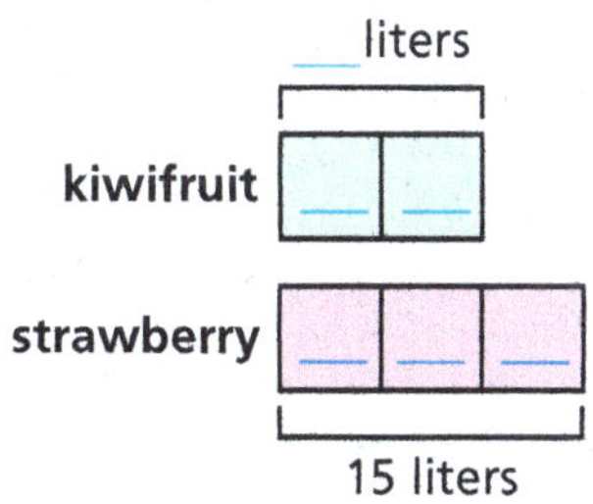

	1	
k	2	☐
s	3	15

$\frac{2}{3} = \frac{x}{15}$

2. How many liters of strawberry juice should be mixed with 50 liters of kiwifruit juice to make KiwiBerry juice? ______ liters

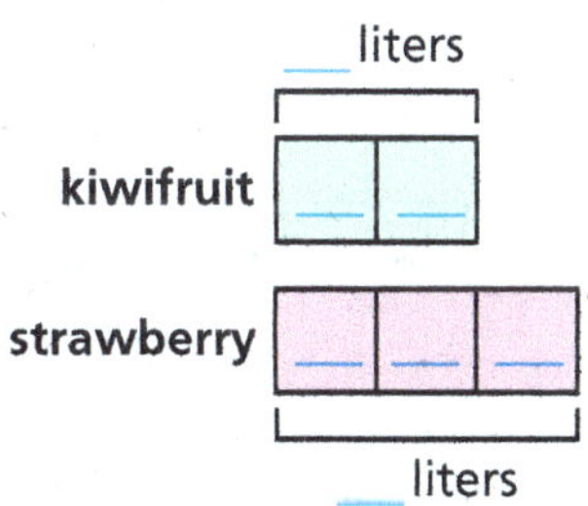

k		
s		☐

3. How many liters of kiwifruit juice should be mixed with 20 liters of strawberry juice to make KiwiBerry juice? ______ liters

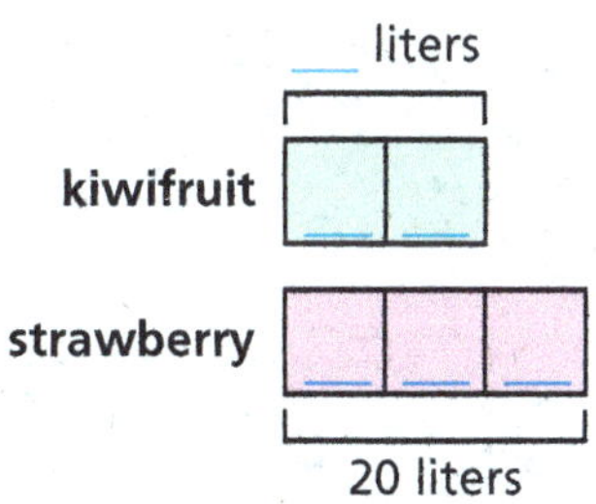

k		☐
s		

Name ______________________________

Part-to-Whole Ratios

Remember that KiwiBerry juice is made by mixing 2 parts kiwifruit juice with 3 parts strawberry juice.

We can solve problems involving the total amount of juice or the total number of parts.

Solve each problem three ways: using the tape diagram, using a Factor Puzzle, and using cross-multiplication.

7. How many liters of kiwifruit juice should be used to make 50 liters of KiwiBerry juice? ________ liters

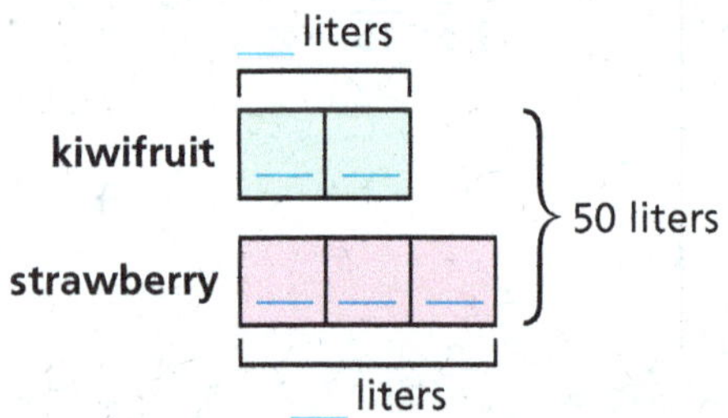

	1	
k	2	
KB	5	50

$$\frac{2}{5} = \frac{x}{50}$$

8. How many liters of strawberry juice should be used to make 20 liters of KiwiBerry juice? ________ liters

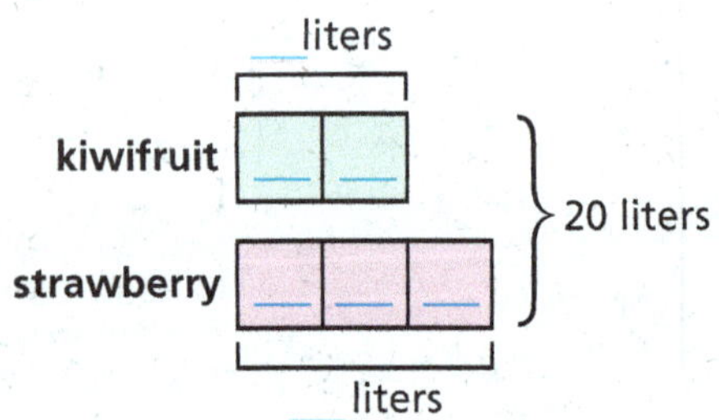

9. If 7 liters of kiwifruit juice are used, how many liters of KiwiBerry juice can be made? ________ liters

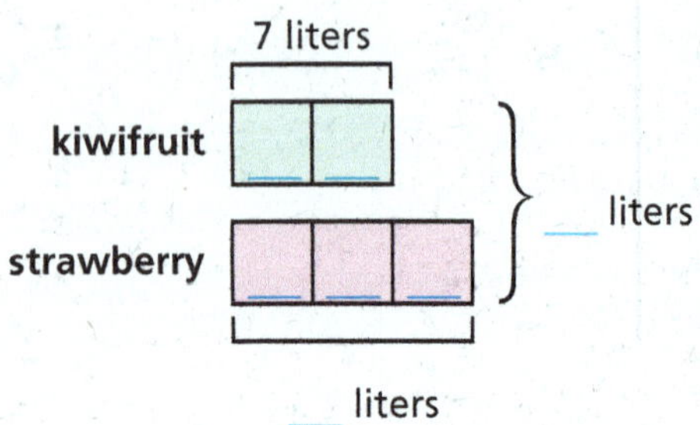

Name ______________________________

Different Portions Can Be One Whole

10 Complete each tape diagram.

Green sand is 1.

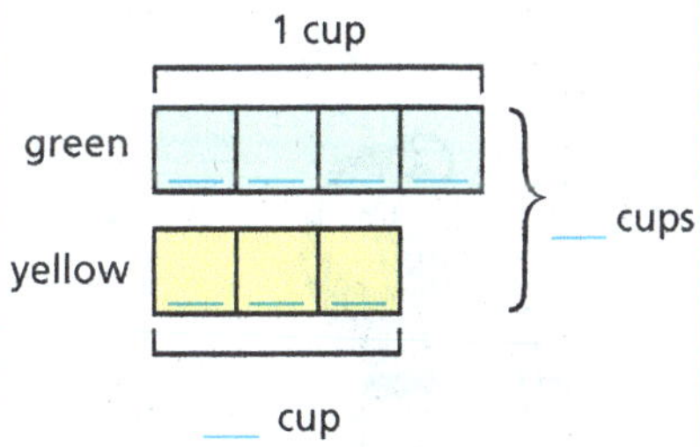

Yellow sand is 1.

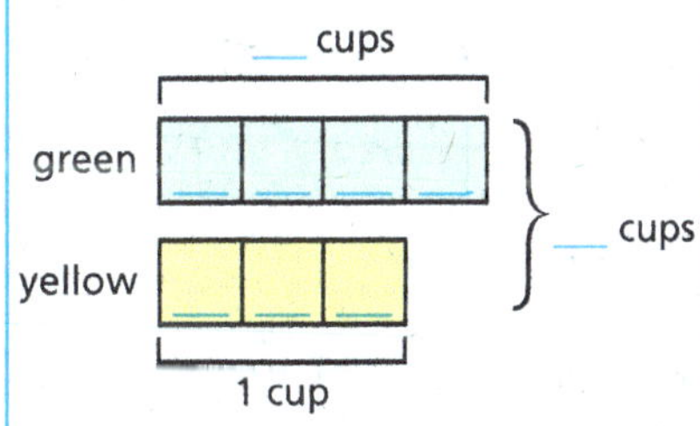

Total sand is 1.

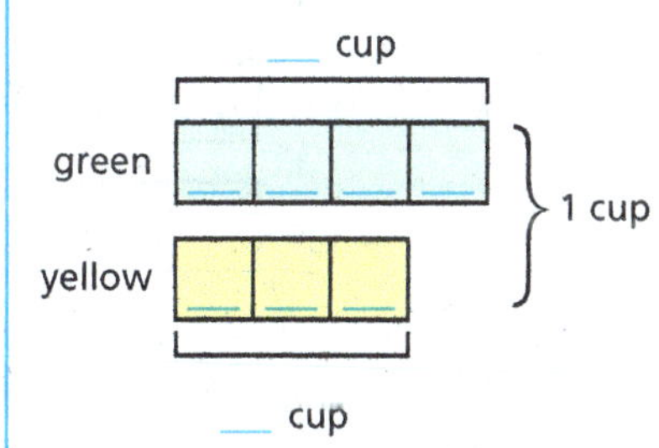

Unit Rates

Write a fraction to complete each unit rate.

11 __________ cup of yellow sand for every 1 cup of green sand in the mixture

12 __________ cups of green sand for every 1 cup of yellow sand in the mixture

13 __________ cup of green sand and __________ cup of yellow sand for every 1 cup of mixture

14 __________ cups of mixture for every 1 cup of green sand

15 __________ cups of mixture for every 1 cup of yellow sand

Multiplicative Comparisons

Write a fraction to complete each multiplicative comparison.

16 The amount of yellow sand is __________ times the amount of green sand.

17 The amount of green sand is __________ times the amount of yellow sand.

18 The total amount of mixture is __________ times the amount of green sand.

19 The total amount of mixture is __________ times the amount of yellow sand.

Name ______________________________

What's the Error?

Dear Math Students,

I made my own sand mixture. I mixed 2 parts purple and 5 parts orange.

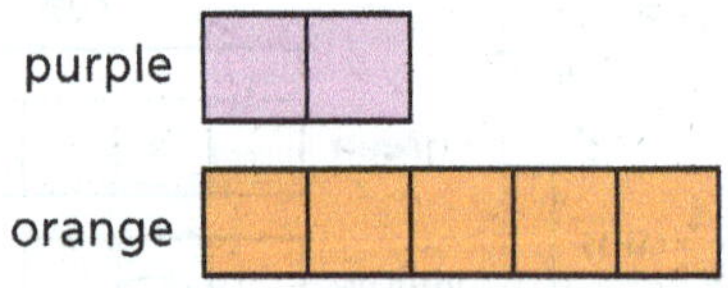

Then I wrote this multiplicative comparison.

- The amount of purple sand is $\frac{2}{5}$ times the amount of the total mixture.

My friend says that I made a mistake. Did I? If I did, can you tell me what mistake I made and help me correct it?

Your friend,
Puzzled Penguin

20 Write a response to Puzzled Penguin.

____

____

____

____

____

____

Use Equations to Relate Quantities

21 Let g be the number of cups of green sand in Seth's ratio. Let y be the number of cups of yellow sand in Seth's ratio.

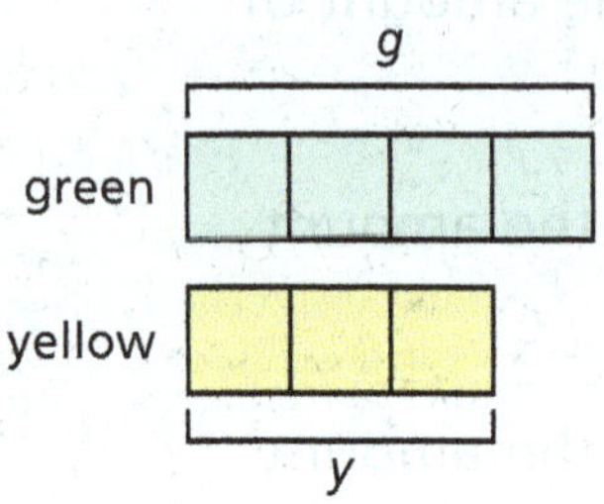

$\frac{4}{3} = \frac{g}{y}$

$y = \frac{3}{4}g$

$\frac{4}{3}y = g$

Discuss why these three equations can all be used to relate g and y.

Name ______________________________

Solve.

Show your work.

1. In a laboratory, Solution A will be mixed with Solution B in a ratio of 3 to 2. What amount of Solution A is needed to mix with 750 mL of Solution B?

____

2. It takes a maintenance person 36 minutes to replace all of the fluorescent light bulbs in 2 identical classrooms. At that rate, how long would it take him to change the bulbs in 12 identical classrooms?

____

3. Apple and cranberry juice are mixed in a ratio of 5 to 3. What amount of each juice would be needed to make a 64-fluid ounce pitcher of apple-cranberry juice?

____

4. A juice mixture is 3 parts pineapple juice to 5 parts orange juice. For every pitcher of the mixture, what fraction of the pitcher is each type of juice?

____

5. If a 3-pound bunch of bananas cost $1.50, how many pounds of bananas should you be able to buy for $5.25?

____

Fluency Check 16

Name ____________________

PATH to FLUENCY

1. 72.60 − 3.55 =

2. 40.38 − 5.41 =

3. 14.09 − 4.29 =

4. 86.12 − 6.63 =

5. 27.72 − 14.8 =

6. 50.04 − 23.7 =

7. 31.44 − 30.9 =

8. 65.01 − 5.28 =

9. 782 − 0.08 =

10. 507 − 0.05 =

11. 3,782 − 0.06 =

12. 7,013 − 0.15 =

13. 2,902 − 0.29 =

14. 4,883 − 4.17 =

15. 1,657 − 6.38 =

Name ______________________________

VOCABULARY
percent

Define Percent

Percent means "out of 100" or "for each 100." The symbol for percent is %.

> 37% is read "37 percent."
>
> It can mean the fraction $\frac{37}{100}$, the ratio 37:100, or the rate 37 *per* 100.

The fans at a sold-out concert are in 100 equal sections of seats. Each small rectangle in the diagram represents one section of fans.

1. Color one section blue.

   What fraction of the fans is this?

   ____

   What percent of the fans is this?

   ____

2. Color three sections red.

   What fraction of the fans is this?

   ____

   What percent of the fans is this?

   ____

3. Color 23% of the sections green.

   What fraction of the fans is this?

   ____

4. Color 37% of the sections yellow.

   What fraction of the fans is this?

   ____

5. Shade some sections in purple. What percent did you shade?

   ____

Name ______________________________

Percents of Bar Diagrams

The bars in Exercises 6–9 are divided into 100 equal parts.

6. Shade 5% of the bar.

7. Shade 15% of the bar.

8. Shade 45% of the bar.

9. Shade 85% of the bar.

10. Label each section with the percent of the whole bar it represents. Under the section, write the fraction it represents.

Bar A

___%	___%
___	___

Bar B

___%	___%	___%	___%	___%	___%	___%	___%	___%	___%
___	___	___	___	___	___	___	___	___	___

Bar C

___%	___%	___%	___%	___%
___	___	___	___	___

Bar D

___%	___%	___%	___%
___	___	___	___

11. Shade 70% of Bar B.

12. Shade 60% of Bar C.

13. Shade 75% of Bar D.

Name ______________________________

Relating Percents, Decimals, and Fractions

14 Label each long tick mark with a decimal, a percent, and a fraction with a denominator of 10. If the fraction can be simplified, write the simplified form as well.

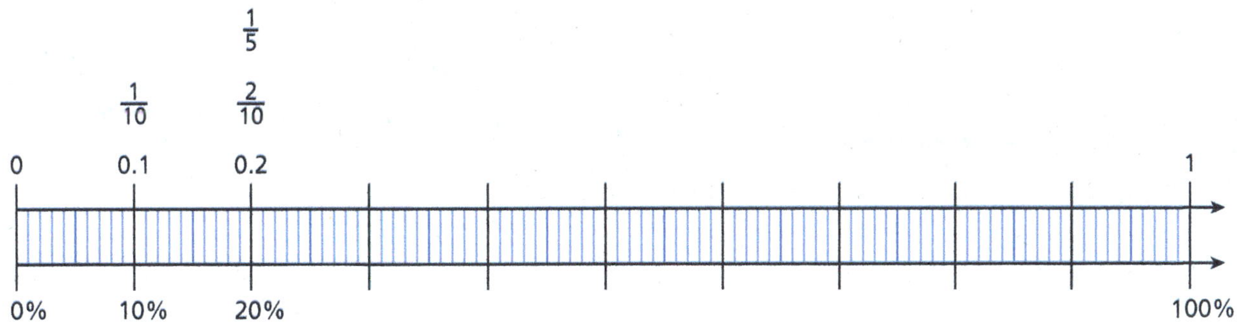

15 Write each percent as a fraction with denominator 100 and as a decimal. Then place the percents and decimals on the number lines.

Percent	83%	51%	46%	6%	60%	27%	127%	3%	30%	130%
Fraction	$\frac{83}{100}$						$\frac{127}{100}$			
Decimal	0.83						1.27			

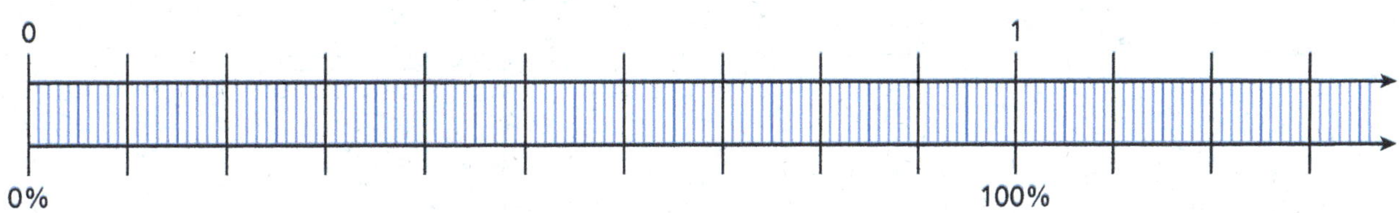

Name ______________________

What's the Error?

Dear Math Students,

I said that 7% is 0.7, but my friend said that I am not right. Why not? Please help me understand how percents and decimals are related.

Thank you.
Puzzled Penguin

16 Write a response to Puzzled Penguin.

____

____

Percents and Area

What percent of the figure is shaded?

17 ____________

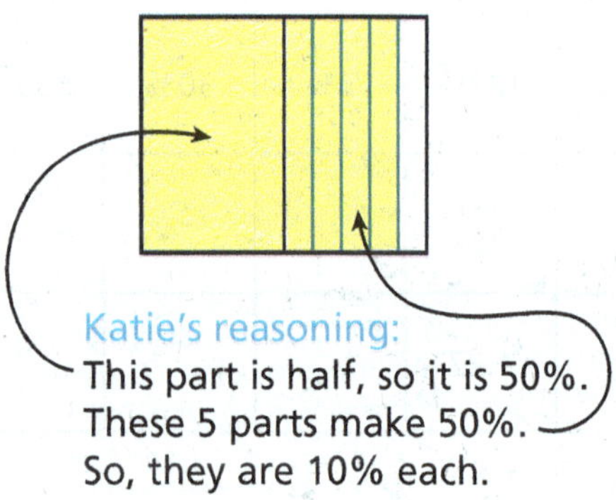

18 ____________

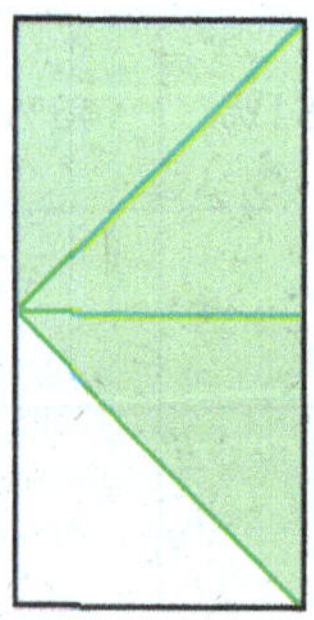

19 ____________

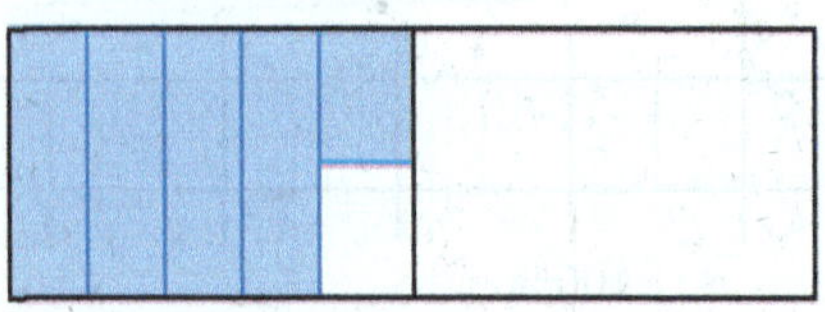

20 ____________

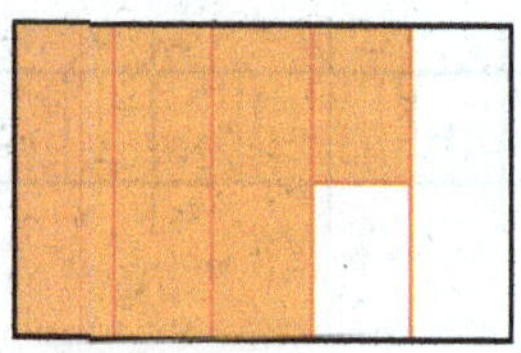

Check Understanding

Explain what the word *percent* means and how percents are related to fractions and decimals.

Name ______________________

Model Finding a Percent of a Number

The 300 students at a school are in 100 groups of 3.

1. Color one group blue.

   What percent of the students is this?

   ____

   What number of students is this?

   ____

2. Color four groups red.

   What percent of the students is this?

   ____

   What number of students is this?

   ____

3. Color 17 groups green.

   What percent of the students is this?

   ____

   What number of students is this?

   ____

4. Color 9% of the students yellow.

   What number of students is this?

   ____

5. Color 24% of students orange.

   What number of students is this?

   ____

6. Color 35% of the students purple.

   What number of students is this?

   ____

Name

Percent as a Ratio

Now the students at the school are in 3 groups of 100.

12 Circle one student from each group in blue.

What percent of the students is this?

What number of students is this?

13 Circle four students from each group in red.

What percent of the students is this?

What number of students is this?

14 Circle 45% of the students in green.

How many students is this? Why?

15 Circle 82% of the students in yellow.

How many students is that? Why?

Name

Methods for Finding a Percent of a Number

Five students had different ideas about how to solve the problem below.

Of the 300 students at a school, 99% say they are going to the school party. How many students is this?

Use each idea to solve the problem.

Show your work.

16 Hilda's idea: 99% means 99 for each 100. So, I will use a 99% ratio table.

99% ratio table

portion	99		
whole	100	200	300

17 Anna's idea: I will divide 300 by 100 to find 1% of 300. Then, I will multiply that answer by 99 to find 99% of 300.

18 Rantavious's idea: I will use the fact that 99% of 300 means $\frac{99}{100}$ times 300.

19 Jon's idea: If p is the number of students going to the party, then the fraction of students going is $\frac{p}{300}$, and it is also $\frac{99}{100}$. I can write and solve a proportion.

20 Gregory's idea: 99% is 100% minus 1%, so I will take 1% of the 300 students away from 100% of 300.

Solve.

21 What is 51% of 600 students?

Check Understanding

What is 49% of 500 students?

Name ______________________

Percents of Numbers

The adult dose of a medicine is 8 milliliters. The child dose is 75% of the adult dose. How many milliliters is the child dose?

1 Complete the double number line to help you solve this problem.

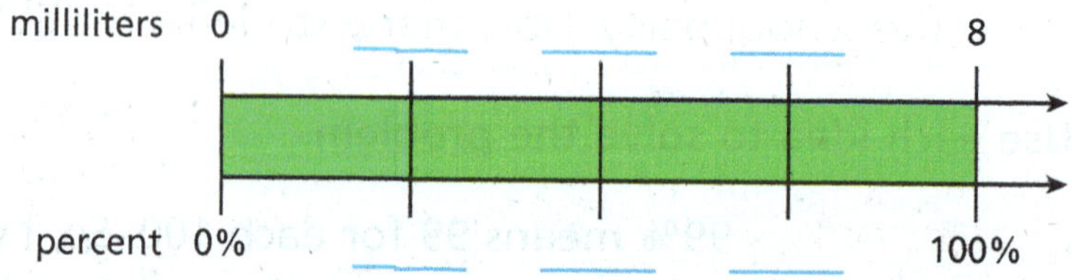

2 Discuss and complete these solutions.

Trey's Reasoning About Parts

100% is 4 parts, which is 8 mL.

25% is 1 part, which is 8 mL ÷ 4 = 2 mL.

75% is 3 parts and is ______________

Quowanna's Factor Puzzle

	percent	milliliters
	25	
portion	75	☐
whole	100	8

Tomaslav's Equation

m is 75% of 8.

$m = \frac{75}{100} \cdot 8 =$ ______________

Jessica's Proportion

	percent		milliliters
portion / whole	$\frac{75}{100}$	=	$\frac{m}{8}$
	$\frac{3}{4}$	=	$\frac{m}{8}$
	m	=	______

Solve in two ways.

3 The adult dose of a medicine is 6 milliliters. The child dose is 75% of the adult dose. How many milliliters is the child dose?

____

4 A chemist needs 20% of the 120 milliliters of solution in a beaker. How many milliliters of solution does the chemist need?

____

Name ______________________________

Find the Whole from the Percent and the Part

If 12 milligrams is 60% of the recommended daily allowance for niacin, then what is the recommended daily allowance for niacin?

5 Complete the double number line to help you solve this problem.

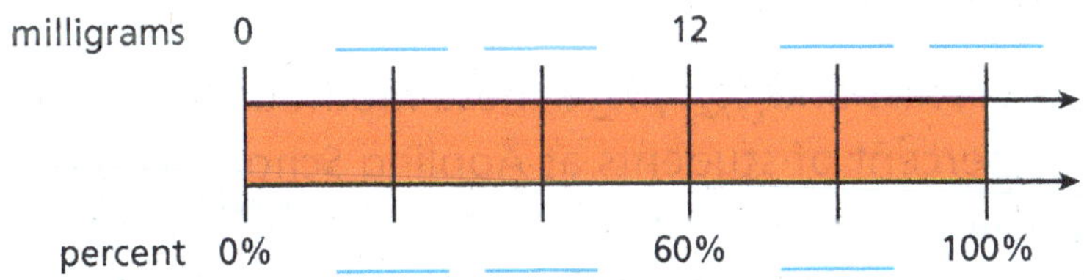

6 Discuss and complete these solutions.

Trey's Reasoning about Parts

60% is 3 parts and is 12 mg.

20% is 1 part, which is 12 mg ÷ 3 = 4 mg.

100% is 5 parts, which is ______________.

Quowanna's Factor Puzzle

	percent	milliliters
portion	60	12
whole	100	

Tomaslav's Equation

60% of g is 12.

$\frac{60}{100} \cdot g = 12$

Jessica's Proportion

	percent		milliliters
portion / whole	$\frac{60}{100}$	=	$\frac{12}{g}$

Solve.

7 What is 40% of 70? ________

8 40% of what number is 70? ________

9 30% of what number is 120? ________

10 What is 30% of 120? ________

11 If 75% of the recommended daily allowance of vitamin C is 45 mg, what is the recommended daily allowance of vitamin C? ______________________

Check Understanding

Make a Factor Puzzle to solve the following problem.
12 is 80% of what number? ________

Name ______________________________

Use Percents to Compare

Using percents can help you compare two groups when the sizes of the groups are different.

Appling School has 300 students and 45 students ride a bus to and from school each day. Baldwin School has 500 students and 55 students ride a bus.

1 Discuss and complete these methods for calculating the percent of students at Appling School who ride a bus.

Alex's Equation

$f\%$ is $\frac{45}{300}$.

$\frac{f}{100} = \frac{45}{300}$

Jordan's Equation

$f\%$ of 300 is 45.

$\frac{f}{100} \cdot 300 = 45$

Aliya's Factor Puzzle

	percent	students
portion		45
whole	100	300

Rachel's Idea of Going through 1%

300 students is 100%.

$300 \div 100 = 3$; 3 students is 1%.

$45 \div 3 = 15$; 45 students is 15 groups of 3 students, which is ________%.

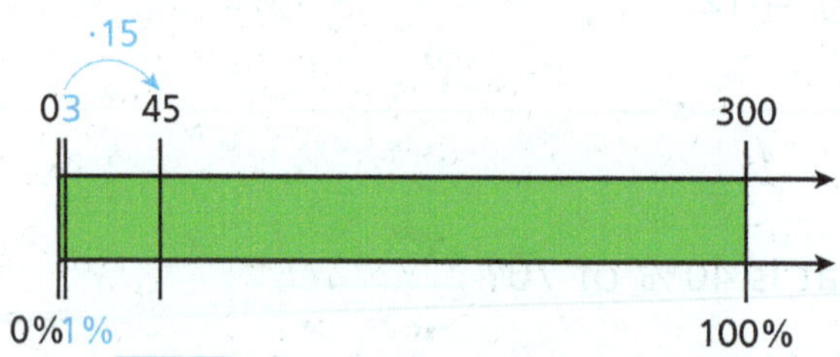

2 Use two methods to calculate the percent of students at Baldwin School who ride a bus.

____

Unit 7
Quick Quiz 3

Name ______________________________

Solve.

1 Complete the double number line below. Then explain how it can be used to find 80% of 25 pounds.

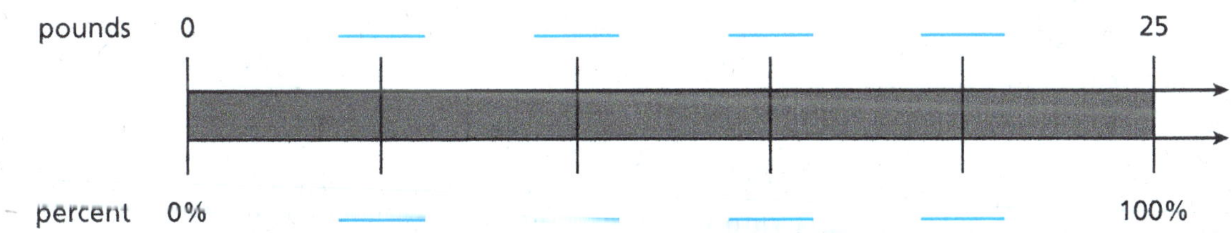

____

____

____

____

Solve.

Show your work.

2 40% of what number is 84?

____

3 Of the 190 students in an elementary school, 57 students had perfect attendance during the second semester. What percent of the students had perfect attendance that semester?

____

4 A mortgage payment represents 21% of a family's monthly budget. If the mortgage payment is $756 per month, what amount of money is the family's monthly budget?

____

5 Of the 820 residents of a town, 35% are children. How many children live in the town?

____

Fluency Check 17

Name ______________________

PATH to FLUENCY

1.
$$\begin{array}{r} 0.623 \\ +\ 0.178 \\ \hline \end{array}$$

2.
$$\begin{array}{r} 0.527 \\ +\ 0.387 \\ \hline \end{array}$$

3.
$$\begin{array}{r} 0.824 \\ -\ 0.736 \\ \hline \end{array}$$

4.
$$\begin{array}{r} 0.209 \\ -\ 0.134 \\ \hline \end{array}$$

5.
$$\begin{array}{r} 2.783 \\ +\ 1.098 \\ \hline \end{array}$$

6.
$$\begin{array}{r} 4.257 \\ +\ 2.789 \\ \hline \end{array}$$

7.
$$\begin{array}{r} 1.062 \\ -\ 0.748 \\ \hline \end{array}$$

8.
$$\begin{array}{r} 1.329 \\ -\ 1.255 \\ \hline \end{array}$$

9.
$$\begin{array}{r} 12.451 \\ -\ 8.073 \\ \hline \end{array}$$

10.
$$\begin{array}{r} 18.362 \\ -\ 17.259 \\ \hline \end{array}$$

11.
$$\begin{array}{r} 20.752 \\ -\ 19.153 \\ \hline \end{array}$$

12.
$$\begin{array}{r} 40.146 \\ +\ 8.075 \\ \hline \end{array}$$

13.
$$\begin{array}{r} 11.108 \\ +\ 8.473 \\ \hline \end{array}$$

14.
$$\begin{array}{r} 15.419 \\ +\ 14.675 \\ \hline \end{array}$$

15.
$$\begin{array}{r} 23.056 \\ +\ 14.176 \\ \hline \end{array}$$

Name ______________________

Convert Between Centimeters and Millimeters

1 Label the double number line to show how centimeters (cm) and millimeters (mm) are related.

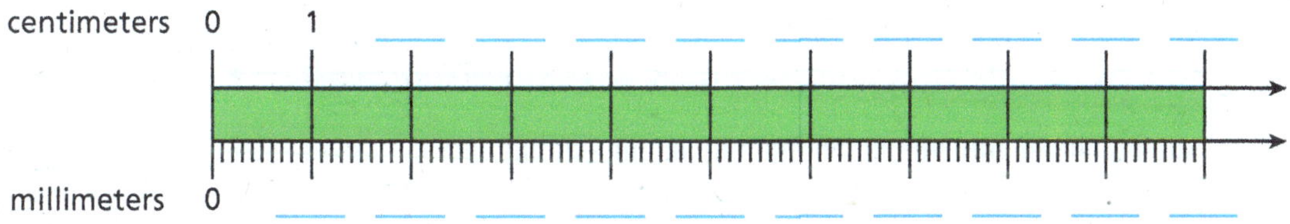

We can write two unit rates comparing centimeters to millimeters.

There are 10 millimeters per centimeter.

We can write this unit rate as $10 \frac{\text{mm}}{\text{cm}}$.

There is $\frac{1}{10}$ centimeter per millimeter.

We can write this unit rate as $\frac{1}{10} \frac{\text{cm}}{\text{mm}}$.

Unit rates are helpful for converting measurements from one unit to another.

2 Compare these methods of converting 52 centimeters to millimeters.

Write and Solve a Proportion

$$\frac{1 \text{ cm}}{10 \text{ mm}} = \frac{52 \text{ cm}}{x \text{ mm}}$$

$$52 \cdot 10 = 1 \cdot x$$

$$520 = x$$

So, 52 cm = 520 mm.

Use a Unit Rate

$$52 \cancel{\text{cm}} \cdot 10 \frac{\text{mm}}{\cancel{\text{cm}}} = 520 \text{ mm}$$

There are 52 cm, and there are 10 mm in each cm.

The unit cm cancels, leaving the unit mm.

3 Complete these methods for converting 85 millimeters to centimeters.

Write and Solve a Proportion

$$\frac{1 \text{ cm}}{10 \text{ mm}} = \frac{x \text{ cm}}{85 \text{ mm}}$$

So, 85 mm = ________ cm.

Use a Unit Rate

$$85 \cancel{\text{mm}} \cdot \frac{1}{10} \frac{\text{cm}}{\cancel{\text{mm}}} = \text{\_\_\_\_\_\_\_\_ cm}$$

There are 85 mm, and there is $\frac{1}{10}$ cm in each mm.

Name ______________________________

Convert Between Feet and Inches

4 Label the double number line to show how feet and inches are related.

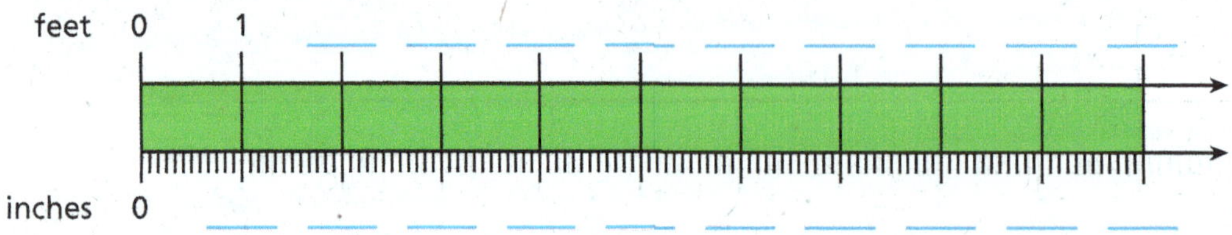

5 What are the two unit rates in this situation?

________ $\frac{\text{in.}}{\text{ft}}$ and ________ $\frac{\text{ft}}{\text{in.}}$

6 Convert 132 inches to feet by multiplying by a unit rate. Show your work.

132 in. = ________ ft

7 Convert $6\frac{1}{2}$ feet to inches by multiplying by a unit rate. Show your work.

$6\frac{1}{2}$ ft = ________ in.

Practice Converting Units of Length

8 What two unit rates relate centimeters (cm) and meters (m)?

____

9 Convert 7.9 meters to centimeters using any method.

7.9 m = ________ cm

10 Convert 42 centimeters to meters using any method.

42 cm = ________ m

11 What two unit rates relate feet (ft) and yards (yd)?

____

12 Convert 16 feet to yards using any method.

16 ft = ________ yd

13 Convert 24 yards to feet using any method.

24 yd = ________ ft

Name ____________________

Practice Solving Area Problems

Solve.

18 A rectangle has a base length of 3 meters and a height of 15 decimeters. Find the area of the rectangle. Be sure to specify the unit in your answer.

____

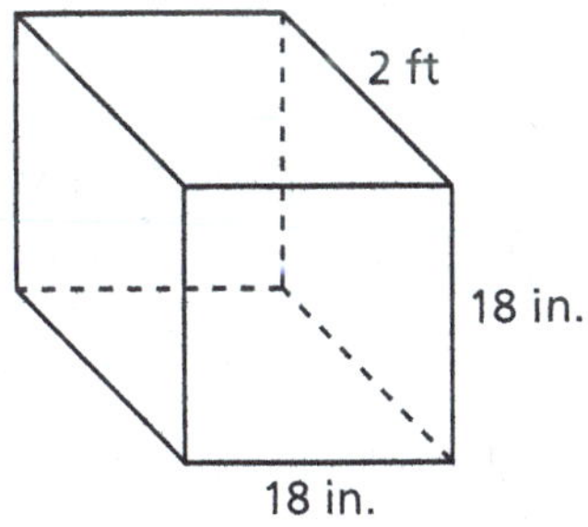

19 Find the surface area of the rectangular prism at the right. Be sure to specify the unit in your answer.

____

What's the Error?

Dear Math Students,

The school nurse said that I am 42 inches tall. I wanted to figure out how many feet this is. Here's what I did:

$42 \text{ in.} \cdot 12 \frac{\text{in.}}{\text{ft}} = 504 \text{ ft}$

I know I am not 504 feet tall! Please help me figure out what I did wrong and help me find my real height in feet.

Thank you,
Puzzled Penguin

20 Write a response to Puzzled Penguin.

____

____

____

____

Check Understanding

Explain how to convert units of length using a proportion and using a unit rate.

Name ______________________

Converting Metric Units of Liquid Volume

The most common metric units of liquid volume, or capacity, are milliliters and liters.

5. Label the double number line to show how liters (L) and milliliters (mL) are related.

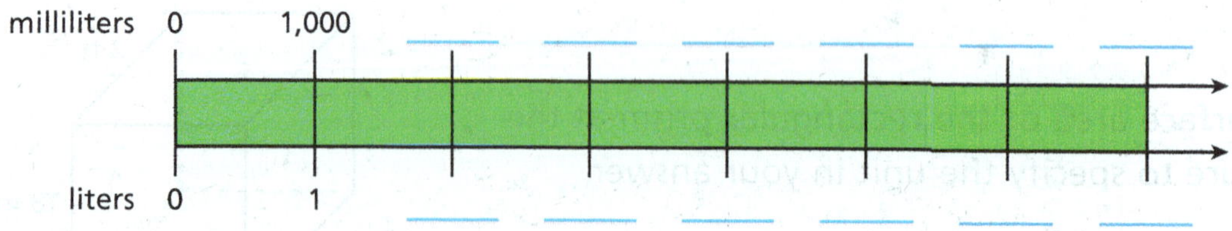

6. What two unit rates relate liters and milliliters?

____

7. A can holds 344 mL of seltzer. How many liters is this? Find your answer in two ways: by writing and solving a proportion and by using a unit rate.

Write and Solve a Proportion	**Use a Unit Rate**

344 mL = ________ L

Solve using any method.

8. A bottle contains 1.89 liters of water. How many milliliters is this?

____

9. A soap dispenser holds 220 mL of soap. A refill bottle of soap contains 1.76 L. How many times can the dispenser be refilled from the bottle?

____

Unit 7
Quick Quiz 4

Name ______________________

Solve.

Show your work.

1. Write two unit rates relating millimeters (mm) and centimeters (cm).

____

Convert 450 millimeters to centimeters.

____

2. Write two unit rates relating meters (m) and kilometers (km).

____

Convert 2.9 kilometers to meters.

____

3. How many juice glasses, each having a capacity of 125 mL, could be filled from a pitcher containing 2 L of juice?

____

4. The floor of a classroom is shaped like a rectangle and has a length of 42 feet. The carpet that covers the entire floor has an area of 168 square yards. What is the width of the classroom in feet?

____

5. Shauna's favorite breakfast cereal was on sale, so she bought 12 boxes. Each box contained 12 ounces of cereal. How many pounds of cereal did Shauna buy?

____

Fluency Check 18

Name ___

PATH to FLUENCY

Add or subtract.

1. $\begin{array}{r} 45.6 \\ +\ 3.52 \\ \hline \end{array}$

2. $\begin{array}{r} 15.644 \\ -\ 4.951 \\ \hline \end{array}$

3. $\begin{array}{r} \$12.75 \\ +\ \$\ 6.48 \\ \hline \end{array}$

4. 819.2 + 43.6

5. 17.24 − 5.6

6. 7 + 0.15

7. $\begin{array}{r} 0.168 \\ +\ 0.275 \\ \hline \end{array}$

8. $\begin{array}{r} 518.39 \\ +\ 6.12 \\ \hline \end{array}$

9. $\begin{array}{r} 78.61 \\ -\ 12.9 \\ \hline \end{array}$

10. 41.92 − 8.64

11. 238 − 0.31

12. 36.9 + 1.21

13. $\begin{array}{r} \$35.12 \\ -\ \$31.60 \\ \hline \end{array}$

14. $\begin{array}{r} 27.56 \\ -\ 4.81 \\ \hline \end{array}$

15. $\begin{array}{r} 1.521 \\ +\ 4.806 \\ \hline \end{array}$

Name ______________________________

1 Dotti's potato salad uses 5 large potatoes and 2 eggs.
Choose True or False for each statement.

1a. The salad uses potatoes and eggs in a ratio of 5:2. ○ True ○ False

1b. The salad uses 2 potatoes for every 5 eggs. ○ True ○ False

1c. The salad uses $\frac{5}{2}$ potatoes for each egg. ○ True ○ False

2 How are comparing two fractions and comparing two ratios alike? How are they different?

Alike:

Different:

3 The double line graph shows that 100% of a quantity has a mass of 24 grams.

Part A

Complete the double number line and explain your method.

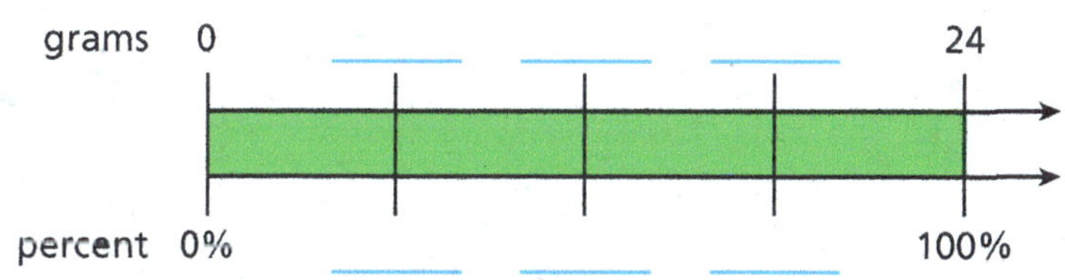

Part B

Explain how you can use the double number line to find 75% of 24 grams.

Name ________________________________

4 Fill in the bubble next to the measure that makes the sentence true.

4 quarts = 1 gallon, so _______ = 1 quart.

○ $\frac{1}{4}$ gallon ○ 0.4 gallon ○ $\frac{4}{1}$ gallons

5 Select Yes or No to indicate if the expression is equivalent to the ratio 3:2.

5a.	$\frac{3}{2}$	○ Yes	○ No
5b.	6:3	○ Yes	○ No
5c.	$\frac{9}{4}$	○ Yes	○ No
5d.	12:8	○ Yes	○ No
5e.	$\frac{2}{3}$	○ Yes	○ No

6 There are 420 pumpkins in Jennifer's pumpkin patch. She picked 15% of them. How many pumpkins did Jennifer pick?

Ⓐ 15 pumpkins
Ⓑ 28 pumpkins
Ⓒ 42 pumpkins
Ⓓ 63 pumpkins

7 Carly buys 4 pounds of strawberries for $9.00. What is the unit cost of the strawberries?

_____________ per pound

8 Choose numbers from the number tiles to write two fractions that will make the statement true. You may write a number more than once.

4	5	9

A paint mixture is 4 parts red and 5 parts white. For every 1 gallon of paint, _____________ gallon is red and _____________ gallon is white.

Name ______________________

Solve. Show your work.

9 $\frac{4}{x} = \frac{3}{5}$

$x =$ ______

10 $\frac{1}{7} = \frac{b}{18}$

$b =$ ______

11 14 is what percent of 56? ______

12 25% of what number is 35? ______

13 Which distance is equivalent to 8 meters? Select all that apply.

Ⓐ 80 cm

Ⓑ 800 cm

Ⓒ 0.08 km

Ⓓ 0.008 km

14 Convert 8,900 mL to L.

______

15 Orange and pineapple juice are mixed in a ratio of 4 to 5. Choose one number from each column to show the amount of each juice that is needed to make 36 gallons of orange-pineapple juice.

orange	pineapple
○ 12 gal	○ 16 gal
○ 16 gal	○ 18 gal
○ 18 gal	○ 20 gal
○ 20 gal	○ 24 gal

16 Savitri buys 3 pounds of sliced turkey for $12. At that rate, how much sliced turkey can she buy for $25? Show your work.

______ pounds

Name ______________________________

17 If 35% of a company's advertising budget is $7,000, what is the full advertising budget? Show your work.

$ __________

18 A rectangle has a base of 4 feet and a height of 18 inches. The area of the rectangle is:

Ⓐ 34 square inches

Ⓑ 72 square inches

Ⓒ 6 square feet

Ⓓ 4.5 square feet

19 An empty bottle of olive oil has a capacity of 750 mL. How many empty bottles could be filled with 4.5 L of olive oil? Show your work.

__________ bottles

20 In a lab, Chemical A and Chemical B are mixed in a ratio of 2 to 3.

Part A How much of Chemical B is needed to mix with 18 liters of Chemical A? Explain your answer.

__________ liters

Part B What percent of the mixture is Chemical A? Explain your answer.

__________ %

Part C Suppose the ratio of Chemical A to Chemical B is 4 to 5. Would the percent of the mixture that is Chemical A be greater or less than the percent in the 2 to 3 ratio? Explain.

____

Name ______________________

21 On Friday, Pizza Place sold a total of 120 pizzas.

Part A

30% of the pizzas sold were plain cheese pizzas. How many plain cheese pizzas were sold? Show or explain how you got your answer.

__________ plain cheese pizzas were sold

Part B

Thirty of the pizzas sold were vegetarian pizzas. What percent of the pizzas sold were vegetarian pizzas? Show or explain how you got your answer.

__________ %

Part C

On Saturday, Pizza Place again sold 30 vegetarian pizzas, which was 10% of the total number of pizzas sold on that day. What was the total number of pizzas sold on Saturday? Show or explain how you got your answer.

__________ pizzas sold on Saturday

Name ________________________________

22 Arun's honey-mustard sauce has 3 cups honey and 4 cups mustard. Ben's honey-mustard sauce has 5 cups honey and 8 cups mustard.

Part A

Graph and label a line to represent each ratio.

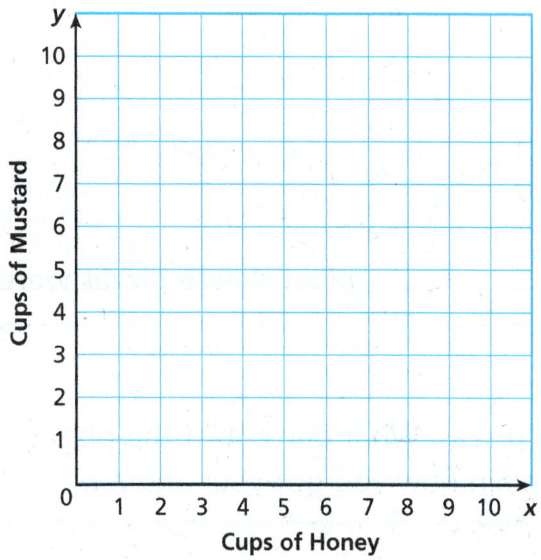

Part B

Explain how to use the two lines and a straightedge to determine whose honey-mustard sauce is more honey-tasting.

Part C

Jenna makes a sauce with 4 cups of honey and 6 cups of mustard. Order the three sauces from most to least honey-tasting. Explain your reasoning.

Name ______________________________

Are You Listening?

Suppose your school has a license to operate a low-power radio station, and you are the program director for the station. (The broadcast of a low-power station only travels a few miles.)

Your station will be on the air for 50 minutes each day after school. Your job is to plan programming for 50 minutes. You must include time for:

- public service announcements for your community
- announcements about just-completed and upcoming school events
- an interview with a teacher, student, or other member of the community
- a commercial about a local business
- music

You can also include other types of programming that your listeners may like.

1. In the first column of the table below, list the different types of programming your 50-minute broadcast will include.

Program Description	Length in minutes	Fraction of 50 minutes	Percent of 50 minutes
Total	50 minutes		

Unit 7
Performance Task

Name ____________________

2. In the second column of the table, write the length of time, in minutes, for each program. (Each program must be a different number of minutes.)

3. In the third column of the table, write a fraction for the portion of the broadcast each program represents. Write each fraction in simplest form.

4. In the fourth column of the table, write a percent for the portion of the broadcast each program represents.

5. Calculate the sum of your fractions and the sum of your percents, and write the sums in the Total row at the bottom of each column in the table. Show your work.

6. Explain how you can use these sums to be sure your calculations from Exercises 3 and 4 are correct.

7. Choose one program from your broadcast. In a school year of 180 days, about how many hours will be used for that program? Show or explain how you got your answer.

Dear Family:

The math unit your child is beginning to study now involves numerical data in the form of statistics and probability.

Some of the important words we will be working with in this unit are shown at the right. Some of the data displays we will be working with are shown below.

Important Words

Statistics
mean or average
median
mode
range
interval
quartiles
clusters
peaks
gaps

Probability
sample space
outcomes
event
relative frequency
experimental probability
theoretical probability

Histogram

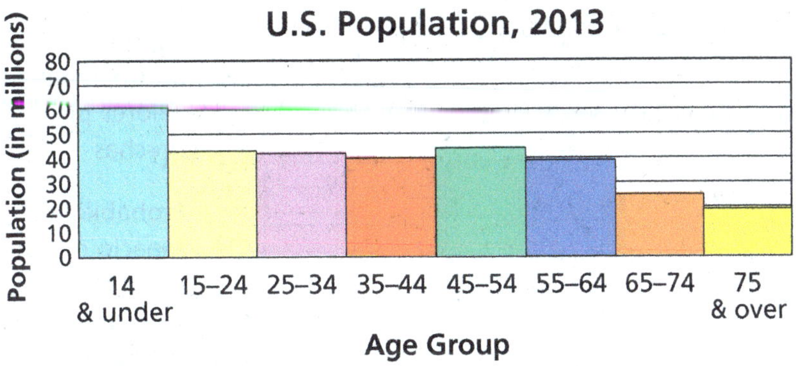

Dot Plot

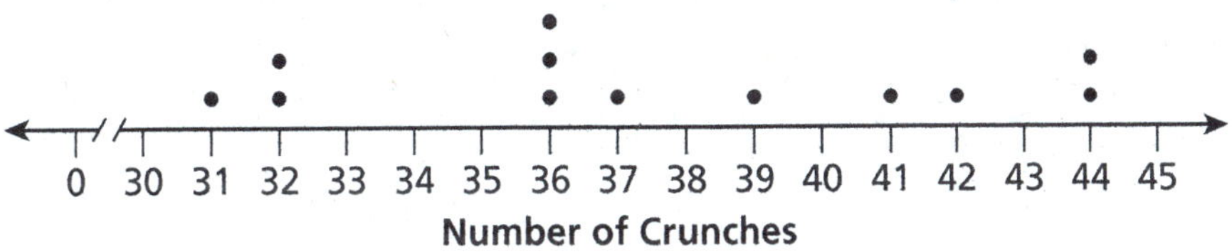

Box Plot

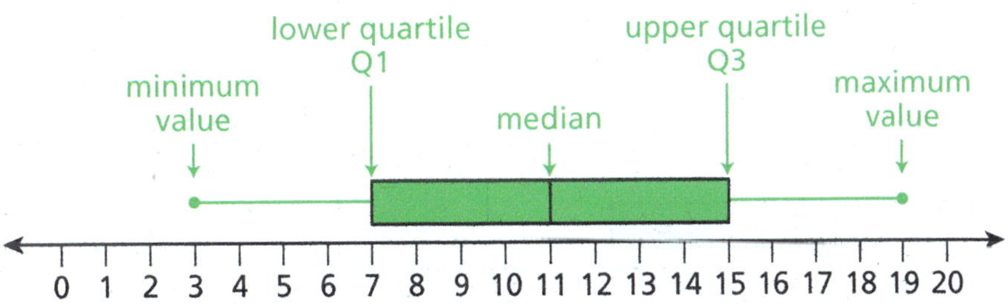

In addition to learning about ways to display data, your child will be learning about ways to analyze and summarize it.

Your child will also be introduced to the basic concepts of probability.

If you have any questions or comments, please contact me.

Sincerely,
Your child's teacher

Estimada familia:

La unidad de matemáticas que estamos comenzando a estudiar trata de datos numéricos en forma de estadísticas y probabilidad.

Algunas de las palabras importantes que usaremos en esta unidad se muestran a la derecha. Algunas de las representaciones de datos que estaremos usando se muestran debajo.

Palabras importantes

Estadísticas
media o promedio
mediana
moda
rango
intervalo
cuartiles
agrupamientos
valores pico
brechas

Probabilidad
espacio muestral
resultados
suceso
frecuencia relativa
probabilidad experimental
probabilidad teórica

Histograma

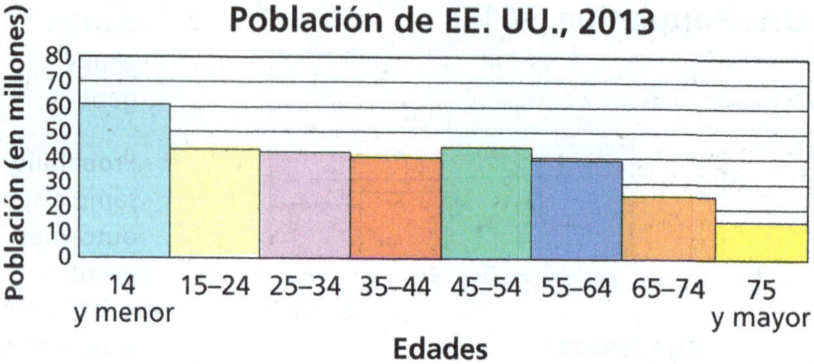

Diagrama de puntos

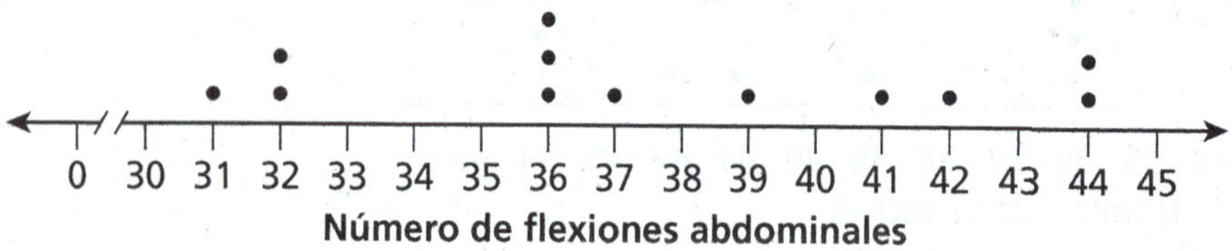

Diagrama de caja y brazos

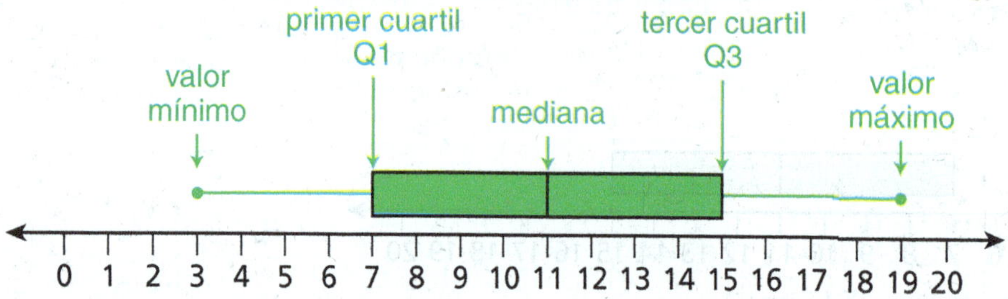

Además de aprender acerca de diferentes maneras de representar datos, su hijo aprenderá cómo analizarlos y resumirlos.

Se le presentará también a su hijo los conceptos básicos de probabilidad.

Si tiene preguntas o comentarios, por favor comuníquese conmigo.

Atentamente,
El maestro de su hijo

box plot	equally likely
cluster	event
dot plot	experiment

All the outcomes of an event have the same chance of occurring.

A graphic summary that shows the median, quartiles, and minimum and maximum values of a set of data.

Example:

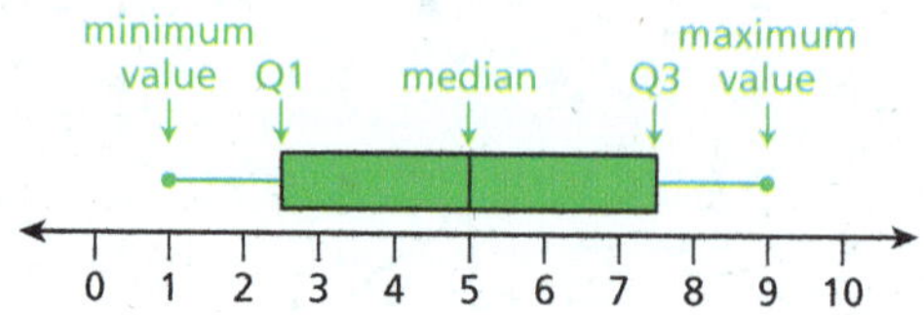

A set of possible outcomes resulting from an experiment.

A group of data values. A data set may have no clusters, one cluster, or more than one cluster.

Example:

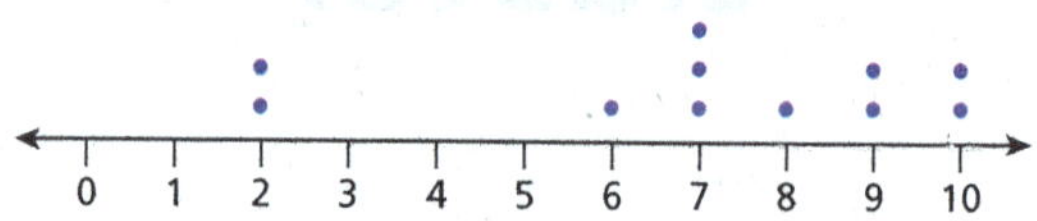

The data cluster from 6 to 10.

A situation involving probability that results in outcomes.

A display showing the frequency of numerical data. A dot plot uses a number line and dots to show how often the numbers in a set of numerical data occur. Also called a **line plot**.

Example:

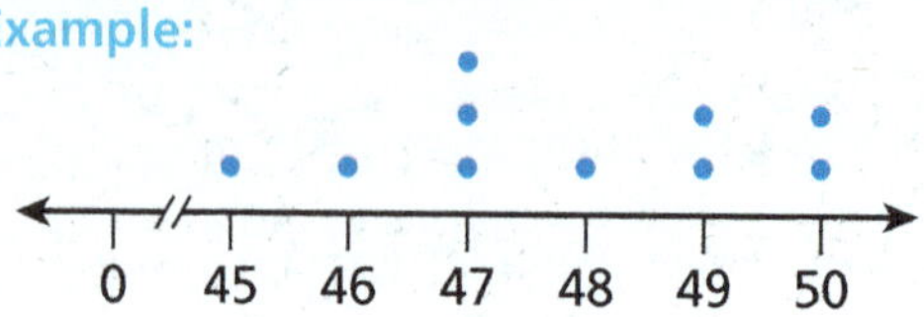

experimental probability	gap
first quartile (Q1)	histogram
frequency	interquartile range (IQR)

An interval with no data. A set of data may have no gaps, one gap, or more than one gap.

Example:

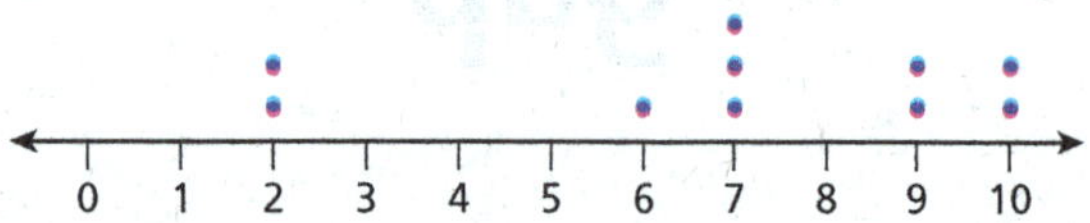

The data have a gap from 3 to 5 and at 8.

In a probability experiment, the relative frequency for an outcome.

A frequency display that uses bars to show the distribution of data in a set. Each bar represents an interval, or range, of data.

Example:

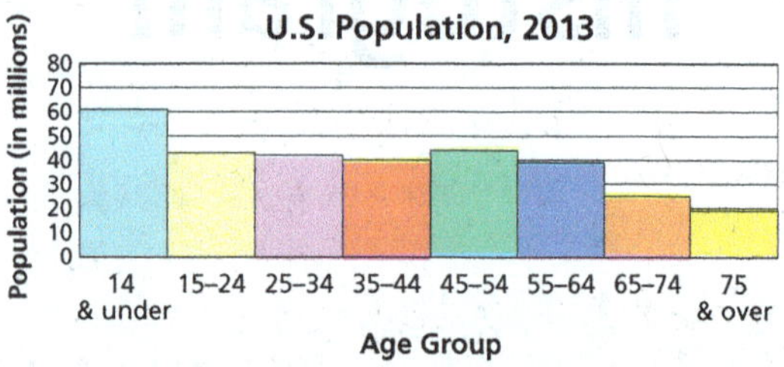

The middle number, or mean of the two middle numbers, of the lower half of a set of data.

Example:

1 2 3 4 5 6 7 8 9 10 11 12

first quartile (between 3 and 4) median (between 6 and 7)

So, Q1 = 3.5.

A measure of the difference between the upper and lower quartiles. IQR is a way to describe the spread or variability of the data in a set.

Example:

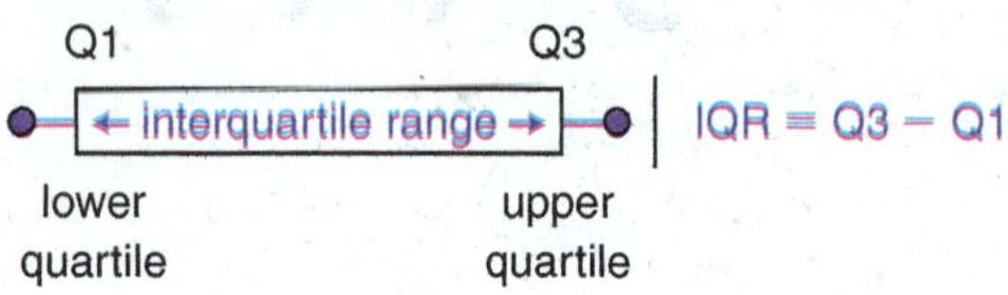

The number of times an outcome occurs during a probability experiment.

interval	**mean**
likelihood	**mean absolute deviation**
likely	**median**

A single number that summarizes all of the values in a set of numerical data. A mean is a measure of center that shows what the common data value would be if all of the data values were the same. A mean is calculated by adding the data values and dividing the sum by the number of values.

A range of numbers in a frequency display such as a histogram. An interval is sometimes called a *bin*.

A measure of variability that shows the average distance the data values in a set are from the mean.

Example:

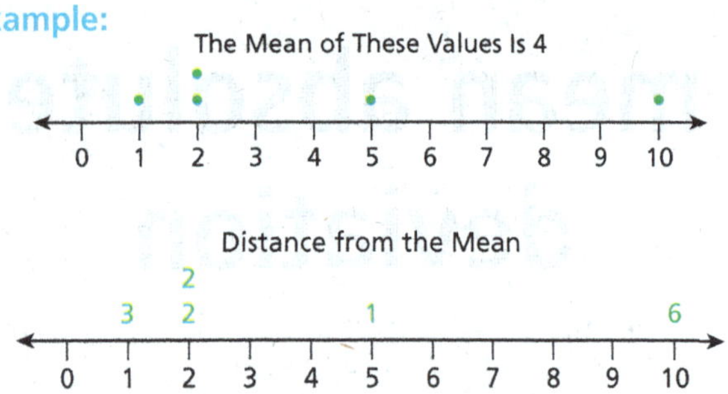

The mean absolute deviation is
$(3 + 2 + 2 + 1 + 6) \div 5 = 2.8$.

A description of the chance that an event will occur.

A single number that summarizes the center of a set of numerical data. The median is the middle number, or the mean of the two middle numbers, when data have been arranged from least to greatest or from greatest to least. After the median has been calculated, one-half of the remaining numbers in the set will be less than the median and one-half will be greater.

The description of an event that has a greater chance of occurring than of not occurring.

numerical data	peak
outcomes	probability
outlier	quartiles

The value (or values) that appear most often. A set of data may have no peaks, one peak, or more than one peak.

Example:

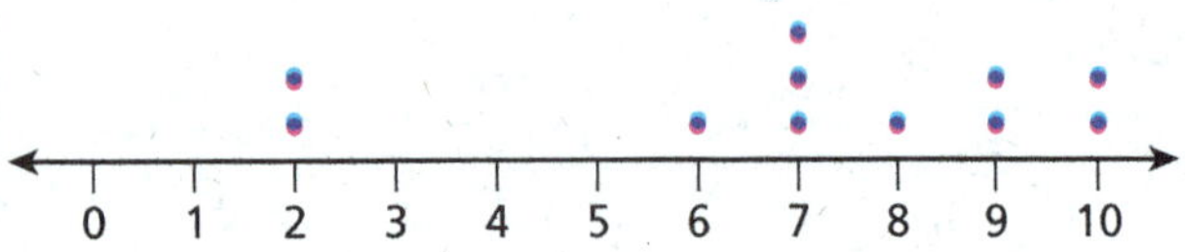

The data peak at 7.

Data involving numbers and quantities.

Examples:

- The number of students in each class in a school.
- The population of a city each year for the last ten years.

A number from 0 to 1 inclusive that describes how likely it is for an event to occur.

The possible results of a probability experiment.

The values of the points that separate a set of data into four approximately equal parts.

An extreme or distant value. A set of data may have no outliers, one outlier, or more than one outlier.

Example:

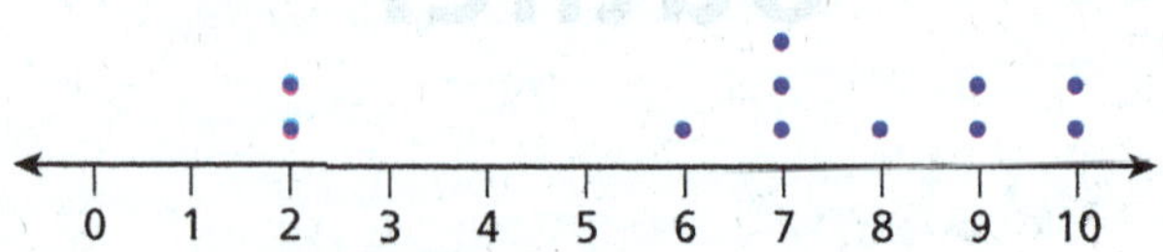

The values at 2 are outliers.

range

symmetric data

relative frequency

theoretical probability

sample space

third quartile (Q3)

A data distribution that has a line of symmetry. The shape of the data on one side of the line of symmetry is the same as the shape of the data on the other side of the line.

Example:

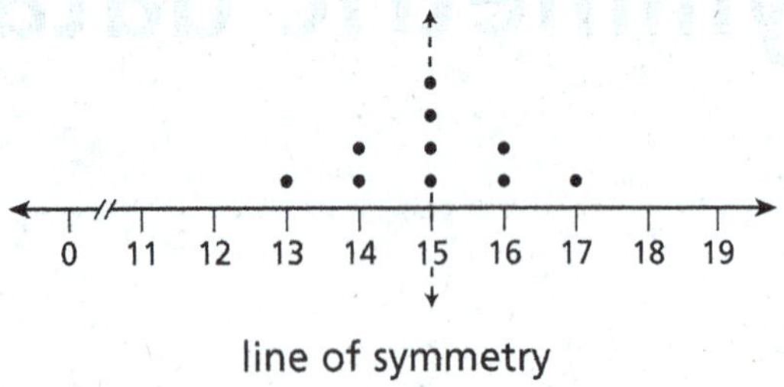

A single number that summarizes the variability of the data in a set. The range is calculated by subtracting the least number in the set from the greatest.

Example:

{5 2 16 10} ← The greatest value in this set is 16. The least value is 2.

$16 - 2 = 14$ ← Subtract. The range of the data is 14.

In a probability experiment, the ratio of the size of an event to the size of the sample space.

In a probability experiment, the ratio of the frequency of an outcome to the total number of trials.

The middle number, or the mean of the two middle numbers, of the upper half of a set of data.

Example:

1 2 3 4 5 6 7 8 9 10 11 12

↑ median (between 6 and 7) ↑ third quartile (between 9 and 10)

So, Q3 = 9.5.

The set of all possible outcomes of a probability experiment.

trial

unlikely

A procedure that can be repeated in a probability experiment.

The description of an event that has a greater chance of not occurring than of occurring.

Name ______________________________

Make a Dot Plot

The data below show the number of hours a group of students spent doing homework last week.

5, 4, 1, 6, 0, 5, 3, 3, 5, 6, 1, 3, 8, 5, 4

1. Draw a dot plot to represent the data. Title your display.

2. How many students does your dot plot represent? Explain how you know that number of students is correct.

3. **Analyze** Why are no dots shown at 2 and at 7?

4. **Analyze** Why do you think 5 hours is the most frequent number of hours? Explain.

5. **Predict** The data represent 15 students. Would the scale of the plot change if it included more students? Explain.

6. **Predict** Suppose the data represent sixth grade students. Would the data change if it represented high school students? Explain.

Name ____________________

What's the Error?

Dear Math Students,

The dot plot at the right displays data about kites that were seen at the beach.

I interpreted the dot plot to show that 2 kites had tails with five bows on each tail, and 4 kites had tails with one bow on each tail.

Did I interpret the dot plot correctly? Explain.

Your friend,
Puzzled Penguin

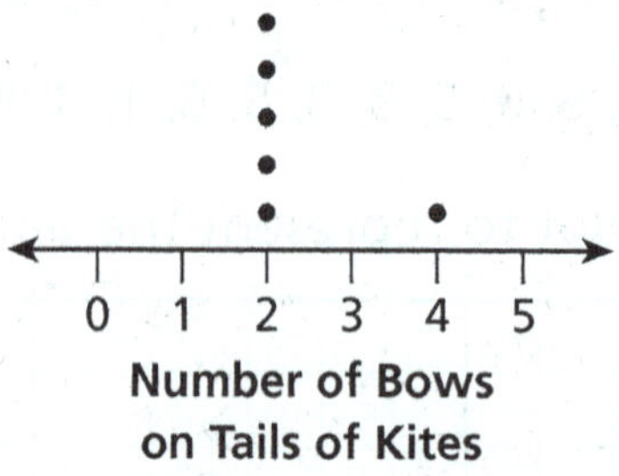

7 Write a response to Puzzled Penguin.

____

____

____

Dear Math Students,

Five of my friends made a dot plot to show the number of times they ate hot lunch at school last month.

My three friends represented by the dots on the left side of the plot said that altogether they ate hot lunch more times than my two friends represented by the dots on the right side of the plot.

Can you help me decide if they are correct?

Your friend,
Puzzled Penguin

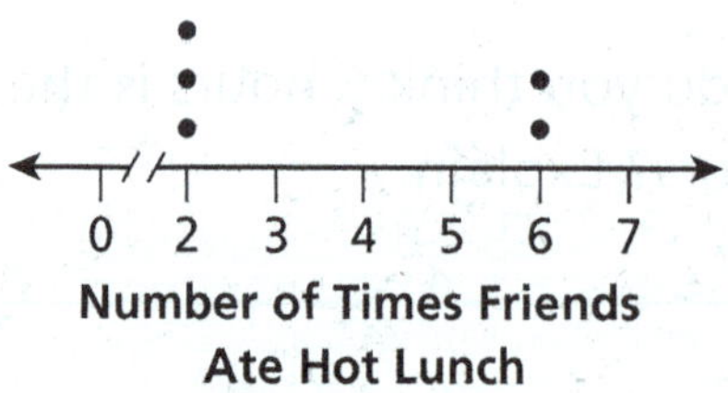

8 Write a response to Puzzled Penguin.

____

____

____

Name ______________________________

Make a Histogram

The table below shows the lengths of various U.S. rivers.

Selected Rivers of the United States

River	Length (miles)	River	Length (miles)
Connecticut	407	Savannah	314
Hudson	306	Illinois	273
Mobile	45	Roanoke	410
Potomac	287	Yazoo	169
Apalachicola	90	Saint Johns	285
Monongahela	129	Kanawha	97
Sacramento	374	Delaware	367

14 On the grid below, draw and label a histogram of the data.

Check Understanding

Compare and contrast dot plots and histograms and describe advantages and disadvantages of each display.

Unit 8
Quick Quiz 1

Name ______________________________

Solve.

1. Write a statistical question that is likely to show variability in its answer. How do you know you are correct?

____

____

____

____

Use the data below for Exercises 2 and 3.

The students in a science class earned the following scores on the first quiz of the year.

92	96	100	94	100	92	94
94	100	98	92	90	94	98

2. Draw a dot plot of the data.

Scores – Science Quiz 1

3. How many students does the dot plot represent? Explain how you know.

____

____

____

____

Unit 8
Quick Quiz 1

Name ______________________________

Use the data below for Exercises 4 and 5.

The estimated populations of the 16 largest cities in Wyoming are shown in the table.

City	Population
Rock Springs	18,708
Lander	6,867
Evanston	11,507
Sheridan	15,804
Torrington	5,776
Riverton	9,310
Cheyenne	53,011
Rawlins	8,538

City	Population
Worland	5,250
Gillette	19,646
Cody	8,835
Casper	49,644
Douglas	5,288
Green River	11,808
Powell	5,373
Laramie	27,204

4 On the grid below, display the data in a histogram.

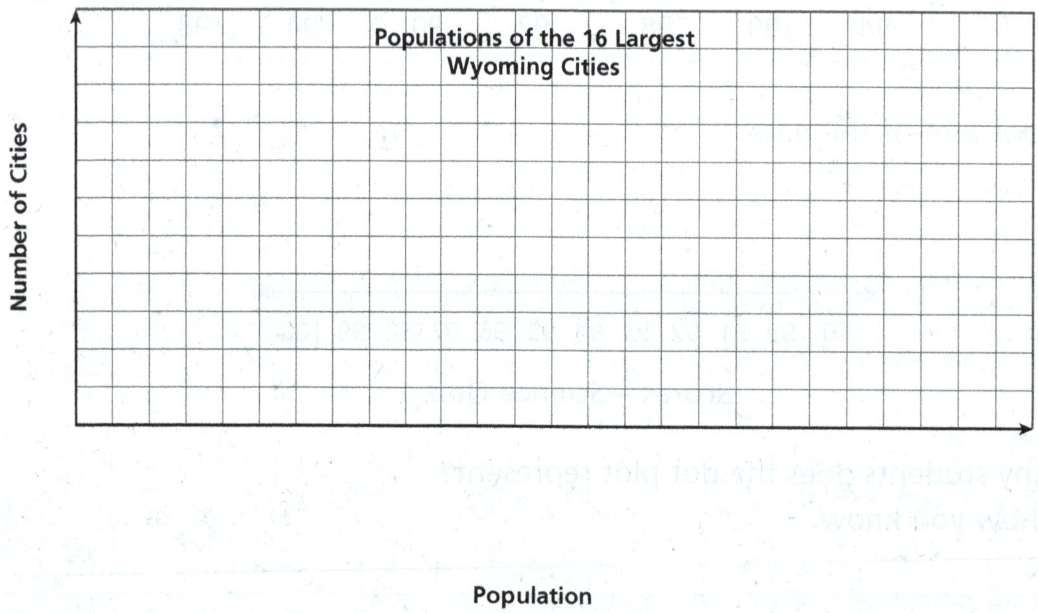

5 What interval, or range of populations, did you choose for your histogram? Explain why you chose that interval.

____

____

____

Name ______________________________

What's the Error?

Dear Math Students,

I was asked to find the mean of the numbers 3 and 6.

I know that finding the mean is the same as rearranging cubes so there are the same number of cubes in each group.

When I rearrange the cubes, there are too many cubes to make two groups of 4, and not enough cubes to make two groups of 5. So I don't think there is a mean for the numbers 3 and 6. Am I correct?

Your friend,
Puzzled Penguin

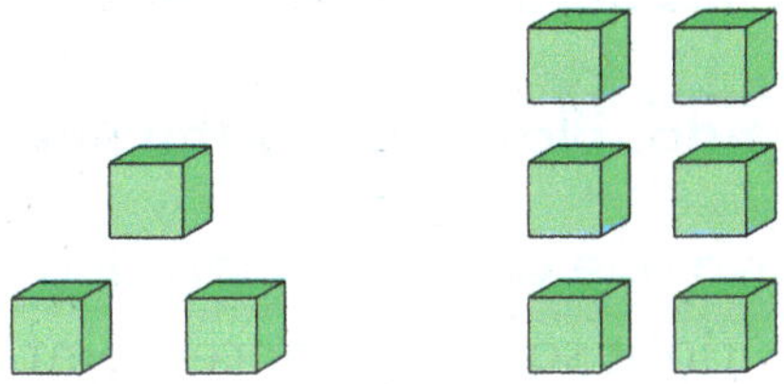

5 Write a response to Puzzled Penguin.

____

____

Dear Math Students,

I was asked to find the mean of the numbers 12, 1, and 2.

When I used addition and division to calculate the mean, my work produced an answer of 5, which didn't seem right because the set of numbers doesn't contain the number 5. Can you explain what I did wrong?

Your friend,
Puzzled Penguin

6 Write a response to Puzzled Penguin.

____

____

Check Understanding

Explain how leveling out different groups of cubes to produce fair shares relates to finding a mean.

Name ______________________________

Draw Models to Balance Data

In this lesson, the mean is shown as a balance point.

Draw a dot plot to show the new arrangement of dots.

1. Move one dot to the left and move one dot to the right so the balance point remains the same.

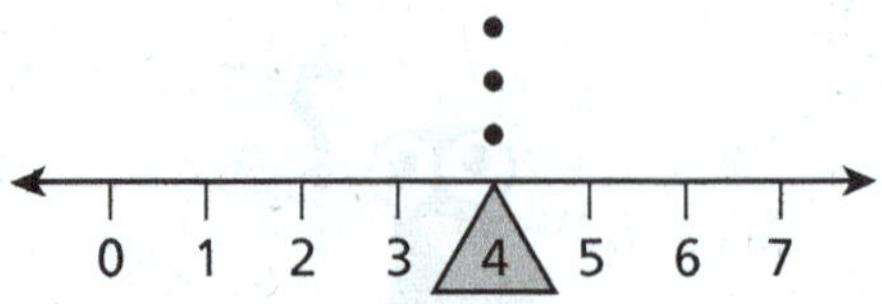

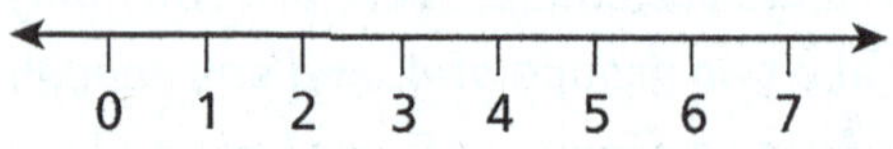

2. Move all of the dots so the balance point remains the same.

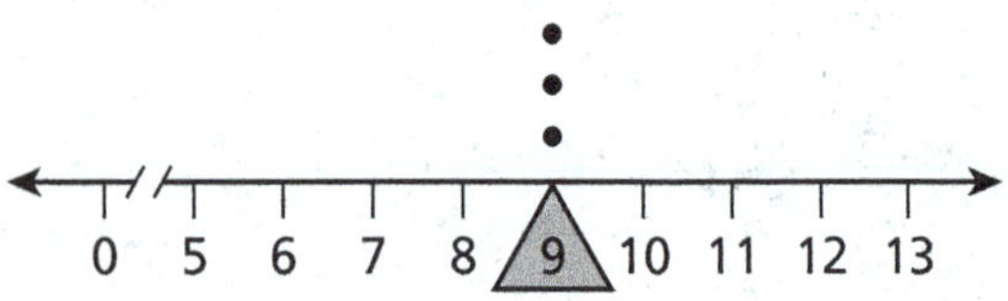

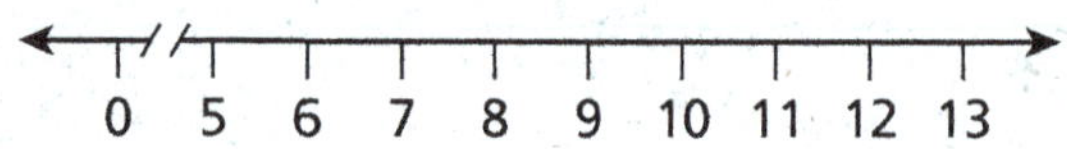

3. Move all of the dots so that the balance point changes to a different whole number. Draw the new balance point.

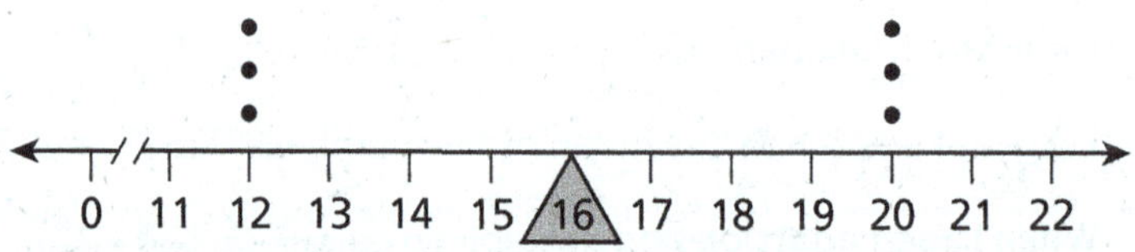

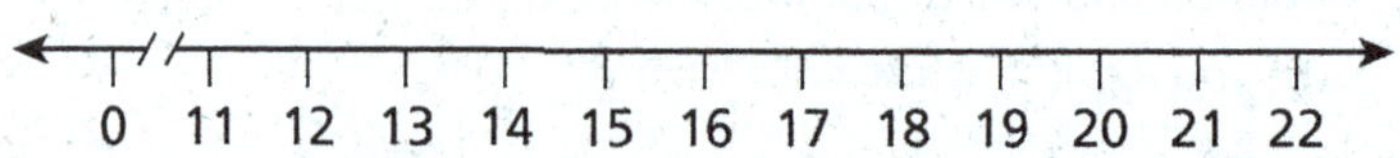

4. Move all of the dots so that the balance point is 6.

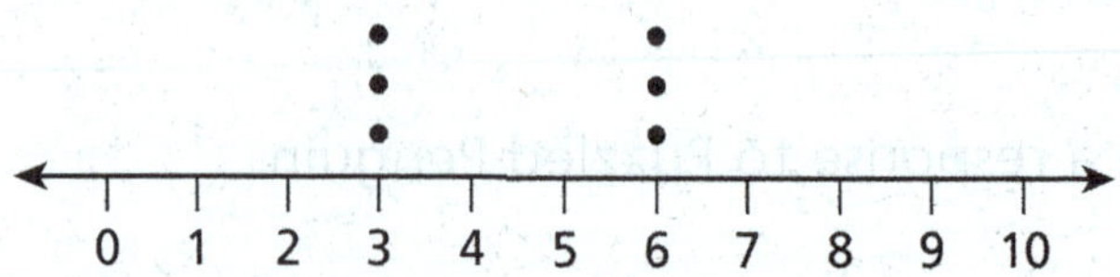

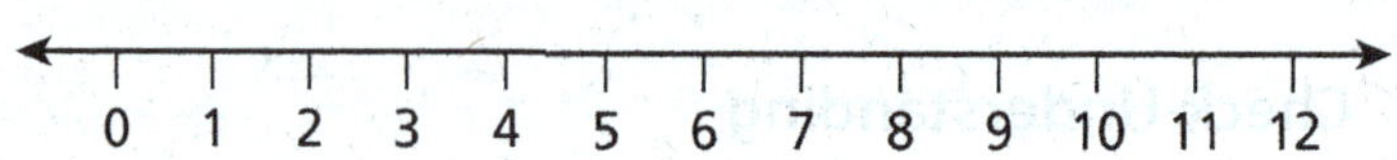

Name ________________________________

Predict the Mean

Plot the given data. Draw a balance point to predict where you think the mean will be located. Then calculate the mean to check your prediction.

5. 10, 17, 9, 18, 11

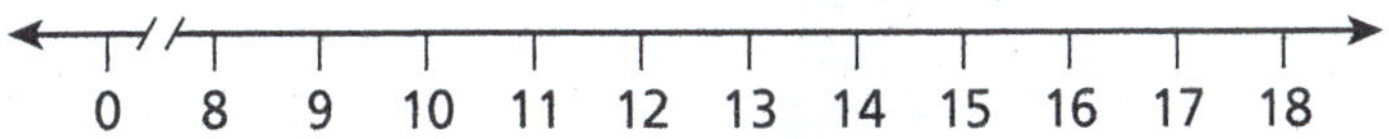

mean: ____________________

6. 8, 10, 7, 5, 10, 2

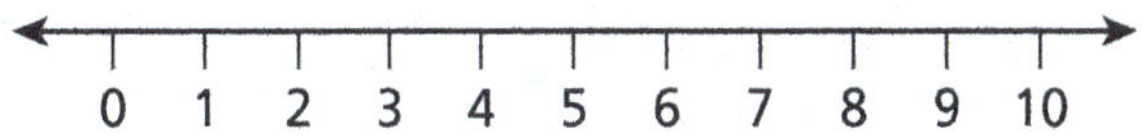

mean: ____________________

What's the Error?

Dear Math Students,

I was asked to decide if the balance point of the dot plot at the right was correct.

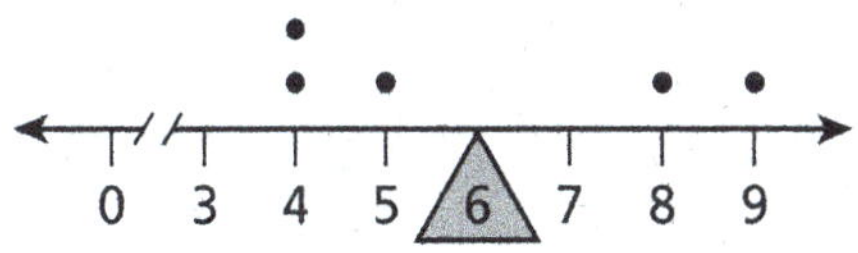

The numbers to the left of the balance point are 4, 4, and 5, which add to 13. The numbers to the right of the balance point are 8 and 9, which add to 17.

I decided the balance point is not correct because the total on one side of the balance point is not the same as the total on the other side. Can you help correct my thinking?

Your friend,
Puzzled Penguin

7. Write a response to Puzzled Penguin.

____

____

____

____

Check Understanding

Plot the given data, and draw the balance point to predict the mean. Then calculate the mean to check your prediction.
4, 5, 7, 8, 5, 7

Name

What's the Error?

Dear Math Students,

I was asked to find the median of the set of numbers at the right.

7 4 5 1 6 8 9

By counting, I discovered that there are three numbers to the left of 1 and three numbers to the right of 1. So I decided that 1 is the median because it is the middle number.

Can you tell me what I did wrong?

Your friend,
Puzzled Penguin

6 Write a response to Puzzled Penguin.

Dear Math Students,

5 5 5 6 8 8 8 9 9

I was asked to find the mode of the set of numbers at the right.

There are 9 numbers and 8 is the middle number. So, I decided that the mode is 8 because it is the middle number.

Can you tell me what I did wrong?

Your friend,
Puzzled Penguin

7 Write a response to Puzzled Penguin.

Unit 8
Quick Quiz 2

Name ______________________

Use the numbers below for Exercises 1–3.

10	14	5	11	8	1	9	14

1. Find the mean. mean = ________
2. Find the median. median = ________
3. Find the mode. mode = ________

Use the dot plot for Exercise 4.

A class of 12 students took an end-of-year spelling test. The dot plot below shows the score each student earned.

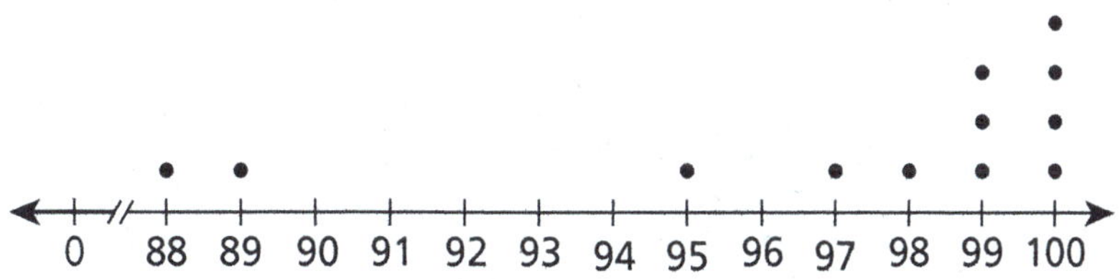

End-of-Year Spelling Test Scores

4. Which is greater—the median or the mode of the scores?

____

Use the dot plots below for Exercise 5.

Plot A

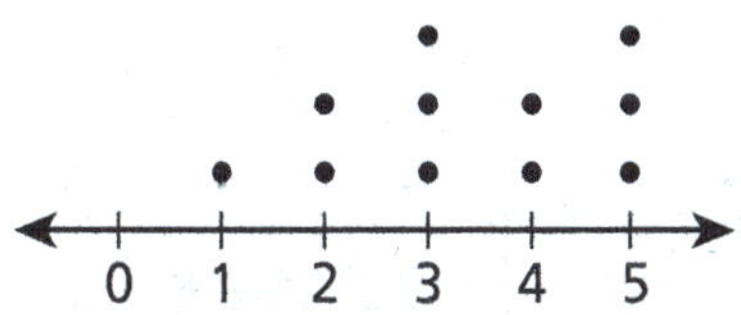

Plot B

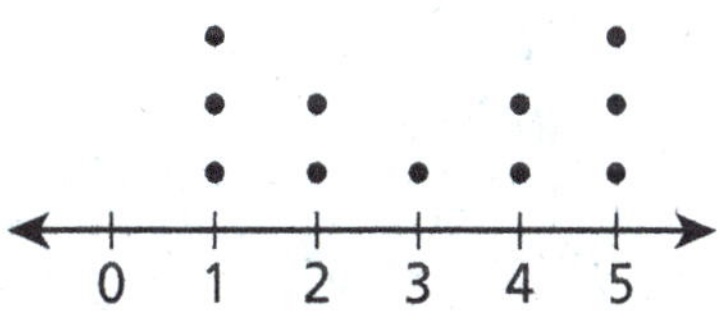

5. Identify the dot plot that displays symmetric data. Explain how you know your answer is correct.

____

____

____

Fluency Check 19

Name ____________________

PATH to FLUENCY

Add or subtract.

1. $\begin{array}{r} 56.32 \\ +5.91 \\ \hline \end{array}$

2. $\begin{array}{r} 119.26 \\ -15.7 \\ \hline \end{array}$

3. $\begin{array}{r} \$10.45 \\ +\$\ 8.79 \\ \hline \end{array}$

4. $59.21 - 7.6$

5. $1.08 + 6.39$

6. $43 - 0.86$

Multiply or divide.

7. $3.2\overline{)185.6}$

8. $\begin{array}{r} 0.12 \\ \times\ 45 \\ \hline \end{array}$

9. $14\overline{)218.4}$

10. $3.6\overline{)93.96}$

11. $\begin{array}{r} 5.1 \\ \times\ 1.6 \\ \hline \end{array}$

12. $92\overline{)197.8}$

13. $\begin{array}{r} 0.63 \\ \times\ 84 \\ \hline \end{array}$

14. $43\overline{)402.05}$

15. $\begin{array}{r} 2.2 \\ \times\ 4.9 \\ \hline \end{array}$

Name ______________________

What's the Error?

Dear Math Students,

I can use mental math to calculate the range and the median of the numbers at the right.

10
30
40
50
70

The range is 60 because $70 - 10 = 60$. And the median is 30 because $60 \div 2 = 30$. Is this correct?

Your friend,
Puzzled Penguin

16 Write a response to Puzzled Penguin.

Dear Math Students,

I was asked to calculate the first quartile of the set of data that is shown at the right.

2,	2,	3,	4,	4,	6,	8,	8,	8,	10

To calculate the first quartile, I divided the range by 4, like this:

First Quartile $=$ Range $\div 4$
First Quartile $= (10 - 2) \div 4$
First Quartile $= 8 \div 4$
First Quartile $= 2$

So I decided that the first quartile is 2. Can you explain what I did wrong, and explain how I can correctly calculate the first quartile?

Your friend,
Puzzled Penguin

17 Write a response to Puzzled Penguin.

Check Understanding

Explain how to find the quartiles of a set of numerical data.

Name ______________________________

VOCABULARY
box plot

Compare a Dot Plot and a Box Plot

The dot plot and box plot below represent the same set of data. A **box plot** is a graphic summary that shows the median, quartiles, and minimum and maximum values of a set of data.

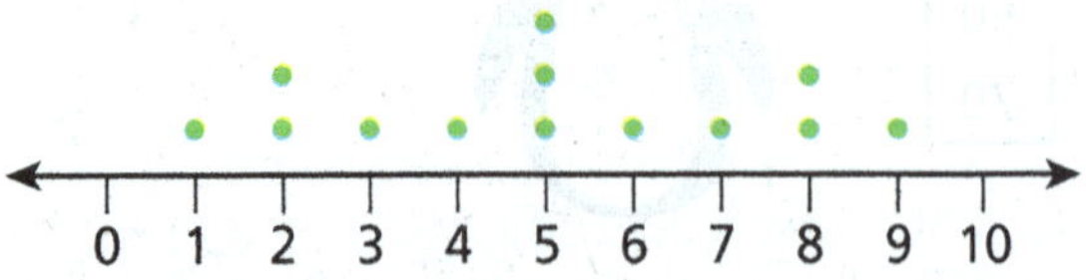

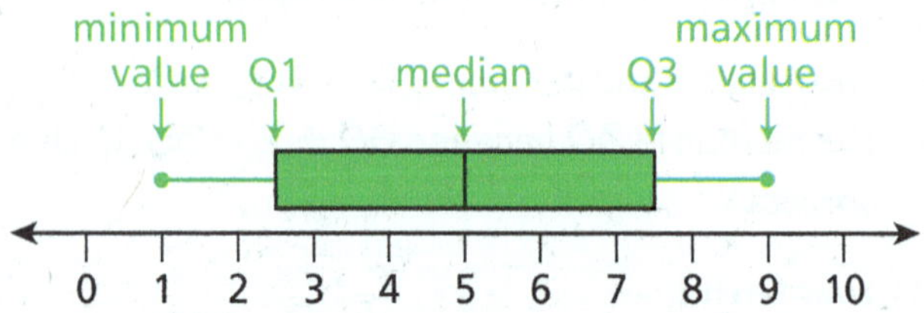

1. In which display, the dot plot or the box plot, is it easier to identify the median and quartiles of the data? Give a reason to support your answer.

____

____

2. Use the box plot to name the median, the quartiles, and the minimum and maximum values of the data. Explain how you know.

____

____

____

3. In which display, the dot plot or the box plot, is it easier to identify the range into which one half the data can be found? Explain your answer.

____

____

Make a Box Plot

4. Make a box plot to represent the dot plot data.

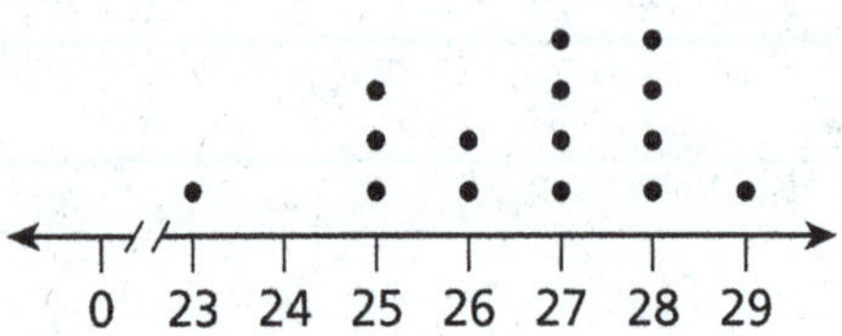

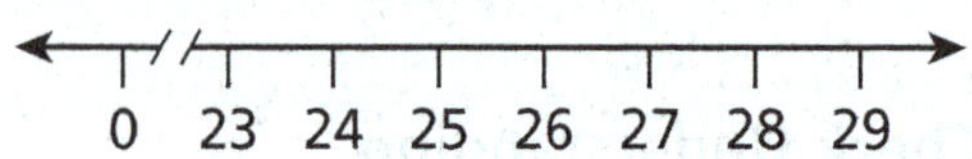

Name ______________________________

What's the Error?

Dear Math Students,

I was given this set of data. 21 21 22 23 24 25 26 26 26 29 30

Here is the box plot I made to represent the data. Can you help me understand what I did wrong?

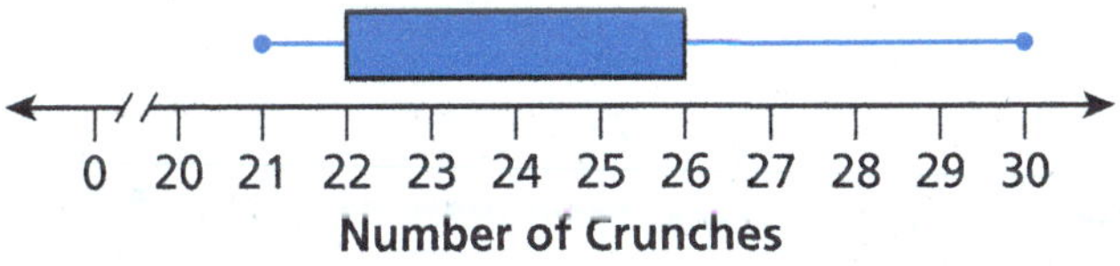

Your friend,
Puzzled Penguin

13 Write a response to Puzzled Penguin.

____

____

Dear Math Students,

203 204 205 206 207 208 209

I was asked to draw a box plot to display the set of data at the right. The box plot I made is shown below. Can you help me understand what I did wrong?

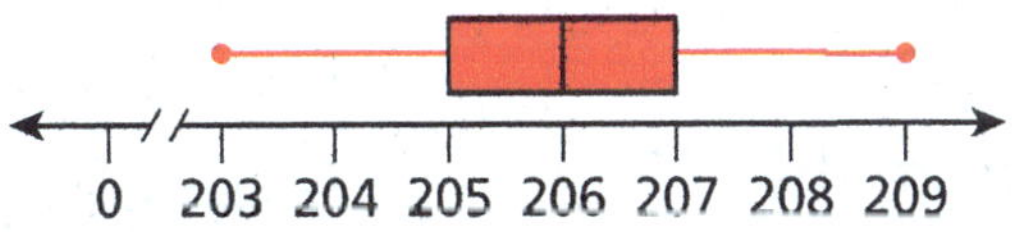

Your friend,
Puzzled Penguin

14 Write a response to Puzzled Penguin.

____

____

Check Understanding

Explain how the interquartile range of a box plot is related to the spread of the data.

Name ____________________

Determine Distance from the Mean

This dot plot shows six values. The mean of the values is 5.

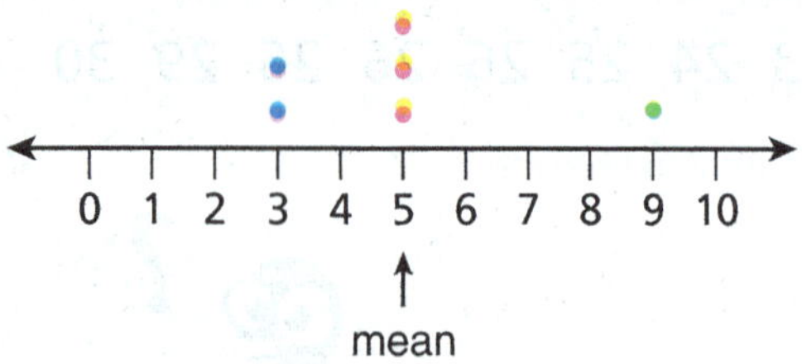

The numbers below represent each dot's distance from the mean.

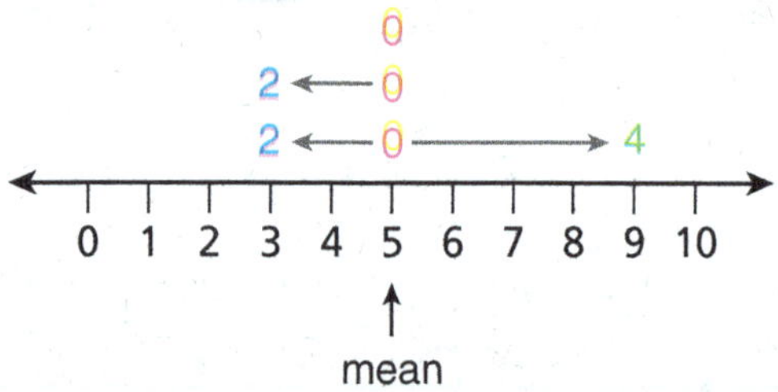

1. Why is 5 the mean?

____

2. What subtraction is used to calculate distance from the mean to each blue dot?

____

3. What subtraction is used to calculate distance from the mean to the green dot?

____

4. Calculate the mean of the dot plot below and label it. Then on the number line on the right, write a number for each dot that represents the dot's distance from the mean.

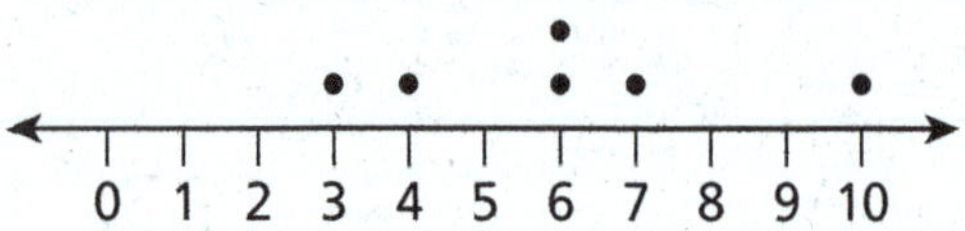

Name ______

Compare Mean Absolute Deviations

A basketball team consists of two groups of players with five players in each group. The tables below show the number of points the players have scored so far this season.

Group A	Points Scored
Nick	10
Kurtis	31
Raul	68
Cory	26
Hector	45

Group B	Points Scored
Casey	29
Pedro	43
Zack	32
Andre	45
Tommy	31

13 Calculate the mean number of points scored by the players in each group.

Group A mean: ______

Group B mean: ______

14 Calculate each player's distance from the mean number of points scored and write the distances in the tables below.

Group A	Distance from Mean
Nick	
Kurtis	
Raul	
Cory	
Hector	

Group B	Distance from Mean
Casey	
Pedro	
Zack	
Andre	
Tommy	

Name ______________________

What's the Error?

Dear Math Students,

On the last day of school, the students in a sixth grade class were asked how many days they were absent that year.

The table shows the data that were collected.

I calculated the mean absolute deviation for each set of data.

I concluded that the data for the girls showed more variability than the data for the boys.

I was told my conclusion was wrong. Can you tell me why?

Your friend,
Puzzled Penguin

Number of Days Absent	
Boys	Girls
2	0
0	3.5
8	1
5	3
0	4
3	0
0	4.5
9	3
0	5
1	2

18 Write a response to Puzzled Penguin.

Number of Days Absent	
Distance from the mean	Distance from the mean
Boys	Girls

Check Understanding

Describe what a mean absolute deviation is a measure of, and explain how it relates to the spread or variability of the data in a set.

Unit 8
Quick Quiz 3

Name ______________________________

Solve.

1. A box plot displays five numerical summaries of a data set. What are they?

____

Use the box plot at the right for Exercises 2 and 3.

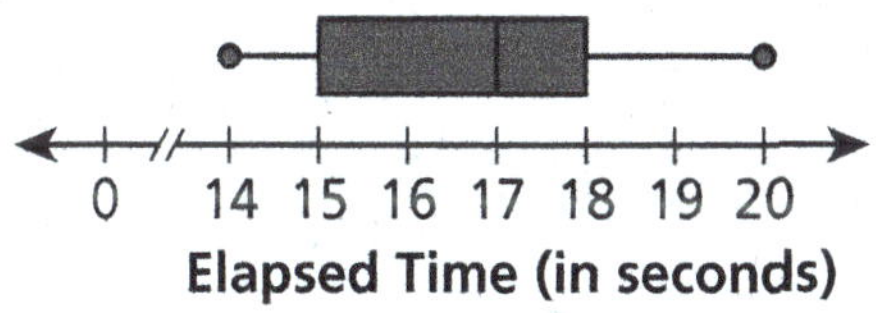

2. Calculate the range of the data.

   range = __________

3. Calculate the interquartile range (or IQR) of the data.

   IQR = __________

Use the dot plot for Exercise 4.

The students in Mr. Jackson's math class recorded their homework scores. The dot plot at the right shows the number of A's the students earned on their homework last week.

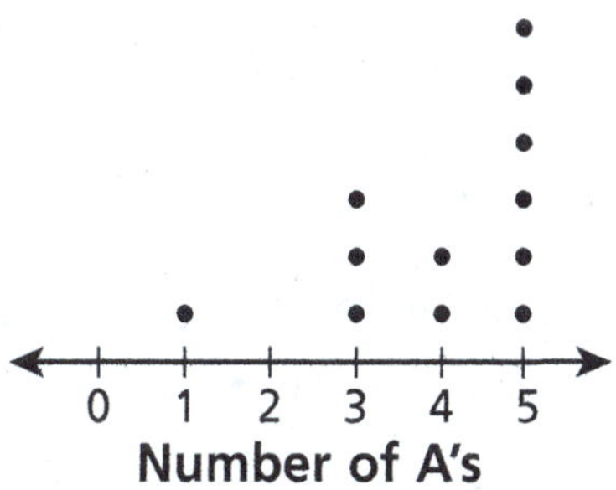

4. Calculate the mean absolute deviation of the data.

   mean absolute deviation = __________

Use the dot plot at the right for Exercise 5.

5. Describe the overall shape of the data. Include the words *cluster(s)*, *gap(s)*, *peak(s)*, and *outlier(s)* in your description.

____

____

____

____

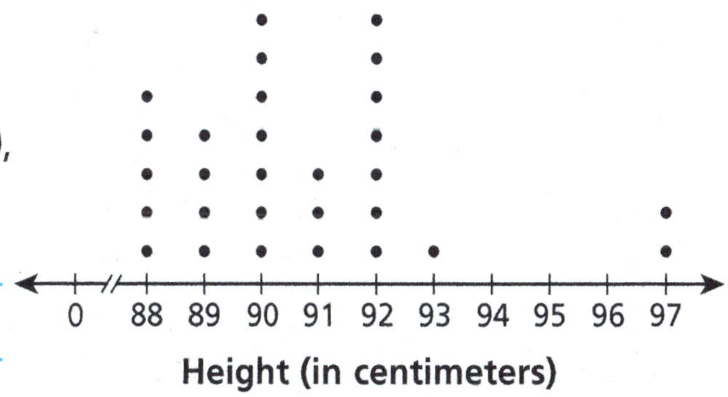

Fluency Check 20

Name ______________________

PATH to FLUENCY

Add or subtract.

1. $\begin{array}{r} 5.218 \\ +\ 2.942 \\ \hline \end{array}$

2. $\begin{array}{r} 136.74 \\ +\ 2.55 \\ \hline \end{array}$

3. $\begin{array}{r} \$15.62 \\ -\$\ 3.08 \\ \hline \end{array}$

4. 29.5 + 0.38

5. 412.61 + 0.73

6. 59 − 0.17

7. $\begin{array}{r} 45.024 \\ -\ 3.671 \\ \hline \end{array}$

8. $\begin{array}{r} 48.74 \\ +\ 19.2 \\ \hline \end{array}$

9. $\begin{array}{r} 0.825 \\ +\ 0.197 \\ \hline \end{array}$

Multiply.

10. $\begin{array}{r} 0.73 \\ \times\ \ 45 \\ \hline \end{array}$

11. $\begin{array}{r} 8.1 \\ \times\ 2.6 \\ \hline \end{array}$

12. $\begin{array}{r} 0.24 \\ \times\ 0.9 \\ \hline \end{array}$

Divide.

13. $34\overline{)537.2}$

14. $92\overline{)51.52}$

15. $8.3\overline{)365.2}$

Name ______________________________

Ways to Represent Sample Space

A drawing, a table, and a tree diagram are all ways to represent the sample space for an experiment.

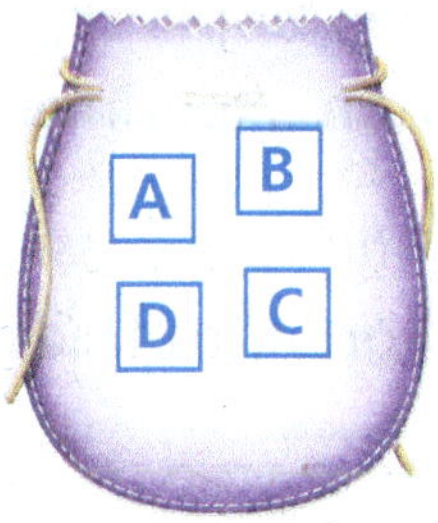

Rick takes one letter tile from a bag and rolls a 1–6 cube for a probability experiment. He puts the tile back in the bag each time. Rick wants to represent the sample space.

5. Rick makes this drawing to show the outcomes.

A 1   A 2   A 3   A 4   A 5   A 6

B 1   B 2   B 3   B 4   B 5   B 6

C 1   C 2   C 3   C 4   C 5   C 6

D 1   D 2   D 3   D 4   D 5   D 6

Explain how Rick's drawing represents the outcomes.

____

____

6. Complete the table of outcomes for Rick's experiment.

Tile / Number	1	2	3	4	5	6
A	A 1	A 2	A 3	A 4		
B	B 1					
C	C 1				C 5	
D						D 6

7. Rick also draws a tree diagram of the outcomes.

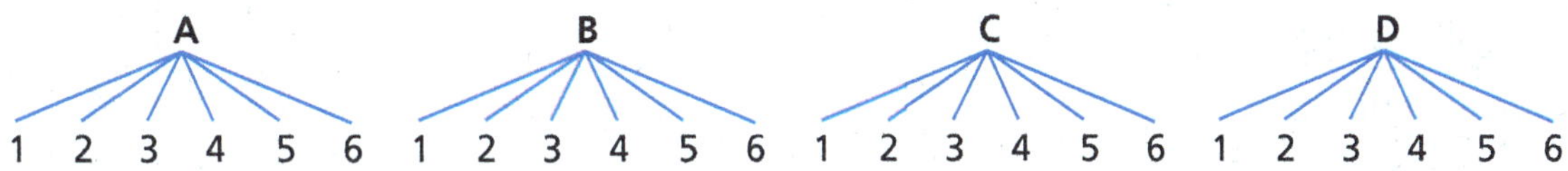

Explain how the tree diagram represents the outcomes.

____

____

8. How many possible outcomes does Rick's experiment have? ________

Name ______________________________

VOCABULARY
event

Solve Problems About Sample Space

The size of the sample space is the number of possible outcomes for an experiment.

For an experiment of tossing 3 coins in a row, you can use a tree diagram to find the size of the sample space.

9 Complete the tree diagram to show the outcomes.

```
First coin:              H                   T
                        / \                 / \
Second coin:          H     T             H     T
                     / \   / \           / \   / \
Third coin:         __ __ __ __         __ __ __ __
```

10 Count the possible outcomes of the experiment to find the size of the sample space. ______

11 What is the sample space?

____

____

12 Find the size of the sample space for an experiment of rolling two 1–6 number cubes. ______

What Is an Event?

An experiment, such as rolling a 1–6 number cube, may have different events. An **event** is a set of outcomes that includes all related members of the sample space.

Sample Space: {1, 2, 3, 4, 5, 6}

Event	Related Members of the Sample Space
Roll a 1	1
Roll an even number	2, 4, 6
Roll 3 or 5	3, 5

13 What members of the sample space for rolling a 1–6 number cube are related to the event *Roll an odd number*? ______

14 What members of the sample space for tossing two coins are related to the event *Two heads or two tails*? ______

Name ____________________

Analyze an Experiment

Josie wants to do a probability experiment that involves spinning a 4-part spinner and tossing a coin. The four colors of the spinner are **R**ed, **Y**ellow, **G**reen, and **V**iolet.

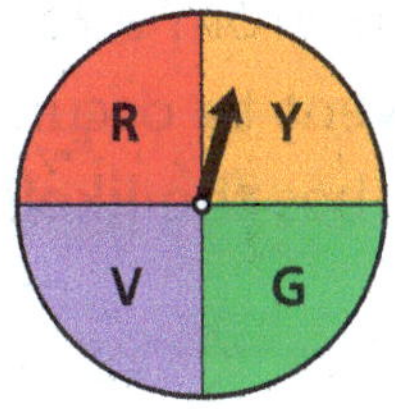

15 Make a drawing, a table, or a tree diagram to represent the possible outcomes.

16 Explain why your work represents all possible outcomes.

____

____

____

17 Write the sample space for this experiment.

____

18 What is the size of the sample space for this experiment? ________

19 For each event of this experiment, name the related members of the sample space.

Event	Related Members of the Sample Space
Spin Yellow, Toss H	
Spin Red, Toss H or T	
Spin Yellow or Violet, Toss T	
Spin Red, Yellow, or Green, Toss H	
Spin Yellow or Violet, Toss H or T	

Check Understanding

Draw a tree diagram to represent the possible outcomes of rolling a 1–6 cube and tossing a coin.

Name ______________________________

VOCABULARY
probability
likelihood
likely
unlikely
equally likely

Probability and Likelihood

A **probability** is a number from 0 to 1 inclusive that describes how likely it is for an event to occur. This number line shows how a probability describes the likelihood of an event.

impossible	unlikely	equally likely or unlikely	likely	certain
0		$\frac{1}{2}$		1

1 For each event in the table, use the words on the number line to describe the likelihood.

Event	Likelihood
A rolled 1–6 number cube lands with 8 up.	
A rolled 1–6 number cube lands with 3 up.	
A tossed coin lands heads up.	
A rolled 1–6 number cube lands with 3, 4, 5, or 6 up.	
A tossed coin lands heads or tails up.	

For all outcomes of an experiment to be **equally likely**, each outcome must have the same chance of occurring.

- When you roll a 1–6 number cube, each number from 1 through 6 has the same chance of being rolled, so the outcomes 1, 2, 3, 4, 5, 6 are equally likely.
- When you roll a number cube with two 2s, two 4s, and two 6s, each number from 1 through 6 does not have the same chance of being rolled, and the outcomes 1, 2, 3, 4, 5, 6 are not equally likely.

2 Write *equally likely* or *not equally likely* to describe the outcomes of spinning each spinner.

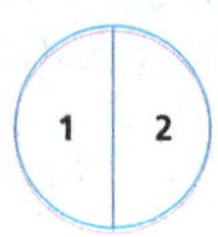

____

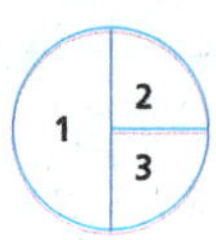

____

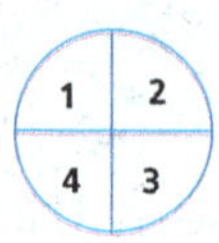

____

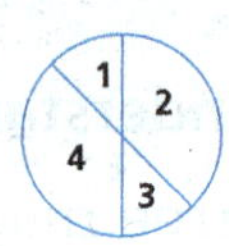

____

Name ______________________________

Relative Frequency and Probability

VOCABULARY
trial
frequency
relative frequency
experimental probability
theoretical probability

During a probability experiment, the outcome of each **trial** is recorded. The **frequency** of an outcome is the number of times it occurs. Then the **relative frequency** of each outcome is found. The relative frequency is the ratio of the frequency of an outcome to the total number of trials.

Jeff rolled a 1–6 number cube 24 times. He used tallies to record the outcomes.

1	2	3	4	5	6
||	卌 |	卌 ||	卌	|||	|

1. Complete this frequency table for Jeff's experiment. Record the frequency of each outcome. Find the relative frequency of each outcome as a fraction and as a decimal rounded to the nearest thousandth.

Outcome	Frequency	Relative Frequency
1	2	$\frac{2}{24}$ or $\frac{1}{12}$, 0.083
2		
3		
4		
5		
6		

When you carry out a probability experiment and find the relative frequency of an outcome, the relative frequency is the **experimental probability** for that outcome.

When you know the outcomes that make up an event and the sample space of a probability experiment, the ratio of the size of the event to the size of the sample space is the **theoretical probability** of that event.

In an experiment with a very large number of trials, the experimental probability is usually very close to the theoretical probability.

2. How do the relative frequencies in Jeff's experiment compare to the theoretical probability of each outcome?

Name ______________________________

Carol used a computer simulation to carry out a probability experiment of rolling a 1–6 number cube 2,400 times.

3 What is the theoretical probability of rolling a 1?

____

4 Carol recorded the outcomes in a frequency table. Calculate the relative frequency of each outcome as a fraction and as a decimal rounded to the nearest thousandth.

Outcome	Frequency	Relative Frequency
1	396	
2	398	
3	400	
4	402	
5	404	
6	400	

5 What is the relative frequency of rolling a 1 in Carol's experiment?

____

6 How do the relative frequencies in Carol's experiment compare to the theoretical probability of each outcome?

____

7 Compare the relative frequencies from Jeff's experiment to those from Carol's experiment. Explain any differences.

____

____

____

____

____

8 How are a relative frequency and a theoretical probability similar?

____

Name ___________________________

Find Relative Frequencies for an Experiment

9 If you roll two 1–6 number cubes and add the numbers you roll, do you think that one sum will be rolled most often? If so, what sum?

____

10 Roll two 1–6 number cubes, add the numbers you roll, and put a tally under the sum in this chart. Do 20 trials.

2	3	4	5	6	7	8	9	10	11	12

11 Enter your data and the class data in this frequency table and calculate the relative frequencies as decimals.

	My Experiment		Class Data	
Sum	Frequency	Relative Frequency	Frequency	Relative Frequency
2				
3				
4				
5				
6				
7				
8				
9				
10				
11				
12				

12 Compare your data and the class data. What do you observe?

____

Name ______________________

Compare Relative Frequencies and Theoretical Probabilities

13 Complete this table to find the sample space for rolling a sum with two 1–6 number cubes.

+		First Cube					
		1	2	3	4	5	6
Second Cube	1	2					
	2						
	3						
	4						
	5						
	6						

14 What is the size of the sample space?

____

15 What sum will likely be rolled most often?

____

16 What is the size of the event of a sum of 7?

____

17 What is the theoretical probability of rolling a sum of 7? ______________

18 Compare the theoretical probability of rolling a sum of 7 with the relative frequency of rolling 7 in your experiment.

____

____

19 Compare the theoretical probability of rolling a sum of 7 with the relative frequency of rolling 7 in the class totals.

____

____

Check Understanding

What is the theoretical probability of rolling an even number when you roll a 1–6 number cube? ______________ If you roll a 1–6 number cube 100 times, about how many times would you expect to roll an even number?

____

Name ______________________________

Use Experimental Probability to Make a Prediction

Jennifer has a bag containing 20 centimeter cubes. The cubes are red and blue. She does a probability experiment to predict how many of each color are in the bag.

For each trial, she reaches into the bag, mixes up the cubes, draws out a cube, records its color, and returns it to the bag. In 25 trials, she draws 4 red and 21 blue cubes.

1. Complete this frequency table for the 25 trials.

Outcome	Frequency	Relative Frequency
Red		
Blue		

2. Find the experimental probability (as a percent) of drawing a red cube.

____

3. Find the experimental probability (as a percent) of drawing a blue cube.

____

4. Predict the number of red and blue cubes in the bag.

____

5. Jennifer continues her experiment to include 250 trials. She has drawn a red cube 55 times and a blue cube 195 times.

Outcome	Frequency	Relative Frequency
Red		
Blue		

Complete the frequency table for these results. Use the new data to predict the number of red and blue cubes.

____

When Jennifer looks at the cubes to check the predictions, she finds that the prediction with 250 trials is true.

Name ______________________

Compare Experimental and Theoretical Probabilities

Work with a partner to carry out a probability experiment. You will spin two numbers and find their sum.

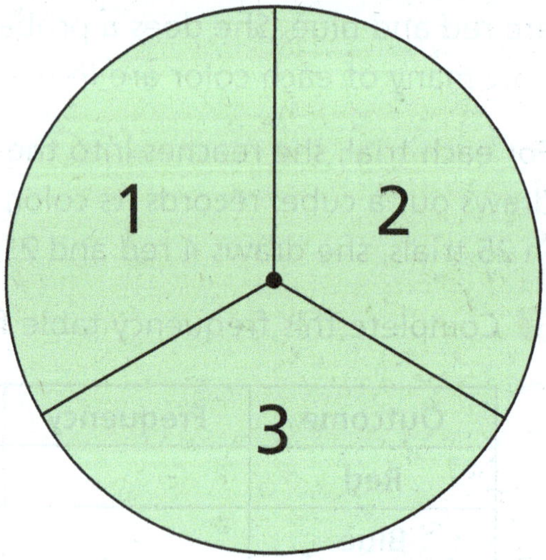

Begin by placing a spinner over the circle, being sure that the center of the spinner is exactly over the center.

6 Carry out at least 25 trials.
To carry out 1 trial:

- Each partner spins a number.
- Find the sum of the numbers.
- Record the sum in the table below.

Calculate the relative frequency for each sum.

Sum	Tallies for This Sum	Frequency	Relative Frequency
2			
3			
4			
5			
6			

7 Find the experimental probability for a sum of 6. ________

8 Find the theoretical probability for a sum of 6. Round to the nearest thousandth. ________

9 Compare the theoretical and experimental probabilities for a sum of 6.

____

____

Name ______________________________

Use Relative Frequencies

The outcomes for spinning a color on this spinner are not equally likely because the parts are not all the same size. You can do an experiment to find the experimental probability of spinning each color.

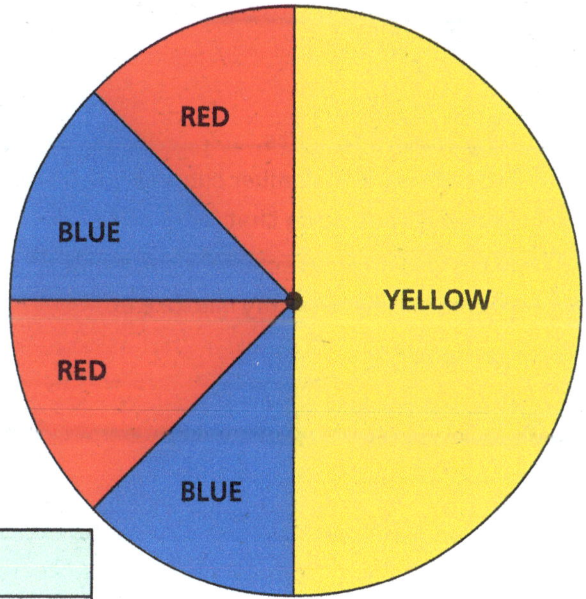

10 Place a spinner over the circle. Record the results of at least 24 spins.

Color	Times Spun
RED	
YELLOW	
BLUE	

11 Find the relative frequency for spinning each color. Write the experimental probability of spinning each color as a fraction, a decimal, and a percent.

Color	Frequency	Relative Frequency	Experimental Probability
RED			
YELLOW			
BLUE			

12 The yellow part of the spinner is $\frac{1}{2}$ of the circle. The red parts are $\frac{2}{8}$ of the circle, and the blue parts are $\frac{2}{8}$ of the circle. How closely do the experimental probabilities you found for each color match the fractions of the circle?

____

____

____

Name ____________________

What's the Error?

Dear Math Students,

I rolled two 1–6 number cubes. I rolled two 2s. I think the probability of doing that is $\frac{2}{12}$ or $\frac{1}{6}$.

Is my thinking correct? If I made a mistake, please tell me what my mistake is.

Your friend,

Puzzled Penguin

13 ____________________

____

____

Dear Math Students,

I tossed a coin 20 times. I tossed Heads 8 times and Tails 12 times. I wrote the ratio of Heads to Tails to find an experimental probability for tossing Heads of $\frac{8}{12}$.

I think I made a mistake. Please explain my mistake and tell me how to find the experimental probability.

Your friend,

Puzzled Penguin

14 ____________________

____

____

Check Understanding

For a given event, the theoretical probability is the ____________ of the sizes of the event and the ____________, and the experimental probability is the ____________ of the event.

Unit 8
Quick Quiz 4

Name ______________________

Jenna is doing a probability experiment that involves picking a shape tile from this bag and rolling a 1–6 number cube.

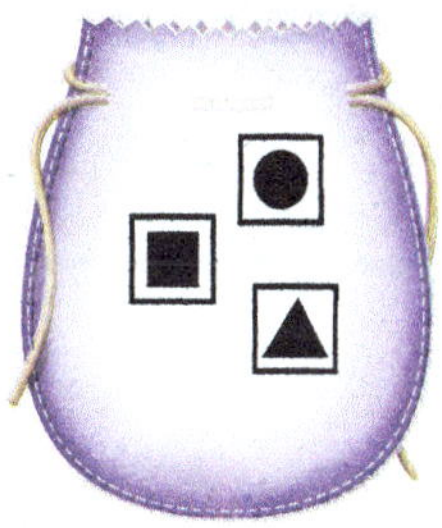

1 Make a drawing, an organized list, a table, or a tree diagram to represent the possible outcomes.

2 What is the size of the sample space for this experiment?

____

3 What is the theoretical probability of choosing the triangle tile and rolling an even number? Write your answer as a fraction.

____

4 Jenna does 30 trials of her experiment. She picks the circle tile 12 times. How does Jenna's experimental probability of choosing the circle tile compare to the theoretical probability of choosing the circle tile?

Fluency Check 21

Name ______

PATH to FLUENCY

Add or subtract.

1. $\begin{array}{r} 4.482 \\ +\ 3.319 \\ \hline \end{array}$

2. $\begin{array}{r} 127.92 \\ +\ \ \ 4.69 \\ \hline \end{array}$

3. $\begin{array}{r} \$17.71 \\ -\$\ 4.52 \\ \hline \end{array}$

4. 30.6 + 0.32

5. 718.66 + 0.41

6. 49 − 0.12

7. $\begin{array}{r} 57.087 \\ -\ 4.331 \\ \hline \end{array}$

8. $\begin{array}{r} 56.65 \\ +\ 17.7\ \\ \hline \end{array}$

9. $\begin{array}{r} 0.745 \\ +\ 0.116 \\ \hline \end{array}$

Multiply.

10. $\begin{array}{r} 0.65 \\ \times\ \ \ 31 \\ \hline \end{array}$

11. $\begin{array}{r} 9.7 \\ \times\ 1.6 \\ \hline \end{array}$

12. $\begin{array}{r} 0.11 \\ \times\ \ 0.5 \\ \hline \end{array}$

Divide.

13. $32\overline{)454.4}$

14. $22\overline{)74.8}$

15. $6.6\overline{)481.8}$

Name ______________________________

1 Is the question a statistical question? Select Yes or No for each question.

1a. How many pets do you have in your home? ○ Yes ○ No

1b. How tall are basketball players? ○ Yes ○ No

1c. Who is the tallest 6th grade student? ○ Yes ○ No

1d. How many minutes long is a lunch period in a school? ○ Yes ○ No

1e. How much time do 6th grade students spend doing homework every night? ○ Yes ○ No

2 What is the probability of rolling an odd number on a 1-6 number cube? Write your answer as a decimal.

____

3 Suppose the data in one dot plot are symmetric and the data in a related dot plot are not symmetric. Explain how the dot plots would look different.

4 Why do the quartiles of a set of data divide the data into four equal parts?

Name ______________________

5 Explain why you can think of finding a mean as unleveling and leveling data.

6 Norberto collected the data shown.

21	16	10	6	12	4

6a. Find the mean. ______________________

6b. Find the median. ______________________

6c. Find the mode. ______________________

7 Trina's final math grade is the average of five scores—four quarterly tests and a final exam. Her quarterly test scores were 72, 80, 84, and 76. What is the lowest score she can earn on her final exam if her goal is to have an average score of 80?

Choose the correct answer.

7a. ○ 80

7b. ○ 84

7c. ○ 88

7d. ○ 92

8 Choose a number from the number tiles to show the median, first quartile (Q1), and third quartile (Q3) of the data on the dot plot.

2	3	4	5
6	9	10	11

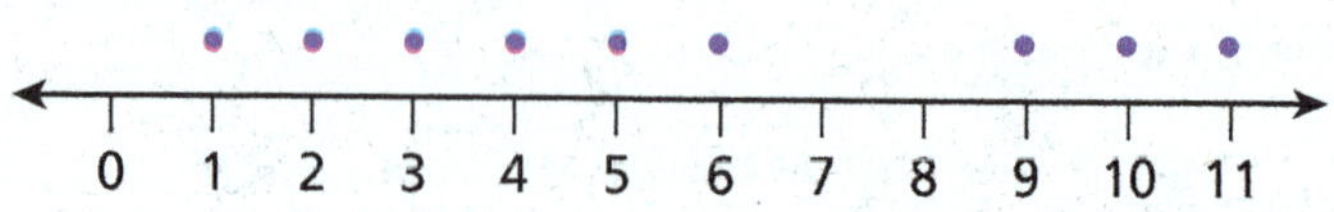

Median: ☐ Q1: ☐ Q3: ☐

Name ____________________

9 The dot plot below shows the number of correct answers a group of students scored on a quiz.

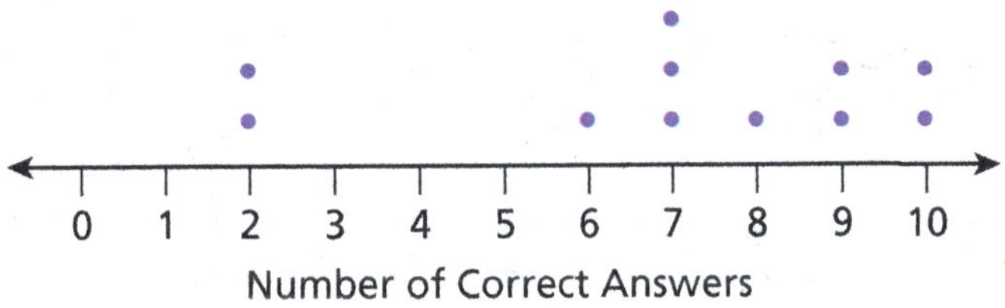

9a. Calculate the mean absolute deviation of the data.

9b. Consider the shape of the data in the dot plot above. Does the dot plot display a *cluster or clusters* of data? Explain.

10 Using the dot plot from Problem 9, categorize each data value as a peak or a gap. Not every data value will be used.

1	2	3	4	5	6	7	8	9	10

GAP	PEAK

11 Are any of the data values outliers? Explain why or why not.

Name ______________________________

12 Look back at Problem 9. In the space below, make a box plot display of the data.

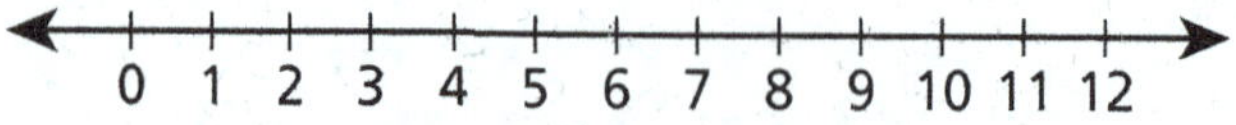

13 The table below shows the length of the shorelines of various states.

13a. On the grid, draw a histogram of the data.

Shorelines of Selected States

State	Length (miles)
Texas	3,359
Rhode Island	384
Georgia	2,344
California	3,427
Hawaii	1,052
Alabama	607
New Jersey	1,792
Maine	3,478
Oregon	1,410
South Carolina	2,876
Connecticut	618
Massachusetts	1,519
Washington	3,026
New York	1,850

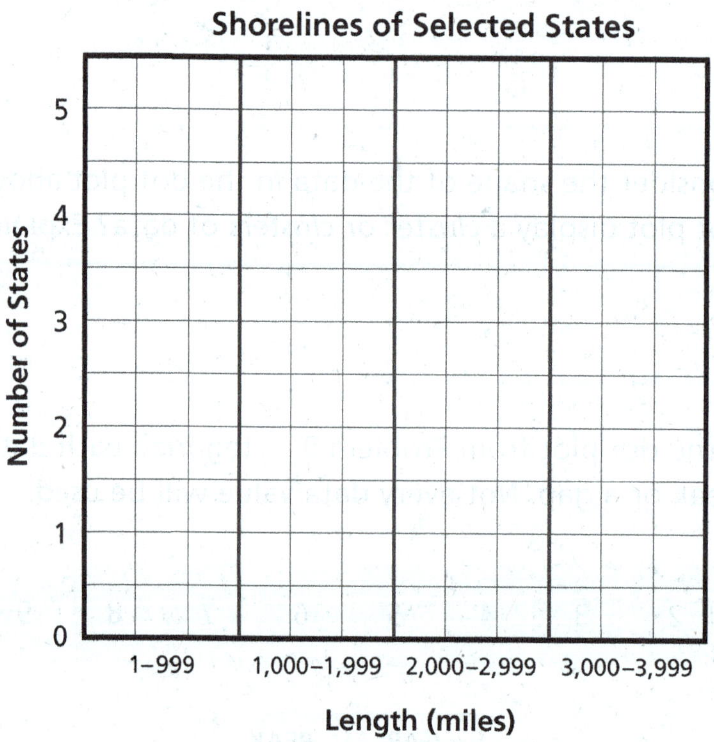

13b. In your histogram for Problem 13a, which length interval has the greatest number of states?

- ○ 1 – 999
- ○ 1,000 – 1,999
- ○ 2,000 – 2,999
- ○ 3,000 – 3,999

Name ______________________________

14 Calculate the range and interquartile range of the dot plot data.

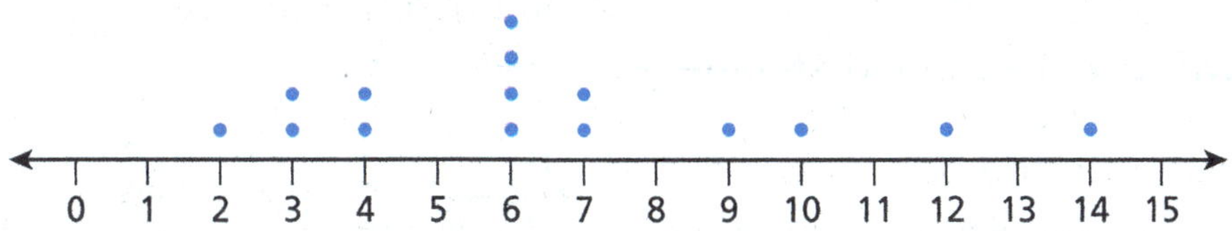

Range: ______________ Interquartile range: ______________

15 In the box plot below, the data value at 15 represents a(n) [cluster / gap / outlier / peak].

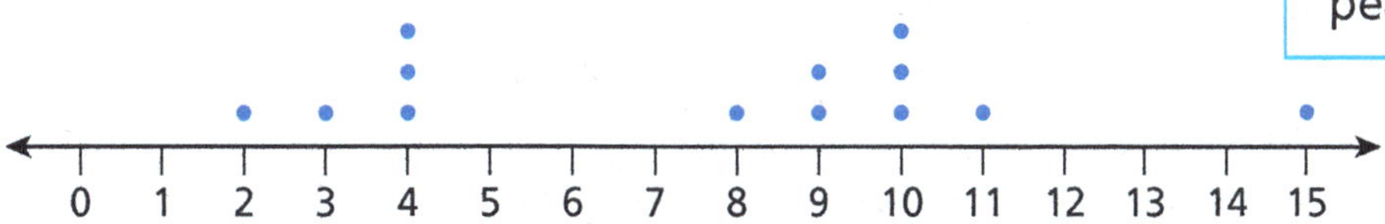

16 Suppose you wanted to investigate the size of a typical sixth grader's foot.

16a. What unit of measure would you use?

____

____

16b. How would you do the measuring?

____

17 Calculate the range and interquartile range for the data displayed in the box plot.

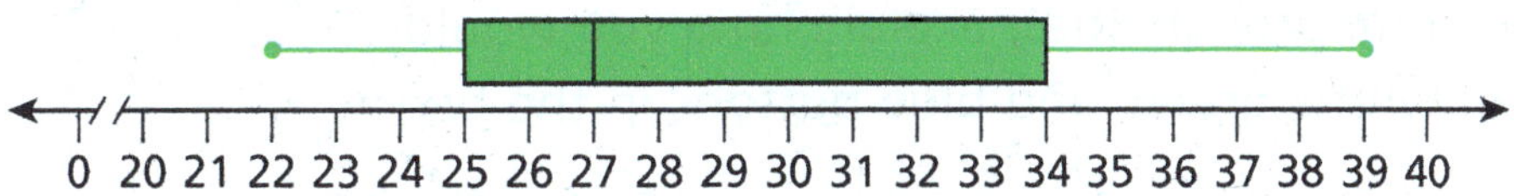

Range: _____ Interquartile range: _____

Name ______

Use the information below for Exercises 18–20.

Maya does a probability experiment. She has a bag of 30 buttons that are all the same size—12 white, 8 green, and 10 blue.

For each trial, she reaches into the bag, draws out a button, records its color, and returns it to the bag. This table shows the results of her first 20 trials.

Outcome	Tally
White	~~IIII~~ ~~IIII~~
Green	~~IIII~~ I
Blue	IIII

18 Write the theoretical probability of each event as a fraction, a decimal, and a percent. Round decimals to the nearest hundredth.

Drawing a white button: ______

Drawing a green button: ______

Drawing a blue button: ______

19 Complete the following for the 20 trials.

19a. Complete the frequency table. Write the relative frequency as a fraction and a decimal.

Outcome	Frequency	Relative Frequency
White		
Green		
Blue		

19b. Write the experimental probability as a percent.

Drawing a white button: ______

Drawing a green button: ______

Drawing a blue button: ______

20 Based on the experimental probabilities, explain how you would predict the number of white, green, and blue buttons in the bag.

Name ____________________

In the Blink of an Eye

Have you ever wondered how many times people blink in one minute? This activity will help you answer that question.

1. Collect data about the number of times ten of your classmates blink in 1 minute.

2. Display your data in a dot plot.

3. Describe the shape of the data in your dot plot, using terms such as symmetric, gap, peak, outlier, and/or cluster.

4. Find the first quartile Q_1 and the third quartile Q_3 of the blinks per minute. Show or explain how you got your answer.

5. Draw a box plot of the data you collected.

Name ______________________________

6 Which graph is more appropriate to display the data? Is there another graph that might better show the information? Explain.

7 Find the mean, median, and mode of blinks per minute. Show or explain how you got your answer.

8 Name the measure of center that you think best describes the data you collected. Explain your reasoning, and explain how the measure you named is related to the context of the data.

9 What answer would you give to the question "How many times does a typical person blink in 1 minute?" Explain your answer.

10 If you collected the same data for all the students in your school, do you think the data would be nearly the same? Explain your reasoning.

Dear Family:

Your child will be learning about numbers throughout the school year. The math unit your child is beginning to study now introduces rational numbers. A rational number can be positive, negative, or zero. Examples of rational numbers include integers, fractions, and decimals.

Some of the lessons and activities in the unit will involve number lines. An example of a number line is shown below.

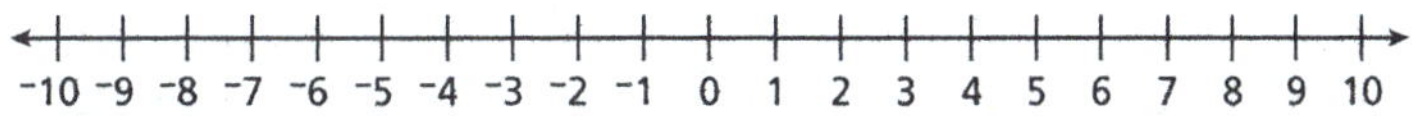

Your child will learn to plot and locate points on a number line, and use a number line to compare and order numbers.

This unit will also introduce your child to a four-quadrant coordinate plane, shown below. The plane is formed by the intersection of two number lines.

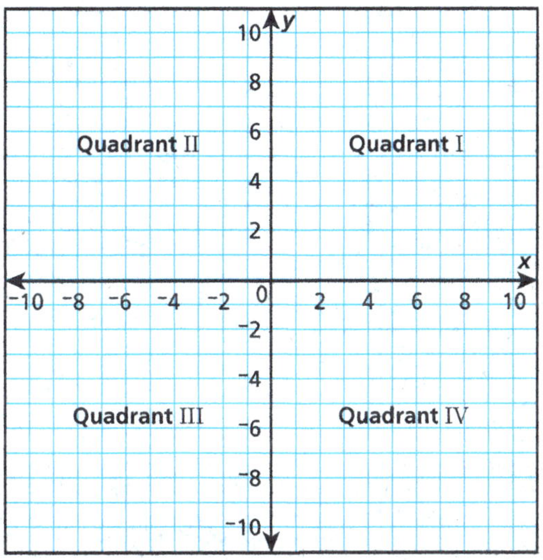

In previous units, your child has plotted and located points for ordered pairs in Quadrant I of the coordinate plane. In this unit, your child will be working in all four quadrants of the plane.

If you have any questions or comments, please contact me.

Sincerely,
Your child's teacher

Examples of Rational Numbers

Integers

$^{-}8$ $^{+}3$ 0

Fractions

$^{-}\frac{1}{2}$ $\frac{3}{4}$

Decimals

$^{-}0.5$ 6.29

Examples of Ordered Pairs in the Coordinate Plane

(2, 1) (x, y) ($^{-}7$, $^{-}4$)

Estimada familia:

Su hijo aprenderá diferentes conceptos relacionados con los números durante el año escolar. La unidad de matemáticas que estamos comenzando a estudiar presenta los números racionales. Un número racional puede ser positivo, negativo o puede ser cero. Ejemplos de números racionales incluyen enteros, fracciones, y decimales.

Algunas de las lecciones y actividades tendrán rectas numéricas. Abajo se muestra un ejemplo de una recta numérica.

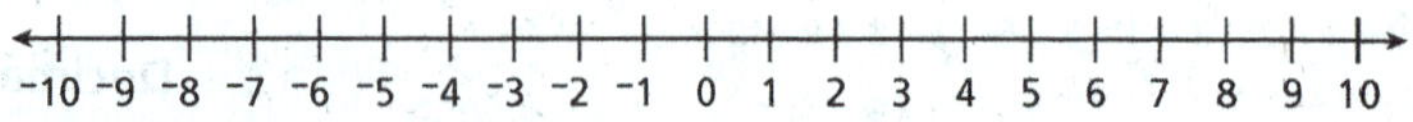

Su hijo aprenderá a localizar y marcar puntos en rectas numéricas. También aprenderá a usarlas para comparar y ordenar números.

En esta unidad también se introduce un plano de coordenadas dividido en cuatro cuadrantes, como el que se muestra abajo. El plano se forma por la intersección de dos rectas numéricas.

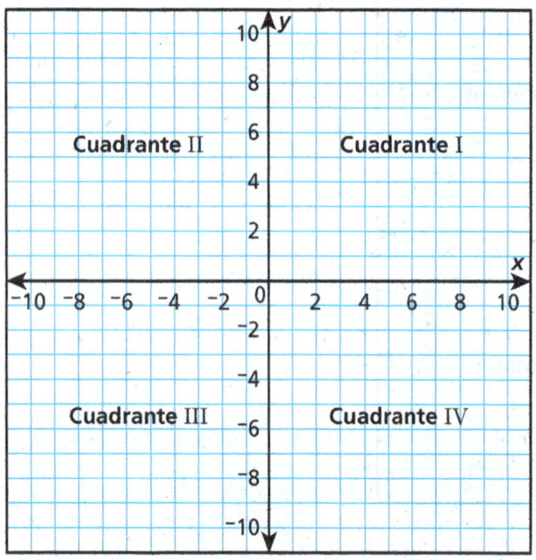

En unidades anteriores, su hijo ha localizado y marcado puntos para pares ordenados en el Cuadrante I del plano de coordenadas. En esta unidad trabajará en los cuatro cuadrantes del plano de coordenadas.

Si tiene preguntas o comentarios, por favor comuníquese conmigo.

Atentamente,
El maestro de su hijo

Ejemplos de números racionales

Números enteros

−8 ⁺3 0

Fracciones

$-\frac{1}{2}$ $\frac{3}{4}$

Decimales

−0.5 6.29

Ejemplos de pares ordenados en el plano de coordenadas

(2, 1) (*x*, *y*) (−7, −4)

absolute value	negative numbers
coordinate plane (four quadrants)	opposites
integers	origin

Negative numbers are to the left of zero on a horizontal number line, and below zero on a vertical number line.

A measure of the distance a number is from zero on a number line.

Two numbers are opposites if they are the same distance from zero on a number line, but in opposite directions.

Examples:

$^-5$ and 5
12 and $^-12$

A plane together with two perpendicular number lines that intersect at 0 on each number line. The coordinate plane is divided into four quadrants by the *x*- and *y*-axes.

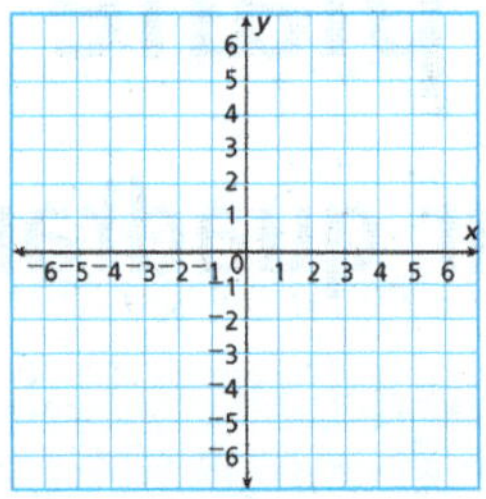

The origin of a number line is the point at 0. The point of intersection of the *x*-axis and *y*-axis is called the origin of the coordinate plane.

The set of integers includes whole numbers, their opposites, and zero.

positive numbers	reflected point
quadrant	
rational number	

A given point and its reflected point are mirror images across the *x*-axis or *y*-axis of the coordinate plane.

Example:

Point *N* is a reflection of point *M* across the *x*-axis.

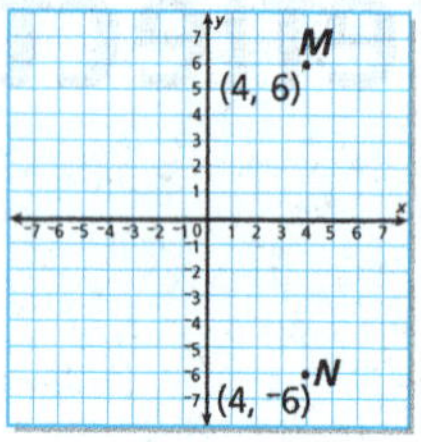

Positive numbers are to the right of zero on a horizontal number line, and above zero on a vertical number line.

The *x*- and *y*-axes divide the coordinate plane into four regions called *quadrants*. Beginning in the upper right quadrant and moving in a counterclockwise direction, the quadrants are numbered using the Roman numerals I, II, III, IV.

Example:

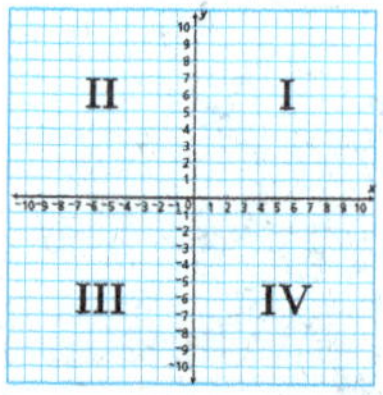

Any number that can be expressed as a fraction $\frac{a}{b}$, where *a* and *b* are integers and $b \neq 0$.

Name ______________________

Distance and Points on a Number Line

One way to represent distance on a number line is to circle unit lengths. Another way is to mark points. The number lines on this page use tick marks and points to show the origin and unit lengths.

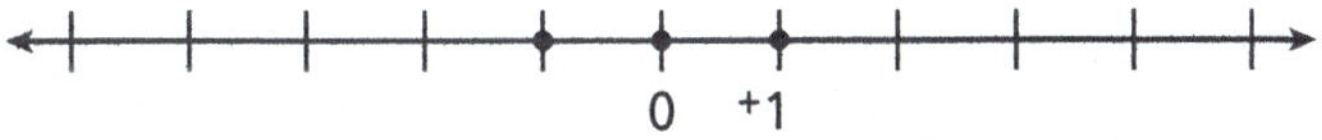

7 One point on each number line is not labeled. Label each point with an integer, and explain why you chose that integer.

____

____

8 On each number line, draw a point at each tick mark. Label each point.

What's the Error?

Dear Math Students,

Today I drew two number lines to show the integers from $^{+}2$ to $^{-}2$.

Number Line *A*

Number Line *B*

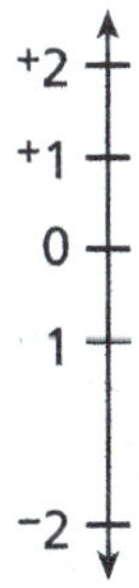

My friends say that I did not draw either number line correctly.

Can you tell me what I did wrong?

Your friend,
Puzzled Penguin

9 For each number line, write a response to Puzzled Penguin.

Number Line *A*: ______________________

____

Number Line *B*: ______________________

____

Name ______________________________

Integer Number Line Game

____

Player's
Initials

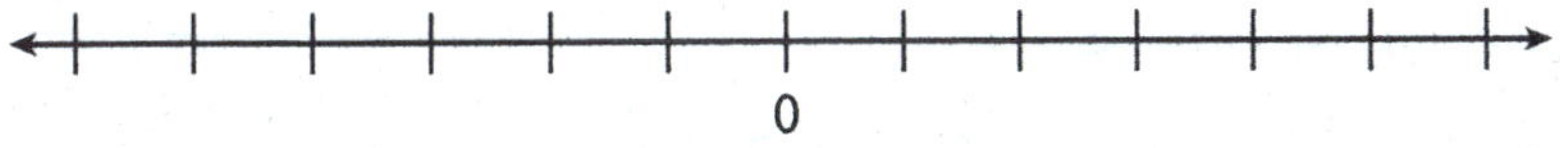

____

Player's
Initials

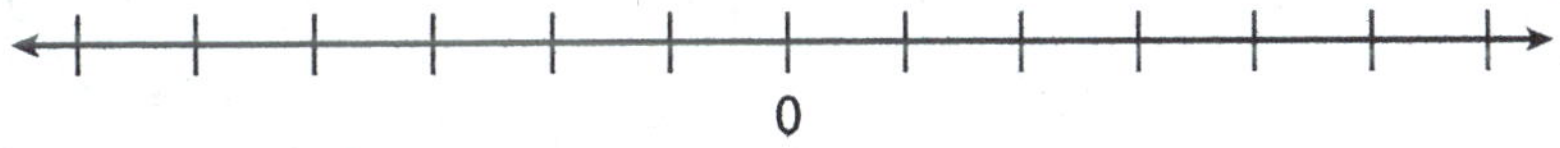

Instructions for Each Pair

Using stickers, label one blank number cube with the integers from 1 to 6, and label another blank cube with three + signs and three − signs.

Each player labels one horizontal number line with the integers from $^{-}6$ to $^{+}6$.

With your partner, take turns rolling both cubes and plotting a point on your number line to show the outcome. Say:

- *I am plotting a point at* (say your integer).
- *My integer is* (say *positive* or *negative*), *so it is to the* (say *right* or *left*) *of zero*.
- *It is* (say the number) *unit lengths from zero.*

If the outcome is a point you already plotted, roll the +/− cube if you need the opposite outcome, and say:

- *I want a negative sign so that* (say your integer) *changes to its opposite, which is* (say the opposite integer).

If you roll a point that is already plotted, roll again until you get a different point.

If you roll a negative sign, draw a point at the opposite of your original integer.

The first player to draw a point at every positive and negative integer on the number line wins the game.

Name ______________________________

Integer Number Line Game (continued)

Repeat the game using the vertical number lines.
This time say *above* or *below zero*
instead of *to the right* or *to the left of zero*.

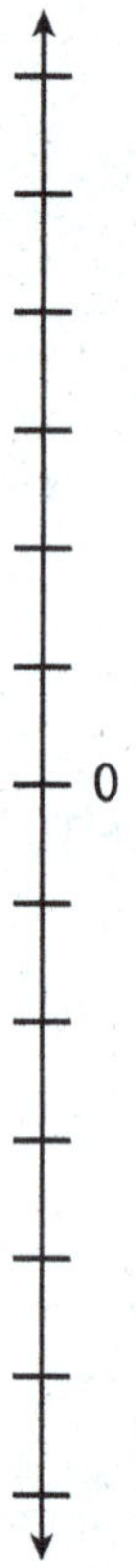

Player's Initials

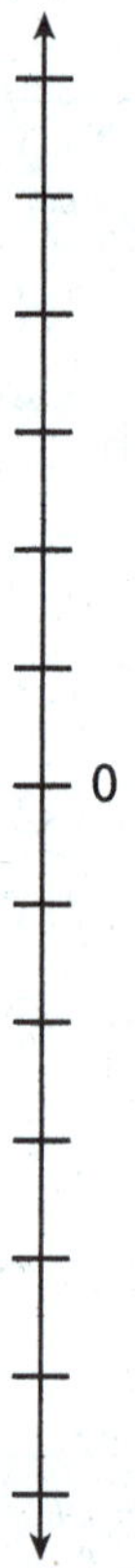

Player's Initials

✓ Check Understanding

Explain the relationship that distance shares with integers on a number line.

Name ______________________________

Absolute Value and Opposites

Use the number line below for Exercises 35–37.

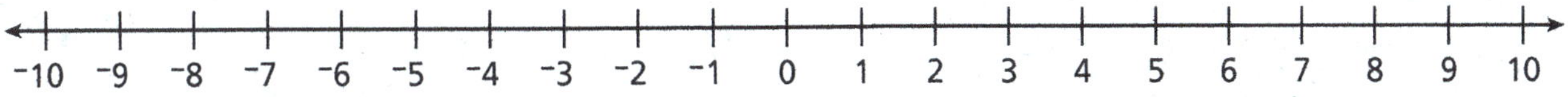

35 Plot a point at 8 and plot a point at $^-8$.
What is the absolute value of each number? $|8|$ = ______ $|^-8|$ = ______

36 Are 8 and $^-8$ opposite integers? Explain why or why not.

____

37 Write a generalization about the absolute values of opposite integers.

____

Use Absolute Value to Compare

Use absolute value to compare the numbers. Then write <, >, or =.

38 $^-5$ ◯ $^-4$

39 $^-1$ ◯ $^-3$

40 $^-2$ ◯ $^-5$

41 $^-6$ ◯ $^-6$

What's the Error?

Dear Math Students,

I was asked to use absolute value to compare two positive integers and two negative integers. The positive integers were 10 and 5, and the negative integers were $^-10$ and $^-5$.

I know that 10 is the absolute value of both 10 and $^-10$, and I know that 5 is the absolute value of both 5 and $^-5$.

I decided that the greater absolute value is the greater number. So I wrote 10 > 5 and $^-10$ > $^-5$.

Can you explain to me what I did wrong?

Your friend,
Puzzled Penguin

42 Write a response to Puzzled Penguin.

____

____

Name ________________________________

What's the Error?

Dear Math Students,

I was trying to evaluate the expression $|5 - 2|$. I thought that the absolute value meant that I should change the minus to a plus, so I wrote $5 + 2 = 7$.

The teacher marked this one wrong. Can you help me understand my error? What should the correct answer be?

Your friend,
Puzzled Penguin

55 Write a response to Puzzled Penguin.

____

____

____

____

____

Dear Math Students,

I am having a rough day. So now I was trying to evaluate the expression $|{}^{-}a| - |{}^{-}b|$ for $a = 6$ and $b = 3$.

I substituted the values for a and b, and wrote $|{}^{-}6| - |{}^{-}3|$.

So then I continued evaluating, and wrote that $6 + 3 = 9$.

Again, the teacher marked this one wrong. Can you help me understand my error? What should the correct answer be?

Your friend,
Puzzled Penguin

56 Write a response to Puzzled Penguin.

____

____

____

____

Name ______________________

VOCABULARY
coordinate plane

Graph in the Coordinate Plane

A **coordinate plane** is formed by two perpendicular number lines that intersect at the origin, 0.

Use the coordinate plane at the right for Exercises 1–8.

Write the location of each point.

1. Point *A* ________
2. Point *B* ________
3. Point *C* ________
4. Point *D* ________

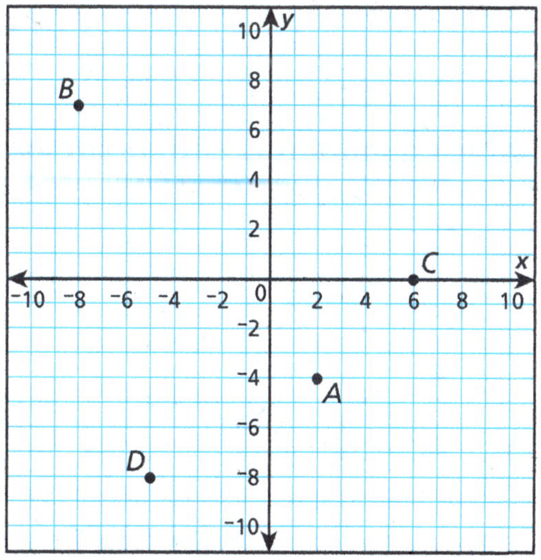

Plot and label each point.

5. Point *E* at (0, 4)
6. Point *F* at ($^-9$, $^-2$)
7. Point *G* at (7, 9)
8. Point *H* at (9, $^-6$)

What's the Error?

Dear Math Students,

I was asked to graph a point at ($^-3$, $^-6$) in the coordinate plane. My work is shown at the right.

I was told that I did not plot the point in the correct location. Can you explain to me what I did wrong and explain how to plot the point correctly?

Your friend,
Puzzled Penguin

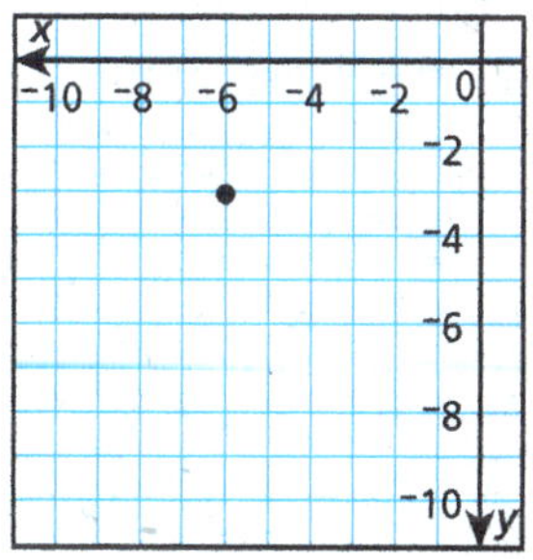

9. Write a response to Puzzled Penguin.

Name ______________________

Quadrants of the Coordinate Plane

VOCABULARY
quadrant

The two perpendicular number lines (the *x*- and *y*-axes) divide the coordinate plane into four regions called **quadrants**. Beginning in the upper right quadrant and moving in a counterclockwise direction, the quadrants are numbered using the Roman numerals I, II, III, and IV.

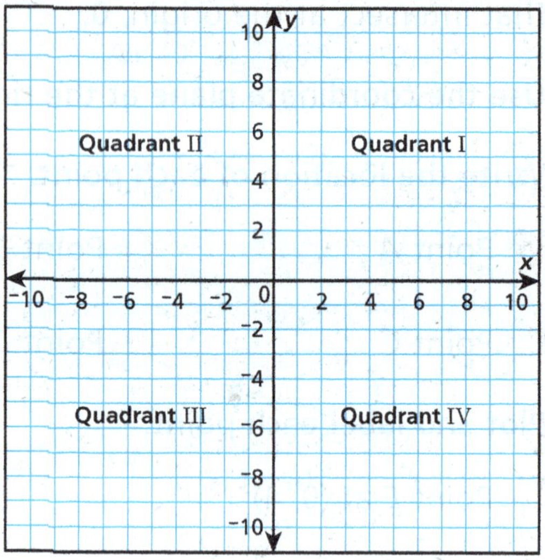

In which quadrant is each point located?

10 (5, 4) ______________

11 $(^-5, ^-4)$ ______________

12 $(5, ^-4)$ ______________

13 $(^-5, 4)$ ______________

A coordinate is a number that determines the horizontal or vertical position of a point in the coordinate plane. An ordered pair consists of two coordinates.

14 The signs of the coordinates of an ordered pair are (–, +). In which quadrant is the point located? Explain your answer.

____

____

____

15 The signs of the coordinates of an ordered pair are (+, –). In which quadrant is the point located? ______________

16 The signs of the coordinates of an ordered pair are (–, –). In which quadrant is the point located? ______________

17 The signs of the coordinates of an ordered pair are (+, +). In which quadrant is the point located? ______________

18 On the coordinate plane above, plot Point *T* at (0, 0).

Name ____________________

The Coordinate Plane and a Map

The coordinate plane below represents a map. Use the map to solve these problems.

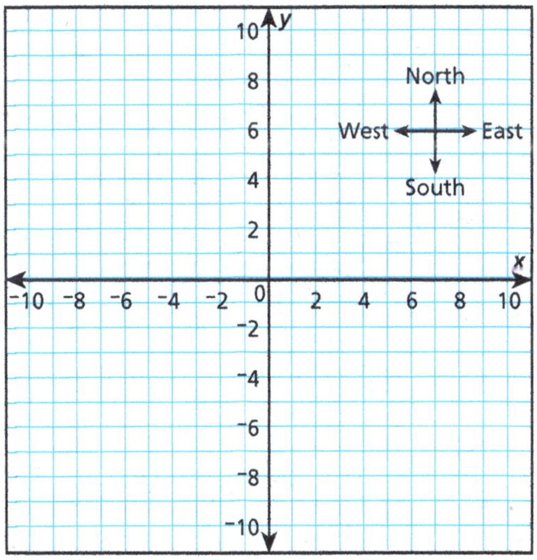

24 A family's home is located at $(4, {}^-5)$. Draw a point at that location, and write "Home" next to the point.

25 The family begins their vacation by leaving home and driving to a restaurant at $({}^-7, {}^-5)$. Draw a point at that location, and write "Restaurant" next to the point. In what direction did the family drive?

____

26 From the restaurant, the family drove to a campground at $({}^-7, 1)$. Draw a point at that location, and write "Campground" next to the point. In what direction did the family drive?

____

27 From the campground, the family drove to a rest area at $({}^-3, 1)$. Draw a point at that location, and write "Rest Area" next to the point. In what direction did the family drive?

____

28 From the rest area, the family drove to $(-3, 9)$, to $(2, 9)$, and then to their destination at $(2, 10)$. Plot points at each location, and write "Destination" next to the point at $(2, 10)$. During this portion of the trip, in which directions did the family *not* drive?

____

29 Starting from home, draw line segments to show the path the family traveled. Suppose that each side of every unit square represents 25 miles. What is a reasonable estimate of the number of miles the family traveled from home to their destination?

____

Check Understanding

Use your Mathboard to plot and label the following points. Then find the distance between the points: Point *A* at $({}^-7, {}^-4)$ and Point *B* at $({}^-7, 8)$.

Unit 9
Quick Quiz 1

Name ______________________

Write the opposite integer.

1. $^{-}7$ ____________

2. 3 ____________

Use the number line below for Exercises 3 and 4.

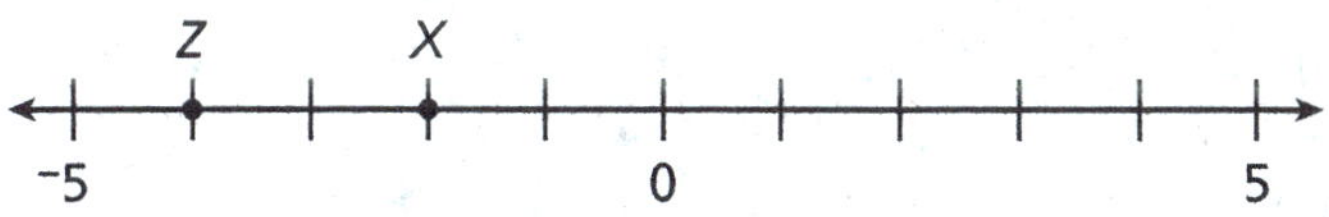

3. Write the value of Point *X*. ____________

4. Write the value of Point *Z*. ____________

Compare. Write <, >, or =.

5. $^{-}3$ ◯ $^{-}1$

6. 5 ◯ $^{-}5$

7. Evaluate the expression for $a = -10$ and $b = 2$.

$|-a| - b^2$

____

The coordinate plane at the right shows the locations of some buildings in a historical village.

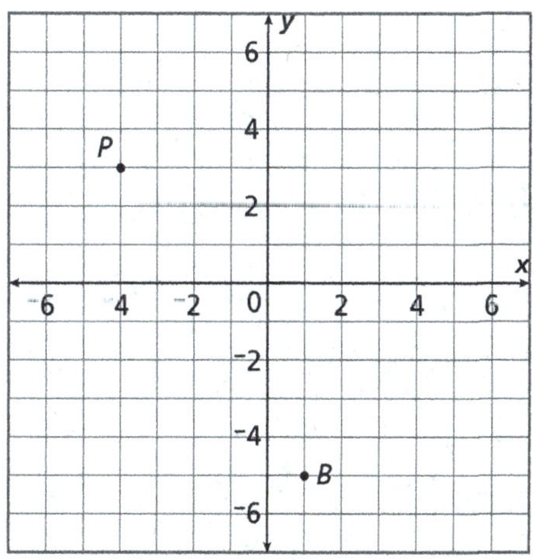

Use the coordinate plane for Exercises 8–11.

8. Point *P* is the physician's office. Write the location of Point *P*.

____

9. Point *B* is the bank. Write the location of Point *B*.

____

10. Point *M* is the location of the merchant. Plot and label Point *M* at ($^{-}3$, $^{-}3$).

11. Point *W* is the location of the wagon maker. Plot and label Point *W* at (3, 2).

Fluency Check 22

Name ______________________________

PATH to FLUENCY

Add or subtract.

1. $\begin{array}{r} 8.415 \\ -\ 2.623 \\ \hline \end{array}$

2. $\begin{array}{r} 0.724 \\ -\ 0.356 \\ \hline \end{array}$

3. $\begin{array}{r} 5.96 \\ +\ \ 8.5 \\ \hline \end{array}$

4. 28.59 − 2.6

5. 583 + 0.24

6. 86.7 + 19.43

Multiply.

7. $\begin{array}{r} 0.56 \\ \times\ \ 38 \\ \hline \end{array}$

8. $\begin{array}{r} 7.4 \\ \times 1.2 \\ \hline \end{array}$

9. $\begin{array}{r} 0.35 \\ \times\ \ 0.6 \\ \hline \end{array}$

10. $\begin{array}{r} 6.8 \\ \times 4.2 \\ \hline \end{array}$

11. $\begin{array}{r} 0.91 \\ \times\ \ 0.7 \\ \hline \end{array}$

12. $\begin{array}{r} 0.29 \\ \times\ \ 15 \\ \hline \end{array}$

Divide.

13. $21\overline{)747.6}$

14. $52\overline{)39.52}$

15. $4.16\overline{)249.6}$

Name ______________________

VOCABULARY
rational number

Fractions on a Number Line

Use the number line below for Exercises 1–8.

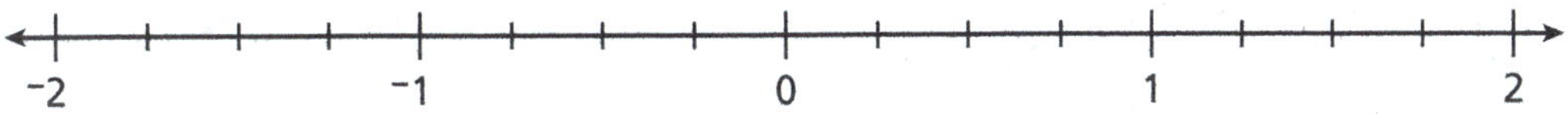

1. How many equal lengths are between 0 and 1? ______________
2. What fractional unit does the number line show? ______________
3. Label each tick mark of the number line with a fraction or mixed number in simplest form.
4. Draw a point at $^{-}\frac{1}{4}$. Label it *A*.
5. Draw a point at $\frac{3}{4}$. Label it *B*.
6. Draw a point at $^{-}1\frac{1}{2}$. Label it *C*.
7. Draw a point at $\frac{6}{4}$. Label it *D*.

A **rational number** is any number that can be expressed as a fraction $\frac{a}{b}$, where *a* and *b* are integers and $b \neq 0$.

8. Do Points *C* and *D* represent *opposite* rational numbers? Explain. Draw arrows above the number line to justify your answer.

____

____

Write the opposite rational number.

9. $^{-}\frac{2}{3}$ ________
10. $\frac{7}{10}$ ________
11. $\frac{-11}{12}$ ________
12. $\frac{1}{6}$ ________

Simplify.

13. $^{-}(^{-}\frac{3}{5})$ ________
14. $^{-}(1\frac{3}{4})$ ________
15. $^{-}(^{-}1\frac{2}{5})$ ________
16. $^{-}(\frac{4}{7})$ ________

Draw and label a number line from ⁻2 to 2 by thirds. Then use it to plot and label each point.

17. Point *E* at $^{-}1\frac{2}{3}$
18. Point *F* at $1\frac{1}{3}$
19. Point *G* at $\frac{2}{3}$
20. Point *H* at $^{-}\frac{1}{3}$

Name ______________________

Decimals on a Number Line

Use the number line below for Exercises 21–26.

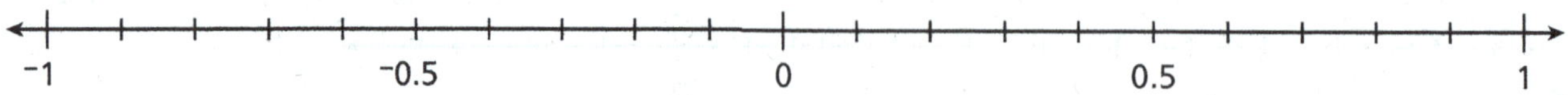

21 How many equal lengths are between 0 and 1? ______________

22 What decimal place does the number line show? ______________

23 Label each tick mark on the number line with a decimal.

24 Draw a point at ⁻0.3. Label it *B*.

25 Draw a point at 0.7. Label it *C*.

26 Draw a point at 0.2 and label it *M*. Draw a point at its opposite and label it *N*. Draw arrows above the number line to show that the numbers are opposites.

What's the Error?

Dear Students:

I was asked to write a sentence about opposite numbers. Here's what I wrote:

A number and its opposite are the same number.

I wrote the sentence because I know that the opposite of zero is zero. Since the opposite of zero is zero, I thought it made sense for me to say that a number and its opposite are the same number. Can you help correct my thinking?

Your friend,
Puzzled Penguin

27 Write a response to Puzzled Penguin.

____

____

____

Name ______________________________

Rational Numbers Number Line Game

____
Player's Initials

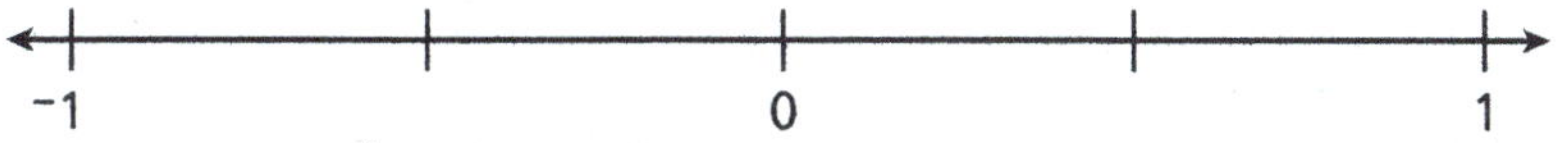

____
Player's Initials

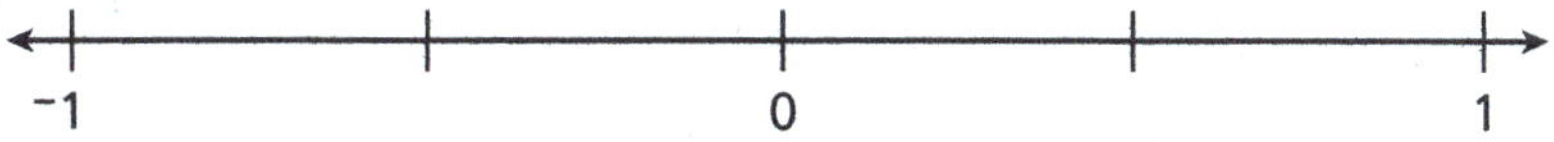

Instructions for Each Pair

Label a blank number cube with these stickers: $^{-}1$; $^{-}0.5$; 0; $\frac{1}{2}$; 1; Roll Again.

Each player labels the tick marks on one horizontal number line with a decimal and a fraction in simplest form.

With your partner, take turns rolling the cube and plotting a point on your number line to show the outcome. Say:

- *I am plotting a point at* (say your rational number).
- *My rational number is* (say *positive* or *negative*), *so it is to the* (say *right* or *left*) *of zero.*
- *It is* (say the number) *unit length(s) from zero.*

If you roll a point that is already plotted, roll again until you get a different point.

If you roll 0, draw a point at 0. *Roll Again* gives you another turn.

The first player to draw a point at every tick mark on the number line wins the game.

Name ______________________________

Rational Numbers Number Line Game (continued)

Repeat the game using the vertical number lines. This time say *above* or *below zero* instead of *to the right* or *to the left of zero*.

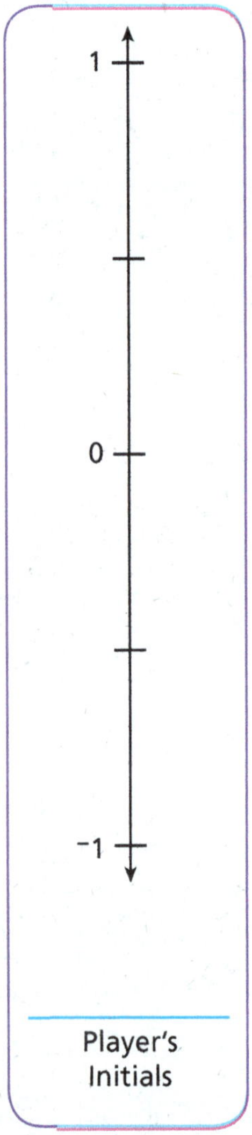

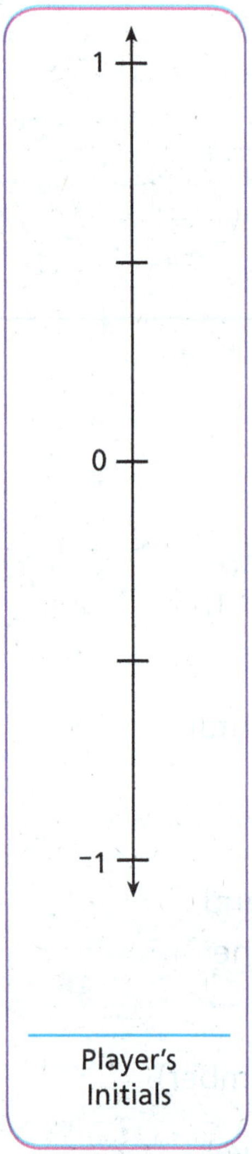

Check Understanding

Explain the relationship that distance shares with rational numbers on a number line.

Name ____________________

Graph Real World Situations

Victor's checking account has a balance of $10 and is charged a $2 service fee at the end of each month.

7. Suppose Victor never uses the account. Complete the table below to show the balance in the account each month for 6 months. Then use the data to plot points on the coordinate plane to show the decreasing balance over time.

Month	Balance (in dollars)
0	10
1	8
2	6
3	
4	
5	
6	

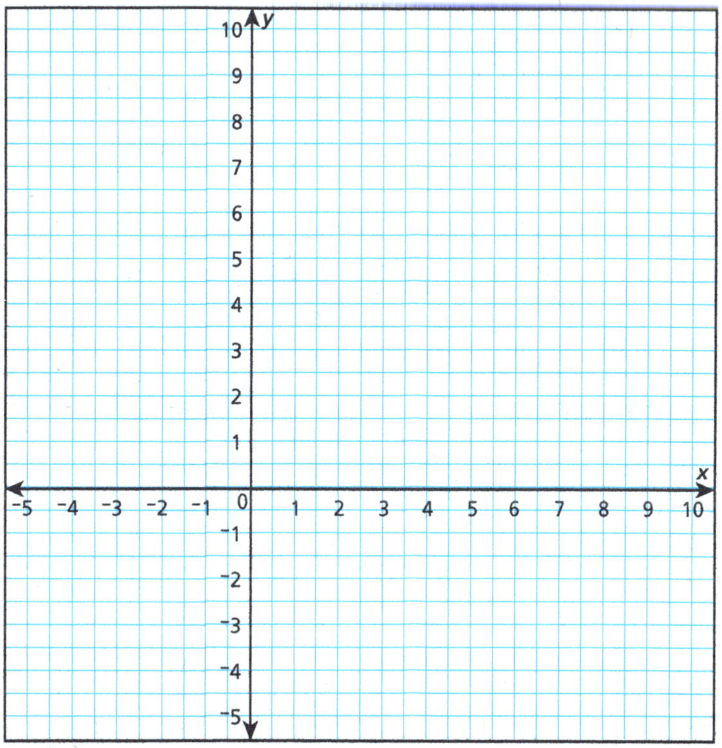

8. Add points to the graph showing what Victor's balance would be each month if the service fee was $2.50, instead of $2.00.

9. How do the graphs for the $2.00 service fee and the $2.50 service fee compare?

____

____

____

____

Name ______________________________

Coordinate Plane Game

Instructions for Each Pair

Using stickers, label each of two blank number cubes 0.25, 0.5, 0.75, 1, 1.25, and 1.5.

With your partner, take turns rolling both cubes and shading a circle or circles on your grid to show the result. For example, if you roll 0.25 and 1.5, shade the circle at (0.25, 1.5) and the circle at (1.5, 0.25).

The first player to shade all of the circles on his or her grid wins the game.

Use the grids below to play the game two more times.

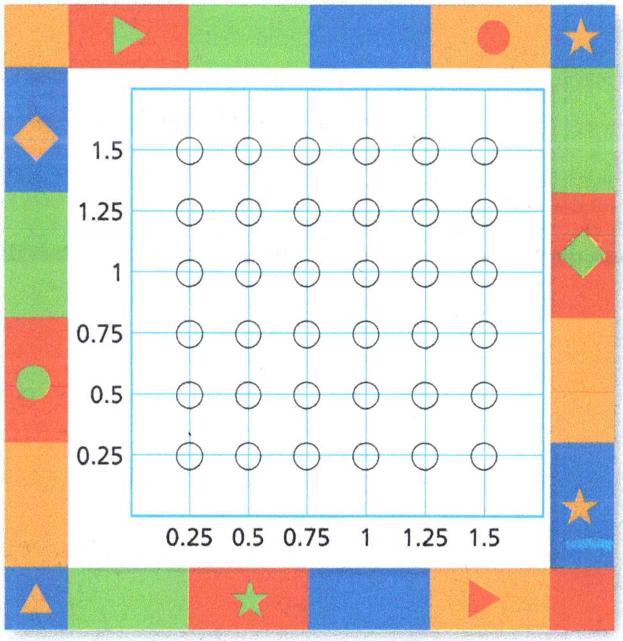

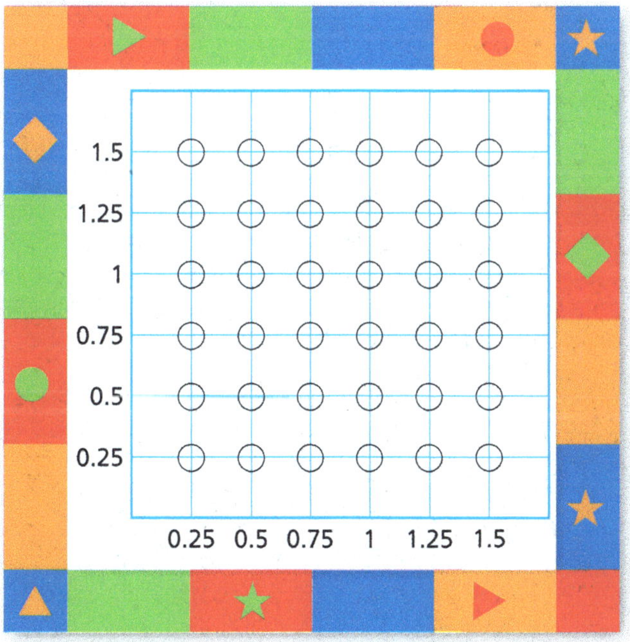

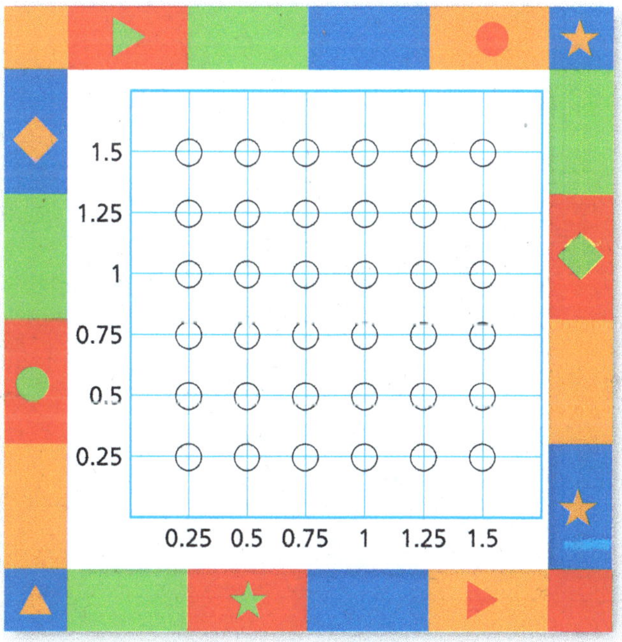

Check Understanding

Explain how subtraction can be used to find horizontal or vertical distances between points in Quadrant I of the coordinate plane.

Unit 9
Quick Quiz 2

Name ______________________________

Write the opposite rational number.

1. $\frac{-3}{8}$ ______________

2. $^-1.5$ ______________

Write the value of Point *K* and Point *Q* as a fraction and as a decimal.

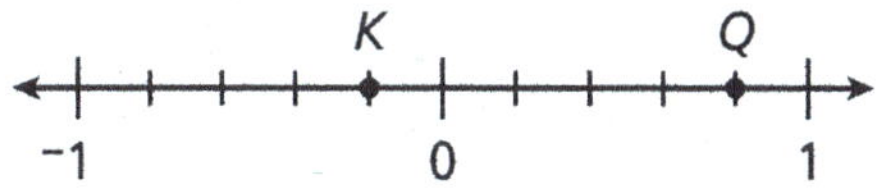

3. Point *K* ______________

4. Point *Q* ______________

Compare. Write <, >, or =.

5. $\frac{-3}{8}$ ◯ $\frac{-5}{8}$

6. $|^-0.75|$ ◯ 0.75

A city planner is sketching a park on the coordinate plane at the right.

Use the coordinate plane for Exercises 7–10.

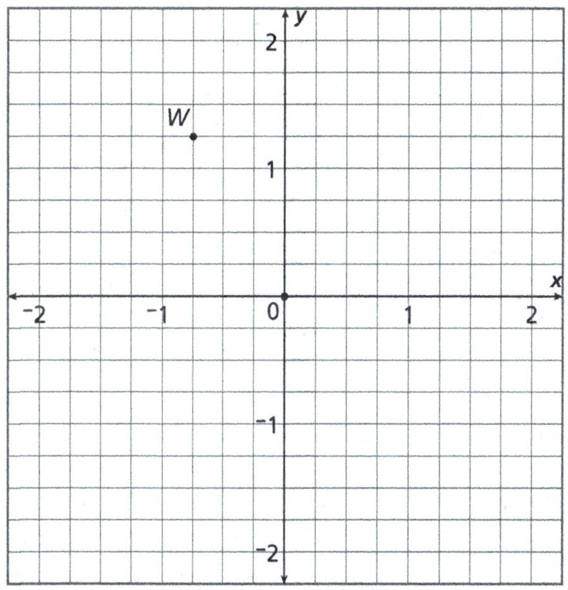

7. The planner will locate a wooded area at Point *W*. Write the location of Point *W*.

____

8. The location of a flower garden will be a reflection of Point *W* across the *x*-axis. Plot and label Point *F* at that location.

9. The location of a picnic area will be a reflection of Point *W* across the *y*-axis. Plot and label Point *P* at that location.

10. Explain how absolute value and the coordinates of the points can be used to find the distance from Point *W* to Point *F* and from Point *W* to Point *P*. How do the signs of the coordinates change when a point is reflected?

____

____

____

____

Fluency Check 23

Name ______________________

PATH to FLUENCY

Add or subtract.

1. 4,750 − 8.3
2. 31 + 2.75
3. 15.67 + 26.54
4. $\begin{array}{r} \$5.32 \\ -\ \$0.78 \\ \hline \end{array}$
5. $\begin{array}{r} 21.049 \\ +\ 6.583 \\ \hline \end{array}$
6. $\begin{array}{r} 92.56 \\ -\ 3.8 \\ \hline \end{array}$

Multiply.

7. $\begin{array}{r} 2.7 \\ \times\ 3.4 \\ \hline \end{array}$
8. $\begin{array}{r} 0.75 \\ \times\ 2.6 \\ \hline \end{array}$
9. $\begin{array}{r} 0.14 \\ \times\ 65 \\ \hline \end{array}$

Divide.

10. $6.3\overline{)1{,}386}$
11. $29\overline{)\$1{,}046.90}$
12. $31\overline{)24.18}$
13. $4.5\overline{)325.8}$
14. $87\overline{)20.01}$
15. $1.26\overline{)94.5}$

Name ____

1. Write each number on the tiles in the box below the term that describes it.

$^-3$	0
0.3	$^-3.5$
$\frac{1}{3}$	3

Integer	Non-Integer

2. Which expressions simplify to 6? Select all that apply.

Ⓐ $^-(6)$

Ⓑ $^-(^-6)$

Ⓒ $^+6$

Ⓓ $^-|^-6|$

Ⓔ $5 + |^-1|$

Ⓕ $3^2 + |^-3|$

3. Rene identified the numbers in each number pair as opposites.

1.5 and $^-1.5$

4.1 and 1.4

Is Rene correct? Explain your answer in terms of a number line.

Name ______________________________

4. Circle the numbers that are less than $^-3$.

$^-7$	0	$^-1$	1	$^-2$	$^-3.5$	2	$^-5\frac{1}{2}$

5. Suppose two points in the coordinate plane have the same *x*-coordinate but different positive *y*-coordinates. Explain how subtraction can be used to find the distance between the points.

6. How will the *x*- and *y*-coordinates of a point in Quadrant I of the coordinate plane change if the point is reflected across the *x*-axis?

Unit 9 Review/Test Name ____________________

7 For Exercises 7a–7c, select True or False for each statement.

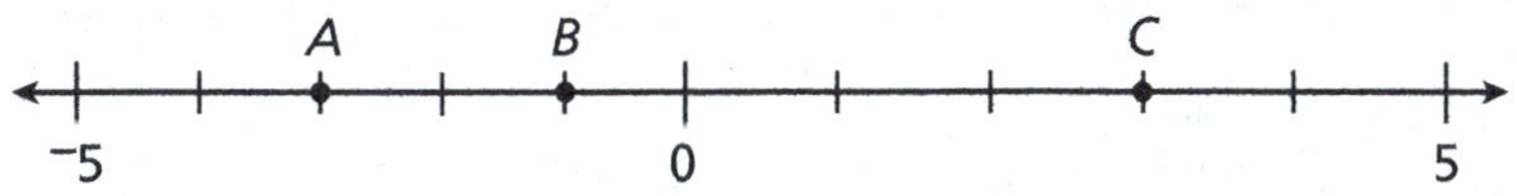

7a. Point *A* is located at 7. ○ True ○ False

7b. Point *B* is located at $^{-}1$. ○ True ○ False

7c. Point *C* is located at 2. ○ True ○ False

8 Where is each number located on the number line? Write the letter.

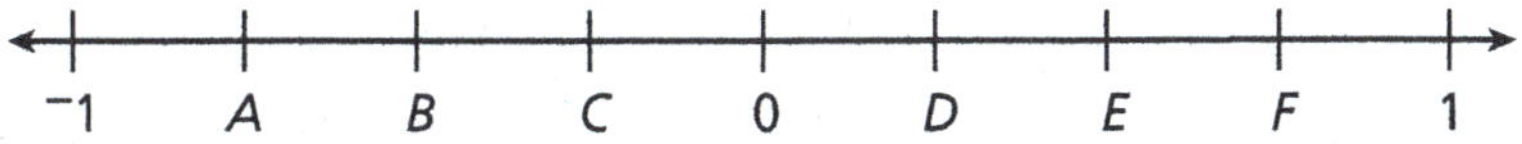

0.25 ____________ $^{-}\frac{1}{2}$ ____________

0.75 ____________ $^{-}\frac{3}{4}$ ____________

$^{-}\frac{1}{4}$ ____________ 0.5 ____________

For Exercises 9–12, select Yes or No for each question.

9 Is $^{-}3.1 > {}^{-}6.8$? ○ Yes ○ No

10 Is $2 > {}^{-}2$? ○ Yes ○ No

11 Is $^{-}10 > 114$? ○ Yes ○ No

12 Is $^{-}({}^{-}5) > {}^{-}5$? ○ Yes ○ No

Name ______________________________

13. A thermometer shows a temperature of $^{-}8.5$°F. A nearby thermometer shows a temperature of $^{-}7.5$°F. Explain how absolute value can be used to find the *warmer* temperature.

14. Suppose that the ordered pairs (p, q) and (r, q) represent two points in the coordinate plane, and p, q, and r represent positive integers. If $p < r$ and $q = 2$, what expression represents the distance between the two points? Explain your answer.

Name ______________________

Use the coordinate plane. Write the ordered pairs for Exercises 15–17.

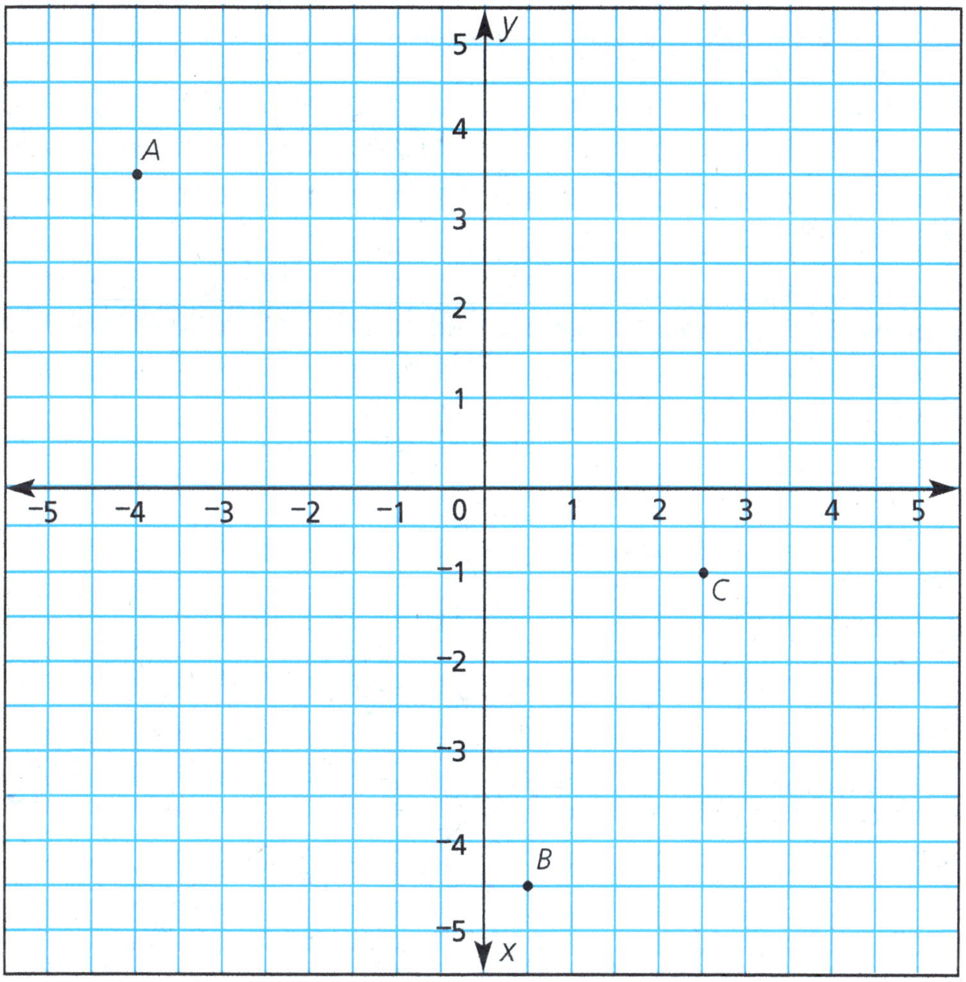

15 Point *A*

16 Point *B*

17 Point *C*

18 Reflect Point *A* across the *x*-axis. Label it Point *X*. Name its location.

19 Reflect Point *A* across the *y*-axis. Label it Point *Y*. Name its location.

Name ______________________

20 Look back at the coordinate plane for Exercises 15–19. Use absolute value to find the distance from Point *A* to Point *X*. Show your work in the space below.

Use the table for Exercises 21–23.

Becca recorded the high temperature each day for five days. The table shows her data.

Day	Temperature (°C)
Mon	⁻1
Tue	4
Wed	8
Thur	0
Fri	⁻3

21 What is the opposite of the temperature recorded on Monday?

Ⓐ ⁻1

Ⓑ 1

Ⓒ ⁻4

Ⓓ 4

22 How can you use a number line to order the temperatures from greatest to least?

23 Which lists the days from coldest to warmest?

Ⓐ Thur, Mon, Fri, Tue, Wed

Ⓑ Mon, Fri, Thur, Tue, Wed

Ⓒ Fri, Mon, Thur, Tue, Wed

Ⓓ Thur, Fri, Mon, Tue, Wed

Name ______________________________

Making a Plan

Brenda is planning to turn part of her backyard into a rectangular vegetable garden. She uses grid paper to sketch a plan of her garden.

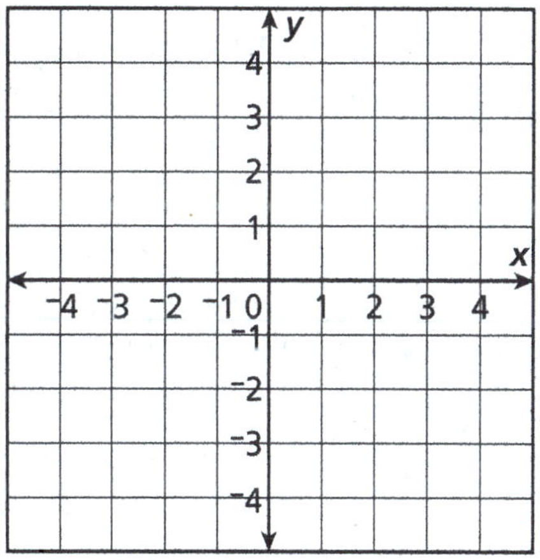

1. Brenda wants the corners of her garden to be located at the following coordinates: (4, 3), (⁻3, 3), (⁻3, ⁻2), (4, ⁻2). On the coordinate grid, plot and label the corners of the garden, then shade the region that the garden will cover. (Note: 1 unit in the grid equals 1 foot.)

2. What are the measurements of Brenda's garden? Show or explain how you know.

3. What is the area of Brenda's garden? Show or explain how you know.

4. On the coordinate grid, sketch a rectangular garden whose area is 40 square feet. Label the vertices of your rectangle with their coordinates, and show or explain how you know the area.

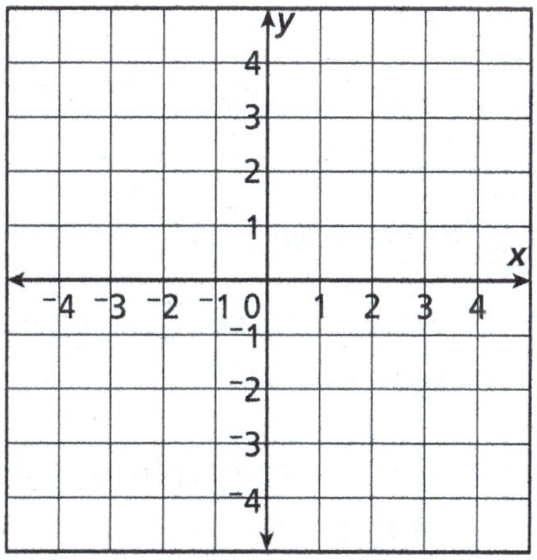

□ = 1 square foot

5. If the scale on the grid were to change so that each square represented 4 square feet, what would be the area of the rectangular garden you sketched for question 4? Show or explain how you know.

Unit 9
Performance Task

Name ______________________

Planning a park before it is built helps maximize the enjoyment visitors have when they visit the park. Use the grid below to sketch a plan for the park.

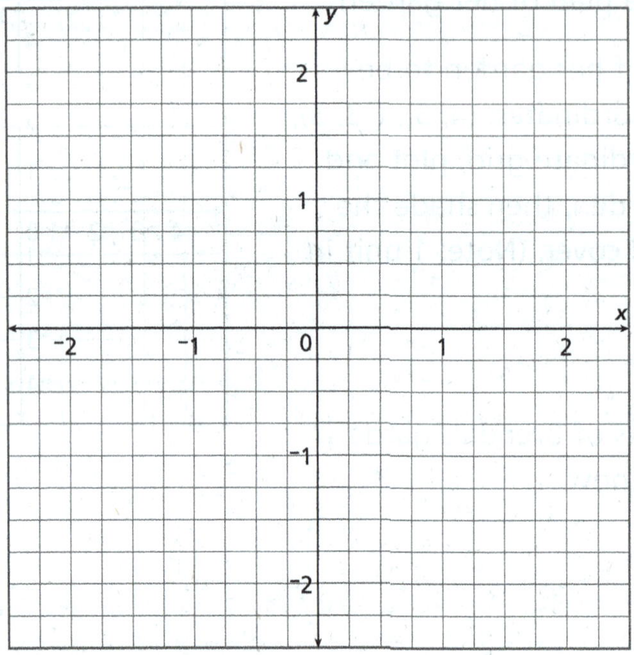

□ = 100 square yards

6 On a separate sheet of paper, list five features you would like your park to have. For example, one feature might be a soccer field.

7 Shade an area of the grid to represent each feature, and write its name.

8 On your list,

- write the vertices (as ordered pairs) and the area of each feature.
- write the percent of the park area that each feature represents.
- write the percent of the park area that has no features.

Be an Illustrator

Illustrator: Josh Brill

Did you ever try to use shapes to draw animals like the toucan on the cover?

Over the last 10 years Josh has been using geometric shapes to design his animals. His aim is to keep the animal drawings simple and use color to make them appealing.

Add some color to the toucan Josh drew. Then try drawing a cat or dog or some other animal using the shapes below.

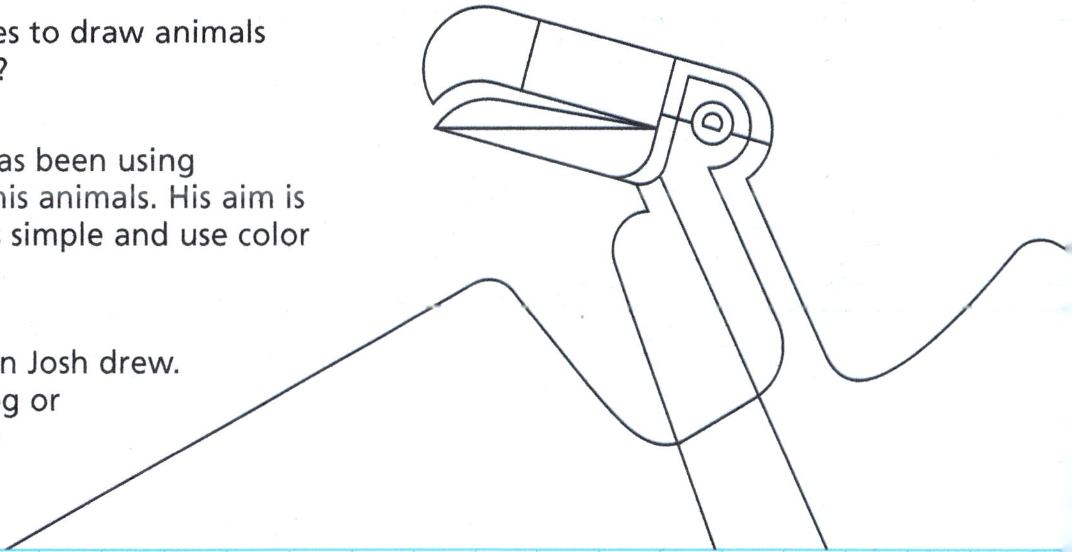

Shape Toolbox

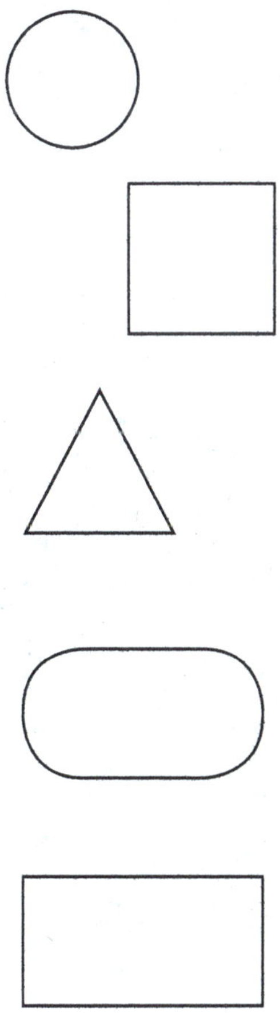